Volume 64

BANTU PROPHETS IN
SOUTH AFRICA

D0555196

BANTU PROPHETS IN SOUTH AFRICA

BENGT G. M. SUNDKLER

Routledge
Taylor & Francis Group

LONDON AND NEW YORK

First published in 1948 by Lutterworth Press and as a second edition in 1961 by Oxford University Press for the International African Institute.

This edition first published in 2018
by Routledge
2 Park Square, Milton Park, Abingdon, Oxon OX14 4RN

and by Routledge
711 Third Avenue, New York, NY 10017

Routledge is an imprint of the Taylor & Francis Group, an informa business

© 1961 International African Institute

British Library Cataloguing in Publication Data
A catalogue record for this book is available from the British Library

ISBN: 978-0-8153-8713-8 (Set)
ISBN: 978-0-429-48813-9 (Set) (ebk)
ISBN: 978-1-138-59853-9 (Volume 64) (hbk)
ISBN: 978-1-138-59859-1 (Volume 64) (pbk)
ISBN: 978-0-429-48629-6 (Volume 64) (ebk)

Publisher's Note
The publisher has gone to great lengths to ensure the quality of this reprint but points out that some imperfections in the original copies may be apparent.

Disclaimer
The publisher has made every effort to trace copyright holders and would welcome correspondence from those they have been unable to trace.

A BANTU JOHN THE BAPTIST.

The white shirt with a green cord have been revealed to the prophet by an "Angel" in his dreams as a means of overcoming and preventing illness. In his hand a staff of palm leaves.

BANTU PROPHETS IN
SOUTH AFRICA

by
BENGT G. M. SUNDKLER

Second Edition

Published for
THE INTERNATIONAL AFRICAN INSTITUTE
by the
OXFORD UNIVERSITY PRESS
LONDON   NEW YORK   TORONTO
1961

Oxford University Press, Amen House, London E.C.4

GLASGOW   NEW YORK   TORONTO   MELBOURNE   WELLINGTON
BOMBAY   CALCUTTA   MADRAS   KARACHI   KUALA LUMPUR
CAPETOWN   IBADAN   NAIROBI   ACCRA

First published 1948
(Lutterworth Press)

Second Edition 1961
(Oxford University Press)

*This book has been printed in Great Britain by
litho-offset at Taylor Garnett Evans & Co. Ltd.,
Watford, Herts.*

PREFACE

Dr. Sundkler has rendered missionary work in South Africa a signal service by his study of the Bantu separatist churches. It is a subject on which much is known in loose terms, but little with any accuracy. Here we have the facts set out before us in a spirit which is critical in the best sense of the term, objective, and full of a kindly understanding such as the subject undoubtedly merits. There are elements in the life of some of the Bantu separatist churches which are not Christian in any normally accepted sense of the word—there are elements of true faith and vision. It is doubtful whether any human being can wholly separate the wheat from the tares in this luxuriant field of religious activity, but Dr. Sundkler has done his best.

It is clear from the study which follows that nationalism plays a great part in Bantu separatist church organization and that the spirit of separatism, in spite of quite sincere attempts at union, is very strong. European Christianity in South Africa must face the fact that it is partly responsible for these phenomena. There has been a strong element of nationalism in certain fields of European Christianity and an emphasis on denominational differences which has done harm. It is probable that the very area which Dr. Sundkler surveys so thoroughly is, if one may coin a word, the most over-denominationalized missionary area in Africa. To-day the spirit of comity and co-operation has gone a long way to remove differences between missions. They still exist, but the unedifying competitiveness which was to be found in some areas in the past has been greatly lessened. Europeans none the less must bear their share of the responsibility for a good deal of the separatist church movement and, even when separation has sprung from worldly motives of hurt pride or ambition, it is to be remembered that European missionary superintendents have not infrequently, through an overbearing manner or through lack of understanding and imagination, contributed to secession.

So far I have spoken of separatist churches, but Dr. Sundkler rightly speaks of "independent Bantu churches", reminding us that not all the denominations which are studied have their origin in secession from established missionary churches. Not only in independent churches, but also in those which in their origin were separatist, there are elements which spring, not from the faults and defects of European missionary work, but from the desire of the Zulu people to find some synthesis between their own tribal religion and Christianity. Dr. Sundkler's researches into this side of the movement are among the most interesting parts of his book.

I should not, of course, like to commit myself to every opinion or conclusion of the author, but I should like to pay tribute, in closing, to the spirit in which he has written; not merely an unbiased scientific spirit, but a spirit which shows true kindness, a positive attitude and a sympathetic understanding of Zulu ideas and aspirations.

EDGAR H. BROOKES.

FOREWORD TO THE SECOND EDITION

This book on Bantu Churches in South Africa first appeared in 1948, and South Africa has changed considerably since then. Yet, when looking at South African society from the standpoint of the particular Bantu religious groups analysed in this study, the change in the political field in 1948 does not appear as sudden or as drastic as it does from the account of other observers. Apartheid, or separate development, as a term may have been coined with the advent of the Nationalist Government; but the fact was of course there long before 1948: the fact of a society divided according to colour lines and of a Church similarly divided. The first edition of this book dealt in fact with church apartheid and its results and consequences prior to 1945–48. The important event in that development was the Natives Land Act of 1913: both Separatism as such and the ensuing religious ideology on Bantu lines are an outcome of the deep malaise felt throughout the African masses in the years after 1913.

Thus, when "apartheid" arrived, the Bantu Separatist Church found itself already *apart*. Its problems in the 1950's were of course part of those of the African population as a whole, but these problems could, in the world of the Separatist Churches, be approached from the standpoint of apartheid already arrived at, rather than apartheid enforced. In order to understand the post-1948 development in the great number of Bantu Separatist Churches, this fact must be borne in mind.

4

On the invitation of the International African Institute and its Director, Professor Daryll Forde, I had the opportunity of revisiting South Africa for eight months in 1958, with a view to preparing a second edition of this book. My research was once again concentrated on the Separatist Church conditions among the Zulus: on the Rand, in Natal, and in Zululand proper. But there was some widening of the scope of our research. Through the help of Dr. J. F. Holleman, Director of the Institute for Social Research of the University of Natal, I was given the chance of visiting Swaziland. I paid attention to Swazi Zionist and Ethiopian Churches in Swaziland and on the Rand. Here was a cultural and religious situation very similar to that of the Zulus—as Northern Nguni they are closely related. Yet there are significant differences in the fundamental factors: land, kingship, political situation.

The brief chapter on "Bantu Christ" in our first edition is now found to be inadequate. Bantu Messianism's increasing significance and its particular, ambivalent relationship to "Zionism" requires us to develop our typology and refine our approach to the problem. This we have attempted to do in the last part of the new additional chapter.

We have retained the "Special Bibliography" as it stood in the 1948 edition; within the rich growth of studies in the last few years we would draw attention to G. Parrinder, *Religion in an African City* (1953), dealing with West Africa; G. Balandier, *Sociologie Actuelle de l'Afrique Noire* (1955); Efr. Andersson, *Messianic Popular Movements in the Lower Congo* (1958). Of great importance also for the history of the South African movement is G. Shepperson—T. Price, *Independent African, John Chilembwe and the Origins, Setting and Significance of the Nyasaland Native Rising of 1915* (1958).

The first attempt at a general survey of the Separatist movement in South Africa was Allan Lea's book of 1926, included in our Special Bibliography. His book is now of less interest for what it tells of the Bantu Independent Churches, which is very little, than as source material illustrating the attitude of a whole generation of missionaries to "Native Separatism".

Dr. Katesa Schlosser, of the Kiel Ethnological Museum, in 1958 published a series of personality studies of Bantu Church leaders under the title *Eingeborenenkirchen in Süd- und Südwestafrika. Ihre Geschichte und Sozialstructur.* She has a valuable and interesting chapter on Shembe. The book also includes a study of the great modern Zulu revivalist Nicholas Bhengu;

5

it should be stressed that Rev. Bhengu and his "Back to God" movement must not be identified with the Churches discussed in this book. Special value must be attached to L. Mqotsi— N. Mkele's study on Bishop Limba's Church: "A Separatist Church", *African Studies* (5), 1946. The two African authors are to be saluted as forerunners in a field where contributions by African sociologists should prove to be of particular importance.

For considerations of space the supplementary chapter in this edition, *Developments* 1945–1960, had to be limited to some 35 pages. They must be regarded as a brief preliminary report, giving an outline to be followed, as soon as circumstances allow, by another volume in which we hope to analyse in some detail our groups and personality cases from 1958, together with relevant texts.

The International African Institute, London, gave a grant towards my travel and field expenses. The National Council of Social and Educational Research, Pretoria, and the Institutes for Social Research, Durban, gave grants to our research in the Union, including African research assistants. I am much indebted to officials of the Native Affairs Department, Pretoria, among whom I mention particularly Dr. N. J. van Warmelo, Chief Ethnologist, and to the officials of the Administration in Swaziland. I am particularly indebted to the Institute for Social Research of the University of Natal, whose Director, Dr. J. F. Holleman, gave me unfailing help.

BENGT SUNDKLER

Uppsala University
June 1960

CONTENTS

7

8

CONTENTS

9

CONTENTS

ACKNOWLEDGMENTS

I have had the privilege of discussing some of the problems and viewpoints of this book with Professor R. Firth, Dr. Hilda Kuper, Dr. A. I. Richards, Professor I. Schapera and Dr. N. J. van Warmelo. I owe a particular debt of gratitude to Dr. Richards for helpful advice. I thank Professor C. P. Groves, Selly Oak Colleges, whose unfailing interest in this study has been a constant source of encouragement to me. Dr. A. Wilkie, lately of Lovedale, has read à set of proofs. The Rev. R. Barton, S.P.G., Arogyavaram, South India, and Allen Skipper, Esq., Friends Mission, Tananarivo, Madagascar, have brushed up my English. I should, perhaps, exonerate the International Missionary Council, of which I became Research Secretary in January, 1948, from any responsibility for this book.

The Olaus Petri Foundation, Uppsala, Sweden, gave a grant to the expenses of Zulu assistants for the field research. The S. African Council for Educational, Sociological and Humanistic Research, Pretoria, contributed towards travelling expenses in South Africa, and the Colonial Social Science Research Council, London, gave a grant in connexion with the final stage of the writing of the book. I am also grateful to the Board of the Church of Sweden Mission for their readiness to grant me some time of leave for the period of writing the manuscript. Thanks are due to the Editor of *Libertas* magazine, Mr. T. C. Robertson, Johannesburg, for permission to use some of the photographs which Miss Constance Stuart, Pretoria, took for an article I wrote, in 1945, for *Libertas*. I feel that Miss Stuart's close-ups contribute to a fuller understanding of the personalities of the Bantu Church leaders who are discussed in my book.

Lastly, my wife's help has meant more to this book and to my work in Africa than can be expressed here.

ILLUSTRATIONS

A BANTU JOHN THE BAPTIST   *Frontispiece*
The white shirt with a green cord have been revealed to the
prophet by an "Angel" in his dreams as a means of overcoming
and preventing illness. In his hand a staff of palm leaves.

Facing page
FROM DARKNESS TO LIGHT; FROM ILLNESS TO HEALTH   62
"Before, I was ill; the Zionists prayed for me; now I am well",
is her message. The green and blue cords in front, and the
wooden croziers in her right hand, guarantee health and
ritual purity.

THE APOSTOLIC JERUSALEM CHURCH IN SABBATH OF
SOUTH AFRICA   63
Bishop E. M. Morupa addressing his group in preparation
for a baptismal service. The bishop claims to be associated
with a [fictitious] Ethiopian-Abyssinian Legation in South
Africa.

THE CHIEF OF HIS CHURCH   110
Rev. J. Mdelwa Hlongwane, founder and president of the
Bantu Methodist Church, nicknamed the "Donkey Church".
The photo taken from a rally of Independent Bantu Churches
in Pimville, Johannesburg, on which occasion the Rev.
Hlongwane gave a "charge" to the assembled ministers.
Banners with inscriptions in English and Zulu are carried in
procession.

ZULU MESSIAH   111
Isaiah Shembe (d. 1935), a man of a magnetic personality,
founder of the Nazarite sect. He wielded a deeper and wider
influence than any other Zulu prophet. He wears a black
dress—all others in the church are dressed in white—with
a white collar, necklace of Zulu beadwork and European
sun-helmet. (Photo: Lynn Acutt, Durban, abbr. L. A.)

A MOTHER IN ISRAEL   126
The widow of Rev. Paul Mabilitsa, a prominent Zionist
church leader. As mother of the present Church leader she
wields a considerable influence.

BISHOP L. M. MAKHOBA   127
The President of the African Congregational Church.

DANCING BEFORE THE LORD   190
Isaiah Shembe, in sun-helmet and umbrella, leading the men's
section dancing through the Ekuphakameni village. (Photo:
L. A.)

APPROACHING THE PROBLEM

During the last decades leaders have appeared in various parts of Africa, calling to life new religious organizations, formed partly by secessions from White Mission churches, and partly by spontaneous growth. The prophet movement on the lower Congo; the role of the Watch-Tower movement instigating disturbances in Northern Rhodesia, Nyasaland and Belgian Congo; the emergence of Independent Schools in Kenya; Separatist Church movements in an embryonic stage in Tanganyika and Uganda; a fairly rich flora of African sects on the West coast of Africa; and, above all, the hypertrophy of African churches in the Union of South Africa: the whole of this development presents the Protestant missionary undertaking in Africa with one of its most baffling practical problems, and we are hitherto very poorly informed as to the very nature of the movement. The present study is an attempt to analyse the sociological and religious problems within the "Separatist Church" movement in South Africa, on the assumption that the development of the movement in South Africa may have its bearing upon and be relevant to similar movements among other Bantu further north.

There was a time in South Africa when the "Ethiopian Problem" was discussed with interest and almost with anxiety, not only by missionaries, but also by politicians, scholars and others interested in the welfare of the country. This occurred in the years after the Boer War (1899–1902) and in the days of the Zulu Rebellion, 1906. It was then feared that the Ethiopian movement was an African political underground movement aiming at ousting the White man from South Africa, or, at least, that it might establish a pan-African National Church which would cause harm by hampering the evangelization of the Bantu peoples.

If the problem now—after forty years—seems to have lost its primary interest, as far as the general public in South Africa is concerned, this is not due to any decline of the Bantu Independent church movement as such. The movement is now numerically very much stronger than a generation ago. Further, the history of this African movement in recent years, full of

13

dramatic points and vicissitudes, elucidates more clearly than anything else an important phase in the ascendancy of the Bantu peoples. The fact that all this has remained, and still remains, very much a hidden world to those who otherwise have the cause of the Africans at heart, is significant of the general development in the Union at the present time; the gulf separating the races is much wider now than at the beginning of the century.

This study pertains almost exclusively to conditions within one South African tribe, the Zulus. This limitation has been made for definite methodological reasons. With my experience from ten years of investigation into this subject I would now claim that the research area could advantageously be limited still further. One could have concentrated on one particular Independent Zulu church, or on an area geographically more circumscribed than that of a whole tribe stretching—as the Zulu language area does—from the Natal coast line to Johannesburg.

In planning the study on lines such as those drawn in this book, one is in a position of being able to define clearly the tribal, cultural and religious background of the problem, and to relate the phenomena of Bantu church life to definite social conditions in different communities (reserve, farm and urban areas).

The material on which my conclusions are based consists of my own direct observations in the field, together with local observations over a certain period (1941–45) made by Zulu assistants. I have been privileged in having had full access to rich and instructive material in the official archives in South Africa. My knowledge of the Independent Zulu churches was gained in the course of my missionary activity in South Africa, 1937–42, and during six months of special study of the problem on the Witwatersrand in 1945. As a missionary in Central Natal (farm and coal-mining districts) and in Northern Zululand (a tribal reserve), I had daily opportunities of coming into contact with the leaders and common people of these Independent Zulu churches, meeting them, as I did, wherever I went. In 1942 I went for three years to Tanganyika, and this *trek* to the north helped me, I believe, in letting me see the South African situation more in perspective than would otherwise have been the case.

From time to time I arranged meetings where Independent Church leaders met with pastors, evangelists, and ordinary lay members of Mission Churches. We had very stimulating talks, sometimes friendly, sometimes arguing rather heatedly, in the end agreeing to differ on fundamental theological and religious questions, such as the interpretation of the Bible, the role of baptism and purification rites, the Black Christ and the Whites' Christ, and scores of other problems. Sometimes our Lutheran Church at Ceza, Northern Zululand, was filled with hundreds of "Zionists" in their colourful vestments. I attended preaching and purification services and other meetings of the Independent Churches whenever my own regular mission work allowed me to do so.

I was greatly helped by the competent and keen co-operation of some ten Zulu assistants. Teaching theology for a short while at a Lutheran college in Natal, I attempted to interest the students in a thorough study of this subject, of which they already had considerable practical knowledge. After some initial training in the art of observation and note-making, they were in two consecutive years, 1940 and 1941, posted in different areas of Natal and Zululand, for a period of some weeks at each place. Detailed life stories of local leaders and ordinary church members were recorded, Church services, dreams and visions related. All their notes were, as in the case of my own fieldwork, written in Zulu. In certain cases, these observations revealed new issues and tasks of field research to which we would turn our concerted action. Three of my helpers—now pastors in Lutheran Mission Churches— proved to be exceptionally good and reliable observers, and I owe them a very real debt of gratitude. For reasons which they have pointed out to me, their names are not published here.

Prior to undertaking this study, I had certain forebodings that in my capacity as a missionary of one particular church I should be handicapped in establishing friendly contacts with Independent church leaders—contacts without which they would not give information about themselves, their work, ambitions and aspirations. But my fear on this point was unnecessary. In an overwhelming number of cases I found that the very fact that I was known as a missionary, genuinely interested in their church life as well as in their personal life-histories and activities was a help when trying to elicit the information I wanted. Almost without exception, my African assistants and I were received as honoured guests at their church services. I was invited to preach in their churches, an invitation which I hardly ever refused. I count some of these Zulu leaders as good friends. Experience of related problems in the work of one's own mission church opened up new avenues of inquiry and research.

And yet, I am fully conscious that my account does not reach the heart of the matter. I doubt whether any outsider can achieve that. However sympathetic an attitude the White observer may take, he remains—an outsider. The Bantu churches of South Africa have not yet got—as the Negroes of the United States have—their own Richard Wright to record the rhythm of black voices and to feel the heart-beat of the Black Man's longings and aspirations.

I was at a disadvantage sometimes with the Zulu Christians of my own mission church (Church of Sweden Mission, Lutheran), who of course found my intense and sympathetic interest in the ways of "Ethiopian" archbishops and "Zionist" prophets somewhat out of place, although generally speaking, they were forbearing towards this peculiarity of mine.

The reader should be fore-warned that in an investigation of this kind there obviously enters *the problem of bias.* A subjective emphasis is bound to affect any student of these phenomena. This can be gauged by putting the question, what would have been the outcome of this investigation if the observer had been, let us say, a Pentecostal soul-winner, or an African nationalist, or a sociologist who would not necessarily have to be a professing Christian. Obviously the writer's valuations and ideals enter into the investigation—from the collecting of the material itself, which is the fundamental stage, to the final presentation with its balancing of one viewpoint against another. I readily accept the engaging frankness and honesty with which the eminent Swedish sociologist Gunnar Myrdal in his book on the Negro problem declares that "a disinterested social science is pure nonsense. It never existed, and it never will exist."[1] Value premises do enter into our arguments. So they should not be hidden, as tacit assumptions, but explicitly stated. A subjective emphasis is bound to affect the valuations of any missionary dealing with a problem of this nature, implying a definite criticism of his own ideals and life-work. No doubt, I am myself, both as a Protestant missionary and as an investigator, a part of the problem, and I affect its future development by my missionary activity or inactivity.

The value premises on which—as far as I am aware—the argument of this book is based are the following two:

1. As a motto of the book I have chosen a statement by Bishop Gore at the World Missionary Conference in Edinburgh, 1910: "What I mean is that we have got to put into all bodies of Christians the consciousness that continuous life depends upon continuous principles." The significance of that statement is seen by Dr. Gore's grave warning expressed on the same occasion: "On almost all sides I notice in respect of what might be called in the broadest sense, the religion of Protestant Christianity, a tendency to drift. Men are conscious that what they used forcibly to assert was essential to Christianity they no longer are willing to assert."

Hardly anywhere is there, of course, such a cruel example of this tendency to drift as in the Bantu Independent Churches, and I shall attempt to show in this book to what this tendency seems to lead. The material of this investigation is therefore also organized as a contribution to the discussion of the central problem and main dilemma of the Protestant missionary cause: the founding of an "independent", self-supporting, self-governing, self-propagating Church. My contention is that there has been altogether too much stress on the "*self*" and much too little emphasis on what the *Church* is. Without those "continuous principles" which have been delivered to the Church, "continuous life" is not to be expected.

2. This investigation is also a study of the impact of racial discrimination upon the life of the Christian Church. In South Africa, there have been two Protestant traditions in this respect: First, the S. African Calvinist "golden rule" claiming "*geen gelijkstelling*" (no equality) between White and Black in Church and State. And secondly, a liberal interpretation of the Bible proclaiming equal opportunity for all men, regardless of race and colour. Neither of these policies, if left unhampered by any conflicting views, would seem to lead to secession. The problem arises when the more repressive view tacitly or openly becomes dominating in churches which, in principle, are equalitarian and liberal, but which by "practical necessity"—consideration for the race-conscious White membership of a particular church— have to conform to a general segregation policy within the church.

The very reason why I first undertook this study was *practical*: my interest in it was based on the assumption that, in these churches, one could be able to see what the African Christian, *when left to himself*, regarded as important and relevant in Christian faith and in the Christian church. By such

17

a study I hoped to be able to discern tendencies that could be utilized in the practical task of building Christ's Church in Africa.

Instead of the official name, "Native Separatist Churches", which is obviously not a very happy term, I speak of "Bantu Independent Churches". The word "Native" is not liked by the Africans, and to apply the term "Separatist" only to Bantu secessionists as if White secessionists were not "Separatists" in much the same degree, does not seem fair. Although conscious of the fact that *"Independent"* in English usage often stands as a synonym for "Congregational", I shall here use the word *"Bantu Independent"* in a wider sense, as referring to such religious organizations as, in their desire for independence from the Whites, have seceded from mission churches. I also notice that D. Westermann, in his *Africa and Christianity*, refers to these churches as "Independent".

One difficulty which is encountered when describing the activities of certain Bantu church leaders is the necessity of *anonymity*, so as not to offend contemporary individuals and also to avoid legal actions which might otherwise follow. Some North American sociologists have encountered the same problem when publishing their Indian or Negro material (cf. M. Mead, *The Antlers*, and Dollard, *Caste and Class in a Southerntown*). On the other hand, in the case of the Zulu prophet and Church leader, Isaiah Shembe, for instance, such precautions are not necessary to the same degree, because his ideology is expressed in the official hymn-book of his church. I believe I can honestly say that I have tried to show all appropriate personal consideration—without jeopardizing the analysis of the actual problems.

CHAPTER I

RELIGIOUS AND SOCIAL BACKGROUND OF THE ZULUS

The White man's God and the White man's gold have influenced and changed Zulu belief and behaviour to a very considerable extent. As far as the results of the mission work go, the South African Native Churches Commission of 1925 could state with reason: "The rapidity and ease with which the South African Native has received the teachings of Christianity is one of the most remarkable phases in his acceptance of European civilization." Yet the word "ease" is perhaps not altogether accurate in this connexion. In fact, the African has put up a strong resistance to the mission's attempted conquest. The independent Zulu Churches may well be regarded as a symptom of an inner revolt against the White man's missionary crusade, and in these Churches we shall see many proofs of the vitality of the religious and cultural heritage of the Zulus, which in them is given a more honoured place than in the Mission Church. In order to make clear the influence of this African heritage I shall set out very briefly some of the main points in the system of myth, ritual and magic which makes up traditional Zulu belief.

(I) ZULU BELIEFS

(a) High God

It is not possible here to enter into a discussion of the controversial problem of the high-gods of the Bantu. The Zulus refer to their high-god by different names: *uNkulunkulu* ("the great, great one", or "the old, old one"), a term which together with the Xhosa name *Thixo* has been taken over by the Christian churches as the name for God; *uMvelingqangi* ("the one who emerged first") and, in an alternative form *uHlanga* (i.e. the "bed of reeds", from which mankind broke off) are terms used by pagan Zulus referring to this high-god.

But while these names refer to God as a vaguely conceived Creator or First Cause, there is another set of names—or perhaps better, another layer of tradition, possibly another cultural influence altogether—which refers to "Heaven" or the

"Lord of Heaven" (*inkosi yezulu* or *inkosi phezulu*). This has been largely overlooked in the literature on the subject. Callaway, one of the outstanding authorities on pagan Zulu religion, tried to show "how utterly indistinct and undeveloped is their notion respecting a heavenly Lord",[1] but this I cannot wholly accept. I suggest that a study of modern half-Christian prophetic movements in Africa may be a methodologically new approach towards a discernment of what has been vital and important in the old primitive religion.

The *inkosi phezulu* is the sky-god. Naturally, he is particularly connected with thunder and lightning. When it thunders, the Zulus say: "The king is playing". He could strike by lightning anybody who had angered him.[2] In Zulu magic, fat of the so-called lightning-bird and earth from the place where lightning has struck are considered to be particularly powerful materia.[3] The lightning magicians, the "shepherds of heaven" (*a6elusi 6ezulu*)—who in actual fact are, of course, the priests of the sky-god-cult—have to lead lives of strict ritual purity in order to influence weather phenomena. They do not appear to derive their power from the ancestors, but by being magically treated with medicines known to contain "heaven" in a concentrated form.[4]

A lesser deity who should be mentioned even in this brief account is *Inkosazana* or *Nomkhu6ulwana*, a personification of spring, the Zulu Ceres. Gluckman sums up the essential parts of the ceremonies consecrated to Nomkhu6ulwana in the following five points:

(i) the dominance of women and girls in the ritual;

(ii) the soliciting of a good harvest from the Queen of Heaven;

(iii) the festivities, songs and dances in her honour;

(iv) the herding of cattle by the girls who wear men's garments; and

(v) the planting of consecrated fields and the offering of beer in the fields to the goddess.[5]

Nomkhu6ulwana appears dressed in white to the women who are hoeing. She moves with the mist, being on one side similar to a human in form, on another side a river, on a third side overgrown with green grass. When revealing herself to her female followers, she gives them some new law or predicts things which will happen in the future. This cult (*uNomdede*) is particularly interesting because of the central part played in it by women.

(b) Ancestors

"The real, vital religion of the Zulus is their ancestor worship."[6] The spirits of the departed (Zulu: *idlozi*, plur. *amadlozi*) become the guardian spirits of their descendants. Vaguely localized at the grave or the kraal or in some subterranean abode ("those who are below", *aɓaphansi* or *umhlaɓa*) the spirit wields great influence over his people. He is believed to look after their well-being in all respects. Illness, misfortune or death in the kraal are sure signs that he regards himself as neglected. The spirit, therefore, must be appeased by various means, especially by sacrifices in order to restore health, happiness and harmony in the kraal and among his kinsmen. The spirits of chiefs and the royal ancestors are naturally more important than ordinary, common spirits. They are "the source of communal well-being and prosperity".[7] A spirit may often choose to reveal himself to his people in the form of a snake, appearing in the cattle kraal or the hut. Another important channel of the self-revelation of the Spirit is in dreams, by which he warns and leads his descendants. The royal ancestors kept in touch with the Zulu tribe largely through the king, one of whose principal functions was to be the priest in various ancestral rites.

Formerly, the king was not only the great medicine man of the tribe, he was also by his specially close relationship with heaven responsible for the growth of vegetation.[8] The king was the greatest rain-maker of the tribe, and he would procure rain by calling upon his ancestors for assistance. The royal spirits were specially cared for on the occasion of the great national festival of the year, the Zulu New Year festival, or the first-fruit ceremonies.[9]

These ceremonies included sacrifice and were accompanied by recitations of praise of the king and his forefathers and, by the use of various magical means, strengthened the king. There was also a ritual bath of the king. Decorated with garlands and fruits, the king went at dawn to a river, accompanied by doctors carrying ashes of a sacrificial bull. When he was in midstream, the doctors poured the ashes into the water just above the king. As they floated by downstream, the king washed himself with ashes and water. His soldiers, who had entered the water further downstream, washed in the water which had passed over the king. Through the ablutions they were both purified and at the same time filled with the power of the royal ancestors.

The most powerful and spectacular self-revelation of an ancestral spirit takes place in the initiation of the diviner (*isangoma*). While in the later routine activities of the diviner, magic and religion are blended, the actual initiation process is predominantly religious because of the role of the ancestors. During the initiation period (*ukwethwasa*) the novice carefully avoids all things that could ritually defile her.[10] She must go through daily purification rites by vomiting and by ablutions in a river. She adorns her body with white strips (*imiqwamba*) from the skin of a sacrificial goat. White is the diviner's colour. The purification rites and the whiteness of the dress are all part of the same process to "make the initiate see", to give her a clear vision, and to cause her to become totally possessed by the spirit. Together with her instructor, who is an experienced *isangoma*, and other initiates, she gives much time to rhythmical dancing which is an essential feature of the initiation. Each diviner has her special song, with its particular lilt and rhythm. The repeated performance of singing and dancing to this tune is required in order to please and materialize the spirit in whose honour the song is composed.

The urge to be possessed by the spirit and to become a diviner is felt as an irresistible force. Few are those who consciously wish to become possessed, but once the spirit has made known his intention to enter the person concerned, he must have his way. A prayer woman, Saulina, in our Ceza congregation suddenly disappeared from our church services, and it was reported that she was about to *ukwethwasa*. I went to the kraal and tried to persuade her to abandon such an idea, but both she and her pagan husband had definitely resigned themselves to her fate. "Leave me for some years, Mfundisi", she said. "I can do nothing about this possession. It must have its course. My *idlozi* wants me. But after, perhaps, two years, I will be back again". Although in this way the *idlozi*-possession is experienced as an irresistible force which most would prefer not to experience, yet Gluckman is correct in stating that to become diviners is for pagan Zulu women the only socially recognized way of escape from an impossible situation in family life; it is also the only way an outstanding woman can win general social prestige.[11]. In recent times the number of the *izangoma* has been greatly on the increase (Shaka, who resented their influence, had most of them killed).

A modern form of ancestor-possession is the *amandiki* or *amandawe*-possession. The phenomena connected with this have been scientifically described as far as the Vandau, the Venda and the Lovedu are concerned.[12] Quite recently—about 1910—they appeared in Zululand. It is characteristic that the two most serious epidemics in recent times among the Zulus— "influenza" in 1919–20 and malaria in 1933—were among the causes of the rapid spread of this form of possession. Like the *izizwe*-hysteria (see p. 248), the *amandawe*-possession is directed at curing some illness, and initiation into the cult is regarded as a healing agency, for it is believed to be therapeutic. As with *idlozi*-possession, dancing is an important feature of the more modern cult. However, whereas the *isangoma* novice is most often of an hysterical constitution, and the symptoms of the initiation (*ukwethwasa*) are quite violent, the initiates of *amandawe*-possession are relatively quiet. An *amandawe*-doctor is called to heal the patient. This is done by rites and dances designed to cause one of the patient's ancestral spirits to materialize. The initiate goes through many days of an exhausting dance, until at last the spirit enters her. It speaks through the initiate and expresses itself in a reputedly foreign tongue, as, for instance, a so-called "Indian" or "Thonga" language. In actual fact it may only be a series of meaningless sounds, which are thought by the audience to be some foreign language. Sometimes two or even as many as seven different ancestral spirits may take up their abode in the person concerned and speak in different languages.[a]

(c) *Magic*

Medicine, magic and religion are closely connected in Zulu pagan beliefs. We have, for example, just seen that the diviner receives her supernatural powers by being entered into by the spirit of one of her ancestors. In cases of illness and ill-fate, the diviner is called in to make a diagnosis. There are two other orders of doctors besides the diviner (*isangoma*)—namely, the

[a] The Zulus have had no well-known counterpart to the famous Xhosa prophets of the last century. The best known heathen "prophet"-influence among the Xhosa is, of course, the movement instigated by Mhlakaza and Nongquase in 1856. Apocalyptic expectations caused the people to slaughter 200,000 head of cattle and led to economic and social disaster. Willoughby mentions that a "prophet" was known as a *modimo* (god) in Bechuanaland before the Europeans came (*The Soul of the Bantu*, 1928, p. 113), a fact which is of importance for an understanding of the "Black-Christ-theology" in the Zionist churches.

herbalist or the leech (*inyanga*, plur. *izinyanga*) and the lightning magician. While the profession of diviner is not
hereditary and most of them are women, that of the herbalist
is handed down from father to son.[13] The actual call to follow
in the father's footsteps may be extended to a young man
through a dream. There is co-operation between diviner and
herbalist: when the former has concluded her diagnosis she
sends her patient to some herbalist to get treatment by a
specialist. An important development in the therapeutic
technique of the herbalist has taken place in recent years.
Many cases of hysteria which the *inyanga* is required to heal
nowadays are being treated with such medicines (*umuthi*, pl.
imithi) as are supposed to replace or supersede the hysteria with
some form of possession, called *indiki*, *indawe*, or *izizwe*. The
Zionist prophet movement, as we shall see, violently opposes
these practices and claims to be able to heal the *inyanga*-
induced possession by a new state of mind, possession by the
"Holy Spirit", as they describe it.

We have seen that the diviner-novice has to pass through a
lengthy process of initiation by which an ancestral spirit finds its
way into her being. As distinguished from this, the lightning-
magician, the priest of the sky-god, arrives much sooner and
more easily at proficiency in his particular speciality. A narrow
escape from being killed by lightning shows him that he is
specially favoured by the heavens. An older heaven-doctor will
smear him with the required medicines: fat of a heaven-bird
(an imaginary bird supposed to be found in the lightning) and
so-called *intelezi*-charms. Treated in this fashion, he acquires
the power necessary to perform his particularly dangerous work
for the benefit of the whole society.

All three categories of doctors are engaged in a struggle
against lurking dangers and destruction brought about by
ubuthakathi in all its forms of witchcraft and sorcery. "Black"
and "white" medicines of the *inyanga* strengthen the patient
against being smitten down by these malignant influences, or
are supposed to cure him if he has already fallen prey to them.
The main task of the diviner is to find out where sorcerers have
hidden their destructive and deadly poisons. In a society where
a sorcerer is supposed to be able to direct the very lightning
against the enemy by magical means, the heaven-doctor is kept
busy in placing magically prepared pegs (*izinkhonkwane*) which
will attract the powerful impulse of the sky-god and thereby
save the lives of men.

24

The belief in *u6uthakathi* is of fundamental importance to pagan Zulus. We shall see how this belief is taken over by the independent Bantu churches, and later shall discuss the means by which the various aspects of the *u6uthakathi* are blended with the new Christian belief taken over from the Whites.

(2) WHITE MISSIONS, HISTORY AND POLICY

(a) *1835–85: "Bantu-Boer-Briton"—and Boston*

William Shaw, the first Wesleyan missionary in Kaffraria (Cape Province), surveying in 1823 the tremendous expanse of the unknown African continent, said: "There is not a single missionary station between the place of my residence and the northern extremity of the Red Sea." Shaw was probably the first Protestant missionary to plan an "apostolic road" in Africa, a chain of mission stations to stretch from Salem, Shaw's first mission station, to what is now known as Durban (then Port Natal).[14]

This was in 1823. The situation has changed considerably since then. The advance during the first fifty years of missionary activity among the Zulus was slow but steady and definite. This advance must be seen against the general political background. The great expansion of Zulu political power under Shaka (murdered in 1828) was checked under the reign of Dingaan by the Dutch Voortrekkers at Bloedrivier on December 16, 1838. This clash between Bantu and Boer synchronized with the arrival of the first missionaries representing Britain and Boston (the headquarters of the American Board were situated in Boston). Distrust, sullen resistance and even violent opposition met Allen Gardiner, the Anglican missionary, and the American Congregationalists in the beginning of their work. This opposition was partly caused by the fear which the threatening political and military advance of the Europeans inspired among the Zulu leaders. Only in 1846 was the first Zulu, Umbulazi, baptized by Dr. Newton Adams, the physician in the team of the first American Board missionaries.[15]

These missionaries were able to secure a foothold in Southern Natal round Durban and Pietermaritzburg, but Zululand proper was closed to the missions. In 1850 the Norwegian missionary H. P. S. Schreuder succeeded, however, in overcoming King Mpande's resistance on this point. So much impressed was

25

Mpande by Schreuder's medical cure of one of his royal ailments that he at once gave the Lutheran missionary land at Empangeni (Zululand) and permission to build a mission station there. "Thus was Zululand opened to the Gospel—by the medicine bottle!"[16]

The mission work of the American Board developed rapidly. The principle of self-support and self-propagation by the Zulu Church was stressed by the missionaries from the beginning. In 1860 a "Native Home Missionary Society" was organized by and for the Zulus for the support of Zulu workers, and in 1870 the first Zulu pastor was ordained. The young Church accepted in 1879 the so-called "Umsunduze Rules", drawing a sharp line between the old heathen customs and the new Christian ethics. Dr. J. D. Taylor has described these rules as "an ironclad code of conduct which was used to stiffen the moral backbone of Christians".[17] A decisive stride forward was taken in the last year of this period, 1885, with the formation of the so-called "*Abaisitupa*" (The Six), a committee of six Zulu members who were entrusted with the Home Missionary Movement. This was a bold step towards devolution of responsibility to the African Church. At about the same time (in 1883) the mission succeeded in giving the Zulus that precious gift, the whole Bible translated into Zulu.

The evangelistic advance was supported by successful educational work, especially through the institutions at Amanzimtoti and Inanda. The American Board was also particularly instrumental in negotiating with the Natal Government in 1856 about so-called "Mission Reserves", which are large tracts of land in the immediate vicinity of mission stations. Zulu converts were invited to settle upon these reserves which have proved to be of great importance for the building of a Christian community in Natal.

Of the British Societies the Wesleyans eventually took up the challenge of their missionary, William Shaw. Important links in the chain of mission stations which he had visualized were welded from about 1847. A characteristic feature of the rapid development of their work during this first period is the *Unzondelelo*[a] revival movement, beginning in 1866.[18] At the outset, the Zulu leaders of this movement were not encouraged by the missionaries, who had their apprehensions of the possible separatist trends of the *Unzondelelo*. In 1878, however, the movement received authoritative approval. It has proved to be

_____
[a] *Unzondelelo*: zeal.

"a striking example of Bantu initiative wisely used" (Brookes).[19]

The Anglicans under Bishop J. W. Colenso laid the foundations of their mission work among the Zulus. The diocese of Natal was formed in 1853. Colenso, through his linguistic ability and ethnological interest, was well equipped to wield a great influence among the Zulus. In 1870 the first Bishop of Zululand was consecrated and the new diocese became separate from the diocese of Natal. The Free Church of Scotland began their work among the Zulus in 1864, the first missionary being James Allison, earlier working in connexion with the Wesleyan Methodist Mission Society.[20] Lutheran Societies from the Scandinavian countries and from Germany also constituted a strong missionary force in Natal. Through Schreuder's influence the Norwegians concentrated their efforts in Zululand itself. German societies (Berlin and Hermannsburg) followed about 1850, while the Church of Sweden Mission began its work at the end of the period, in 1878.

The first half-century is thus the period of the laying of the foundations. At the same time it is a period of serious crises in the Mission Churches. Two of the great leaders during this time, Colenso and Schreuder, played important parts in these crises. Colenso, that "attractive if wayward personality", was deposed from his episcopal see in 1864 because of his radical views pertaining to Biblical problems and questions of Church discipline (he favoured baptism of polygamists).[21] The Colenso controversy shook the colony of Natal for a considerable time. Schreuder, the rugged Norwegian Viking, was consecrated bishop in 1866. Seven years later he left the Norwegian Missionary Society as it was too Low-Church for his liking, and formed his own organization under the Church of Norway.

(b) 1885–1915

A decisive factor for mission as for other work during these thirty years was the discovery of the gold mines around Johannesburg in 1885. The "Witwatersrand" became not only the gravitation point of African labour but also an important centre for missionary activity. A host of new mission organizations were attracted to this field from Europe and America. William Shaw had during the 'twenties stated that there was not a single missionary station between his residence and the northern extremity of the Red Sea. Two generations later his successors were confronted with a problem

27

of an altogether different order: the "multiplication of mission-ary agencies" and "overlapping" of efforts in Natal and Zululand.

Most of these new mission organizations were the outcome of radical revivals in Europe and America of the "Holiness", Pentecostal and Apostolic Faith type; others belonged to the Seventh Day Adventists (from 1892); others again represented the Salvation Army. An important organization in Natal was the South African General Mission, the leader of which was Rev. F. Suter. He became especially well known as the principal of the Dumisa Training Institute for Pastors and Evangelists, an interdenominational institution. Several Zulus who later were to become Separatist Church leaders received their initial theological training at Dumisa.

The Ethiopian problem, or the Separatist Church movement, was felt as a disturbing element during this period. We should, however, also remember the positive consequences on mission work of this situation. The threat of the Separatist Church movement on the one hand and the rapid growth of the number of missionary societies on the other hand became strong in-centives towards missionary co-operation. A platform for this co-operation had already been built in 1881 through the forma-tion of the Natal Missionary Conference, and the scope of co-operative endeavour was widened by the institution of General Missionary Conferences for the whole of South Africa from 1904 onwards.

All the same, the World Missionary Conference in session at Edinburgh in 1910, when referring to the conditions of mission work in South Africa, did "bewail the extent of overlapping, which has prejudicial influence on the attitude of the Natives affected by it, and tends to neutralize that wise and careful discipline which is so necessary in the upbuilding of a Native Church".[22] Towards the end of the period, after seventy-five years of mission work in Natal and Zululand, eighteen different societies were united in the Natal Missionary Conference. The number of European missionaries represented in the Conference was 263. African ministers were forty-six, and full members 60,000. The probable total of adherents of all societies was 200,000. To this should be added certain undenominational societies not attached to the Natal Missionary Conference, and a considerable number of missionary agencies operating only in Johannesburg, although from this central position influencing Zulus also elsewhere than on the Witwatersrand.[23]

(c) After 1915

The tendencies towards "multiplication of missionary agencies", on the one hand, and on the other towards more co-operation between the societies has been accentuated during this last period. The *Christian Handbook of South Africa* (1938) enumerates forty societies as engaged in mission work in Natal and Zululand, ranging in size from Mission churches of 100,000 members and more (Methodists, Anglicans, Lutherans) to small groups of less than 1000.[24] We should also mention the Roman Catholic Missions. The work in Natal has been entrusted since 1882 to the Trappist Order (Congregation of Mariannhill), and that in Zululand to the Benedictine Order since 1923. The Roman Catholic advance among the Zulus during this last period has been both extensive and intense.

The outstanding fact about church co-operation during the period was the formation in 1936 of the Christian Council of South Africa. The Council is doing its most valuable work through its seven sectional committees on Education, Evangelism, Literature, Medical Work, Native Welfare, Women's Work, and Youth Movements. Although not envisaging any federation or union of the constituent Churches, the Christian Council acts as the mouthpiece of the œcumenical cause in South Africa.[25]

Missionary policy

A brief analysis of the missionary policy followed in the leading missionary societies is necessary at this point. In concentrating our attention upon the period which saw the rise of the Separatist Church movement—approximately 1890–1910 —we stress that this summary is simply meant as a background for the main problem which we are discussing in this book.

Henry Venn, Rufus Anderson, and Gustaf Warneck expressed the programme of modern Protestant missions, as far as the "Native Church" is concerned, in the slogan: "A self-supporting, self-governing, and self-propagating church."[26] This was taken to mean that the young Church in China, India, or Africa should be independent and indigenous. This policy was, however, so far of only theoretical interest. It was discussed in the transactions of the Mission Boards in London or Boston. It had not yet been tried out in the field. When this mission policy was brought to the South African mission field it caused some consternation among the missionaries, whether Britishers or Americans. I mention three examples of this.

29

When John Kilner, a secretary of the Wesleyan Methodist Missionary Society, went on a "kind of deputational hurricane" to South Africa, he was impressed by the "amazing modesty" of the missionaries. "He marvelled at the modesty which prevented them from putting forward some of the Native leaders who were fit for the work."[27] He emphasized the need of an African ministry, and no less than fifty or sixty names were registered of men who might be ordained as "Native Ministers on Trial". Kilner met, however, with opposition from some of the "modest" missionaries, who "felt that the action was too hasty and there were serious misgivings on the part of some".[28]

The conference of Foreign Mission Boards of the United States sent a circular in 1895 to the missionaries in the Zulu field stressing the need for a self-supporting Church. When this circular was translated into Zulu, the words for self-support (*ukuzondla*) and self-government (*ukuziphatha*) were not clearly understood. Some of the African leaders, reading the circular in Zulu, "believed that the missionaries were withholding from them the rights of Congregational Churches" (that is, of forming independent, self-governing congregations).[29] They resented missionary control. This was one of the reasons for the formation, in 1896, of the separatist Zulu Congregationalist Church.

Something of the same problem was felt by Presbyterian mission leaders. Dr. Stewart of Lovedale was not altogether willing to follow the lead from Edinburgh urging the ordination on an increased number of African ministers. In an agitated moment, he seems to have claimed that the main cause of Ethiopianism was to be found in the interference of European mission boards in the matter of ordination of Africans.[30]

One should perhaps not draw too far-reaching conclusions from these three examples. But they are not insignificant. They show that some missionaries in the field—representing some of the most influential missionary societies working in South Africa at the time—felt the danger of a too hasty application of Henry Venn's and Rufus Anderson's principles.

Ten years later the situation had changed. Missionaries of a younger generation, filled with the ideals of a self-governing African Church, had begun their work. They were in the years 1905–10 confronted with a situation where the Ethiopian problem was felt as most disturbing and perplexing. This was bound to affect mission policy very definitely. At General Missionary Conferences in 1904 and 1909 the problem was tackled by two missionary leaders, E. Jacottet of the Paris Mission in Basutoland and J. Lennox of Lovedale (United Free Church of Scotland).[31]

Jacottet urged that missions had to adapt themselves to the new situation created by Ethiopian secessions. "Let us take what is good in the programme of Ethiopianism, and be truer to it than the Ethiopians themselves." This would be accomplished by making the Mission Church indigenous and at the same time separate from the European Church. "A little less Presbyterianism, a little less Anglicanism, a little less Lutheranism (not to speak of all the other larger or smaller South African *isms*) would do no harm, and a little more Africanism would do a great deal more good. Christianity must lose its European form and colour, it must become as African a religion to the Africans as it is to-day a European religion to the Europeans." In order to achieve this aim, "complete separation" between the European and African churches was of paramount importance. This separation, or segregation as we should say to-day, was made "quite imperative" because of two considerations, according to Jacottet: (1) "The general feelings of the European towards the native" in South Africa. (2) Only in a segregated church would the African be allowed full scope for self-development. Experience had proved to Jacottet that Africans who were connected with a European church "would always have to play second fiddle". To him the aim which the mission had to strive to attain was the independent native church, although *ad hoc* European supervision and help was necessary: "I do not mean that the native churches should be *at once* completely independent and self-governing."

The segregated African Church was discussed by Lennox five years later. He referred to the discussions which had taken place in the Anglican Church of the Province at that time. While certain Anglicans asked for special bishops for "Native" work, the majority were for "maintaining visibly the unity of the whole Catholic Church, white and black".[32] Lennox opposed this "incorporating union" of the European and African sections of the Church. With such an arrangement "everything which gives outward expression to the belief and permanent form of the Church is imposed from above on that which is below". Lennox stated the consequences of his supposedly more democratic approach: in the South Africa of race conflict, Lennox emphasized, this implied a segregated church divided into one White section and another, African section in order to give to the latter freedom of expression and opportunity for development and leadership.[33]

The most notable result of these views, as expounded, for instance, by Lennox, was the formation in 1923 of the Bantu Presbyterian Church. The Church of Scotland Missions then decided to accept the consequences of the mission policy professed by them and other Protestant missions in making the experiment of this autonomous and segregated or "parallel" Bantu Church. The first African Moderator of the General Assembly of the Bantu Presbyterian Church was Right Reverend Y. Mbali. From 1923 to 1946 there have been altogether twenty one moderators, of whom ten have been European missionaries and eleven African ministers. The enrolment which in 1923 was some 24,000 has now (1946) risen to 30,000. The Bantu ministers have received a sound theological education, first at Lovedale and latterly at Iona House, Fort Hare. The number of European missionaries compared with that of African ministers is small. They have no power of veto in the General Assembly, but have equal votes with the African brethren. The African moderators have a very considerable influence in the Church.[34]

Some Protestant missions in South Africa have followed the example of the Bantu Presbyterian Church; others have not. Anglicans and Roman Catholics oppose the policy of parallel and segregated churches, claiming that the Catholic Church is indivisible.

(3) "NET VIR BLANKES—FOR EUROPEANS ONLY"

If it is a fact—and I believe that it is—that nowhere else has the Separatist church movement grown to such dimensions as in the Union of South Africa, this must mean that there is in South African society some particular root cause not found elsewhere, at least to the same extent, which leads to this result. This root cause is the colour line between White and Black. Nothing more than a cursory glance at the history and sociology of racial discrimination in South Africa can be given here, but it is obvious that any inquiry into the life of the independent Bantu churches must give some consideration to the racial caste system in that country.

Public and private life in South Africa is dominated by the colour problem. Everything, from public conveyances and conveniences to national legislation, is literally or figuratively

32

stamped with that warning sign of racial segregation, expressed in the two official languages of the country: *"Net Vir Blankes—* For Europeans Only.*"* There are differences in the general attitudes of Boer and Briton to the Bantu, but there is now in essence a common front, a common attitude.

(a) *Land and labour*

It may seem strange to start a discussion of this problem with a few notes on the land question. However, as has been rightly said, "the Native question *is* the land question" (W. M. Macmillan), so it can be argued that even the Separatist church problem is a corollary of the land problem.[35] The increase in the number of Bantu independent churches could be shown on a diagram as a parallel to the tightening squeeze of the Natives through land legislation. Some of the African land-buying syndicates before 1913 were composed of Ethiopian leaders, and even to-day one of the highest ambitions of a successful church leader is to find land for the founding of a church colony of his own. Professor Jabavu, one of the most level-headed and best known of African spokesmen, uses very strong language when characterizing the Natives Land Act of 1913 in an article about "Bantu Grievances." He there stresses that the Act of 1913 was felt as the worst of their grievances.[36] This Act, the first link in the chain of segregational legislation, lays down that no Native, *qua* Native, may purchase or even hire land except in certain scheduled areas. This meant that in Natal, with its 25,000 square miles of territory and its European population of 132,000 (Census 1921), the one million Zulus were restricted to the purchase of land in an area of less than 4000 square miles.[37] For South Africa as a whole it meant that one million Europeans held a larger share of the land than the approximately five million Africans, who were restricted to the so-called Reserves. It is fair to record here that only 15 per cent. of the Union is cultivable.[37a] The passing of the Natives Land Act of 1913 explains the bitterness with which African agitators at that time used to accuse the Whites: "At first we had the land, and you had the Bible. Now we have the Bible, and you have the land." The effect of the Native Trust and Land Act of 1936 has not yet been widely enough felt as to alleviate substantially the hardships experienced by Africans.

The result of the 1913 Act was that many Africans moved from Natal, either to the Reserves or to the towns, especially Johannesburg. The taxation policy was another cause of the city-ward trend of the Africans. Then the Urban Areas Act of 1923 (amended in 1930) further emphasized the segregation policy begun in 1913: it aimed at "the segregation of Natives *from* the towns, and the segregation of Natives *in* the towns",[38] the reason being that European farmers wanted to secure farm labour. No wonder that the Africans, debarred by such restrictive legislation both from the land and from the towns, asked themselves almost in despair, "*Siyangaphi?*" — "Where are we to go?"

In 1926, the legislation in a Joint Session of the two Houses put the placard "*Net Vir Blankes*—For Europeans Only" on any skilled labour in the mining industry.[39] This made the existing industrial "Colour Bar" legal. The result has been "loss in the earning power and opportunity for the Native, the growth of anti-White prejudice, and the general embitterment of race relations throughout the Union".[40] Because of this "Colour Bar Act" the unemployed problem during the economic crisis in the early 'thirties was neatly "solved" by substituting "white" for "black" labourers wherever possible.[41] These socio-economic factors directly affect the argument in this book: many of the outbursts of the Independent Church movement occurred during this period of bitterness caused by African unemployment. The existence to-day of a considerable number of Independent Church leaders who prior to the enforcement of the "Colour Bar Act" were occupied as skilled artisans and craftsmen, seems to point to an important relation between these two phenomena in the life of Africans at the present time. It is pertinent to our subject to observe that these restrictions were most strongly felt on the Witwatersrand, the most important centre of the Independent Church movement.

So far African labour has not had much help from the South African trade unions, which are practically "lily-white", as they put it in the Southern States of America. There are only a few African trade unions, in which the urbanized African's leadership urge can find some outlet and where his organizing abilities can be developed. But African Trade Unions are not recognized by the law, and—to make the White domination technique fully effective—the African, by the Native Labour Regulation Act of 1911, is deprived of the strike weapon. Native strikes are, as such, illegal. The resort to strikes was "for Europeans only—*net vir Blankes*".

The "Industrial and Commercial Workers Union", often referred to as the "I.C.U.", did attain a certain degree of influence in the 'twenties, especially among the Zulus, under its Nyasa leader, Clemens Kadalie, and the Zulu politician, A. W. G. Champion.[42] "Official and unofficial deliberate repression", together with bad administration of the affairs of this union, led to its early downfall.[43] The same has come to be the fate of the African National Congress, an organization which grew out of the resentment against the passing of the Natives Land Act. Its organ is the newspaper *Abantu-Batho*. The Congress reached the peak of its influence about 1918–24; it later lost its grip on the masses.[44] Some Ethiopian church leaders have played a part in the deliberations of the Congress.

(b) Social relationships

In the matter of social relations, a missionary friend of mine told me of an incident which is very revealing for the situation as a whole. She worked as a secretary in the office of a missionary institution out in the country in Natal. One day she visited Durban, and in the fashionable West Street met a Zulu pastor, whom she knew from her mission station. She greeted him, they stopped for a while, chatted, and parted. Two days later she received a letter from the minister. He wished to express his gratefulness to her, for he knew very well, he said, that an African could be treated as an ordinary human being when on the peaceful mission station out in the country, but that meeting in West Street, Durban, was a different matter. She had honoured him by her act of greeting him in the street in a quite natural way.

Relations between the two races are generally only casual. One is reminded of the American Negro leader DuBois' famous simile of the plate glass: "Some thick sheet of invisible but horribly tangible plate glass is between the Negroes and the world. They get excited; they talk louder; they gesticulate. Some of the passing world stop in curiosity; these gesticulations seem so pointless; they laugh and pass on. They still either do not hear at all, or hear but dimly, and even what they hear, they do not understand."[45] Segregation and colour bar have indeed raised up a plate glass wall between White and Black also in South Africa.

Casual contact is regulated by a well-defined deference system. The "Master-and-Servant" attitude gives its particular taint to such contacts. Hat in hand, the African is supposed to say "Yes, Sir" to anything that a White man, *qua* White, tells him to do. The educated, urbanized African is regarded as

35

"cheeky" and disobedient because he may not duplicate the *khonza*-attitude of his uneducated fellow Africans in detail.[a] "Give me the raw Kaffir every time!" is therefore a stereotyped and popular White retort to what is thought to be pro-Native ranting. And—such is the sequence of this White argument— why bother about the social and religious welfare of the African; look at the African in the street, how happy he is! So he may appear—struggling along, smiling, laughing, boisterous—but the smile may be misleading. The American Negro poet, Langston Hughes, has interpreted for the whole of his race, what may be the hidden feeling behind that broad smile:

> Because my mouth
> is wide with laughter
> and my throat
> is deep with song,
> You do not think
> I suffer after
> I have held my pain
> so long.
>
> Because my mouth
> is wide with laughter
> You do not hear
> my inner cry;
> Because my feet
> are gay with dancing
> You do not know
> I die.[b]

(c) White Christianity and the colour bar

The Christian Church in South Africa is represented not only by the missions, the history and policy of which we have just referred to, but also by the three million Whites, most of whom profess to be Christians. I believe W. M. Eiselen is right when, in a brilliant survey of *Christianity and the Religious Life of the Bantu*, he says that "contact with a population of White Christians has raised the quantity and has lowered the quality of Bantu Christians."[46] Eiselen sees the reason for this second effect—the lowering of the quality—in the discrepancy between the missionary's Christian message and the European's Christian life, which is said to have led to religious indifferentism

[a] *Ukukhonza* is the Zulu verb for "serving one's lord as a subject". Bryant, *Zulu Dictionary*, p. 318. For the modern use of the term, see Hoernlé, *S.A. Native Policy and the Liberal Spirit*, 1939, p. 51.

[b] Reprinted from *The Dream Keeper*, by Langston Hughes, by permission of Alfred A. Knopf, Inc. Copyright 1932 by Alfred A. Knopf, Inc.

among the modern Bantu. This discrepancy is above all revealed in the colour bar within the Christian Church. *"Net vir Blankes*—For Europeans Only" is figuratively but no less virtually written on many church doors in the Union. And this fact is one of the reasons for the emergence of Independent Bantu Churches. One of the leading Zulus of a younger generation has recently expressed the position thus:

> For a long time the church acted as a mellowing influence in African life. Whatever inequalities existed in the harsh every-day world, the Africans firmly believed that these would not exist within the church. But in many cases these hopes have not been fulfilled. The result has been racial bitterness and the ultimate formation of Bantu separatist churches. Even where this has not happened there is a general acceptance of the inevitability of an African National Church, unless relationships between African and European take a turn for the better.[47]

The old "golden rule" of South African Calvinism, *"geen gelijkstelling*—no equality between Black and White in Church or State", has in fact and in every-day practice been accepted by many other White churches. As a rule, an African cannot with impunity enter a White church for an ordinary religious service. I have listened to scores of Independent church leaders who have related instances of how they have been turned away from White church services because of their black skin. The resentment over these pinpricks has added to the general aversion to the White man's Christianity. It should be underlined that some Churches with firm episcopal authority have broken with this rule, both on principle and also in actual practice. I have no doubt that this is one reason why such churches do not come up against the problem of separatism to the same extent as do other Churches. Senator E. H. Brookes has rightly stated: "Separatism has been the result, to a very large extent, of the presence of the colour bar within the Christian Church."[48]

CHAPTER II

THE RISE OF THE INDEPENDENT CHURCH MOVEMENT

The Bantu independent Church movement in South Africa already has a history. It is a history of bold aspirations and of baffled endeavours. With all its weaknesses it is part of the story of Christian Missions. I shall here limit myself to the *general trend* and the main *types* of the independent church movement.

(1) HISTORY OF CHURCHES OF ETHIOPIAN AND ZIONIST TYPE

The first so-called "Ethiopian" church was founded on the Witwatersrand in 1892. Before that date there had, however, occurred certain attempts at Bantu emancipation from mission authority. We begin by recording briefly these apparently sporadic movements.

In the Hermon congregation of the Paris mission in Basutoland there was in 1872 a minor secession, caused no doubt in part by the changes in ecclesiastical organization which the mission underwent in that same year.[1] Of greater importance was the tribal church, organized in 1884 by the Wesleyan minister, Nehemiah Tile. This man was one of the group of prominent African leaders within the Wesleyan Mission Church who had·been ordained as a result of John Kilner's "deputational hurricane" in 1880.[2] As Tile was criticized by a European missionary because of his strong Tembu-nationalistic sympathies, he left the church in 1882. Two years later he formed the "Tembu Church", with Ngangelizwe, the Chief of the Tembu, as its visible head. The cause of this important secession was not only opposition to European control, but also a positive desire to adapt the message of the Church to the heritage of the Tembu tribe. As the Queen of England was the head of the English Church, so the Paramount Chief of the Tembu should be the *summus episcopus* of the new religious organization. When Ngangelizwe's successor, Dalindyebo, got into difficulties with the Government authorities of the Cape Colony because of this Church, he withdrew his support and returned to the Mission fold. Of a similar character was a secession from the London Missionary Society at Taung, Bechuanaland, in 1885.

38

The tribal chief Kgantlapane took an active part in the founding in that year of the Native Independent Congregational Church, and he appointed ministers of his own choice to lead this tribal Church. In 1889 a young and over-zealous missionary of the Berlin Mission to the Bapedi, J. A. Winter, anxious to give the African Church leaders more responsibility, formed a secessionist church, the Lutheran Bapedi Church. And in the same year an evangelist of the Anglican church in Pretoria, Khanyane Napo, formed his own organization, the "Africa Church".

These few attempts, within various tribes, to found national or tribal religious organizations, as distinct from the denominational and inter-tribal Churches organized by the missions, were so far, however, sporadic. When these ideas spread to the Witwatersrand the whole movement took a new momentum. Among the thousands of African labourers who were attracted to the work in the gold mines there were also small groups of Christian workers, mostly Wesleyan local preachers. In 1895 there were in Johannesburg no less than sixty-five such voluntary preachers of the Wesleyan Church, coming from various parts of the country.[3] Some of them had had relatively responsible positions in the rural districts from which they came. In the Golden City they were unknown and grew restless. One of their leaders, a Wesleyan minister, Mangena M. Mokone, opposed what he regarded as racial segregation within the church, as seen by there being one conference for European leaders, and another for African leaders.[4] He resigned from the Wesleyan Church in 1892, and together with other malcontents in Pretoria formed a new religious organization (ministers, evangelists, teachers and ordinary adherents of the Wesleyan Church). The name of the new Church was of great significance —the *"Ethiopian Church"*. Mokone's group was not limited by any mere tribal interest. The Church leader on the Rand had a wider horizon and appealed to many tribes. There was a programme in the very name of the new Church. Mokone had heard missionaries who referred in their sermons to Ps. 68: 31, *"Ethiopia shall soon stretch out her hands unto God"*, and to other references such as Acts 8: 27, and who interpreted this as a promise of the evangelization of Africa. Mokone took this to mean the self-government of the African Church under African leaders. Among Mokone's colleagues were some of those destined to take a leading part in the future of the Ethiopian movement, such as Khanyane Napo, S. J. Brander, Jonas Goduka (Tile's successor), and James M. Dwane.

39

The one outstanding leader among them was Dwane, a Gaika of a chief clan. Like Tile and Mokone, he was an ordained Wesleyan minister (born 1848, ordained 1881). Gifted as a speaker, he was sent to England in 1894–95 to represent his Church and solicit financial support for the work. On his return to South Africa, he quarrelled with his mission authorities about the disposal of this money, and left the Mission Church. In 1896 he joined forces with Mokone and Brander, and because of his ability and forceful personality, at once became the leader of the new movement.

Both Mokone and Dwane had through different sources heard of the African Methodist Episcopal Church among the Negroes of the United States. At a conference in Pretoria in 1896—a momentous year in the history of South Africa and the Rand—all the independent Church leaders met, and they decided to seek affiliation with this Church. Dwane was chosen to go to America in order to obtain such affiliation. A few facts should be mentioned here about the Church in question.

The African Methodist Episcopal Church was founded in Philadelphia in 1816 by the Negro preacher Richard Allen († 1831) who already in 1787 had withdrawn from the White Methodist church because of the colour bar practised there.[5] Allen is said to have been consecrated to the episcopate when the new church was founded in 1816. Allen's church started mission work in Liberia in 1820. At the time of Dwane's visit to the United States this Negro Church in America had grown to include some 800,000 communicants. It was relatively well organized, and its church paper, *Voice of Missions*, was read by Ethiopian leaders in South Africa. Through Dwane's representations the Ethiopian Church was formally incorporated in the African Methodist Episcopal Church. Dwane was appointed General Superintendent of the South African work.

On his return to South Africa he succeeded in persuading all the Ethiopian leaders to follow him into the A.M.E. fold. Together with Khanyane and Mokone, he approached the Government of the Transvaal for formal recognition of the Church, which was granted. Dwane's ambitions took him further. He asked Cecil Rhodes for the right to extend his church to Rhodesia and the Zambezi, and he planned to collect funds to be sent to King Menelik of Abyssinia in order to extend mission work to the Sudan and Egypt.[6] This expansion caused much upheaval in the work of the mission societies. Congregationalists, Presbyterians and others felt the repercussions of

Dwane's broad advance. Thus, to the unrest caused by war and rumours of war in South Africa was added the Ethiopian tension within the Mission Churches.

In 1898 the A.M.E. bishop, H. M. Turner, paid a five weeks' visit to South Africa. In this short time the Negro bishop was accorded a triumphant welcome by the Ethiopians. He managed to achieve some startling results: the work was organized in regional conferences, Turner ordained sixty-five ministers, consecrated Dwane as assistant bishop, and bought a site for a future centre for higher learning (in Queenstown). Through Turner's visit the membership figure of the church was more than doubled, mainly through affiliating malcontent groups and congregations from Mission Churches. The membership was suddenly inflated to over 10,000.[7]

In the following year, 1899, Dwane went to America once again. His aim was both to get financial support from the Negro Churches of the United States for the work in South Africa, and to have Turner's consecration of himself confirmed by the Negro Church as a whole. He was not content with being only an assistant bishop, a position which emphasized the inferior status of the African Church as compared with the Negro Church. He had discovered that the Ethiopian programme, "Africa for Africans", conflicted with the linking up of his church with an American (Negro) Mission Church. The fact that Turner's action in consecrating Dwane as assistant bishop did not receive the full recognition of the other Negro bishops made Dwane finally realize that he should break with the African Methodist Episcopal Church.

On his return to South Africa Dwane took an extraordinary step. He sought contact with the authorities of the (Anglican) Church of the Province, and was informed by them that the African Methodist Episcopal Church "could not hand on Episcopal Orders because they had never received them".[8] The outcome of Dwane's deliberations with the Anglicans was the formation in 1900 of the "Order of Ethiopia" as part of the Church of the Province. On the part of the bishops of the Province this step was an act of real statesmanship and of great promise. Dwane was eventually ordained a deacon and later for some years was Provincial of the Order. Energetic efforts were made to give theological instruction to those of Dwane's sub-leaders who had followed him into the Anglican Church. Dwane did not, however, succeed in carrying the majority of Ethiopians with him. The main stream of the Ethiopian movement

41

continued in the channels of the African Methodist Episcopal Church or of other independent groups that sprang up during and after the Boer War.[9] In 1908 the adherents of the Order were only some 3500.[10] Dwane died in 1915 and was succeeded by another African as Provincial. Generally speaking, the Order of Ethiopia can hardly be said to have succeeded in attracting the broad masses of Ethiopians. Furthermore, it has remained mainly Xhosa. As an attempt on the part of a great Mission Church to tackle the Ethiopian problem in a spirit of understanding and deep concern, it is, so far, unique in the mission history of South Africa.

At the same time as Dwane left the Ethiopian movement, the importance of the American connexions of the African Methodist Episcopal Church was emphasized by the United States Negroes sending one of their ablest men, L. J. Coppin, to South Africa as their first resident bishop. The A.M.E. as it is called among the Zulus has had some good leaders, such as Bishops D. H. Sims and R. R. Wright. They have shown a keen interest in Native education. The Wilberforce Institute, near Johannesburg, with Teachers Training and Theological Departments, is aiming at becoming a South African "Tuskegee".

American Negro missionaries were, however, just as much foreigners and strangers in the eyes of the Ethiopians as the White missionaries. Therefore the same kind of propaganda was directed against the A.M.E. as against the "white" missions. Thus, for instance, Brander, one of the oldest Ethiopian leaders, claims that the A.M.E. "took, like the old 'Papae Romanorum', all moneys collected for the interests of the church in Africa to America, and there expended them obviously on purely American interests and not on Ethiopic interests".[11] Because of this, and for similar reasons, Brander founded his own church called the Ethiopian Catholic Church in Zion, in 1904, breaking away from the African Methodist Episcopal Church.

Another important Ethiopian Church must be mentioned, the African Presbyterian Church founded in 1898 by P. J. Mzimba of the United Free Church of Scotland. Mzimba was, like Dwane, widely travelled. He represented his race at the Jubilee Assembly of the Free Church of Scotland in 1892, and after founding his Church he visited America in 1902. One of the reasons why Mzimba broke with his mission and with that great missionary statesman, Dr. J. Stewart of Lovedale, was that he had been given considerable sums of money in Scotland. On returning to South Africa, he claimed the right to allocate these sums to such objects as he pleased, without regard to the opinion of the Lovedale presbytery.[12] His position as a respected pastor of the Presbyterian mission congregation at Lovedale made his secession the more serious. Two-thirds of this congregation followed him. The fact that Mzimba—himself of the Fingo tribe—only carried the Fingo people with him, whereas the Xhosa section of the Presbyterian church remained unmoved by his approach, throws an important light on secessionism. Like Tile's Tembu church, Mzimba's organization was not only Ethiopian, but tribal.[13] Characteristically, the leadership of the Church was inherited by his son, L. M. Mzimba, who had had some years' education in America.[14] In parenthesis, one may mention in this connexion that a surprising number of Ethiopian leaders have for a shorter or longer time studied in America. A Natal Native Affairs Commission of 1906–7 found that up to that time at least a hundred and fifty Africans from South Africa, some of them with definite Ethiopian affiliations, had gone to America for studies. Of these, twenty or more were from Natal and were, presumably, Zulus.[15] Also in more recent times Zulu Ethiopian leaders, such as Walter Dimba and others, have had a background of some years of study in America. On this point, the Ethiopian movement opened the eyes of many Europeans in South Africa to the desirability of a Bantu centre for higher learning nearer home, and has thereby some relation with the decision to create the Bantu University College at Fort Hare, opened in 1916.[16]

Against this general background of the first beginnings of the Ethiopian movement in South Africa, I shall now sketch some of the main developments, in so far as secessions are concerned, within certain leading Protestant churches, giving special emphasis to such developments among the Zulus.

(2) GENEALOGICAL TABLES OF REPRESENTATIVE CHURCHES

"Few discoveries are more irritating than those which expose the pedigree of ideas", Lord Acton has said.[17] In seeking the root of the separatist problem we shall have to suffer such irritation. The problem in fact lends itself to a treatment in terms of genealogical tables of Churches. In a short period of time the growth of the number of Churches has been as if by geometrical progression. I choose three examples of such genealogical tables, two representing in the main Churches

43

which I shall describe as of Ethiopian type, whereas the third
is an attempt to show the pedigree of "Zionist" Churches.

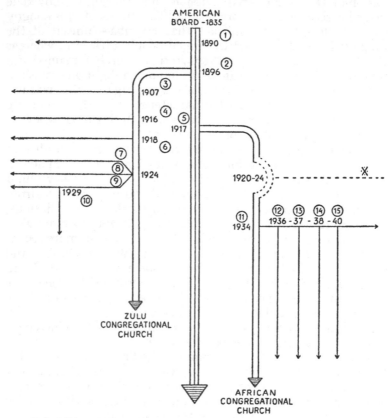

1. Zulu Mbiyana Church.
2. Zulu Congregational Church.
3. African Mission Home Church.
4. African United Zulu Church.
5. African Congregational Church.
6. Zulu of African Ethiopian Church.
7. Shibe's section of Zulu Congregational Church.
8. Zulu Shaka Church.
9. African Free Congregational Church.
10. African Free Congregational Church, competing section of.
11. Gardiner Mvuyana African Congregational Church.
12. African Congregational Church lika Mvuyana.
13. N. Laudon's section of No. 11.
14. African Native Faith Healing Church.
15. Native Primitive Church.
✗. Ephemeral union with African Congregational Methodist Church.

(a) Congregational offshoots (see diagram, p. 44)

Apart from one insignificant secession as early as 1890, representing Mbiana Ngidi's Zulu Mbiana Congregational Church, there are two main branches in the tree of Congregational secessions: the Zulu Congregational Church founded in 1896, and the African Congregational Church of 1917. These are the main offshoots from the Mission Church itself. All the following secessions are the result of fission of independent Zulu Churches. I do not need to draw attention to the main stem of the diagram: the American Board Mission in spite of these secessions has continued its richly blessed mission work with its strong emphasis on the educational uplift of the Zulu people.

The Zulu Congregational secession in 1896 is bound up with the history of Congregationalism in South Africa. In the 'nineties the American Board attempted to establish close co-operation with the (English-South African) Congregational Union of South Africa. A missionary of the latter organization was to take over the "Table Mountain" mission station in Natal, founded by the American Congregationalist missionaries. The African leader of that congregation, Samungu Shibe, opposed this to him incomprehensible transfer and seceded. At the same time two African leaders on the Rand broke off from the Mission over a matter of church property. They were, however, reconciled to the mission after some time.[18] The Zulu Rebellion ten years later added new recruits to the Zulu Congregational Church. After some time, the founder of the Church lost his grip over his followers, and new secessions followed. The leader's death in 1924 led to three new secessions. The Church seceding in 1918 introduced "Baptist" (which in this particular case is identical with Zionist) practices, whereas one of the secessions of 1924 called itself the Shaka Zulu Church. The very name "Shaka Zulu Church" denotes the nativistic tendencies which necessarily enter an independent Church when it is sufficiently distant from the influence of sound Bible teaching.

The African Congregational Church had as its founder one of the most powerful leaders and best preachers that Zulu Congregationalism has known, Gardiner B. Mvuyana. Born in 1866, he became a teacher in 1886, evangelist in 1890, and was later ordained. As a minister in the mission in Johannesburg he wielded a considerable influence. When the missionary in charge took him to task for certain actions which he regarded as irreconcilable with Christian standards, Mvuyana left and founded his own Church. It is characteristic that this important secession took place on the Rand. The repercussions in Natal and Zululand were also considerable. On the diagram I have pointed out the attempt to unite his Church with another separatist body, the African Congregational Methodist Church. This attempt was abortive however. Mvuyana died in 1925. Since his death the church has been led by other able and powerful men, M. S. Dube († 1942) and L. M. Makhoba, the latter elected president in 1943. The Church was awarded Government recognition in 1937. In 1932–34 difficulties were caused by an interesting but restless leader of "Young Intellectual" type, Walter M. Dimba, who had had four years' training in America. It is significant that in his effort to arouse the enthusiasm of his followers he called his Church "African Congregational Church *lika Mvuyana*" (Mvuyana's). The clan name of the strong man and church father of the organization from which he is seceding is here used as a propitious name for the new Church. Dimba's attempts at church leadership have so far been unsuccessful. It is worth while observing that one subsecession calls itself African Native Faith Healing Church: this shows the influence of Zionist practices on an Ethiopian offshoot—and it corresponds to similar developments just referred to, on the outer fringes of the Zulu Congregational Church.

Returning to Lord Acton's remark on the "pedigree of ideas" one is reminded, when studying this development of Church secessions from a congregational body in a mission area, of what Malcolm Spencer, himself a good Congregationalist, says of the Congregational churches: "The core of the claim for the religious autonomy of the individual group or person has been the belief [of the Congregationalists] that the most real embodiment of the divine is in the religious individual. Life is more unquestionably evident in that which is original, novel, individual." But he warns: "It can be seen and admitted now that an undue emphasis on the significance of the individual person or group may lead to an undue disparagement or neglect of the value of tradition, order, and restraint."[19] We shall see presently in the chapter on Leadership how certain African leaders coming from this camp now attempt to build up a new tradition of order and restraint. In fact, that is the core of their leadership problem.

(b) Methodist offshoots

The Methodist mission work in South Africa is of such dimensions and stretches to so very many tribes that it is not possible to do justice to the secession problem within this group of churches by a simple diagram. I limit myself to a few characteristic developments which are related to the theme in this book, Tile's secession and the Bantu Methodist Church.

Tile's Tembu Church, founded in 1884, suffered a serious crisis in 1892 through the death of the founder. On his deathbed, Tile is reported to have told his followers that he would have a worthy successor in a man of the Gaika tribe. As many Tembu people did not accept Gaika leadership, they joined the Ethiopian Church under Dwane and Mokone instead. The Gaika leader who took over the remnants of Tile's church was Jonas Goduka, also a Wesleyan. He drew up a new Constitution calling the Church the African Native Mission Church. In order to secure his hold over the Church he persuaded his followers to declare in 1904 that he should be a leader for life. After the death of Jonas Goduka, when his son inherited the leadership, there occurred in 1919 a new crisis, as one section opposed the principle of the church leadership being inherited. This was branded as "poperism". It is characteristic of the development which we are tracing in this book that one section breaking off from Goduka eventually called itself the African Faith Healing Mission. Here again an Ethiopian Church is showing an example of the strong pull from Zionist healing practices.[20]

The *Bantu Methodist Church* or the "Donkey Church" founded on the Rand in 1932–33 is one of the most spectacular secessions in recent times. The leadership problems involved in this crisis are analysed on p. 172. The interesting point about it is the role of the broad mass of urbanized church people in this upheaval. There was an unmistakable nationalist spirit which fired leaders and followers with enthusiasm for the break, as well as dissatisfaction with the financial policy of the Mission.[21] Within a year of the formation of the new Church there was a split into two main sections, the Bantu Methodist Church and the Bantu Methodist Church of South Africa. Each of these has within a period of less than ten years suffered losses through two or three secessions. A rather dismal feature of the development has been the many long drawn-out legal cases which these leaders and contra-leaders have fought in the courts of the Witwatersrand.

(c) The Zionist movement

A perusal of the list of Bantu independent Churches shows a bewildering preponderance of Churches calling themselves with the names "Zion", "Jerusalem", "Apostolic", "Full Gospel", "Pentecostal" and so forth. There are a host of such groups among the Zulus alone. But in spite of the apparent complexity of the situation it is possible to reduce the problem to a few main facts.

The initial force behind this movement was an apocalyptic Church in the United States, the Christian Catholic Apostolic Church in Zion, founded in 1896 by John Alexander Dowie, "First Apostle and General Overseer". The main teaching of the Church was "divine healing", "triune immersion", and the conviction that the second coming of the Lord was "near at hand". In 1906 this "theocracy", as they called it, in Chicago passed through a crisis from which the organization never recovered. Dowie's second-in-command, W. G. Voliva—described in a sermon by him as "that scoundrel Voliva, miserable little cur, traitor and thief"—took the lead.[22] He is known for his predictions of the Return of the Lord on certain recurrent dates and for the fervour with which he opposes Copernicus: the earth is flat according to Voliva's Bible. The Zion "theocracy" in Chicago eventually split up into six different American groups.

And that was the kind of Church which was to attempt to save the Africans lingering in utter darkness. One "overseer", Daniel Bryant, baptized the first group of twenty-seven Africans on May 8, 1904, in Johannesburg by "triune immersion".[23] A European, P. L. le Roux, also joined the Church. He was to attain a certain prominence in the movement. In 1908 three Pentecostal or Apostolic Faith missionaries arrived in Johannesburg from the United States. It was now discovered that "Zion taught immersion and divine healing, but *not* Pentecost". Le Roux "received his Pentecost" or "baptism in the Holy Spirit" in 1908. The Africans of the Zion Church were not slow to follow. They all received their "Pentecost". But as they had a great liking for the name "Zion", it was decided to call the Church in its new stage the Zion Apostolic Church.

About 1915 Le Roux concentrated on the Pentecostal work among the Europeans and left the care of the African congregation on the Rand in the hands of his African helpers.[a]

It is out of this first group of African Zionist leaders that eventually the whole series of Zionist Churches has emerged.

[a] This information was given to me in an interview with Rev. Le Roux in 1940.

The main secessions—naturally only the chief offshoots are mentioned here—took place at about 1917-20.

(1) Paulo Mabilitsa († 1942) was the best educated of these men and had a knowledge of English, so he at first represented the group before Government. He called his Church the Christian Apostolic Church in Zion (1920). Mabilitsa was of a prominent chief's clan. He gave me the impression of being a fine, almost distinguished personality. He was certainly much respected on the Rand and in the Reserves, and was widely known. He took an active part in the building up of a solid school work in Alexandra, Johannesburg. The work is now carried on by his son, Rev. Philip Mabilitsa, B.Sc.

(2) Daniel Nkonyane, a Zulu, was probably the most impressive of the leaders among those who started the Zionist movement. His church, the Christian Catholic Apostolic Holy Spirit Church in Zion, was on his death inherited by his son, Stephen Nkonyane, Charlestown.

(3) J. G. Phillipps, a Nyasa, founded the Holy Catholic Apostolic Church in Zion. He took over this church from one American Zionist, F. M. Royall. After his death, Phillipps was succeeded by the present leader, M. G. Koza.

(4) Elias Mahlangu, a Zulu, started the Zion Apostolic Church of South Africa.

(5) Fred Luthuli became prominent in a Seventh-Day Adventist offshoot with Zionist tendencies.

The ramifications of Zionist churches can in one way or another be traced back to these beginnings. It would be neither entertaining nor particularly edifying to show in detail how the hundreds of small or large Zionist Churches have split up. The amazing feature is, of course, that the message of a church of this kind could make such an effective appeal to Africans. The nature of the appeal will be analysed in various ways in this book. The fanciful names of the Zulu Zionist Churches are only individual variations on a theme once intoned on the shores of Lake Michigan, United States. The practices of these Churches, as they are seen to-day, show, however, that much has happened in the transfer from Lake Michigan to the streams and the ponds of Zululand.

In this historical survey the *"ama-Nazaretha"* Church should also be mentioned. In certain respects it belongs to what I propose to call the "Zionist" type of Zulu Churches, although it is more deliberately nativistic in its approach than the Zionist Churches referred to above. The founder and prophet of this

49

church, Isaiah Shembe, was baptized in 1906 by the Rev. W. M. Leshaga of the African Native Baptist Church. This was probably an offshoot from the Negro Baptist groups which had begun their work in Natal in 1899, and who as "Cushites" practised the new sacrament of foot-washing.[24] In Shembe's system of purification rites this sacrament occupied a prominent place.[25]

(3) ATTEMPTS AT CO-OPERATION

It is not unfair to say that any Zulu leader who breaks away from his parent Church is immediately ready to become a champion of Church union. One of the most spectacular moves in this direction, the "United Churches of Christ", was initiated by a Rev. X. Y., who in 1924 seceded from the Apostles and Brethren Church in order to form the African Pentecostal Church of South Africa. After one year, in 1925, he was expelled from the presidency of the latter Church and retained only part of his former following. Four years later, in 1929, he was the organizing power of the United Churches of Christ, a group of seven Ethiopian organizations on the Rand, which hoped through such a federation to obtain the privileges attached to Government recognition. After another year the Rev. X. Y. could style himself "Chaplain of the Transvaal African National Congress", and he then left the United Churches of Christ in order to unite all Separatist Churches in the name of the Congress. This linking of the independent Church movement to the Congress was a new development, but the urge for a nation-wide union of all Separatist organizations was at least ten years older.

As far as I am aware, it was the Rev. E. L. Mkhize, an Anglican Zulu minister of the Diocese of Pretoria, who first convened a conference for Church union. A meeting was held in Bloemfontein in 1919, bringing together African ministers and laymen. It was agreed "that the doctrine of one United Native Church is essential". In a "Humble Appeal" of the same year, Mkhize broadcast this view in order "to preach the Union to all people and the chiefs in particular".

When the matter was taken over by the African National Congress, hopes were raised that something more durable and tangible would result. The programme was generous enough. Constituent members of the proposed "United National Church of Africa" would be any Separatist Church with a minimum of 250 members, "which can also be lessened to 100". The organizing committee would consist of "all leading ministers", and the constituent members would have the right to appoint and ordain their own bishops, ministers and evangelists. In order to propagate the union scheme, certain powers should, however, be delegated to "National Leaders, and Chief Organizers and Messengers of the Formation of the Church". It would be a prerequisite for these leaders that they should be "fully competent in different creeds and doctrines of various denominations in Africa"—in the circumstances quite an ambitious claim. It need not be said that denominational questions were never raised. Even the matter of baptism—a bone of contention between Ethiopians and Zionists—was left to "the individual freedom for all members". It is characteristic that this appeal for Church union under the ægis of the African National Congress was dated December 16, 1931, Dingaan's Day, which was suggested as the Annual Day of the Church. The response to these appeals was very poor, and even when the Methodist spokesman, Z. K. Makgato, took up the same slogan of Church Union under Congress auspices, nothing came of it.

An ambitious Church union programme was launched in 1939 by an influential group of African intellectuals, one of them being the African Methodist Episcopal Church leader, Dr. J. Nhlapo. A United African Church is here described as "an urgent practical necessity", and it is pointed out that such a union would be "the efflorescence of European missionary enterprise in Africa". As an initial step, the formation of a federation was suggested and such a federation was to be "merely an anvil on which to hammer the various sects into one African church". A Bloemfontein conference to discuss these problems was suggested.

Appeals of this kind stirred the imagination of church leaders and political leaders among Africans. Professor Jabavu, in a pamphlet of 1942, *An African Indigenous Church*, sees the Bloemfontein appeal as a practical result of œcumenical deliberations from Edinburgh 1910 to Tambaram 1938:

> To-day, I feel, is that time and opportunity, because the air is ringing with schemes for post-war reconstruction, and there are many more who, like myself, recognize the need for such a development.

The ringing in the air was also perceived by Zulu church leaders. In 1937 "The Bantu Independent Churches Union of South Africa" was formed by Zulu ministers from Congregational offshoots and various other Ethiopian and Zionist groups.

They were above all interested in an attempt to persuade Government to extend recognition and subsequent privileges to a much greater number of churches than before. They even declared themselves as prepared to act as an Advisory Board to Government, vouchsafing which churches were "doing good and constructive work" (none of these churches themselves was recognized by Government!). They associated themselves with the influential Councillor A. W. G. Champion (a Zulu by birth) and approached Government in 1943 with a view to securing some alleviation in the procedure for recognition of Separatist Churches.

Mr. Champion called a conference of Zulu ministers in April, 1944, at Durban. Some African ministers of Mission Churches took part, but the majority were independent church leaders. The conference showed the deep differences which existed between the groups represented. When a committee of the conference suggested that in order to put an end to the many divisions of Zionists all such groups should be joined into one big, all-embracing organization, violent opposition was raised by those Zionist leaders who felt their position endangered by the plan. And when Mr. Champion proposed as an alternative that they should all join with independent Churches that were already recognized by Government, Zionist leaders of course objected that they could never contemplate being unequally yoked with people who, though Christians, ate medicine or pork.

In Zulu society, also, politics is the art of the possible. The Durban conference proved that union was outside the scope of possible attainment. When Mr. Champion brought the matter of the independent Churches to the attention of the Native Representative Council in Pretoria, 1944, he did not therefore advocate Church union, but "freedom of worship".[26] When asked whether this implied that one should "encourage any man who falls out with the head of the Church to start his own sect", the Zulu politician cheerfully replied: "In that way only can we increase the worship of God in this country. In that way only can we hope to have the full Gospel of Christ taught."

The motion led to a very interesting debate in the Council. On the one side were men like Champion and Mosaka, who believed that the "Atlantic Charter" and "freedom of worship" implied an unbridled splitting up into an infinite number of Churches. On the other side were leaders like the Editor of *Bantu World*, Councillor S. Thema, who opposed the motion, because it would encourage the policy of disunity among the

Africans: "What we ourselves as people should encourage is a Church of our own."

A noble plea for the second point of view was also expressed in sincere and moving words by the Paramount Chief of the Zulus, Mshiyeni ka Dinuzulu:

> Let me say that I think it is desirable that there should be an African National Church—a church for the whole of the African people. Let me say this—and I say it very seriously—there is nothing worse than to be isolated. A man who is isolated and alone can be regarded as a sort of discarded person, he is a man cast out of society and that type of man, under our old customs and traditions, used to be killed. If this man, this separatist, is at all efficient, why does he leave the church, and if he leaves the mother church, why does he not join some African Church which is recognized, instead of starting a new church of his own. . . . If we go on in this way we shall eventually find thousands of Sects— almost every family will have its own Sect. If new churches are started, let them be of good repute, able to lead our race.

The debate in the Native Representative Council thus revealed the characteristic moods and attitudes to be found among African leaders. On the one hand are those who, like P. Lamula, lightheartedly declare that "separatist churches are very much fewer in this country than in America. It seems that there, to-day, they number 36,000. But in this country it is said that there are only [!] about 600 of these separatist organizations."[27] On the other hand are those responsible Africans— church leaders, chiefs and politicians—who sincerely deplore the fission of African church life and who advocate a nation-wide Church union. The interested onlooker would remark that whereas the former are much too lighthearted, or perhaps cynical, in their acceptance of the *status quo*, the latter are Utopian in their approach if they really believe that union of these Churches will ever be possible through some kind of federation.

(4) TYPES AND CHARTERS

We shall distinguish between two main types of independent Bantu Churches. I propose to call them the "Ethiopian" type and the "Zionist" type. Anticipating results in later chapters I shall here define the two types in broad outlines.

As *Ethiopians* I classify such independent Bantu Churches as have (*a*) seceded from White Mission Churches chiefly on racial grounds, or (*b*) other Bantu Churches seceding from the Bantu leaders classified under (*a*). These share the racial outlook of the other leaders, but they have quite often split off on other issues, chiefly the struggle for prestige and power. Their programme as far as their relation to the White Churches is concerned, is characterized by an interesting ambivalence: on the one hand, it includes the slogan "Africa for Africans" and it is a reaction against the White mission's conquest of the African peoples; on the other hand, their church organization and Bible interpretation are largely copied from the patterns of the Protestant Mission Churches from which they have seceded, even if, as this book will show, these patterns have become of necessity modified by African stress on rank and ritual.

Although they do not all call themselves Ethiopians, this does not mean that they do not generally conform to a type with something of the same outlook and ambitions. They share also to a large extent the same "mythical charter" which gives the clue and the key to an understanding of their activities and behaviour.

I should add here that some of these "Ethiopian" Churches fall outside the type I am defining. The African Methodist Episcopal Church which played so considerable a part in the first years of the Ethiopian movement is, of course, strictly speaking a Mission Church, with its centre in the United States. As I am concerned with purely Zulu Churches, I only occasionally refer to this important Negro Mission Church. Even within the Zulu Ethiopian Churches there is a wide scale of difference ranging from a right wing comprising Churches which in their structure and outlook are "carbon copies" of their parent Mission Churches,[a] to a left wing where Zionist tendencies loom large.

To the other main type of independent Church belong most of the organizations which call themselves by some of the words "Zion", "Apostolic", "Pentecostal", "Faith" (this word sometimes misrepresented as "Five", "Fife", "Fifth"). I describe these organizations as *Zionists*, which word of course has nothing to do with any modern Jewish movement. The reason for the use of this term is simply that the leaders and followers of these Churches refer to themselves as "*ama-Ziyoni*", Zionists. Historically they have their roots in Zion City, Illinois, United States. Ideologically they claim to emanate from the Mount of

[a] As examples of these I mention the important African Congregational Church (recognized by Government), United National Church, Independent Methodist Church.

54

Zion in Jerusalem. Theologically the Zionists are now a syncretistic Bantu movement with healing, speaking with tongues, purification rites, and taboos as the main expressions of their faith. There are numerous denominational, local, and individual variations in Zionist groups, and every Zionist prophet is anxious to point out some speciality through which his Church stands out from the rest. On careful analysis, however, Zionists show an amazing uniformity, caused no doubt by certain fundamental needs and aspirations in the broad masses of these Churches, which needs and aspirations find their satisfaction in the behaviour patterns of the movement.

Their attitude towards the heritage of the White Missions is different from that of the Ethiopian Churches. Whilst their contact with White missionaries has generally speaking been very casual and ephemeral, they may yet combine a general dislike of the Whites as being ritually unclean, with a high esteem of some American Zion Church leaders. John Alexander Dowie, "First Apostle", and to a lesser degree, W. G. Voliva, are on their way to becoming modern church fathers in Zululand.ᵃ As far as their attitude to the Zulu religious heritage is concerned they combat the use of the *inyanga's* medicines and they fight against the diviner's demons of possession. But the weapons with which they fight the struggle belong to an arsenal of old Zulu religion. One strong section of the Zionists is deliberately nativistic, and Churches of this kind in the end become the bridge over which Africans are brought back to the old heathenism from whence they once came.

I hasten to add, however, that some Zionist Churches are gradually becoming more and more "Ethiopian" in ideology and behaviour. There are cross-relations and constant interdependence between these organizations. And further, within one particular organization which is in principle either Zionist or Ethiopian there may be strong local tendencies towards the other type of independent Church.

The list of names of the eight hundred independent Bantu Churches appears to the European as merely fanciful and funny. To the people concerned this is not so. The naming of the Church

---

ᵃ In 1942, the Lord Bishop T. M. Msibi of the "Congregational Catholic Apostolic Church of Zion in South Africa" made the following pronouncement on the faith of his church: "We as members of the 'C.C.A.C. of Zion in S.A.' declare and make known to all and sundry that our faith rests on the version of the old and new Testaments embodied in the Holy Bible and we believe in the doctrine and teachings of our former leaders John Dawi and Wilbur B. Voliva who extracted their doctrine from Zion name of Books."

is an important factor. Many Zionist leaders claim to have received their particular name through supernatural revelation in a dream. To both Ethiopians and Zionists the name of the Church has a special significance. It contains the charter of the Church.

When Mokone in 1892 called his organization "The Ethiopian Church" he thereby alleged that the new Church was related to the Ethiopia mentioned in the Psalms and in the Acts of the Apostles. It is not possible now to define the more precise implications of this term as used by Mokone and his successors, for the reason that the word "Ethiopian" is used rather loosely. The meaning of the term seems to oscillate between two interpretations or associations:

(a) A general reference to the programme "Africa for Africans", with a corresponding aversion to White domination. The fact that "Ethiopia" is mentioned in the Bible gives antiquity to the claim of the African's Church, and is thought of as a sanction of this claim.

(b) On the other hand, the word "Ethiopian" can be more specific, referring to a particular African country under an African Christian king—Abyssinia or Ethiopia.

These interpretations are now intermingled in a way which often makes it impossible to disentangle them. As a general rule, however, one finds that the more educated Ethiopian leaders use the term in the first sense, while some Ethiopian leaders, most Zionist leaders, and the broad masses of independent Church people use the two meanings fairly indiscriminately. We should also note that those who use the term "Ethiopian" in the former, more general sense, may also use other synonyms such as African, Bantu, National, Uhlanga (*Ibandla lohlanga*, meaning the National Church, or the Church of the Black Race), or some generic tribal name as Zulu, Sotho.

I have not gone into the problem of how far Abyssinia may have been known to educated Africans in the eighties of the last century, although it is quite possible that Sir Robert Napier's expedition to King Theodore III in 1867 may have been discussed by African nationalists at that time. Obviously Mokone interpreted Ps. 68: 31 as referring to Africa as a whole. The first occasion on which this Ethiopia-mythology was projected to Abyssinia seems to be the occasion when Dwane wrote to King Menelik, asking him to take oversight of the religious conditions in Egypt and the Sudan and that he, Dwane, had tried to collect funds for this purpose among the

Negroes in America.[28] The Abyssinian victory over the Whites at Adowa in 1896 was of some importance in stirring up the hopes of South African Ethiopians in the first beginning of the movement. The Zulu followers of the American Negro Baptists —who began mission work in Natal in 1899—called themselves right from the beginning *Ama-Kushi*, the Cushites.[29] In their circles there must have been theological discussions on the relation of Ethiopia and Cush. Accepting the challenge of the Whites in South Africa who claimed that the Africans were under the curse of Ham, these Ethiopians found that they appeared in the Bible: Cush, son of Ham, became their first ancestor, and the Bible taught them that Cush and Ethiopia were identical.

I have not followed the channels through which this Ethiopian mythology has gradually spread among the Zulus and other tribes. I have to limit myself to a few statements about recent developments which have led to the emergence of a "mythical charter" of the Ethiopian Churches.

The Italo-Abyssinian War of 1935 strongly encouraged the spread of these ideas. Ethiopian and Zionist Churches in many parts of Natal and Zululand received thousands of new followers, brought into the Church by the nightly prayer meetings which were held in those days on behalf of Abyssinia's cause. Ethiopian leaders sought the advice of Native Commissioners as to whether the Churches should sponsor collections of money to be sent to Abyssinia.[30] Names of Churches founded at this time and later are: the Ethiopia Star Church of God; the Melchizedek Ethiopian Catholic Church; the Abyssinian Baptist Church; the Ethiopia Church of Abyssinia; and the Coptic Ethiopian Church Orthodox of Abyssinia. One church leader claims that he has communicated by letter with the "Bishop of Abyssinia", but that he was prevented by the war (1939–45) from going to Abyssinia for his theological training. Great stir in Ethiopian circles has been caused by the not-so-innocent activities of a certain "H. R. Highness Ras Michael Sultan D—— of the Ethiopian Imperial Legation Office, organizing unity between South Africa and Abyssinian chiefs", an African living in one of the cities of South Africa and pretending to be the head of the Abyssinian Legation to South Africa. In actual fact, the Abyssinian Government has no such representative in South Africa. His followers are given a membership card called "The Coptic Church of Ethiopia, Church of Abyssinia, United Church of Bantus (!) and Abyssinians, Capital Temple Aksum:

Addis Abbaba". The bishop of the Apostolic Jerusalem **Church** in Sabbath of South Africa (Zionist type) writes jubilantly to Government in 1944 about his connexion with this organization: "We report ourselves that to-day we are united with the General Commander in Chief of Abyssinia H. T. H. Ras Mikael D.M.P. C.O.C. Ethiop. Imper. Legation Office in Union of South Africa —— [place name]. The Ethiopian Church of Abyssinia Existant 10 Century B.C." In an interview this bishop told me that the union referred to in his letter to the Government was the fulfilment of a dream: before the Italo-Abyssinian War he had a dream, in which he met the King of Abyssinia at a station. The king shook hands with the Bantu bishop and invited him to join his Coptic Abyssinian Church. No wonder that the regalia and vestments of this and similar Churches are supposed to be copied from the "Capital Temple, Aksum".

The Abyssinia-ideology of the Ethiopians, shared also by most Zionists, is in essence an attempt to give to the independent Church an ancient apostolic succession and a charter, linking their Church with the Bible—which speaks of "Ethiopians"—and with a Christian African kingship. As we shall see in Chapter V, the kingship pattern of the Zulus is the foundation of the leadership ideals of the bishops and presidents of these Churches. But Zulu kingship pattern is heathen; the "mythical charter" of the apostolic succession from the Ethiopian Church in Abyssinia does "Christianize" this Zulu pattern, and that is why this charter is so necessary.[31]

Influences from Negro Churches in America sometimes introduce a decidedly anti-White note into this Ethiopian ideology. The influence of Marcus Garvey—the Negro prophet, visionary and agitator—is strong in the Afro-Athlican Constructive Church, centred in Kimberley and with but few contacts with Zulus. The creed of this Church easily out-Ethiopians the Bantu Ethiopians: "We believe in one God, Maker of all things, Father of Ethiopia, and in his Holy Laws as it is written in the book Piby [the Ethiopian Bible], the sincerity of Angel Douglas and the power of his Holy Ghost. Who did Athlyi, Marcus Garvey and colleagues come to save? The down-trodden children of Ethiopia that they might rise to be a great power among the nations."[32]

I have just pointed out that from the beginning of the Ethiopian movement the names "Ethiopia" and "Cush" were used as referring to the same modern African myth. The name "Cush" in Ethiopian ideology and preaching is used in order to prove that the Africans can in fact look back upon a much older, and therefore nobler, ancestry than the Europeans. The name "Children of Cush" gives to the Ethiopians a charter and the assurance of a link with our first ancestors, mentioned on the first pages of the Bible. But this very charter is also an implicit acceptance of the fundamental cleavage in South African life, the difference between White and Black. And, from a theological, nay, from a Christian standpoint, the implications of this mythology are ominous: the first pages of the Ethiopians' Bible supply the dominating viewpoint from which all the following pages are to be regarded: the colour bar is erected in the very charter, and chancel, of the Church.

Whereas the Ethiopian mythology projects the longings of the Africans to a Christian African nation under the "Lion of Judah, King of Kings", the Zionist mythical charter leads their thoughts to the Holy Land itself. The Constitution of the Zion Christian Church defines in the following way the "Basis" of their faith and organization: "The name of the Church shall be designated the Zion Christian Church. But ye are come unto Mount Zion, City of the living God, heavenly Jerusalem, innumerable company of Angels. Heb. 12: 22." There is a more or less holy competition between the leaders for acquiring the most truly Biblical name possible for their Churches. The name gives status to the Church. The *amaNazaretha* claim that they are more important than other Churches, *because* Jesus grew up in Nazareth—and they have through their name a monopoly of that place. The Zionists of various shades claim to be even better because they hail from Mount Zion in Jerusalem itself, according to the name given to them by revelation in dreams. The long, elaborate names are therefore an extremely serious matter: by referring to "Apostles", "Jerusalem" and "Zion", all in one name (e.g. Apostolic Jerusalem Church in Zion of South Africa) they secure for their Church a supernatural bond with these holy guarantees and they signify a charter showing the spiritual strength of the Church.

The name "in Zion", *eZiyoni*, has a technical meaning. By describing his organization by this name the prophet defines it as a New Testament Church which in minute detail carries out the religious programme supposed to have been laid down by the central figure of the Zionists' Bible, John the Baptist. Thereby the prophet gives to his Church a charter, linking baptizing Zulu prophets with that apostolic succession which flows from Jordan, the River of Life.

59

(5) RELATION OF SEPARATIST CHURCHES TO MISSIONS

In connexion with this account of the rise of the independent Church movement, some attention must be given to the problem of contact between purely Bantu Churches and White Mission Churches. The material for such a study is not very rich, for a very definite reason. Once the step of separation from the Mission Church had been taken, there was surprisingly little contact, and few relationships between the independent groups and White missionaries existed. But it is worth while pointing out this *lack* of a meeting-ground between them, because it will serve to set the whole of our problem in a true perspective.

(a) *The relation to missionaries*

We have already referred to Dwane and the Order of Ethiopia being incorporated in the Anglican Church of the Province in 1900. The Ethiopian problem was very seriously discussed by missionaries at that time. Léenhardt quotes one missionary who in 1901–2 anticipated that the Ethiopian movement would in ten to twelve years outgrow all missions in South Africa.[33] At the General Missionary Conference of South Africa in 1904 the whole question was discussed. E. Jacottet of the Paris Mission in Basutoland and F. B. Bridgman of the American Board analysed the problem and a lively debate followed. As the African Methodist Episcopal Church was at that time the most important of what were then called "Ethiopian" Churches, the discussion dealt almost exclusively with the attitude of missions towards this Negro organization. Under the impression created by Bishop Turner's rash ordinations of sixty-five "ministers" and the proselytizing by these men in other missions' districts, the conference passed a strongly worded resolution. In this it was stated: "Ethiopianism is largely a misdirected use of [the] newborn energy" [of the Africans], and it asserted that Ethiopian Churches had often displayed "an utter lack of regard for the principles of Christian comity", while "the lowering of the standard of Christian morals through lax discipline" was deplored. On the other hand the conference thought that perhaps too great importance had hitherto been assigned to the political aspects of the movement. For the moment at least it seemed to require not so much repression as careful guidance.[34]

The matter was not pursued further by subsequent general missionary conferences, apart from the fact that a well-considered paper on the subject was read at the 1925 Conference by Fr. F. Hill, C.R. At the same time the relation of the Dutch Reformed Church to the African Methodist Episcopal Church was discussed in a number of synods, from 1925 to 1937. The problem was whether baptism performed in the latter Church should be recognized by the former. After a period of some indecision the issue was in 1937 decided in the negative.[35]

The only recent official statement on this question was made in a circular of 1940 by the Christian Council of South Africa, which on a suggestion of the Tambaram Conference briefly analyses some of the causes leading to secessions. The Council seems also to have followed with sympathetic interest the attempts made by African leaders to form one African United Church.

An important point in this connexion is the missionary's personality and individual attitude towards secessions and secessionists. Sweeping generalizations on this matter are of course bound to be misleading, but one observation about a certain change of attitude in South African missionary circles over the years may perhaps tentatively be ventured. The patriarchal missionary of the nineteenth century, who personally had baptized and confirmed his flock and who knew every individual by name, has been succeeded by the modern administrator-missionary, who more indirectly—that is, *via* the African ministers and catechists of his Church—is kept in touch with the broad masses of the Church. This change has as its corollary a certain change of attitude towards the possibility of secessions. Look at the missionary patriarchs of the past! Consider Dr. Stewart of Lovedale of whom it is said that the bitter time of Mzimba's secession "left a scar upon his heart that I believe he felt each day until he died".[36] Or consider François Coillard who as an old patriarch won his evangelists back from Ethiopianism and from what he regarded as destruction of all Christian work and of whom his evangelists said: "To despise the counsels of an old man is to be lost."[37] Compare these men and their attitude to secession with the apparent ease which in some cases characterizes those who are to-day responsible leaders in similar crises. One has rather the impression that nowadays there is more often a sigh of relief at the "solution" of a nuisance than the agony of Stewart or Coillard who made the utmost efforts to avoid what to them appeared to be a calamity and catastrophe. One prominent European, now deceased, told me that during the heated deliberations of eighteen months' discussions in his Church, as chairman of the meetings he allowed the malcontents to let off steam, while he read the *Tatler* until the end of the meeting. The deliberations led to a very serious break, the solution of which was certainly not to be found in the *Tatler*. The willingness to walk with the other fellow, not to any lengths, but just that "second mile" in an attempt towards sympathetic understanding, is not always to be found in South Africa where racial superiority permeates much and many. In a few cases the "solution" through secession brings to one's mind some lines of T. S. Eliot, which, with apologies to the author, one might turn thus:

> That is the way the world ends.
> That is the way the world ends.
> That is the way the world ends—
> Not with a whimper
> but with a bang.

The bang of the office door. . . .
Cases are known where leaders of independent Churches have approached their mother Church with a view to co-operation and mutual understanding, and where the answer has been— silence.

At the other extreme there are some mission leaders who claim that it is "a hopeful feature of the separatist trend that it is proving that the Bantu is becoming able to take religious leadership and command a following of his own people. This is all to the good, since the complete Christianizing of the native mind can be brought about only by the Native himself."[38] By these words it even seems to be implied that separatist leadership should be regarded as a wholesome phase of the development in the Christianizing of the Africans.

(b) The relation to African Mission pastors

African ministers in Mission Churches are often placed in a difficult position in deciding what attitude to take towards independent Churches. Here again generalizations are misleading. There are African pastors in the Mission Churches who constantly grumble about Ethiopians and Zionists and who would like to rely on the law and the police in order to have their activities curbed or forbidden. There is also one section among African mission pastors which appears as genuinely accommodating and appreciative in its attitude but they regard secessions rather as a retrogressive step, an escapism from the actual world, the world of the Whites. They have themselves perfected the technique of African deference forms when in contact

FROM DARKNESS TO LIGHT; FROM ILLNESS TO HEALTH.

"Before, I was ill; the Zionists prayed for me; now I am well", is her message. The green and blue cords in front, and the wooden croziers in her right hand guarantee health and ritual purity.

THE APOSTOLIC JERUSALEM CHURCH IN SABBATH OF SOUTH AFRICA.
Bishop E. M. Morupa addressing his group in preparation for a baptismal service. The bishop claims to be associated with a (fictitious) Ethiopian-Abyssinian Legation in South Africa.

with the Whites. One of the best of the many able Zulu ministers who serve in Mission Churches, attended a big conference for independent Bantu leaders in 1944 (p. 52) and pleaded with the Separatists "to return to the Churches of the Whites and ask for forgiveness" (*ukucela uxholo*).[39] He rather hinted that if they did not follow his advice the consequences for their Churches might be very serious. Needless to say, the members of the conference paid no heed to his well meant warning.

There are, however, two circumstances which tend to make African mission pastors incline towards a positive appreciation of the independent Church movement.

1. The dominant cleavage of South African life in general cuts deep into the Christian Church. The African ministers of Mission Churches gallantly attempt to act as interpreters of one race to another, but if they are left to feel that after all they are only the "priest-boys" of the White missionary, they not unnaturally resent this. Their resentment predisposes them to seek to bridge the gap that separates them from their Independent brethren. Many African mission ministers admire the example of self-support and self-government provided by some Ethiopian leaders. Independent Zulu leaders point out to their brethren in Mission Churches that the policy of missions is to establish self-governing Churches. "But", they say, "when your missionaries at some future date will, at last, be prepared to hand over the reins of office to you, we shall have already built up strong churches, and shall have out-distanced all your efforts. So why not be logical and join us now!" On certain occasions, such as annual Ethiopian synods, local African ministers from different Missions are invited and treated as honoured guests. They establish a common meeting-ground for all African ministers (of Mission and independent Churches alike) in local Bantu ministers' associations which assemble from time to time. Two leading Africans on the Rand in the Anglican and Methodist Mission Churches respectively have also pointed out their appreciation of the bold way in which independent Church leaders attempt to interpret Christianity in African behaviour patterns.[40]

2. Where the teaching and the practical example of a White Mission have instilled into the Africans the idea of the Church as some kind of social club or fortuitous association for certain religious interests, they are naturally inclined to appreciate the kind of African religious club which the Independent Churches provide.

E   63

(c) *The relation to broad masses of Mission Church Africans*

The independent Church problem does affect the masses of Africans in the Mission Churches more than it affects leaders. In this book I have attempted to analyse the interdependence of these two sections of Zulu Christians in outline only. A study of this important aspect should be carried out on a sufficiently limited local scale in order to be worth while, and to avoid generalities and platitudes. I have hinted at a local approach of this kind in Chapter IV, p. 92.

As an important over-all observation, I mention that there are no water-tight compartments between the Zulus belonging either to the heathen section or to one of the Christian groups (Missions, Ethiopians, Zionists). In the Reserves one finds them living happily (or unhappily, as the case may be) together, and there is constant interchange of ideas and continuous interdependence. If Mission Christians tend to feel superior to Ethiopians and Zionists because of their generally higher educational standards, and if they deride the nativistic tendencies of the Zionists, there may be situations, such as ill health and misfortune, when Zionist methods of prayer appear more efficacious than those of the Mission Church.

CHAPTER III

GOVERNMENT POLICY

(1) HISTORY OF GOVERNMENT POLICY

In some colonial dependencies even the most embryonic symptoms of independent church tendencies are promptly dealt with and suppressed. The attitude of the South African Government has been different, though not indifferent. The policy in regard to what are officially called Native Separatist Churches has passed through three successive stages:

Pre-Union era, up to 1910. This period is characterized by a repressive policy in Natal, and a more liberal view of the matter in the Cape.

1910–25. After certain attempts in the direction of a Union-wide policy on Cape-liberal lines, the Israelite incident at Bullhoek in 1921 brought about a Government Commission ("the Native Churches Commission") which published a report in which general rules for the recognition of Separatist Churches were laid down for the first time.

After 1925. These rules are applied by the Native Affairs Commission to the rapidly increasing number of Separatist Churches, and Governmental regulations are issued with a view to controlling their activities.

(a) Policy in pre-Union time

1. Cape Colony. It was the African Methodist Episcopal Church ("A.M.E.", as it was called) which first brought the Cape Government into contact with the Separatist Church problem.[1] In the 'nineties their ministers had on various occasions been supplied with official Marriage Registration forms by the Colonial Secretary's office (under the Marriage Order in Council of 1838) and been treated in the same way as European missionaries in this respect.

The visit of Bishop Turner in 1898 and the wholesale ordination of sixty-five African ministers performed by him did cause certain unrest among both Africans and Europeans. The Prime Minister, W. P. Schreiner, who had been struck by the low educational standard of the marriage officers of this Church in 1899, ordered that the issue of marriage forms to these men should cease.

Schreiner seems, however, to have been genuinely interested in the question, and in 1900 he told A.M.E. representatives that their Church should be domiciled in the Colony and should have some fully competent authority with whom Government could deal. When Bishop L. J. Coppin of the A.M.E. Church arrived in the following year, the Colonial Secretary of the Cape Government in a letter of March 26, 1901, recognized the African Methodist Episcopal Church as "a Church within the meaning of the Marriage Order in Council of 1838". At the same time it was verbally arranged between the Colonial Secretary's Department and Bishop Coppin that no more than twelve ministers should be recognized as Marriage Officers in the Cape at any given time. (In 1909 this number was increased to sixteen.)[2]

The Ethiopian movement grew rapidly at this time. Bishop Coppin stated in 1903 that he had some 200 "ministers" (or, rather, ministers *and* evangelists) in his Church.[3] At the same time P. J. Mzimba claimed that his African Presbyterian Church had 6500 members and 20,000 adherents. In this springtime of Ethiopianism the slogan "Africa for Africans" was preached with enthusiasm in these Churches. This caused some concern. An ex-Chief Magistrate of the Cape Colony, J. H. Scott, stated in 1903 that the Ethiopian movement was "a political and social movement, not a religious movement at all" and it is interesting to find that even an African, T. Jabavu, warned the Native Affairs Commission of 1903–5 of Ethiopianism because of its political tendencies: "I think it would be thoroughly bad for the Native."[4]

The Native Affairs Department of the Cape did not, however, allow itself to be alarmed by such warnings. E. E. Dower, who later became Secretary for Native Affairs in the Cape and in the Union, and who had a deciding influence in these matters for a number of years, told the Native Affairs Commission that although he was convinced that certain ministers of the African Methodist Episcopal Church were engaged in political anti-European propaganda, he still favoured the recognizing of Independent ministers who had sufficient educational qualifications: "To endeavour to put the Ethiopian movement down will only have the effect of helping on the movement."[5]

In principle, Dower's point of view dominated the resolutions of the Native Affairs Commission of 1903–5, even if representatives from other colonies, Natal in particular, caused the resolutions to be more apprehensive in form than Dower would have liked them to be:

> The Commission has little sympathy with the movement, as there can be no doubt that its leaders have not yet arrived at a stage when dissociation from the control of European Missionaries is likely to contribute increased wisdom in Church administration, or more ennobling examples of personal self-sacrifice and piety; but so long as it remains unassociated with mischievous political tendencies, members unite in advising that any measure capable of being represented as religious persecution should be avoided. The policy they advocate aims rather to secure such wise control and guidance of the movement that its potentialities may be exerted for good and not for evil. The course which commends itself to the Commission is to accord recognition to such Native Churches as are possessed of sufficiently stable organization to control their pastors and enforce discipline where necessary and to ensure the appointment to the ministry of reliable and worthy men only; but not to encourage those bodies which owe their existence to the discontent, or, in some cases, to the very miscontent, or, in some cases, to the very misconduct of men who have severed connexion with their parent Church, and own no competent central authority.
>
> Licences to solemnize marriages should "depend on the moral character, education and the general fitness of the applicant".
>
> To sum up: The Commission would not advise any measure of legislative repression, unless unforeseen developments render it necessary, considering that effort should rather be directed towards securing efficient constitutional control and organization in order that the influences at work may be wisely directed. To this end the Commission would deprecate the recognition of detached secessionary fragments acknowledging no efficient central authority.

Dower's views were shared by John X. Merriman, Prime Minister of the Cape Colony, 1908–10. Merriman's attention was drawn to the problem by the representations of P. J. Mzimba who was appointed as a marriage officer in 1907 and whose Church was thereby given a measure of recognition. In 1908–9 Mzimba succeeded in obtaining the appointment of four of his ministers as marriage officers for certain areas.

Times were critical and Native opinion in the Cape was very much stirred. The South Africa Act of 1909 which limited membership of Parliament to Europeans and which put an end to the Cape Coloured franchise, had just been published and a deputation of Africans went to London to protest against the Act. In this situation the liberal and practical Merriman, who described himself as "a plain man of business",[6] tried to arrive at a workable solution of the Ethiopian problem which was perhaps somewhat opportunistic in tone, but remarkable in spite of this in view of the repressive ideas held in other parts of the country at that time:

> I am sure that it is not sound policy to repress these religious ebullitions, however inconvenient and absurd they may seem to us. Repression will be like "the blood of the martyrs—the seed of the church". When we come to granting church and school sites, it is a different question. Each must be dealt with on its merits. As a matter of policy I should approve of one or two being granted to Mzimba to make it clear that we do not boycott him on account of colour—an important thing just now—I hope that the Magistrate will recollect Gibbon's account of the Roman attitude in such matters: To the Magistrates, all religions were equally useful.[7]

In accordance with these views, Merriman, together with Dower, laid down the following policy in 1909:

> Applications by Native Separatist Churches for church or school sites should be dealt with on their merits, due consideration being given *inter alia—*
> (a) to the stability of the applicant organization,
> (b) to the danger of discord arising from the introduction of a divisive element into close proximity to established spheres of mission work,
> (c) to the wishes of the people generally,
> (d) to the availability of land.

According to Merriman, three churches were considered to be sufficiently stable to merit consideration, namely: The African Presbyterian Church (Mzimba's), The African Methodist Episcopal Church, and the African Native Mission Church (Goduka's).[8]

2. The Colony of Natal. One consequence of the *laissez-faire* attitude in Native affairs which followed the great Theophilus Shepstone era in Natal was the intense suspicion with which all activities among Natives in Natal and Zululand were viewed by the Europeans of that colony.[9] "Ethiopianism" was generally regarded as being extremely dangerous, and drastic repressive methods were introduced. A blind "Cushite" evangelist, named Johannes, who toured the country preaching "Africa for the Black Man", gave the police much trouble. He was imprisoned three or four times, and eventually deported. J. L. Hulitt, a former Secretary for Native Affairs in Natal, testified in 1903 that Ethiopianism had caused a wave of unrest in the colony and desired that "it should be discountenanced in every way".[10] At this time Natal was the only colony in which the African Methodist Episcopal Church was not recognized.[11] Even an African editor, M. S. Radebe, regarded it as "unwholesome and in some places seditious", and he told the Commission that he was "trying to stamp it out".[12]

These suspicions were, unfortunately, confirmed by the activities of Ethiopian preachers before and during the Zulu Rebellion of 1906. Seditious preaching (of the type which proclaimed: "you shall enjoy ascendancy over Europeans") seems to have been rampant among local leaders of Ethiopian groups. Some of the most enthusiastic leaders of the Rebellion were either preachers and ordinary members of Ethiopian Churches, or for the time being had been swept away from the Mission Churches to join the Ethiopian groups.[13]

It was also observed that at this time many friends of Ethiopianism were working in the interests of Native land syndicates set up for buying Native farms in Natal,[14] and this was another reason why Europeans in Natal became alarmed over the Ethiopian question. One of the principal findings of the Natal Native Affairs Commission 1906–7 (which commission resulted from the Rebellion) refers to the treatment Government had in store for Ethiopian activities:

> The Natives must be made clearly to understand and to realize that the presence and predominance of the White race will be preserved at all hazards, and that all attempts to destroy its hegemony, whether overt or covert, such as the Ethiopian propaganda, will be promptly punished, instead of being disdainfully treated, as in the past (*Report*, p. 5).

3. Natal's policy and the reaction of the other South African colonies. The part played by Ethiopian preachers in the Zulu Rebellion was undoubtedly the primary cause of the strongly repressive action which the Natal Government in 1908 suggested as a basis for a common South African policy in regard to the treatment of Native Separatist Churches. This is a widely different attitude from that of the Merriman–Dower liberal view. Natal's attitude (probably worked out by S. O. Samuelson, who was the Under-Secretary for Native Affairs up to 1909) expressed itself as follows:

No Native Minister of a Church, independent and free from direct and effective European control, shall be registered as a Marriage Officer.

No official recognition in any form by grants-in-aid of schools, or otherwise, shall be given to Native Churches independent of, and free from, European control or to any religious movements amongst Natives embodying race cleavage as a principle;

and, the most repressive clause of all:

That it be made unlawful for any Native Minister or member of a religious movement not under European control and not recognized, whether exempted or otherwise, to address meetings or assemblies of Natives.

Of the other Colonial Governments, only the Orange River Colony agreed in general with these Natal suggestions, whereas the Transvaal Government—which had experience of the Ethiopian movement on the Rand and in Pretoria—opposed the suggested, ban on preaching by Native ministers and, generally speaking, was for a policy of tolerance rather than repression. In 1893 the Transvaal Government had recognized Mokone's Ethiopian Church. The Cape Government, as was to be expected, warned that Governmental interference which aimed at stifling the Separatist movement might "have an effect quite opposite to that intended—as history in other parts of the world has shown".

(b) 1910–25

John X. Merriman's decision in 1909 to remove any reasonable cause of grievance on the part of prominent Separatist Church leaders, secured that three Churches obtained a certain priority when applying for church and school sites.[15] Before their applications had been dealt with, however, the Union was established. The liberal Cape policy was blended with more repressive ideas. In 1913 the Natives' Land Act was promulgated, through which Natives lost their right to purchase land in the Transvaal and Natal provinces. In the same year the Cabinet decided that applications by the Native Separatist Churches for sites could not be entertained, and the Minister of Land formally declined to sanction any application by a Native Church.[16]

Mzimba's African Presbyterian Church, however, was persistent in its demands for sites, and as a result of an interview which Mzimba had with the Native Affairs Select Committee in

1914, Parliament approved that applications made by Mzimba's Church should be dealt with "on their merits".[17] Finally, in 1915, the Acting Minister for Native Affairs extended the privilege given to Mzimba's church to any Native Separatist Church, "subject to careful inquiry and close scrutiny".[18] A similar policy for dealing with the Separatist Churches on their merits was followed in dealing with Separatist ministers who applied for appointment as marriage officers.[19] This resulted in a considerable increase of such officers among Separatist ministers. Whereas in 1910 their number was seventy-two, these being ministers of the three Churches especially favoured by Merriman, the Native Affairs Department reported in 1918 that their number was about one hundred.

One can, presumably, trace Dower's influence in certain alleviations during this period, namely in regard to Pass Laws and Railway concessions. To exclude Separatist Church ministers from privileges given to other Native ministers in these respects "would savour of class legislation and the introduction into such matters of a colour bar—a course the Department would deprecate".[20] With a view, therefore, to giving Separatist Church ministers as well as others "reasonable freedom of movement", it was arranged to give them yearly certificates of registration (in the Transvaal) or special periodical passes (in the Orange Free State). With regard to ministers' concessions on the railways, an agreement was reached between the Native Affairs Department and the Railway Administration, according to which, in the case of new applications, there was to be a joint inquiry into the bona fides of the applicant and the eligibility of his Church for the privilege.

Whilst willing to grant reasonable freedom and facilities to deserving Separatist Churches, Government was, on the other hand, very much aware that the Separatist Church movement was both "a source of serious embarrassment to the Administration, and, what is of infinitely greater importance, a serious hindrance to the spread of true religion among the natives of this country".[21] There were reasons for this indictment: in 1918 seventy-six Separatist Churches were known to the Native Affairs Department. The most fruitful source of fissiparous tendencies among African Church leaders was, according to the Department, to be found in personal jealousies and the scramble for leadership: "Repeatedly these bodies have parted asunder, each side claiming to have expelled the other from the church for insubordination, and both coming separately to the

71

Government with a request for state recognition of the 'church'."[22]

Already at this early stage (1918) the Separatist Church movement had given a bad impression because of its divisions. It is not surprising that in 1918 the Department was complaining that it "is brought most prominently and constantly into contact with the more shady side of native religious activity".

The shadow was to become deeper still. From the North, from Nyasaland and Northern Rhodesia, came disquieting news about the seditious activities of the Watch Tower movement. John Chilembwe's rising in Nyasaland had caused much unrest in 1915, and in 1918–19 Watch Tower prophets in Northern Rhodesia preached the sweet message of the Day when the Europeans would become slaves of the Africans.

When Enoch Mgijima proclaimed that same message to his faithful in the Cape Province, it led to the *Bullhoek incident, of May 24, 1921.*

In 1918, Enoch Mgijima had been excommunicated from the "Church of God and Saints of Christ", an Ethiopian Church of Negro-American origin. The reason for his excommunication was, allegedly, that he used to preach about visions he had had since the appearance of the 1910 comet. One of these visions represented a battle between two white Governments. In his vision he had seen a baboon crush these Governments and destroy them. The interpretation he put upon this was that the white Governments represented the Dutch and the English, and the baboon the Africans. This meant that the white people would be crushed by the Natives. Mgijima was a forceful personality and soon gathered a following around him in the Bullhoek location (near Queenstown), founding there an "Israelite" colony, of which he became "Bishop, Prophet and Watchman". The chief tenets of his creed were: Keeping of the Sabbath; an annual festival of Passover to be observed at Bullhoek; the New Testament to be regarded as a fiction of the white man; the faithful to salute one another with a holy kiss in church; the belief that the Israelites were Jehovah's elected and that Jehovah would deliver them from the bondage of the Europeans as He had earlier delivered His children out of Egypt. Soon the colony consisted of a village of some 300 huts, erected on Crown land without permission. Enoch was ordered by Government to pull down the huts, and promised to comply with the order, but did nothing about it. He was also ordered to compel all the strangers who lived within his colony to leave the place without delay. This he also promised to do, but again did not act. Various officials, even the Native Affairs Commission, tried to impress upon him that he must obey. The Government handled the case with perfect patience, a generosity which was interpreted by Enoch and his followers as weakness and fear on the part of the authorities. When in the end military force was dispatched to the place, the prophet told his people that the bullets of the white men would turn to water; they would all be magically immune to bullets. The outcome was tragic. Some 500 fanatic "Israelites" armed with spears and knobkerries hurled themselves against the machine-guns of the police, and 117 of Enoch Mgijima's Israelites were fatally wounded. Enoch himself did not share the fate of his foolhardy followers.

But the Bullhoek incident had tragic consequences, not only for the Israelite colony built up by Enoch Mgijima. More important was its effect in confirming suspicions long harboured by the Europeans in South Africa and by the Government of the political dangers of the Native Separatist Churches. Such an incident is not easily forgotten. The Government took steps to make an inquiry into the Israelite movement and into the origin, nature and extent of Native Separatist Churches as a whole. A Government Commission was appointed in 1921, among the members being a Dutch Reformed Church leader, the Rev. P. van der Merwe, and the famous expert on Native education, Dr. C. T. Loram. For various reasons, the report of the Commission only appeared in 1925 (*U.G. Report* 39, 1925).

The Commission expressed the conviction that "so long as the movement is not mischievous it should be tolerated and where it springs from a worthy motive and is working in harmony with the Government it should be encouraged". They recommended that some impartial board should be called into being to advise the Native Affairs Department on all applications for recognition. With a view to discouraging fissiparation among the Separatist Churches, the Commission also recommended:

> that it be both the church and the individual Native minister as a servant of the church which are recognized, so that a minister would lose the recognition as soon as he leaves the church organization to which he was attached.

As conditions for recognition, the following points were recommended by the Commission and accepted by the Government:

1. *Age:* As a rule no church should be recognized until it has had a separate and continuous existence for ten years and only then if it is a healthy organization with a constitution, schools, buildings, and other signs of growth.

2. *Size:* During the course of its existence the movement should have spread so that there should be at least six congregations each with its regular meeting place.

3. *Training and Qualification of Ministers:* As a rule no minister should be recommended for a licence who has not passed Standard VI or some equivalent educational test and who has in addition two or three years of special training for the work of a minister.

4. *Ethical Standing of Ministers and Members:* The church must be conducted in accordance with the ordinarily accepted standards of ethical conduct and the ministers should be suitable for the exercise of the civil functions of their office.

To these general requirements there was, however, added an ominous provision; each application should be judged "on its merits". It was left to the then newly formed Native Affairs Commission to advise the Minister of Native Affairs what the merits of the applying Churches were.[23]

(c) *After 1925*

The machinery established through the recommendations of the Native Churches Commission of 1921–25 began to function. A "Form of Application" was issued by the authorities. Quite often a bishop or overseer would not use the prescribed form, but style his application more in accordance with his own personal liking, as a few examples will show.

From the "New Faith Gospel Apostolic Church of Jesus Christ", January 16, 1940:

> DEAR SECRETARY OF NATIVE AFFAIRS,—Here is my case, I have some men here on the farms. We want to build our own church. That is the matter I wish to place before the Native Affairs Department of Pretoria. And I ask you gentlemen to send me your reply.
>
> I am,
>
> (REV.) J. M.

From the "Holy Cross Catholic Apostolic Christian Church in Zion".

> *His Honourable,*
> *Sub-Native Commissioner,*
>
> SIR,—To your worship, we are humbly and submission to present the above Church to your worship. Please will you? As the Church

is now the Holy Cross Catholic Apostolic Christian Church in Zion. We desired it to worship God the Father and God the Son and God the Holy Spirit, here in Johannesburg, all, all over, in Transvaal and South Africa.

> J. E. G.,
> *Founder and Overseer.*

Not seldom there is a touch of trying to win Government's favour by a flattering word or two:

HON. SIR,—I humbly beg to apply for the full Registration and Recognition of my "church" [the inverted commas are the applicant's own]; in which I am the General-Overseer. The Church's name is known as: "The New-Christian-Catholic-Apostolic-Church in Zion."

I know from great and high sources that whenever a church is in touch or known by the Government, such church is ever safe.

Thanking you in anticipation,

I humbly beg to remain, Honourable Sir,

> Your obedient servant,
> E. I. S. X.

And a last example! From "The Poor Christ Church":

MY LORD,—I ask to you to preach the Gospel and to baptize to this Church.

> Good bay,
> Rev. S. N.
> *Benoni.*

Not all applications by far are of this type of course. There is in fact a wide latitude between this kind of supplication and the elaborate memoranda sent in by stronger Churches. In 1916 the African Christian Catholic Baptist Church was helped by a solicitor with its application, and there may be earlier cases of which I am unaware. The Africans with their great interest in legal matters are eager to secure the help of a lawyer in the drawing up of their applications for Government recognition. To-day any Church with self-respect will have a lawyer's assistance even in the formulating of the Constitution. There are included in their applications statistical memoranda on the activities of the Church, and sometimes a bank statement or a balance sheet, certified by a chartered accountant.

In some cases the leader may be so important that he is supposed to be able to get Government recognition for other Churches than his own. I know of a prominent Zionist Church leader on the Rand—his Church is not recognized by Government—who is known to receive from time to time supplicants, seeking his assistance in this respect. It is generally believed that his Church has been recognized for a long time. Such an impression can easily be created. Any application to the Native Affairs Department for recognition is followed by a courteous reply from the Department, stating either that the letter has been received and the matter is under consideration, or that Government has "no objection to the conduct of *bona fide* religious work among the Native people, provided law and order are observed". Adorned with a Government Department letterhead and signed by a high official, such a harmless letter is taken by the Church leader in question to imply that the application has been granted. Or, he may try another method. One Church leader procured a typewriter and at the top of the copy he had received from the Department, typed the words "THERE IS NO OBJECTION". Cases are also known where European lawyers irresponsibly and without authorization from the Department have informed their clients that the Churches concerned have received Government recognition.

The number of Native Separatist Churches which are at all known to Government has risen rapidly from seventy-six in 1918 to 320 in 1932, and nearly 800 in 1945. In its efforts to decide whether they merit recognition or not, Government has been guided by the principle that—

> the conditions prescribed by the Native Churches Commission for the recognition of Separatist Churches were merely intended to serve as a guide on broad lines to the Native Affairs Commission. Each application for recognition, must, of course, be considered on its merits. There may be instances where the age and size of a church are no guarantee of its work.[24]

Through the Native Commissioners a thorough investigation of the quality and extent of the work of the Church concerned and the standing of its ministers is made. A process of winnowing the chaff from the wheat takes place. Most is, however, found to be chaff. Besides the somewhat older Churches which were recognized at an early date, the African Methodist Episcopal Church, Mzimba's Bantu Presbyterian Church, the Ethiopian Church of South Africa and the two Lutheran Bapedi groups, only two new Churches have been recognized since 1925, namely the African Congregational Church in 1937, and the African Orthodox Church in 1941 (cf. pp. 305–6). Thus, so far, *only eight* out of 800 churches are *recognized*, that is, just *one per cent.*[25]

The care given by the Church leaders to their applications to Government for recognition and the fact that, once the application is turned down, another one still more elaborate is handed in, goes to show that Government recognition is a highly coveted privilege, giving status in society. Some Native Commissioners have wisely used this fact as an argument in trying to restrain further fissiparation within Bantu Churches. They have impressed upon competing sect leaders that they will stand no chance of obtaining Government recognition unless they are able to settle their domestic squabbles amicably. Lately there has also been a tendency among smaller unrecognized Churches to seek amalgamation with the few already recognized Bantu Independent Churches. In this way they attempt to secure Government privileges for the smaller group. On the recognition of one Congregational Church (with Zulu leadership) in 1937, an association of African Bantu ministers expressed their appreciation of the Native Affairs Department: "The step taken by the Government by this recognition has not only been highly commendable, but has also been instrumental in reviving the hope that was almost frail and dwindling in relation to the Native Affairs Department among the Bantu ministers."

The chances of obtaining Government recognition being as slight as they are, some Churches of Zionist type make no attempt to secure this privilege. At a meeting of Zulu Church leaders in Durban in 1943, where these questions were discussed, one of the Zionist bishops exclaimed: "The main thing is whether our names are written in heaven, not whether they are written in Pretoria!" Which goes to show that even sour grapes are food.

(2) PRIVILEGES FOLLOWING UPON GOVERNMENT RECOGNITION

Let us briefly consider the main privileges following upon Government recognition of a Church as far as the matter affects Separatist Churches, and with conditions in Natal and Zululand particularly in mind. Such privileges are the possibility of acquiring sites for church and school premises in Native Reserves; the appointment of its ministers as Marriage Officers; the granting of concessions on the railways to its ministers.

The main Government regulations for obtaining a church or school site in Native reserves are that (*a*) the church should be

77

a recognized body, and that (b) the provisions of the so-called five-miles-radius rule should be observed, e.g. a site should be at least five miles from all existing authorized church and school sites situated on South African Native Trust land either in the district concerned or in any adjoining district. (The radius was increased in 1933 from three to five miles.) The primary object of the five-miles-radius rule is to prevent denominational struggles in Native reserves and to guarantee some measure of church homogeneity in different localities. In Natal and Zululand this rule is only too often sidetracked by various devices by which the prophets concerned attempt to safeguard their interests.

On the initiative of a Parliamentary Select Committee on Native Affairs steps were taken in 1935–36 to make a departmental survey of church and school sites in Native areas in Natal and Zululand. The result of this survey was that no less than 225 unauthorized church and school sites were found, as compared with 624 authorized sites. Efforts were made to secure the abandonment of all these unauthorized sites. This action, of course, hit both Mission and Separatist Churches alike, as in many cases recognized Mission Churches had omitted to secure authorization for certain sites, where they had been doing church and school work for a long time.

The reaction of the independent Churches to the Government's enforcement of the rule was to hold regular services on the private allotments of their followers. To these regular services people of that particular church would be invited, and the kraal became to all intents and purposes a church site. Legislation for dealing with cases of this nature was introduced.[26] This regulation was interpreted to mean: No minister or evangelist would be allowed to hold *regularly conducted* services within a Native's private allotment. The consequence was that scores of independent Churches which had put up a chapel or some kind of church building in their followers' kraals, were compelled to pull them down.

An outcry followed. The most vocal of all Zulu Separatist Church leaders protested in no uncertain words:

This sort of thing is absolutely incompatible with the fundamental principle of God found in the Holy Scriptures, and is also incompatible with the principle of all democratic powers of the world. It makes us feel, Sir, that we natives are DELIBERATELY HUMILIATED AND STIGMATIZED under the White rule that professes and confesses Christianity.

As a matter of fact, wartime expediency has prevented any rigid enforcement of the new rule. And as far as one can see, Separatist ministers and prophets in Zululand enjoy all kinds of democratic facilities for preaching their message.[27]

Marriage Officers are appointed by the Secretary for the Interior on the recommendation of the Secretary for Native Affairs. In certain cases African ministers who have seceded from Mission Churches have retained their designation as Marriage Officers, in spite of the fact that their new Churches have received no Government recognition.[28] This anomaly will, however, rectify itself in due course.

Ministers of Religion may, according to Clause 95 of the Official Railway Tariff Book, be granted a railway concession when undertaking journeys *bona fide* on duty. This is a privilege, ensuring reduced travelling expenses for the Church concerned, and therefore one of the reasons why the independent Churches press for recognition.[29]

Difficulties are also experienced by ministers of independent Churches when attempting to purchase wine for sacramental purposes. The Liquor Act (No. 30, 1928) prohibits sale of European liquor to Africans. As only ministers of recognized Churches can be exempted from the provisions of the Act, independent Church leaders feel aggrieved by their Churches being excluded from such privileges. Lately magistrates have received Government instructions to use their discretionary powers to issue such permits also to ministers of unrecognized Churches. In many cases, however, the pastor concerned is told by the local magistrate to write to Pretoria (that is, to the Native Affairs Department there) and by Pretoria he is told to approach his local magistrate, and in the end nothing happens.

The fact that 99 per cent. of the independent Bantu Churches have not been able to secure Government recognition and technically are only tolerated, is fairly revealing as to the Government's attitude to the movement as such.

CHAPTER IV

CHURCH AND COMMUNITY

Western civilization—mines, commerce, education—has revolutionized Zulu society. Suddenly it has been drawn into the magnetic field of the conditions of modern life. These vast changes also affect their church life. The conditions of church development and growth are very different in the tribal area of the Zululand Reserve and the gold mining district on the Witwatersrand, the centre of which is Johannesburg. Still other conditions of Bantu Church life prevail in the farm areas of Natal where Zulus as agricultural "squatters" come in closer contact with their European masters than in the more segregated Reserve.

(1) INDEPENDENT CHURCHES IN THE CITY (JOHANNESBURG)

If Pretoria, according to Dr. Gerdener, "is the birthplace of Ethiopianism and has remained its nursery",[1] the neighbouring Johannesburg is the birthplace of independent Churches of Zionist type. The Rand as a whole, through its central role in the economic and social life of the Union, has had a dominating influence on the development of the independent Church movement. A study of the influence of the urbanization of the South African Bantu on their church life in general and on the emergence and development of independent Churches in particular, would be very much worth-while. Such a study would have to be co-ordinated with a realistic investigation and appraisal of the results of Mission work on the Rand, in order to get the problem in the right perspective. Dr. J. D. Taylor and Dr. Ray Phillips have outlined the situation as it existed in 1926 and in 1936 respectively, but this important subject still waits to be treated in all its implications and in its sociological setting.[2]

I confine myself here to a fairly myopic approach to the problem. To sketch the background of the Separate Church movement on the Rand in its real width would entail repeating over again what was said in the Introduction of the social and denominational conditions of the Church in South Africa as a whole. In Johannesburg the Church of Christ is a *segregated*

Church. An African can generally not worship in a "European" church. It is also a *divided* Church; the "overmultiplication of agencies" of missions has not only led to "wasteful methods"[3] in the actual mission work, but above all to a weakening of the presentation of the Gospel of Christ itself. To these fundamental cleavages—which gape wider in Johannesburg than anywhere else in the Union—are added *tribal* differences, and that refers not only to language, but to the different cultural background of Zulu, Sotho and other tribes. And lastly, different economic and educational attainments of the Bantu are now erecting a *class structure* which is replacing the tribal rank system, as far as the urbanized black caste is concerned.

Of all these factors, which strongly affect the emergence of an ever-increasing number of independent Churches, the colour-bar and racial discriminations are felt by the Bantu as the most damaging. "This is a bad place to worship in", a well-known African minister of a Congregational Mission said of Johannesburg. The number of independent Bantu Churches on the Rand is difficult to compute, mainly because of the great social velocity of the Africans employed for an indeterminate period in the mines and in other capacities. It is difficult to state, with any degree of accuracy, the actual number at any given time.[4] Judging from the fact that in Alexandra Township alone there were in 1944 eighty Bantu independent Churches represented (through their superintendents, bishops or local evangelists) besides fifteen Mission Churches, one realises that the numbers for the whole of the Rand must now be very high. At a conservative estimate, I should put the over-all figure as 350.

As far as membership of Bantu independent Churches on the Rand is concerned, one could classify them in two groups: the few very big congregations and the large number of small congregations. For the sake of comparison, I mention that the African Methodist Episcopal Church reports about 7000 full members on the Rand, with another 1000 "on probation".[5] Ethiopian Churches of Methodist type are influential as far as numbers go: the Bantu Methodist Church and the Bantu Methodist Church of South Africa have each 3000 members on the Rand. The impressive "Quarterly Preaching-Appointment Plan" of the last mentioned Church shows that this organization has services each Sunday at forty-five places on the Rand, and one hundred local preachers to look after the work. The African Congregational Church reports more than 2000, of whom 1000 are full members, 600 children and 400 "on trial". The big

Sotho "Zion Apostolic Faith Mission" has some 3500 members on the Witwatersrand.

Characteristic of most Churches is, however, the fact that they have small numbers in one or many locations and townships. I quote a few examples: The Nations Church of Christ in Africa has fifty-three members, these being in Alexandra only; the Jerusalem Meeting Apostolic Church of Christ Son of God has fifty-four members on the whole of Witwatersrand; the Church of God Apostolic Jerusalem in Zion count fifty members on the Rand; the Christian Apostolic Holy Spirit Church in Zion of South Africa has 230 members in eight locations on the Rand, with a bishop and eleven other (totally uneducated) men to shepherd them, and while the Church has no funds or buildings, the bishop himself is optimistic: "I wish to hear from my Native Commissioner, for my church [is] growing forward, all the weeks and months"; the African Casteroil Dead Church *alias* African Native Mission has seventy members, shepherded by the President himself aided by one minister and two evangelists. To the same category, as far as numbers are concerned, belongs the African Orthodox Church, which claims twenty-three men, forty women and sixty-eight children on the Rand. They have a small church building in Alexandra. This Church is one of the privileged few, as it was recognized by Government in 1941. It is interesting to note that of the 387 members of the Corner Stone of Apostolic Bethlehem in Zion Church (worshipping in five different places on the Rand) only twenty-two are men. Also in Johannesburg the great majority of Zionist Church members are women. In Ethiopian Churches on the other hand a larger percentage are men, a natural development in the City which to such a large extent has drawn the male population away from the Reserves.

The conditions on which an Independent Church is granted a site for erecting church or school buildings in the Johannesburg area are that (a) the church must be recognized by the Native Affairs Department of South Africa, (b) it should possess at least ten church buildings in the Union, (c) its ministers should be authorized marriage officers, and (d) the church must produce evidence of having sufficient funds to erect an approved church building.[6]

For the very few Bantu independent Churches that could meet these conditions another important consideration has been the legal rights to sites and stands in the different "Native Townships". Pimville is the only Municipal Township where

Africans can build their own houses and churches, on land rented from the muncipality. Sophiatown, Martindale and Newclare, where there are native holders of property in European Areas, do not provide such possibilities. And Alexandra Township, "South Africa's number-one problem township— long-standing headache to Union, Provincial and Muncipal authorities",[7] which is established as a private-owned, incorporated company (for 50,000 inhabitants!), offers the independent Churches incredibly expensive conditions: "A stand is cheap at £200. An acre can fetch as much as £1000. An acre in the contiguous European township of Kew £150."[8]*

In such circumstances one is not surprised to find that one well-established Bantu independent Church in Johannesburg reports the value of stand plus church building and manse at headquarters as over £4000, whereas the same Church estimates its property (stand and buildings thereon) at Newclare, Springs, Randfontein, Roodeport, and Benoni as respectively £388, £160, £176, £250 and £63. The church building (without stand) at Orlando and Germiston had cost respectively £575 and £50.[a]

The great number of independent Churches cannot afford expense of this order. The most usual meeting-place for Sunday worship is therefore an ordinary room which becomes during the week a combined bedroom and living-room for a fluctuating number of people. Such a room is adorned with crosses painted on the walls, a bishop's staff in the corner, and perhaps a bright and colourful advertisement of "Studebaker, 1934".

The considerable expense involved in the upkeep of independent Witerwatersrand Churches can be studied in their yearly balance sheet. One amalgamated Ethiopian Church reports that the whole of their "General Missionary Fund"—£200— raised from yearly contributions by members all over the Union, has been exhausted in putting up a church building at Sophiatown (plus the expense of printing the constitution of the Church!). One of the best established Zionist Churches reports for the year ending March 31, 1942, a debit balance of £246 for its congregation at Alexandra and a similar debit balance of £156 for the congregation in Pretoria, incurred because of expenditure for "Rents and Buildings", £264 and £110 respectively at these places. This debit has been met chiefly by

* The Group Areas Act has, of course, changed conditions described here.
a Some well-established churches manage to get substantial financial help in renting their church to the Provincial Council, for school purposes (for use during weekdays only) or for concerts. The church referred to here reports a yearly income of £155 through this source.

the credit balance of £315 from their main rural congregation in Msinga, Natal, which only allowed itself an expenditure of £15 for rents and buildings in order to help the Johannesburg congregations.

This example is chosen at random. If it is anything like typical of the situation within independent Churches of this kind[a]—which is impossible to know, as so few present any financial statements—it reveals shocking conditions. The Africans were drawn to Johannesburg by the alluring promises of the Golden City, but in these Churches the situation stands reversed, and the rural congregations who have but little money, must support City congregations.

In order to improve the financial position of the church, some African ministers are accustomed to solicit money from Europeans in Johannesburg. The kind of situation which may occur because of this is vividly described in a letter of an African minister from Western Native Township, to the Native Commissioner, Johannesburg (May, 1938):

> DEAR SIR,—I thought of writing and let you know of what is taking place in the Location and in Town.
> One day last year I went to town to buy some planks. I went to one of the Albert Street stores. There when the clark saw me coming said: "Go away here I have no money." I felt disgusted as it is indignifying. I answered and said: "Please sir, listen first before you chase me away." So I told him that I wanted some planks. He then said he was sorry he thought I was one of those native ministers who go about collecting money saying they are going to build churches. "I am tired of them," he said.
> Dear Sir, I humbly beg you to see to this and put a stop to it. They are collecting monies for their own use. Please stop them.
> I beg to remain, Dear Sir,
> Your obedient servant,
> W. M. ——.

Responsible leaders of independent Churches oppose strongly their less responsible colleagues who solicit money, and in 1944 the League of the African Bantu Churches of South Africa approached the Native Administration of Johannesburg, pointing out the necessity of having such activities checked.[9] A Coloured manager of a printing press in Alexandra Township, who has followed the development of the Bantu independent Churches with interest, told me: "Christianity is dying out here, because it is only regarded as a money-making machinery."

[a] Some Churches stipulate that their members in urban areas should pay twice as much as the members living in rural areas.

The city congregations are small as a rule. But they must be kept up, for two reasons: firstly, to provide a centre for the members who spend a shorter or longer time in Johannesburg or who may be resident there; secondly, because it is a matter of prestige to have a church in Johannesburg. Although the overwhelming number of church members reside in the Reserve or in Farm areas, the leader, in most cases, lives in Johannesburg. There are exceptions to this rule. The great prophets, for definite reasons (p. 93), reside in the country. Some prominent Ethiopian leaders, like P. Lamula, Ph. Mkhize (Lutheran offshoots) and F. G. Majola (to enumerate only Zulu Church leaders) also live in Reserve or Farm areas. But the number of Ethiopian and Zionist bishops and metropolitans who have chosen the Golden City as their see is great chiefly because both for the leader himself and for his rural church members it is a matter of prestige to do so. "Our President lives in Johannesburg. He lives near Pretoria and Native Affairs Department there. Again and again he speaks to Native Affairs Department about our church. He doesn't just write to them. He goes straight up to the Secretary's [for Native Affairs] office. We will be recognized by Government soon, he says."

For all these thousands, the independent Bantu Church, however weak, takes a central place in their lives and is a (temporary) home for their souls. One of the Congregational leaders on the Rand, upon founding a Church of his own, said in the manifesto in which he invited people to join the Church: "We let the Zulu know that here is his home now." City life may have its particular allurements for the people, but in actual fact social life in the city is, to the Bantu, much less colourful or eventful than life in the country. In this situation the Church becomes a home and a social centre to the Bantu in the city: the mine labourer and the kitchen boy and the policeman and the clerk and the honourable army of those Bantu women who have worked hard all the week, washing and ironing—all these take a pride in the Church which is their very own. Besides ordinary Sunday services, such Churches arrange occasional concerts, when they may be sure to have packed houses, with all enjoying themselves. Zionists have night services between Saturday and Sunday, when Bantu emotional life, subdued and repressed during the week in the artificial world of the Whites, is allowed to break through and find its outlet in song and praise and dance.

The Church follows them, caring for them in the crises of life. Ill-health is rampant in the City, and Zionist prophets gather crowds in the hovels of the slum or out on the veld to pray for the sick and drive out demons. Just off the main road between Johannesburg and Pretoria, near Alexandra Township, they congregate in their hundreds on the Sunday afternoons, laying healing hands on the sick. And death comes to the Bantu location. It comes often. Then the Church is close at hand, and its fellowship, in a strange and bitter world, is reassuring and full of warmth.

The Bantu independent Church in the city is also the centre for a wider social life. Meetings and conferences of the Ethiopian Church follow very carefully a prepared agenda, and are enveloped in an atmosphere of minutes and paragraphs of constitutions and legalistic niceties, thereby offering a substitute for the civic life which is denied to the Bantu in South Africa. By some of them such meetings are used as a training ground for political activities. In one township on the Rand, independent Church leaders managed to get their own people exclusively put on the municipal School Committee, constituted to look after an Anglican school. In the heyday of the African National Congress—that is, during the 'twenties—some Ethiopian leaders on the Rand took an active part in the work of the Congress. During World War II, the Bantu Communist paper *Inkululeko* (Freedom) received letters from Rand Churches which placed themselves at the disposal of the Communist movement. Some class distinctions begin to appear in the independent Church on the Rand. The upper class—the Bantu intelligentsia, editors, doctors, lawyers—will be found in the African Methodist Episcopal Church; whereas at the other end of the scale, Zionist sects take care of the uneducated.

While the independent Churches are a product of social and ecclesiastical separation from the White caste on the Rand, the common front against the other caste has not succeeded in uniting the various Churches. Suspicion of one another is rampant among the African ministers, with the result that quite often ministers, in their clerical collars, avoid greeting colleagues they meet in the street, who wear the same outfit. This avoidance is, of course, as un-African as one could imagine. A Zulu evanglist working in one of the townships—one of my informants—used to break the ice by going up to any African minister he met, greeting him with these words: "Don't you know that it is the instruction (*umthetho*) from the Transvaal Ministers' Association that we should always greet one another as brethren?"

The rivalry between the leaders and the constant breaking

86

away of smaller or larger sections of the Church, which characterizes Bantu independent Churches as a whole, is particularly
common on the Rand. The Native Commissioner's court in
Johannesburg has had to handle a number of cases between
Rand Churches—cases which, after months and years of hear-
ing, are taken to the Rand Division of the Supreme Court. One
Congregational offshoot spent £47 16s. in legal charges for
litigation cases in one year alone, and this example is by no
means unique. Certain European lawyers are busily engaged in
activities for such clients. It is heartening to note that both the
Native Commissioner and judges of the Supreme Court have in
a number of cases used their influence to advise the parties to
settle matters amicably out of court.

To counteract bickering and strife, independent Churches on
the Rand have, with varied success, attempted some measure
of co-operation. There is a Ministers' Association in Pimville
which is supposed to meet every month. Zionist Churches in
various locations may work together for certain practical tasks,
as, for instance, the Independent African Association for
African Widows and Fatherless Children Almsgate, a loose
organization formed in 1939 by twelve Zionist Churches in
Western Native Township. This association seems, however, to
have come to a speedy end.

In the African Ministers' Association, ministers of both
Mission and independent Churches meet together once a month
with a view to discussing church problems on the Rand. The
outlook for this organization has not changed considerably
since R. Phillips wrote of it in 1938: "Genuine co-operation and
sustained interest [are] difficult to attain."[10] Both Mission and
independent Church ministers can be elected chairmen.

So the independent Church lives its rather precarious life in
the City, caring for the thousands and tens of thousands of
Africans, who because of the City's caste distinctions would not
follow the lead of the Mission churches. One of their leaders
once wrote a letter to the Native Commissioner in Johannesburg
asking to be given a site whereon to erect a church, "so that we
can build our Jerusalem". His Church was not recognized, and
he therefore could not have the site. It is hard to build Jerusalem in the City of Gold.

(2) INDEPENDENT CHURCHES ON FARMS

The farm areas of Natal must for our purpose be divided into
three sections, presenting very different conditions to the

87

independent Church. There are the European farms, the Mission Reserves, and the Scheduled Native areas, called "Black Spots in European Areas".

(a) *European farms*. My material on this point is very scanty and provides the basis for only tentative statements. As far as my personal knowledge of the conditions goes, it has been gathered at casual visits to farms and discussions with some Afrikaans and English farmers; and also through rather fuller evidence gained by contacts with African Christians who reside as workers on such farms. In this connexion, I would suggest that it would be helpful to have a Gallup poll among farmers taken by some investigator (of Afrikaans descent). This is needed because we have so far only mutually contradictory impressions to judge from.

One British missionary makes the following statements in a letter of August, 1945:

> The farming areas are more thickly occupied by Sects than the Reserve and even more so are the Urban areas—for the one obvious reason that there are no restrictions of any kind. The majority of farmers have not interested themselves in the establishment of the old established churches on their farms, nor are they interested in Church—or even Secular Schools (for the reason that the latter might affect their child labour!). Thus the African's need for some sort of spiritual satisfaction depends upon his own efforts: hence an open field for him.

This statement needs considerable modification. Here again our typology with its distinction between Ethiopian and Zionist churches, and between two kinds of Church leaders, is important. The farmer has certain definite rules for social rating as applied to the African, and even if tolerant towards one type of independent Church, he may be opposed to the representatives of another type. And in the last resort it is, of course, not a matter of types at all, but of persons and personalities.

The independent Church leader of the *"chief"*-type (p. 106) is, in fact, not uncommon on farms. He may be employed on weekdays as a farm *induna* and the farmer may regard his influence on the other Africans on the farm as wholesome. He must, in order to be tolerated for long by the farmer, make himself known as sound, steady and industrious. That is, steady indeed, but not *too* industrious or enterprising. If, as some do, he becomes conspicuous through attention to the farm work round his own kraal (growing too many peach trees, having a flock of goats which is increasing too rapidly), he may be told that he seems to think he is on a level with the Whites, and that he had better clear out. In such a case the church work he may have built up on that farm and surrounding ones will suffer.

My impression is that the farmer generally prefers to have on his farm Africans who belong to Mission Churches. But the farmer rightly insists that he should know the Church, and that any missionary who wants to do evangelistic work on his farm should present his credentials to him, and not behave as if he, the stranger, owned the farm. Much the same argument applies to the farmer's relationship with Ethiopian Church leaders. One African church leader I knew was accepted by a farmer in spite of protests from a European missionary who claimed that the Zulu preacher might harm the mission's old and established work. In this case the African knew the farmer well, and had certainly seen him more frequently than the European concerned. The personal link was decisive.

In cases where the African church leader is able to win the farmer's confidence, his chances of establishing his church work are greater than they would be in the Reserves, because he may be allowed to build a church, and there is no five-mile-radius rule to be applied on a farm. This accounts for the fact that in certain cases strong independent Churches are able to establish school work. In a few cases such schools on farms may even succeed in getting Government aid from the Education Department, in spite of the fact that the Church concerned is not recognized by Government through its Native Affairs Department.

With one accord farmers are against such Church leaders as are reputed to be political agitators. In the 'twenties and 'thirties this opposition was directed against independent Churches with I.C.U. connexions. There are of course different kinds of politics. One Sotho, the leader of the African Methodist Pentecostal Church of South Africa, claims that he was dismissed from the Anglican Church because he supported his Nationalist farmer's party. He gives as the reason for his secession: "No difference in doctrine from the Anglican church, only the General Parliamentary election of 1924 for G—— seat. I used my influence in support of a Nationalist Candidate and he won." It happened this way, he says: "In 1924 I was badly persecuted to be disgraced among the people—I had to sell *Die Burger* for living—Mnr. B—— gave me a donkey to cart water that I may live (a Nationalist).[a] The part my Church

a *Die Burger* is a Nationalist Party organ.

89

members played was un-Christian—to be suspended without trial."

Zionist prophets have fewer opportunities to establish themselves on the farms. The barbed-wire fence round the farm hinders the roving prophet's wanderings. Some farmers have found that such sects are rather less inclined to beat their swords into ploughshares than to use the farmer's ploughshare as their church bell, and in such circumstances farmers, are hardly favourable to independent Church activities. In certain cases Zionist groups have been evicted from the farms and are dumped in the Reserves. I have come across little Zionist colonies in Zululand, consisting of communities that have been expelled from certain farms in Natal. Under their prophet they have then made the return to the Reserve. One also comes across a few cases where farmers of the Poor White type receive notorious Zionist prophets to squat on their land provided they pay a certain amount every year. With the increasing influence of the "Apostolic" message on lower-class Afrikaans farmers, this tendency to harbour inspired Zionist prophets may even be supported by what they would regard as religious considerations.

(b) *Mission Reserves*. Act No. 49 of 1903 (Natal), Section 6, provides:

> No person, society, or body other than the ecclesiastical or missionary body named in the deed of grant, shall be allowed to establish any mission or undertake religious or educational work, or have any right to use or be upon any such Reserve, saving, however, the rights of occupation [of ordinary residents].

This provision makes it especially difficult for Bantu independent Churches to extend their influence to the Mission Reserve. The usual way of eluding the law is for the prophet to establish himself just on the border of the Mission area. In certain cases, especially on the American Board's extensive Mission Reserves, people who join Congregational offshoots as the African Congregational Church or the Zulu Congregational Church cause considerable difficulty to the Mission authorities with consequent law suits. Already in 1921, a "Committee on Survey and Occupation" of Mission fields in South Africa said about Natal, with a somewhat peculiar wording: "It is difficult to preserve even the Mission Reserves from the encroachment of Roman Catholic and Ethiopian sects."[11] On the whole it is, however, in the Mission Reserves that the influence of a Mission

Church can make itself best felt in shaping the particular community, which is growing up within its borders, and therefore it is here that a Zulu independent Church meets with the most decided resistance.

(c) *Scheduled Native Areas.* Before the Natives Land Act of 1913 and the Native Affairs Administration Bill of 1917 had made it impossible for Natives, either individually or as a syndicate, to acquire land, there were certain areas in Natal, for instance, which had already been bought by Native syndicates and where African communities were established. These are generally referred to as "Black Spots in European Areas". Certain Mission Churches had encouraged their congregations to acquire land in such Native-owned areas and to establish their communities there, and some independent Churches have succeeded either through individual members or through common action in getting a foothold on such farms.

Both the Zulu Congregational Church and the African Congregational Church have acquired their own farms in the Port Shepstone district, the areas being some 400 and 1100 acres respectively. The farms owned by the leader of the Nazarite Church are referred to elsewhere (p. 129). But there are characteristic differences in the conditions on such farms. The Nazarite farm does not belong to the Nazarite Church as such, but to prophet Shembe personally. He can therefore decide whether certain of his people should be allowed to live there or whether they may be evicted. Farms belonging to Congregational offshoots are more constitutional both in principle and practice and small lots are subdivided among members. This again leads to certain unavoidable difficulties. If, for instance, a member of the African Congregational Church who owns some acres of land in its farm area, secedes in order to form a new independent Church, his presence on the farm may disturb the peace of the community. In such a case, lawsuits will follow. The Church tries to reserve its privilege to repay to the seceder the money value of the lot concerned, and to resell it to people whose loyalty is assured. Individual members of independent Churches have succeeded in buying land in "Black Spots" in Natal outside the area of their church farms. From such strongholds they attempt to extend their Church's influence among their neighbours. It is self-evident that on native-owned farm areas, whether they are possessed by syndicates or by individuals, independent Churches have greater opportunities than in other farm districts.

In many cases four, five or more Mission and Independent Churches are represented on the same Native-owned farm. In such places, important problems of local co-operation between the Churches arise. The outcome and success of these efforts towards co-operation depend on the tone that one or two men are able to set for the community as a whole. I quote two examples from central Natal.

On X farm, comprising a total of seventy-five Christian families, the three Mission Churches and the eleven independent groups live in constant strife and in an atmosphere of mutual disregard. These inimical feelings are if anything intensified at the quarterly or annual visits of the superintendent or bishop of any of the Churches.

On Y farm, with fifty kraals, there are three Mission Churches and four independent groups represented. The leader of the most influential of these Churches is at the same time chairman of the Farm Council and Postal Agent—thus holding, besides his church work, the two most important commissions of trust which a man in that community can have. This man's work and the fact that he has established fine co-operation with the other Christian groups on the farm, is the explanation of the atmosphere of happy community living of the whole place. At the death of any Christian, all congregations observe mourning (*ukuzila*) until the time of the burial. Herewith they both revive a time-honoured Zulu tradition and give a declaration of their Christian solidarity: "The burial itself is like a wedding these days; such crowds of people come together." At the suggestion of the Methodist minister, all congregations celebrated a great Thanksgiving festival because of the fact that all children born that year, 1944, were alive and well. When the wives of three brothers got twins, in the same year, this was the occasion for a memorable Thanksgiving-service and tea-party, all the pastors and their groups taking part in the general rejoicing.

Such little incidents show, of course, that human relationships may prevail in spite of all denominational cleavages. It is the women, the mothers, more than the men who push denominational considerations aside and let human relations bring them together. The attraction of a long night's singing and praying and shouting together is too great to be resisted, and the Bantu propensity for enjoying communal living too strong to allow denominational departmentalism to win the day.

92

(3) INDEPENDENT CHURCHES IN THE RESERVE

Whereas the City is the breeding ground of sects, the Reserve is the hatching-ground, and as such it is indispensable also to the City Church. In this respect, however, there is an important difference in the role of the Reserve as between the Ethiopian and the Zionist Churches. To the Ethiopian leader in Johannesburg his congregations in Zululand are just another part of the Church, living under other economic and social conditions than those of the townpeople, but as far as congregational life goes essentially of the same type as the congregation in Johannesburg or Durban. This is not so in the Zionist Church. To them the Reserve is the Canaan with Bethesdas and Jordans, the pools and the rivers where the sick are healed, and Hills of Zion, the holy hilltops where prayers and sacrifices are presented to Jehovah.

I was present at a baptism ceremony led by Bishop Morupa of the Jerusalem Sabbath Church. The baptism took place in a pool, just outside Alexandra Township, Johannesburg. "This is a dirty pool, and its water can hardly be made holy, however much I pray," said the bishop. "Therefore I send my people who are sick away from here to Sibasa, in Vendaland. At my kraal in Vendaland I let them build their own huts, and there they are daily purified in holy water until they recover."

In the same way the Zulu prophet looks to the Zululand Reserve as the only place where the essential business of the Church—healing—can be successfully performed. Here again is the reason why the leading prophets do not live in Johannesburg, as many Ethiopian leaders do, but in the Reserves, as, for instance, E. Lekganyane in Transvaal, and Isaiah Shembe among the Zulus. They stay in the Reserves (or Native-owned farm areas) and establish there the centre of their Churches.

The difference between the status of Ethiopian congregations and Zionist groups is very marked in the Reserves. The very reason why the Ethiopian groups have split away from White Churches—the racial issue—challenges chief and commoner alike in Zululand. Seen from a Zulu point of view, the Ethiopian programme appears as at the same time Christian and African. The ideology and theology appear as roughly the same as those preached in the Mission Church. But the Ethiopians have thrown in their lot with their African kinsmen against the Whites. The Ethiopian Church in Zululand appears as an instrument to vindicate the Zulu cause against all White encroachments upon the over-populated Reserve. The Zulu terms *i6andla lezizwe* (the Native Church) or *uHlanga* (National) or Zulu Congregational Church, used for these Ethiopian churches suggest that in principle and practice they are the Zulu's very own religious organizations. The African Congregational Church has tried to become known as a National Church of Zululand, especially stressing its relations to the Royal family.[12] The idea of a Zulu National Church has not been entirely absent from leading members of that family. The idea of the King, or Paramount Chief, being *summus episcopus* for the tribal Church is, of course, not anything peculiar to the Zulus.[a] R. S. Mahlanga's attempted "National Swazi Native Apostolic Church of South Africa" has possibly had some influence on the Zulu leaders; he said of the Swazi king Sobhuza (who himself is not a confessing Christian): "He is the great and head Minister above you all. He is the King, Priest, Bishop, Minister and President in this the Swazi Church, as he is of Royal Birth". The typical ideology behind such statements would be sure to find an echo in Zulu minds. The Paramount Chief of the Zulus, Mshiyeni ka Dinuzulu, himself a faithful member of the Anglican Church and a man to whom the religious situation among the Zulus is a genuine and grave concern, has however, because of his stand in religious matters, had problems with some of his Zulu people. In order to evade the difficulties caused by the denominational struggles in Zululand, he is reported to have favoured for some time the emergence of a Zulu National Church, and he has repeatedly stressed the need for a Union of all the Churches. As this would come into conflict with certain interests of the Mission Churches, Mshiyeni has not pressed the matter further. He has obviously shown a positive and constructive interest in helping some of the sounder Ethiopian Churches. In one important case Mshiyeni even volunteered to arbitrate (together with Dr. Dube and an African minister) between two Ethiopian leaders, and his intervention was no doubt wholesome and helpful.

Something of the same fundamental difficulty as the one experienced by Mshiyeni is also felt by other chiefs. Gluckman has pointed out that to-day Zulu chiefs are at the same time "Government bureaucrats and centres of opposition to Government",[13] and this conflict may centre in the same individual chief who, torn between his loyalties on the one side to the White Government and on the other to the Zulu community,

[a] Cf. p. 38.

94

is at a loss which side to take. This conflict is often apparent in the attitude taken by chiefs to independent Churches.

The few chiefs who are decidedly and outspokenly anti-White may use the Ethiopian Church as a welcome tool in their stubborn resistance to Government. Thus a chief may refuse to give a Mission Church any land in his ward and instead ostentatiously shield and favour smaller and unrecognized Ethiopian groups. His main purpose is to preserve the *status quo*—or *ukuthula*, peace, as he would call it—in his ward, and support for the anti-White Ethiopian Church which integrates quite well into the life of the community is, according to his view, one method of preserving such peace.

As far as the Zionist Churches are concerned, the attitude of Zululand chiefs is generally speaking negative. The reason for this aversion is, of course, not the chief's views on the Bantu syncretistic tendencies of the Zionists; on the contrary, chiefs may nowadays call upon a Zionist prophet as a diviner in some serious sorcery case, where the traditional heathen diviner has failed. The principal reason for the very definite opposition of the chiefs to the Zionist Churches is the fact that Zionists, according to the chiefs, disturb the community life of the tribe and of the ward.

The Zionists stand out as a separate community in Zululand, as a *tertium genus*, a third race,[14] over against both the heathen and the Christian community. Whereas in their attitude towards the White man they tend to be rather more violent than the Ethiopians, they nevertheless are not easily assimilated to the rest of the Zulu community. Their distinct *mores*—opposition to medicine, medicine-men and hospitals, their food taboos, which are different from the tribal taboos—and their general appearance with their long hair and the Zionist snort and constant cries of "Amen", "Halleluya", single them out as a group by themselves. Furthermore, they themselves are anxious to keep at a distance from "the world"—in this case, other Christians and heathens. If they practise circumcision they do not shake hands with the uncircumcized, who are "unclean". If the whole community come together for a tribal meeting or a prayer meeting for rain, the other people naturally divide themselves according to sex and age class, but the Zionists in their uniforms keep together as a particular group. Zionists do not eat with other men who, whether they are heathen or Christian, are all unclean because they eat pork and therefore are "people with demons", and so on and so forth.

G   95

There must be a social pressure of great weight to get the Zionists to conform to the general pattern of Zulu behaviour. On one important occasion—an *uku6uyisa*-ceremony, or the Bringing Home of the Spirit of a deceased chief one year after his death,[15] an occasion when the whole district met together and royalty were present—there were processions of people, heathen and Christians, coming from all directions to the chief's kraal bringing as gifts for the festival calabashes of beer or *amahewu* (fermented porridge). In these processions there were not a few Zionists who brought their calabashes like the others and drank with them the *amahewu*. The social pressure exercised by the demands of tribal loyalty overcame in this case their fissiparous tendency. But this was a decided exception to the rule.

The outstanding complaint by the chiefs is expressed thus by one in North Zululand: "They take away our wives and daughters to unknown places, and such women become wanderers and lead immoral lives. Our women go to kraals where drums are beaten, and remain away all night with these supposed religious leaders." Or, in the words of the Paramount Chief, Mshiyeni: "I am opposed to people going about preaching in kraals. People come from afar whom we do not know, and say they are Messengers of God. We don't know these people. With our own people it is different. We know them. Even so, no person should preach until he has reported himself to the Chief, who will question him and ascertain his standing and character. Many of these preachers upset our women and young girls and entice them away from their homes."[16]

These complaints become particularly vocal as the Zionist prophets, operating in Zululand, are in many cases not Zulus, but Sotho, Xhosa, or sometimes men from as far away as Nyasaland. One Sotho prophet, Charles P——, one of the most persistent in his anti-White propaganda, wanted to declare his message to the inhabitants of a Mission Reserve. As he was not allowed to enter that Reserve, he lived in the tribal ward on the border, and gave vent to his opinions from this secure spot, as he regarded it. Upon protests from mission authorities and from Africans on both sides of the border, the chief went so far as to threaten the life of the prophet and said angrily: "I do not want this Sotho agitator in this district." I myself have had experience of such a man: he had been expelled from the district by a European policeman because it was proved to all intents and purposes that he had killed a woman by forcing ashes down her throat in order to "heal" her. A couple of weeks later, the same prophet reappeared quite unruffled, and one fine morning I found him shouting in the "Spirit" under a waterfall. When I attempted to bring him to the chief he angrily threatened me with a heavy knobkerry. Eventually he was brought before the chief, who was much perturbed by this defiance of the order of the European police. As the Sotho prophet stood there, scornfully smiling at the chief, the latter barked at him: *"Uyahleka uZulu na?"* ("Are you laughing at the representative of the Zulu nation, man?"). This chief was one of the many who do not wish interference of this kind in his district. The kind of struggle that these heathen chiefs have with Zionist prophets can be gathered from the report of one chief in northern Zululand. When he refused a prophet permission to carry on his church work in his ward, the prophet retaliated by saying that he would call down spirits from heaven which would bring disaster to the chief's kraal.

The healing prophet's meetings in his "Bethesda" or the roving prophet's wanderings from place to place with his married and unmarried female followers are a matter of real concern to the chiefs. The fact that the Zionist groups are somehow beyond the chief's control now causes him much the same concern as when, in the first period of mission work in Zululand, the Mission station appeared to some chiefs as a strange and dangerous place, to which young Zulu girls who wanted to accept this new faith of the Whites ran away against their fathers' wish (*ukweqa*). But in the eyes of the Zulu community and of its official representative—the tribal chief—the Zionist scandal is, probably, more far-reaching.

The instability of the Zionist prophets and followers, the spiritual vagabondage which the movement encourages, characterize their contact with the rural community in Zululand, from the kraal to the *isifunda* (the chief's ward or district) in its entirety. It is a common saying in Zululand of a person who travels a great deal: *"Wa 6ulawa ithambo laseZioni!"* ("He has been 'killed' by his Zionist disposition.") It is of course also a fact that the opposition from chiefs and the heathen community to the Zionist derives from the former group's aversion to the responsible position allotted to women. As we shall see in a later chapter, it is especially in the Reserves that Zionist women tend to acquire a dominating position as prominent office-holders in the Church.

The constant strife and struggle between the local leaders of competing Zionist or Ethiopian groups adds to the instability of the community. It is a rather sad fact that heathen chiefs and headmen have had on occasion to try to reconcile Zionist bishops and local ecclesiastical celebrities who were at logger-heads with one another.

Some chiefs, in order to forestall possible faction fights between Christian groups over the Sabbath issue, have decreed in true Solomonic fashion that in their wards there are two days of rest, Saturday *and* Sunday. Many chiefs are of such an œcumenical spirit so as to embrace all Churches with their sympathy. Chief M—— in the Q—— district, declared that he "loved" all Churches: the Romans, because they had baptized his father *in extremis*; the Anglicans because his chief wife (*inkosikazi*) belonged to that Church; the Lutherans, because he had learned to read and write in one of their schools; the Zionists because they prayed for him when he had been injured by a car, and they had prayed so successfully that he was actually healed when brought to the Swedish Mission hospital in Dundee (Natal)! Thus, when he gives a feast, he is careful to invite people from all Churches.

In spite of the fact that Zionists deliberately segregate them-selves from the community at large, and derive much of their strength by this social separation, they do nevertheless act as a conservative force in so far as the fundamentals of Zulu society are concerned. The heathen belief in sorcery and witch-craft is heartily shared by them, and is even strengthened, though modified, by their Christianized magic and witch-find-ing. Their exclusive stress on "Divine Healing" as the main element of the Christian message is interpreted by the Zionists themselves as revolutionary in relation to the Zulu leech and his medicines. But as we shall find, this Divine Healing has been superseded by Zionist healing through holy water and holy ashes which in the eyes of the ailing Zulu may be even more efficacious than the herbs of the leech. Also in this respect, therefore, and by the very stress on healing as the main thing in religion, Zionists function as a conservative force in Zulu society, in spite of their revolutionary attitude otherwise. Shembe, the leader and prophet of the Nazarite Church, has, more than any other Zulu church leader, deliberately worked upon these lines. The festivals, and the dances at Ekupakemeni, where chiefs are given a special place of honour and where together with the prophet they dance in front of the others, make an appeal to the Zulus because they recognize them as flesh of their own flesh. The monogamy issue, which in most other Churches is a problem of first-rate social importance, does not arise in the Nazarite Church; chiefs are known to have been given additional wives through Shembe's intervention. In many cases the chiefs' wives enjoy special status in the Nazarite Church as *aɓakhokheli* (church stewards) *ex officio*. Because of this, many chiefs, specially on the Zululand coast, call themselves Nazarites and appear, a-dancing and a-singing, at Shembe's festivals. Through such connexions the prophet easily acquires land for his "Bethesda" colonies, in spite of the fact that his Church is not recognized by Government. Isaiah Shembe, himself a leader of great authority, knew how to influence the chiefs: he would not visit locations where the chief was not a follower of his Church, whereas his visit to other wards was hailed as the great and unforgettable happening of the year. If a chief wanted to see him, Shembe might deliberately let him wait for days until he was at last received in audience: a dangerous game of Zulu power politics, but Shembe was influential enough to get away with it.

To quote an example from outside the Zulu-speaking area: when Edmund Sigcu (Xhosa) started his "Church of Christ for the Union of the Bantu and Protection of Bantu Customs, which is the Memorial of Ntsikana" in 1922, he informed Government that he was "going to install a class of Ministers who will work in Harmony with the Chiefs [Native] and who will govern the Church according to Native custom." This meant, to him, apparently, a church which above all recognized polygamy. The church is thus transformed and adapted in order to suit the community.

CHAPTER V

LEADER AND FOLLOWERS

Whereas in the earlier period of the independent Church movement it was the racial issue between White and Black in the Mission Churches which caused secessions, to-day the characteristic feature of this movement is the secession of one African leader from another. The obsession for leadership in the Church is of course only a symptom of other underlying factors, one of the most important being that in the South Africa of racial discrimination and colour-bar it is the church which has provided the only legitimate outlet for the African's strong urge for leadership. In the civic and political sphere there are no openings for African leadership. The Church, in this situation, becomes a kind of psychological safety valve. But even here, the outlet is of limited legality as only eight out of eight hundred Churches are officially recognized by Government.

Margery Perham, when comparing the socio-political situation in South Africa with that of Indirect Rule in Tanganyika, wrote: "I was deeply struck by a contrast in South Africa, where the strong tribal feeling of the Zulus, defeated, restrained, and neglected, made me think of some large power-machine pushed on its side, still working, its energy running to waste, a sad, if not dangerous sight."[1] The statement refers to conditions of fifteen years ago. The power-machine is still working, its energy is still running to waste, and the leadership problems of the Independent Churches are symptoms of this.

(I) THE LEADER

Leadership problems of Independent Zulu churches are here studied in their relation to traditional Zulu leadership patterns, which have influenced and modified the conditions within the church to a marked degree. But it is not a leadership *in vacuo*. It must be seen in constant inter-relation with local subleaders and the great mass of followers.

(a) Zulu patterns of leadership

There are two main elements inherent in the leadership issue, two irreconcilable patterns in competition, both struggling for supremacy and one or the other becoming dominant. The first is a heritage from the Protestant, chiefly Nonconformist missions, where the relation of minister and church is essentially "democratic". The Protestant minister appears to the Africans above all as an evangelistic preacher and a leader of meetings and conferences, not as a priest. The primary importance of the lay element in the Church has been stressed very energetically in Protestant missions, and has been impressed upon Bantu congregations. Theological training of the African ministry has not been the most outstanding achievement of all such missions in South Africa. Up to recent times it has been usual for an African, who by his character and his general spiritual qualities was deemed fit to lead the flock, to be chosen by the Mission and ordained.

The other pattern is the Zulu ideal of leadership. The system of *rank* forms the fundamental pattern of Zulu society.[2] The harmonious life of the nation depended upon a balance of interests between king (and the royal Zulu clan), chiefs and people. In the classical era of Zulu history (Shaka—Mpande) the position of the king was of central importance to both land and people. The people and the land belonged to the king. The name of the king's clan was extended to all people belonging to the other, conquered clans—that is, *a6akwa Zulu*—those of the Zulu clan. He performed the most important religious ceremonies and magical acts on behalf of the nation. Through the first-fruit ceremonies the king was strengthened and cleansed in the name of the nation. Shaka even went so far as to expel all rain-makers, because he alone could control the heavens, and possibly also he was opposed to any rival authorities within the tribe. The king is also the great medicine-man of the tribe. If he fails to heal a case, it is incurable.

The king was the richest man in the nation, rich in cattle and wives. He was supposed to use his riches in feeding and helping his people generously. In approaching the king with ceremonious salutations and respect the Zulus felt that they increased his prestige and thus the prestige of the whole nation. The king listened to important legal cases, and one of his fundamental functions was to maintain the customary law of the tribe. The most efficient instrument in moulding the loyalty of this martial tribe in relation to the king was the institution of the "regiments" (*ama6utho*) according to age-classes: "It was this military orientation of Zulu culture under the king which largely unified his people" (Gluckman). At the military barracks of the royal homestead (*ikhanda*) the regiments served their king, each regiment being on duty for a considerable time. Chanting the king's songs and performing dances, some of which had been invented by the king himself (especially Dingaan), they enhanced the prestige of the king and their own *joie-de-vivre*.

With all his power the king was, however, not autocratic. He delegated some judicial and administrative functions to the chiefs and he had his council, the advice of which he was supposed to follow. This council and the potential powers of his brothers were important sanctions regulating his authority: his brothers and chiefs had to be treated with careful consideration lest they became centres of disaffection against him. There was always the possibility that if the king abused his powers, the people would support one of the other political heads against him. This happened when Shaka was murdered, and in the dramatic struggle between Cetshwayo and his brother Mbuyazi.

The pattern of king-nation-relationship is, to the Zulu, not something solely of the past. Their history is an ever present reality in their lives, moulding their outlook at the present time. In this respect, heathen and Christians form a common front. My Zulu colleague in the mission work, an old gentleman and a fine Christian, was never so pleased as when he was referred to by the name of his Zulu regiment, Dakwa.

At the same time there is, deep in the Zulu's soul, a tragic note in this relation to a glorious history which is gone for ever. In the independent Church and the relationships established there between leaders and followers, the pattern of king and nation, or king-chiefs-nation, is revived again. One of the most important clues to an understanding of the Independent Church is to regard it as an escape into history, into the glorious Zulu history which was brought to an abrupt end by the Whites. In the independent Church history is reborn and redeemed by being projected into an Ethiopian Utopia.

The kingship pattern of Zulu society is imprinted on the leadership in *all* the independent Churches. The leader whether "Bishop", "Overseer" or "President" is a king, *inkosi*, and the church is his tribe. In certain cases this pattern is taken over in a clearly Zulu and nativistic form. But it is characteristic that in other cases this Zulu kingship pattern is being Christianized by being combined with the Ethiopian Abyssinian mythical charter which shows through especially in the bishop's regalia.

One of the main factors in the selective mechanism by which a man in an independent Church may rise to eminence and leadership is descent from or relationship with a royal clan, or with a chief's clan. Both Ethiopian and Zionist leaders are eager to claim that they are of royal blood, or at least have some affinity to Zulu nobility. J. M. Hlongwane of the Bantu Methodist Church related that his mother was adopted by Cetshwayo, and that the *ilobolo*-cattle for her had been paid by the king. Rev. Mabilitsa's brother was a chief of the Bakgatla. When the tribal chief died, the tribe approached Mabilitsa asking him to become their leader, but the answer was: "I am the servant of a great King, I am bigger than a chief." As P. Lamula started his United National Church of Christ and wanted support for this undertaking, he wrote a pamphlet about his Church and about himself: "I am a pure Zulu born. My father was a prominent man during the days of King Mpande. He was ranked among the foremost of Zulu warriors who received the *Ingxota*."[a]

This does not, of course, only refer to Zulu leaders. One finds the same tendency elsewhere. J. M. Dwane could claim that his father was a brother of the reigning chief of the Amantinde, a sub-tribe of the Gaikas, and the Constitution of the Holy Catholic Apostolic Church in Zion is anxious to stress that their founder, the Nyasa minister J. G. Phillipps, was "the son of a Chief, and by right his successor".

It is in line with this tendency that independent Church leaders compete with one another in seeking the favours of the royal house of the Zulus. Gardiner Mvuyana of the African Congregational Church held the 1926 synod of his church at Mahashini, the royal kraal. Shembe was eager to stress his relations with the royal house; he gave Solomon ka Dinuzulu one of his daughters, Zondi. He also built a special house for the Paramount Chief at Ekuphakameni. There is a hymn in Shembe's hymnbook referring to Solomon's relations with the church:

> King Solomon is called,
> He, the son of Dinuzulu
> And the fame of Jehovah
> is in Ekuphakameni.
> (*Nazarite Hymnbook*, No. 116.)

The leader of the ama-Nazaretha Church introduced Christianized first-fruit ceremonies in his Church. Shembe adopted these ceremonies (*ukweshwama*) and they are celebrated in this Church on December 25. No Nazaretha follower may eat the

---

[a] *Ingxotha:* brass armlet as insigne of martial powers.

first-fruits until Shembe has first blessed them. In taking over these ceremonies, which traditionally were the sole prerogative of the king, Shembe made known his claim to be a king of his people. An important trait of the kingship pattern is its hereditary nature of church leadership. This development will be discussed in a special chapter.

As the king of the Church, the leader is the embodiment, the organic representative, of his group. There is an intimate bond between the leader's personality and the Church. His clan's name is extended to the Church which he has founded. So, to mention one instance among many, the official name of Rev. P. Lamula's Church is the "Bantu National Church of Christ (Lamula's)". So far, and in print, the leader's name is put within brackets. In reality, the most important part of the name is that within the brackets.

While the kingship pattern, as stated, is generally formed after the Zulu model, the "mythical charter" of some African apostolic succession from the Ethiopian or Abyssinian past, seems to be one influence resulting in veneration of the Church leader's *regalia*. At the "Induction—Consecration, Instalment and Enthronement of the Founder—President and General Overseer" of the Bantu Methodist Church, this dignitary was solemnly given the following "investitures of office": "Rings, Bibles, copy of Constitution, Pulpit Robes, Key, Hammer, Great Seal of the Church, official Pulpit robes for certain occasions, the necklace of the Cross, Biretta or Mitre, Rod or Staff".[3] Certain Zionist Churches which claim Abyssinian connexions attempt to live up to their claim by an impressive display of liturgical vestments. Some leaders expressly state that they have copied their vestments from a photo of the Emperor of Ethiopia or some Coptic Church dignitary.

The "king" of the Church brings his people back to their promised *land*. The land question is the most bitter grievance of the Bantu in South Africa. The Land Act of 1913 has had a decided influence on the rise of the Independent Church movement. And the tendency of the church leaders to bring their followers together on church farms or in church colonies (in the Reserves) is by them felt as a primary duty of the church chief: that is, to establish his own church tribe on its own land. The church leader is also the supreme *judge* of his Church. That is the reason why, for instance, the Ethiopian Catholic Church in Zion has Judicial Committees, and trial courts, and appellate courts, and clergy courts of appeal, with higher Provincial Court

Ecclesiastical and Supreme Court of Appeal. That is also the reason for the great importance given in the Ethiopian Church to constitutions. A Church can go to almost unlimited expenditure when it comes to acquiring an imposing Code of Constitutions, printed with, if possible, a photo of the President himself, perhaps together with his Supreme Council.

Prominent Zionist Church leaders must be sagacious judges. In the Nazarite Church, appeals from local courts are taken to the "Servant" at Ekuphakameni, "just as if it were the chief's court". Bishop L. S. Moshanyana, of Frankfort, O.F.S., in the Constitution of his Church states his claims in this respect in no ambiguous terms:

> Gal. 3: 24. The Law is a School Master Shepherd, Headquarters: Frankfort. James 4: 14. There is one Lawgiver, the Bishop, with his Chiefs, Minister and Priests. Bishop's Laws will be read in Conference, if complaint to people it should be signed by seven men. Esther 1: 14.

The constitution of the South African National Ethiopian Church of Africa, after lengthy definitions of such matters as trial of members, and prerogatives of witnesses sets out the following "Mode of Trial":

> The following mode of trial should always be adhered to:
> (a) The arraignment.
> (b) Reading the charges and specifications to the accused.
> (c) Demanding his reply to the charges.
> (d) The accused calls and examines his witnesses.
> (e) Cross-examination by the accused.
> (f) The accused puts in his evidence.
> (g) Cross-examination by the accuser.
> (h) Rebutting testimony by the accused.
> (i) Repetition.
> (j) The accuser opens the argument.
> (k) The accused follows in the defence.
> (l) The accuser closes the argument.
> (m) The Committee retires.
> (n) They return and render the verdict.
> (o) Presiding Officer announces the acquittal or expulsion of the accused.

The leader is generally well aware of his eminence. This is well exhibited in the pronouncements of the leader, for instance:

"I say unto you, I Richard Solomon ka Dlamane ka Mubhelebhele Muhlanga Inyati and Ndlavela, I say the Government in Pretoria has authorized this Church on the 9th October 1917 [which, of course, is not true] and I, as the President, I say unto you this church is the church of the —— Nation, as a whole and Grand Children."

One of these men calls himself "General Overseer of the World".

The self-assurance and the authoritative tendencies of the church-chief are sustained by an intricate system for upholding his prestige, similar to that of Zulu kings and chiefs. If somebody wants to speak to the leader, he must first approach him through one of his chaplains. The visitor has to approach the bishop or prophet on his knees, as a big chief was approached in former times (*ukugaqa*). I asked the followers of one prominent prophet whether they showed more respect (*ukukhonza*) to the Paramount Chief of the Zulus or their prophet. The reply was vivid: "*Mshiyeni*—we just pass him like this." They rushed before me without taking any notice. "But our prophet, the Servant! We show him much respect!"—they went down on their knees and crawled slowly as a sign of deepest respect. As the tribal kingship loses much of its importance in the modern world, the kingship pattern is the more energetically projected on the church leader.

But whereas the Zulu kingship pattern in its broad features is applicable to the leaders of most independent Churches, it is however reflected in certain different *types*, according to the different congregational needs and traditions of the Churches represented. The leader does not exercise his authority in a vacuum. He is a leader only in relation to a group of followers, a Church, and the particular aspirations of these groups tend to mould and modify the supreme authority in different ways.

(b) Church leaders of chief-type and prophet-type

Corresponding to the two types of Churches, Ethiopian and Zionist, there are *two types of leaders*, the *chief-type* and the *prophet*. Although I speak of *types*, I am well aware of the existence of hybrids and cross-sections. Broadly speaking, however, this classifying of independent Church leadership is, I believe, pertinent. We shall here analyse these two types in their inter-relation with the Churches they represent.

(i) *The chief-type of leader.* The Ethiopian Churches seceded from the Mission Churches largely because of the colour issue. But there is a strong ambivalence in their reaction to the Whites, with opposition on the one hand, and on the other a desire to copy them and to demonstrate that they can do as well as the Whites. This conflict and double reaction is inherent in the Ethiopian Churches and thereby also in their leader. The flock which he represents has cut away from the European Church. But they have nevertheless strong ambitions and they nurture aspirations to realize, within their sphere, a group life which is adapted to the situation in the world of the Whites. The education of the Whites, and the social life of the Whites—in associations, clubs, trade unions, meeting technique—these ideals are very much alive in the Ethiopian masses. And they influence that selective mechanism by which a man is brought out of obscurity into a leading position in the Ethiopian Church.

The primary requirement for a chief of the Church is *isithunzi*, that indescribable character trait, or sum of traits, which perhaps can be best translated as "prestige". A church chief with *isithunzi* should be a big, bulky, brave man, conspicuous wherever he goes, and a man who receives the acclamation of the mass as a matter of right.[4] He need not be a good preacher, he must not be talkative. A Zulu chief is reserved in his speech, and so should the church chief be.

He should be *brave*. His bravery is, however, tested mainly in the struggle against White domination. And that constitutes the great trial of his career. The leader emerges, conscious of being a Moses freeing his people from their slavery. When the Rev. P. N—— of the Medium Catholic Apostolic Church said of one of his competitors for the presidency, "He feared becoming a Moses for these Israelites", it was a very serious indictment. In the first enthusiasm of the new movement, the leader bitterly opposes taxes, cattle-dipping and similar "white" laws, as a means used by the White man for keeping the African down. He may be able to show his people that he has dared to write to the Government in an official letter: "Your law-abiding black subjects are REPRESSED, HUMILIATED and STIGMATIZED under your honourable Justice, the Union Government." But after a while his followers may find that it is risky to have as a leader a man who is *too* outspoken. They may begin to fear that the advantages they want, especially Government recognition, may not be gained under such a leader. And they may discover that there is more braggadoccio than bravery in his ardent appeal—and he may be ousted from his leadership. In a famous case in the middle of the 'thirties—the two competing leaders had formerly been Lutheran pastors—this very thing happened.

The man who was capable only of embittered protest was superseded by an *accommodating*, safe leader who could be counted upon to represent the followers when the Church grew and became increasingly important.

The standard of education is undoubtedly one of the factors which help in the rise to leadership in the Ethiopian Church. But it is not a primary requirement, even if it adds somewhat to the prestige of the leader. It is more of an embellishment of a position already attained.

Many Ethiopian Churches have in their ranks a certain number of Young Intellectuals, men with six to eight standards in school or men with a teacher's diploma who for some reason or other are out of work. The "Young Intellectual" type of prospective church leader is one of the most interesting phenomena in the modern development of the independent Church. He has been to school and knows all about meeting techniques. Therefore it is rather trying for him to observe the way in which the old President fumbles with minutes and procedure. In the Ethiopian Church, such young men form a potent core of malcontents and will often start their own Churches. Often, however, their attempts are doomed to failure. They have difficulties in getting a following because their people feel that the young intellectual despises the mass of the people. One of them, typical of the frustrated intellectual, who himself had had some years' education in America, in an interview referred to his followers and sub-leaders as "these half-cooked, half-boiled, half-educated Natives who are lowering the standards of Christianity". Even if this was said in an interview with me, a White man, possibly in order to impress me, the frustrated, all-round aggressive attitude behind the statement cannot in the long run be hidden from his followers.

The chief-type of leader should be a good *executive*, well-balanced, willing to listen to what his sub-leaders say, able to come to a successful deal in his deliberations in the interests of the Church. One of the most successful of the Ethiopian leaders belongs to the interesting type of the *outsider*, the stranger, who rapidly rises to eminence. He was educated at a Lutheran Teachers Training School, and was familiar with the traditions of his Lutheran Mission Church. When he joined a Congregational offshoot he soon discovered the great financial potentialities of his new Church, and through his executive ability and business acumen became known as a "level-headed" and judicious man. In this case his education was a positive extra which advanced him still further, until he reached the presidency of the Church.

(ii) *The prophet.* Whereas the Ethiopian leadership pattern is formed under the influence of the ambivalent relation of the Zulu group to the Whites, the congregational aspirations and needs within the Zionist groups are of another order. We shall see in the following chapters how Zionist Churches have built up a syncretistic system of purification rites, taboos, faith-healing and witch-finding. Groups of this type ask for a leader who is a healer and who is in intimate contact with the religious heritage of the African past.

In the Ethiopian Church the kingship pattern is modified by the adaptation of leader and mass to the requirements of the modern White civilization. In the Zionist Church this same kingship pattern is modified by a combination with another strong leadership pattern within Zulu society: that of the diviner or witch-finder (*isangoma*). The outcome of this development is the Zionist *prophet.* We shall see how the specific congregational needs which find their outlet in Zionist organizations have led to the development of a new type of Church, the "Bethesda" type of Church, centred round the purification rites in the sacred pond. This Bethesda type is an adaptation to modern conditions of essential elements in two of the strongest institutions in the history of the Zulus.

(*a*) The temporary huts built at the prophet's kraal and grouped according to status, recall to any Zulu's mind the *ikhanda*, Shaka's military barracks, where the king's followers of both sexes congregated, fulfilling different tasks assigned to them by the king.

(*b*) The second traditional Zulu institution on the pattern of which the Bethesda church is evolving is the traditional community of witch-finders. There is an obvious parallel between the Zulu diviner and the Zionist prophet, a parallel to which heathen and Christian Zulus frequently refer. This parallel in pattern can be followed in minute detail in the following traits:

(i) The initial call to become a diviner or to join a Zionist Church and become a prophet.

(ii) General appearance, behaviour and activities, the Zionists being a modern movement of witch-finders.

(iii) Group pattern of the two associations.[a]

[a] This parallel is shown in detail in Appendix A, "Heathen Diviner and Christian Prophet", p. 313.

In order to understand the position and the particular character of the prophet, I shall here briefly relate salient points in the lives of two prominent Zulu prophets.

The widest known of Zulu prophets was Isaiah Shembe. Dr. John L. Dube has written a short biography of Shembe, in Zulu; and an attempt at a scientific appraisal of his character and his work has been made.[4a] There is very probably no Zulu in modern times who has had such an intense influence over such a large number of people as Shembe. A prominent European, who knew him well, told the writer: "I have never met his parallel among Africans, and with all his tremendous influence over people, he was a man of great charm of manner, benevolence, and tolerance."

Shembe was born in 1870, and died in 1935. According to Dube, his boyhood and youth were characterized by serious moral conflicts. His first revelation was imparted to him when as a young boy he was praying in the cattle-kraal. During a thunderstorm the Word was brought to him by lightning: "Cease from immorality (*ukuhlobonga*)!" Later, as a young man and husband of four wives, he had another vision, also brought by lightning: he saw a multitude of people, or angels, and they pointed to something lying on earth. He saw his own corpse, in a rotten state, evil-smelling. The Word reminded him of his first vision, and the command to cease from immorality. "And that day, though he was an industrious man, he did not work, and he ceased working until Sunday, because he said: I have seen Jehovah." In a third vision it was revealed to him that he should leave his four wives, and though this was so hard that he almost committed suicide, yet he finally followed the divine command.

The decisive, final call to be a prophet was also conveyed by a terrifying storm when lightning killed his best ox and burned Shembe, leaving a scar above his thigh. He was ill three weeks after that, and then Jehovah asked him: "You care for your mother, do you not obey my word?" So he left his mother, and when a Zulu leech came along to cure the wounds on his thigh, he told him: "Jehovah has revealed to me that I must not be healed by medicine, only through His word." And Shembe was cured, because Jehovah saw that he wished to obey Him.

He now went from place to place in Natal, preaching and driving out demons, guided by the Holy Spirit. When he was baptized in 1906 by a minister of the African Native Baptist Church he was already famous as a healer. His gifts as a

THE CHIEF OF HIS CHURCH.

Rev. J. Mdelwa Hlongwane, founder and president of the Bantu Methodist Church, nick-named the "Donkey Church". The photo taken from a rally of Independent Bantu Churches in Pimville, Johannesburg, on which occasion the Rev. Hlongwane gave a "charge" to the assembled ministers. Banners with inscriptions in English and Zulu are carried in procession.

ZULU MESSIAH.

Isaiah Shembe (d. 1935), a man of magnetic personality, founder of the Nazarite sect.
He wielded a deeper and wider influence than any other Zulu prophet. He wears a black
dress—all others in the church are dressed in white—with a white collar, necklace of Zulu
beadwork and European sun-helmet.

preacher and healer were not to be lost to his Church; immediately after his baptism he was ordained a minister, and he started himself to baptize. He took his followers to the sea near Durban to be baptized there. Eventually, in 1911, he broke with his Baptist Church over the Sabbath issue, and started his own organization, called the *ama-Nazaretha*, the Nazarites. He claimed that all verses in the Old Testament, referring to Nazarites, were to be applied to his people.

In 1916 he established his church village, called Ekuphakameni, or the High Place, some eighteen miles from Durban. There he invited his faithful leaders and followers to stay with him. In the same year he had a vision to go to the Nhlangakazi mountain in Natal, which has become the Holy Mountain of the Nazarites. Ekuphakameni is now the centre for the great annual July-festival, Nhlangakazi for the annual January-festival.

Because of Shembe's great reputation as a healer and leader of men, he acquired an ever-increasing influence over Zulu chiefs wherever he went. Dube says (*uShembe*, p. 105) that not even the tribal chiefs were ever shown such respect as that bestowed upon Shembe. At Ekuphakameni I met a young heathen chief who told me that he had come to the prophet's place, not in order to become a Nazarite, but to study the ways of imposing *inhlonipho* (Zulu word for respect) on his people.

When Shembe died he was buried with great honours. One minister called out *"Uyingcwele!"* (He is holy), and the great mass of Nazarites, in their white uniforms, responded with a cry which no one who was there will ever forget: "He is holy." Over his grave at Ekuphakameni there was built a mausoleum which is regarded as sacred by the people of his Church.

The Church leadership was inherited by Shembe's son, Johannes Galilee Shembe. While the father was uneducated and had acquired his position through his great personal qualities, his successor had been given an academic education—he is a B.A. of Fort Hare Native College. Obviously he has not the same leadership qualities as his father, and the struggles within the Church have been bitter and dramatic. These came to a head in a famous case in 1939, when 1500 Nazarites stoned a person to death. In the circumstances, this collective violence was a kind of act of loyalty to the young prophet, who was supposed to have been threatened by the man who was stoned. The veneration shown the present prophet by his church people indicates that the devotional urge of this crowd can be projected on to a leader, even in spite of his deficiences in personal qualities.

Another colourful Zulu prophet is X. When working as a mine foreman in Johannesburg he received, in 1920, a letter from Y, a friend of his, who used to be a teacher in an Anglican school in Zululand. Y had to leave his school work when he began to hear voices and have visions. He went from kraal to kraal, uttering his warning cry: "Woe! woe!" (*nakho, nakho!*). Y claimed to have been translated to heaven on February 15, 1919, and there he was shown by Archangels and Stars and Cherubim the surprisingly geometrical plan of the heavenly places. He was also told what to do on earth. He should (1) put off his shoes for ten years, (2) build the New Jerusalem from stones which he would find at a river nearby, and (3) he would find one precious coloured stone which would reveal the truth in the Scriptures. That stone, if and when found, would save the world, otherwise it would be utterly destroyed. After eight years' search, in 1927, he found the stone, twenty miles away from his home.

Upon receiving his visions Y wrote a letter to X telling him that the Word had chosen X to become a Heavenly Doctor. X did not take any notice at first of this, but his Johannesburg paramour's sudden death a short time afterwards led him into a deep moral crisis. He became very ill and was brought to hospital. There he "died" the first night and had a vision of Satan's angel with long forks prepared to push him into the fire of hell. He saw himself in his bad moral life, and he gazed at his own corpse, rotting on earth. He was addressed by the Word: "Return to earth! Go and tell the ministers to go down from their beds. A minister should not sleep with a woman. A menstruating woman must not prepare food for a minister. If a woman has borne a child, she is unclean, and she must not sleep with men for a while. If she has borne a boy, she must fast seven days; if it is a girl, she should fast for a month. She must be purified by being prayed for by the minister. Ministers must not eat pork or medicine or drink beer. Go and tell the people to marry according to the rules of the Heavenly Marriage with the Lamb."

Then he woke up. When recovering from his illness, he returned to his home in Zululand. He called all the people in the neighbourhood together and proclaimed the heaven-inspired message to them. His relatives who had been with him in Johannesburg could testify that he had been really dead. At first he did not intend to start a new Church. He belonged to the Methodist Mission Church and he did not break this connexion until he was excommunicated. He joined forces with Y and they influenced one another greatly. X prayed for sick people, especially for barren women, which attracted a growing number of people. In order to propagate their ideas, they went in procession during the night from kraal to kraal. As they came to a new kraal, they would encircle it seven times before beginning their service. X and Y expounded the contents and the practical implications of the visions they had seen. X also received some new light on the matter of sacraments and proclaimed that Holy Communion was only an invention of the Whites. Because of these and other irregularities he was excommunicated from his Mission Church, and he then, together with Y, started his own "New Salem" or *Cumane Sande* Church.

He gathered his followers in a community of saints, the number of whom in a year's time had risen to 100, and which at the peak of his influence reached some 250. They built a magnificent church where X, with an episcopal brass staff, was enthroned near the altar, surrounded by hosts of archangels, prophets and apostles, all in different vestments and uniforms. X has a great flair for stage management, his most famous act being the Heavenly Telephone, installed in the vestry. Here he was supposed to receive direct orders from "the Word" about the management of the affairs of the Church.

X had a great influence over his followers. They were instructed to reveal to him all their personal dreams and visions, in order to become full members of the Church. He was regarded as endowed with semi-divine powers. He had, people said, fire on his feet: a woman who came upon him when he washed his feet saw flames of fire rise from the water. No wonder that her child died a couple of days later—she had sinned in witnessing what no eye should see. His great *isithunzi* was generally believed to be derived from his contact with *uMamlambo*, an imaginary being who visited him every morning in the form of a snake, in order to lick his body and therewith impart to him extraordinary powers.[5]

X is a man of an impressive bearing with a penetrating gaze. In the days of his highest power he always used to ride a white horse, and people would kneel to show the prophet their respect and veneration. His companionship with Y was not lasting. They quarrelled over the "Heavenly Marriage" question, and Y started his own religious organization. Some ten years after the first beginning of the New Salem Church at T—— it was closed down by the Magistrate because of certain well-founded charges against X, and he has now gathered another community in another locality.

Shembe and X are undoubtedly among the most prominent of Zulu prophets. In their life-stories there are certain traits which are characteristic of most genuine Zulu prophets, minor or major. Both are regarded by their followers as semi-divine beings. The Prophet becomes the Black Christ, and it is because of this that he acquires his tremendous influence over his followers. For a discussion of the prophet as Black Christ, I refer the reader to Chapter VII. In the current chapter we are concerned with the selective mechanism through which a man emerges from the mass and is singled out as a prophet.

The rise to eminence as a prophet is not, as in the case of the church leader of *chief*-type, dependent on a reputation for possessing a judicial character, executive ability and "drive", or on certain intellectual attainments. The prophet's call must be of a distinctly supernatural kind. He must be able to point to certain dreams in which he has been brought to heaven and where he has received his initial and spiritual ordination for the work. It is of great interest that in both the cases of Shembe and X the call arises out of a moral conflict, and it may be significant that in both call-dreams they saw their own corpses rotting on earth. But I have not found that this combination of moral conflict and prophetic call is very general. The usual dream is a visit to heaven where the person hears himself being addressed by the Word, saying: "You are to become a Heavenly doctor", or something similar. That is why Rev. J. M. of the African Baptized Apostle Church rather jubilantly reports to the Native Affairs Department in Pretoria: "Please, sir, one day I was asleep, I dreamt this church, September 24, 1933, I was dreaming about this church." In so doing he has also received the commission to found the Church and to become its prophet.

The role of lightning as intermediary of Shembe's call is typical of several other supposed prophets. A certain Shelembe was accused by a girl of being responsible for the child she expected. He refused to admit the paternity. "The brothers of the girl became angry and one day when Shelembe returned from the fields they threw lightning on him (*6amphosa ngezulu*) by magical means, and it hit him in the face." The unexpected result of this drastic revenge was that Shelembe was filled with the Holy Spirit. Another minor prophet, Mateu Shabalala, told me how he had received his call. Once when riding his horse, he was struck by lightning. He saw two men in white, one of whom had a book in his hand. This man told Mateu: "Thou shalt enter four doors and at last thou shalt go in through the fifth, and thou shalt find thy rest." This happened exactly as the angel had shown him! Starting as Methodist, he was next for a while a member of an Independent Congregationalist Church, and after that he stayed two years in a Baptist Church. After further time spent in an Apostolic Faith offshoot, he had now come to rest as a prominent prophet in a Zionist church. Certain prophets specialize in anti-lightning practices—just as some Zulu diviners do. J. N——, "General Overseer and Concession Registrar of the Holy New Jerusalem Church in Zion", was an expert diviner of hidden magical poisons and a specialist on how to avert lightning. So great was his knowledge of these things that he found it necessary to adorn his President's Certificate with a specific notice: "This Preaching certificate has been copied by other Native Churches. Members are therefore warned against these imitations which are wholly unauthorized by us. The Zion Church is the True Apostate Church."[a]

Whether the prophetic call has been conveyed by lightning or through dreams or visions, it is always thought of as being a call extended by the Holy Spirit. This is the foundation of the prophet's authority in the Church: the selective principle by which a budding prophet is brought out of obscurity into the limelight and to leadership is the claim to be a man of the Holy Spirit.

His somatic type is other than the heavy, mighty type of the chief. The ideal prophet should be thin, nervous, and highly strung, just as the diviner must be. A certain local prophet I knew was almost blind. This handicap was regarded as an asset by his Church, as it made him conspicuous, and thereby gave him a certain dignity. As opposed to the *chief*-type, the prophet is the revolutionary element in the Independent Church. He will always claim to be the spokesman of the despised, and will avidly keep up a martyr complex concerning himself and his Church.

In order to rise to leadership the prophet must above all be a healer. This is an indispensable requirement. Dubuzana, a young heathen Zulu, had a dream in which he was brought to

[a] The term "Apostate" in the Certificate is a printer's error for Apostolic, but an error which, in this case, is a revelation of a profound truth. The phrase, in this form, appears in many Zionist certificates.

heaven where he was baptized and there he received the call to heal people on earth. When he had succeeded in healing Blind Albert by letting him wash six wooden sticks in water until the sticks rotted and the eyes were somewhat better, he was accepted as an evangelist by the Zionists. But in an interview he expressed his readiness to go further: "Now I am only an evangelist in an out-district, where I pray for many sick people. But now I have healed so many that I wish that they will give me a better position, and I will become a prominent leader."

The nature of the "spiritual" call on which the prophet's authority is based will be studied in Chapter VII. It is important to point out that if in these Zulu Zionist Churches the call of the Holy Spirit is regarded as the only true foundation for the real prophet, this is also derived from the influence by White missionaries of a certain type. Three missionaries who arrived in South Africa in 1908 formulated in the following year, 1909, an Evangelist's certificate with the following wording:

> This is to certify that we recognize Brother E. M. L. of Pretoria has been called by the Holy Ghost as an evangelist in connexion with the —— Mission of Johannesburg for the year 1909 and as long thereafter as he shall maintain the unity of the Spirit with us, to preach the Gospel of Jesus Christ. To lay hands on the sick, To perform Native marriages, To baptize disciples by triune immersion, To administer the Lord's Supper, To concrete [should read "consecrate"] children.

For the sake of the analysis the two types of leaders have here been clearly demarcated the one from the other, as indeed they are in most cases in actual life. There are, however, hybrids where the two types have met together, or cases where there has been a development within certain particular leading personalities from one type to the other.

This development of the individual leader can be seen both in the chief-type and in the prophet. In most cases the development is caused by the *steadying influence of the kingship pattern*. An Ethiopian leader may start out as a revolutionary and a liberator. But as his Church grows and gradually becomes more important and his own position more secure, the character qualities of the kingship pattern become more pronounced. The avalanche of fiery oratory is succeeded by patient listening, wise judgment, and the weighty pronouncements of the chief. And so among the Africans, as in Israel of old, Moses the Liberator is followed by the Judges and then by the King.

The prophet starts out as an eccentric visionary, roving

without fixed abode, preaching his apocalyptic message. As the movement round him grows into an important Church, the kingship pattern has its modifying effects. He mocks at his earlier claim that speaking with tongues or worshipping barefoot are necessary for entrance into the Green Pastures of Heaven, and concentrates on the task of keeping his subleaders and mass of followers together in the common fold. The Book tells of Saul, son of Kish: "When he had made an end of prophesying, he came to the high place." When the Zulu prophet, son of Cush, has come to the high place, he may make an end of prophesying.

These leaders have accommodated themselves to the new order to make their influence lasting, and in order to perpetuate their authority over their Church. In a relationship between. leader and Church which is so largely personal, as in these independent Churches, this problem of perpetuating the leader's influence becomes very pressing indeed.

(c) Inherited leadership

A serious crisis in the history of an independent Bantu Church is caused by the leader's death. This of course is also true of the Mission Church. The European bishop's or superintendent's death has in many cases been one of the deepest causes why certain African ministers have left their parent Church. When such a Church is so intimately connected with a leader that his name is added to the name of the Church, it is only natural that his personal fate is of great importance to the organization he has founded.

That is the reason why the bishop's or president's right to remain in office over a certain number of years, or even indefinitely, becomes an important issue in the independent Churches. Rev. L—— learned that lesson to his dismay. In the Church originally founded by him, the president's term of office was five years, and after two such terms L—— was ousted by a stronger man. L—— had then of course to form a new Church, giving it his own clan's name. In the Constitution it is now expressly stated: "As the Rev. P. L—— is the prime mover and founder of this church, he is appointed the first President of the Church and shall continue in office as such for all times, so long as he adheres to the Constitution." Such precautionary measures are followed by many leaders, and there is now a definite trend in this direction in both Zionist and Ethiopian Churches. This trend also explains, at least to a certain degree, the Ethiopian and Zionist predilection for the episcopal office: it purports to guarantee continuity, at least in the lifetime of the leader. African ministers who have broken away from Wesleyan, Congregational or Baptist Missions where they have been used to electing a new moderator or superintendent either annually or every five years, discuss this system when taking the reins of office in their own hands. Archbishop Potwana, who had split off from the Wesleyans, described the essence of the Church government in his own Ethiopian Catholic Church of Africa: "Strong desire to evolve an African system of religion, thus rescuing some of the Bantu customs and adopting the polity of the Anglican Church." This "Anglican polity" is, however, soon superseded by Bantu customs. The independent Bantu Church tends to have its leadership passing from father to son, this being one of the characteristic ways in which the Independent Church adapts itself to the African heritage.

Margaret Read has pointed out that the *Ngoni* of Northern Rhodesia and Nyasaland in their present environment far away from their origin in Zululand or Swaziland, have succeeded in vindicating their traditional system of "filial succession and inheritance, which supersedes nephew succession".[6] The vitality of this Ngoni institution can be measured also in the independent Church of the present day. This trend towards inherited leadership is an indication that in the long run the *chief*-type of Church leader is more lasting than the prophet-type, because the function of chiefs was inherited, but not that of the diviners.

This characteristic Bantuization of Church leadership is of course safeguarded by various rationalizations from the Bible. Bishop Moshanyana proves himself to be a diligent Bible student on this point: "Every minister after his death, his son will replace him. Num. 20: 28. And Moses stripped Aaron of his garments, and put them on Eleazar his son. Elias L. S. Moshanyana and Jacob L. S. Moshanyana [the bishop's sons] will strip on their father's garments. Gal. 4: 1."

Under the Biblical varnish, the grain of the Zulu pattern shows through very clearly. When the Rev. Hlongwa, bishop of the Christian Apostolic Holy Spirit Church in Zululand died in 1939, it was reported to the authorities by his successor: "He was a headman of this Church, and I am his son, his first-born." Through inheritance from the father and founder of the Church there is transmitted some definite quality which by itself will help the young man to carry on. At least such an assumption seems to explain the apparent ease with which the African

Heaven Baptist Church of South Africa received its new leader. The old leader died on July 30, 1937. In a letter written less than six months after this date, the Church members expressed themselves in the following fashion: "The Congregation and all the full leaders have met and willingly elected W. H. P—— to occupy his father's position as the Minister and Chaplain of the above-mentioned denomination. After his election, he was then sent to a School for Ministry; he has now returned, being fully qualified and recognized as a minister."

This new device of inherited leadership in Church Government in some cases has brought about a certain continuity. But nothing can guarantee that all or even the majority of the old ministers, the father's co-workers, will swear allegiance to the young man. Stephen Nkonyane, a prominent chief-leader type in a Zionist Church, successfully forestalled trouble when inheriting his father's Church, by declaring that he "desired to respect all the ministers who previously had served under his father". Not all by any means fare so well. In Churches both of Ethiopian and Zionist type one could quote a number of cases where the inheritance issue has led to three or four new sects, with bitter litigation between the competing leaders.

Whether the father's *regalia*, as inherited by the son, are supposed to be charged with certain hidden powers which can be transmitted to the new wearer, is a question which I have not studied sufficiently to be able to answer. A faithful conforming to Zulu pattern in this institution would of course predispose the Church leaders to views of this kind. A remarkable indication that something on these lines is bound to develop is the mystical black veil of Isaiah Shembe, which the son has inherited, and which he uses in his healing service (cf. a description of a service led by J. G. Shembe, p. 229). Shembe Jr, a sophisticated B.A., felt the inheritance issue as a problem, when he had to take over the leadership of a Church of this kind. This can be seen in a hymn which he wrote on the holy mountain Nhlangakazi in memory of his deceased father. The father is here supposed to pray:

> Wake another one from my house
> That he may lead thy people.
> Give unto him a heart
> which is similar to Thine.
> Take care of him and anoint him
> with the oil of grace.
> (*Nazarite Hymnbook*, No. 223.)

One of the most amazing and perplexing of recent developments within certain Churches of Zionist type should be mentioned in this connexion. I refer to the way in which the deceased leader is supposed to perpetuate his influence over his Church through a female *medium*. This, of course, only happens in certain prophet-type Churches, namely where the veneration of the prophet has led him to be regarded as a Bantu Christ.

A Zulu woman, whom we shall call Anna, was of a considerably nervous disposition, and Prophet X was supposed to have freed her from her demons (*izizwe*). After a serious illness she had asphyxia and was regarded as dead for some time. In this condition she had a vivid dream about her visit to heaven where she saw herself being helped by X who acted as her intercessor before Jesus. When this prophet died and subsequently rose from the dead, his spirit was reputed to have taken its abode in Anna. Various theories were discussed in the Church as to how she had received the prophet's spirit: whether through her dream-journey to heaven, or through having been laid on X's grave and having, in that position, been charged with his powers, or through having with her own eyes seen him rise from the dead. However it may have happened, it seemed to be a fact that she *had* X's spirit, and she was consequently called *Umphefumulo*, the Spirit.

This woman soon acquired a tremendous influence over the Church. Together with three other young women, who likewise were regarded as media of prophetic revelation, she not only threatened, but actually superseded in personal authority, X Jr who officially was the new leader of the Church. *Umphefumulo* received her revelations by visiting the mausoleum built over the grave of the dead and risen prophet. For such visits she brought two cups of tea, one for herself and the other for the risen prophet. In the secrecy and silence of the mausoleum she was given definite instructions by the prophet about the current affairs of the Church. X Jr together with the Church, for a period of at least three to four years, were completely under her influence; the ultimate authority in the Church was spiritual revelation, and the young official leader could certainly not outbid Anna's claim in this respect. Her influence took a sinister turn when eventually she ordered, on behalf of the risen prophet, the excommunication of a number of old ministers who had served X Sr faithfully for many years. At a big annual meeting she would call out the names of the men of whom she wanted to be rid, and the young leader and the

Church could do nothing but obey. In the end X Jr himself had a revelation from his father who warned him in a dream, showing *Umphefumulo* in the symbol of a dangerous snake; this indicated that she wished to kill X Jr, obviously through sorcery. The revelation was enough, Anna was dethroned and had to return to her obscure position in the house of her long-forgotten husband.

This indication of a highly dramatic crisis within a Church shows how a young prophet struggles to achieve something of the power which had belonged to his father. Revelation through a medium has so far not been common in Zionist Churches. It throws an interesting and rather revealing sidelight, however, upon the struggle for power, prestige and position which in varied guise appears in most of the Independent Churches. And it shows clearly what happens in the Church when the sanction of fundamental authority has been usurped by heathen dream-life.

(d) Educational standards

An investigation of the general educational and theological background of leaders of chief and prophet types, in order to be of the fullest value, should be made against a background of actual theological standards in the ministry of Mission Churches. I have not been in a position to make a survey of the situation over the whole field. The former bishop of Zululand, the Rt. Rev. A. W. Lee, has, however, sketched the history of theological training of Africans in the Anglican Church in South Africa, and the main stages of development as described by him do also apply *ceteris paribus* to other Mission Churches.

During the pioneer days of the Mission, there grew up a "system of using uneducated, almost untrained and unordained men in the ministry of the Church".[7] Despite grave disadvantages, these men were of the people, and they interpreted the new message in a way that could easily be understood by their hearers.

At the next stage emerged the new Africa with the rise of industrialism, nationalism and education, bringing the demand for better training of the African ministry. The various dioceses of the Church of the Province established small diocesan theological colleges or schools such as the college at Isandlwana in Zululand. The co-operating Lutheran Missions in Natal and Zululand, started their theological school at Oscarsberg in 1915. Theological training during this period was in the vernacular.

The present stage in Anglican theological training is characterized by what Bishop Lee calls "unity of effort" through centralizing the theological education at Rosettenville, Johannesburg. The standard of general education required previous to the college course is that of the junior certificate, which in the Union precedes the matriculation examination of the universities. The course is spread over three years, and its academic aim is the examination for a Licentiate in Theology. Some of the students have had matriculation standard behind them when beginning; one was a B.A. from Fort Hare, and his Licentiate of Theology, taken in competition with European candidates, was the best in the Union that year. At the Lutheran school at Oscarsberg the teaching since 1938 has been given in English, and the entrance qualification is a Teacher's Certificate of South African T.4 qualification. The course is completed in four years; and the teaching in exegetical, historical and systematic theology follows much the same textbooks as in Lutheran theological seminaries in America.

A just appraisal of educational standards among ministers in the independent Churches is difficult because these standards vary so much from church to church. On the one hand there is a Church like the African Methodist Episcopal Church, whose bishop when addressing a meeting in Durban, 1939, appealed for "two young Africans who had their B.A. degrees to take them over to America with him for a higher education".[8] The African Methodist Episcopal Church established a theological school at their headquarters at Evaton, Johannesburg, in 1938, and could aspire to Standard VI as an entrance qualification. But the Ethiopian and Zionist Churches have not tackled the problem seriously, a negligence which has proved to be the Achilles' heel of the independent Churches as a whole. The superintendents and bishops generally come from Mission Churches where they have received a catechist's or similar theological education. Thus the independent Churches generally draw upon the limited spiritual capital of Biblical and dogmatic knowledge which their leader received many years previously. In the period 1900–14 some of these leaders had the opportunity of going to Negro colleges in America, and not a few of them have received valuable training there; as for instance the Rev. L. M. Mzimba of the African Presbyterian Church and the Rev. Nyangi of the Independent Congregational Church, the latter having been trained at Lincoln and Howard Universities. Some independent Churches send their men for shorter Bible course to interdenominational Bible institutes, run by certain missions, such as Ezingolweni, Natal, The Union Bible Institute, Sweetwaters, or the Fransson Memorial Bible School, Mhlotsheni, Swaziland.

Of course cases of patent fraud in this respect are by no means unknown. Men who had quite prominent positions may tell high Government officials that they have a B.A. and L.Theol. degree "with distinction" from Fort Hare or some other *alma mater*, at the same time expressing their regret that the certificates unfortunately were burned on such and such an occasion. I know of others who, while hardly able to read and write, claim to possess a B.A. degree. But all the same there is something rather pathetic in the scholastic and theological ambitions of some leaders. The Independent Methodist Church of South Africa, for instance, has established its Board of Examiners before whom candidates for the ministry have to appear and pass both written and oral examinations. The written examination covers "Arithmetic as far as Proportion; English Grammar, including Analysis and Parsing; Geography, Physical and Descriptive especially Europe and Africa; Outlines of English and Cape History; English Composition; Wesleyan Methodist Catechism, Parts I and II". We have reason to believe that the standards are not very exacting, but the attempt is the best they can attain to in the circumstances. I am grieved to think of the many whose ambition leads them to attempt to better their general standard of education by taking exorbitantly expensive courses from some correspondence institute in Johannesburg or elsewhere. Others have taken a less expensive and probably much more satisfactory course under mission tutelage, as for instance the Nyasa leader of a Johannesburg Zionist Church who "was educated at the Headquarters of the Universities Mission (Oxford and Cambridge) of Central Africa". The most startling qualification is perhaps the one given by the head of the "National Church of Africa", whose standard of theological education is defined by himself in the following manner: "Served in Chaplain's Mess during Great War."

It would obviously be of little value to draw up statistical tables of the academic attainments of independent Bantu ministers, as many of the reports of these are unreliable. We offer instead statements of standards in three carefully chosen Zulu Churches, of which the first is a large independent Congregational Church of over 45,000 members with comparatively high standards. The second is a well established Ethiopian Church with some 5000 members, the President of which was earlier a Lutheran pastor; and the third example is representative of the mass of little Zionist mushroom Churches.

(1) Besides the president himself (now deceased), there were forty-eight ministers in the Church. The former, after a Standard VI education (which in South Africa is equivalent to eight school years: two years in the Primary, and Six Standards), claims to have benefited from a two years' correspondence course with Fransson Memorial Bible School in Swaziland. Of the forty-eight ministers one was a graduate from a Negro Teachers' College in the United States; six had South African Teachers' Certificates; one had passed Standard VII; five Standard VI; three Standard V; fourteen Standard IV; eight Standard III; and eight Standard II. As for additional theological training, nine of these men had studied at three different Mission Bible Institutes, while thirteen others had been working in Mission Churches and presumably taken some Bible study there, and twenty-three had had "private studies" in theology. The significance of the term "private studies in theology" when referring to men with a Standard II–III education must not be overrated.

(2) The president himself has a Teachers' Certificate and four years' training at the Lutheran Theological School at Oscarsberg (the theological course during his time was given in the vernacular). His second-in-command has Standard VI plus a "Bible Diploma", and the other nine ministers Standards III–V plus "one year's training by Superintendent".

(3) The Holy Communion Church of South Africa: one of the ministers has attained a Standard IV in school; the bishop himself and the three ministers claim a knowledge of Zulu or Xhosa, but none of them has had any theological training whatsoever.

The great mass of ministers in these Churches have had no more than two to four years in school, often followed by some job with a certain amount of responsibility, such as mine-foreman, policeman, or what they refer to as "commercial education" (in this case a messenger in a store) in Johannesburg. Not a few of the local leaders, and certain superintendents of Churches living in the locations of Johannesburg, are at the same time shop-keepers there, thus offering an interesting sociological parallel to the carriers of the Methodist revival in England.

The *attitude* towards the necessity for theological and secular education for a minister differs considerably within the Independent Churches. As a general observation it is fair to say that while Ethiopian Churches regard "good character" and general leadership abilities as a sufficient substitute for theological training, the Zionists claim inspiration by what they call the "Holy Spirit", as the all overriding requirement. Sometimes this valuation is definitely expressed, as for instance, in Elias Nduli's letter to a Zulu newspaper:

> I see that many ministers have been instructed in colleges and go overseas to learn the minister's work. I have never heard of any place where Christ is supposed to have been taught. I challenge whomsoever it may be of the ministers in European churches to tell me the Bible verse where it is said that Christ was instructed in the Gospel.[9]

In the same manner, a prophet of undisputed influence like Shembe could, without risk, glory in the fact that he had had no schooling. In his case this only served to enhance his achievements. In one of his most important sermons Shembe made a pronouncement supposed to be addressed to missionaries:

> If you had taught him [speaking of himself in the third person] in your schools, you would have had a chance of boasting over him. But God, in order to reveal His wisdom, sent this Shembe, who is a child, that he may speak as a wise and educated man.[10]

But these are exceptions. There is no doubt that supposed education gives status in the Independent Church. Whereas one scarcely ever hears a leader referred to as a "fine Christian" (*ukholiwe kakhulu*), it is very common to speak with awe or admiration of some bishop, who actually may have passed only Standard III and IV, as "very learned", *ufunde kakhulu*. One president, whose claim to have passed Standard VII was made somewhat dubious by his inability to tell the time, spoke in very contemptuous terms of other church leaders, who, he said, "by their lack of education were harming the whole Christian cause in South Africa". This man, who specialized in Zionist lightning magic, was often approached by other Zionist Church leaders with a view to obtaining ministers' certificates from him. But, he said, he was always very careful about first investigating their cases and educational standards, before issuing such certificates. It is significant that when, about 1917, the Bantu Zionist Church leaders definitely split off from their American prophets, leadership over the seceding conglomeration was assumed by P. Mabilitsa "because he knew English", and thus could represent the interests of the Church better than one or two others who might have conformed more closely to Bantu leadership ideals but who lacked education.

While stressing the fact that even Zionist Churches concede status to the supposedly educated man, one should add that this does, of course, apply still more to Ethiopian Churches. The difficulty of a rising church leader in Ethiopian circles, as far as his reputation with regard to education is concerned, seems to be to steer clear of both the Scylla of the Young Intellectual—openly showing contempt for his uneducated subleaders—and the Charybdis of total lack of education.[11]

(e) Ministers' salaries

It is sometimes said that the African starts a Church to get a living out of it, that his motive for organizing a separate Church is economic. In answer to that statement, one must say that it overlooks the fact that to the African prestige matters more than money. And, further, an investigation of the salary position of ministers in independent Churches does not show that this position is particularly enviable. We should add that it is difficult to secure a true picture of the salary scales, as the limits within different Churches and even within the same Church vary so widely.

Generally, the scale of salaries is not a fixed one of so many pounds sterling per month, but varies according to the number of members. Thus, for example, the rate of the African United Native Baptist Church (with some 2500 members) is that one pound a year per member constitutes the salary of the minister, but as the number of members of individual congregations varies between 615 and thirty-seven, it is obvious that with such a rule some ministers get much more than others (on the theoretical assumption that every member is a faithful contributor). The Ethiopian Church in Christ follows a similar rule: a superintendent in charge of both a congregation and a large district is supposed to receive 3s. per quarter from each member of his own congregation, and an additional 6d. from every member in the other congregations of the district. As in this Church the superintendent conducts confirmations, he also gets a fee of half a crown from each member confirmed. The ordinary priests on the other hand are supposed to receive 2s. from every member of their congregations and baptismal offerings as well.

A MOTHER IN ISRAEL.

The widow of Rev. Paul Mabilitsa, a prominent Zionist church leader. As mother of the present Church leader, she wields a considerable influence.

BISHOP L. M. MAKHOBA.
The President of the African Congregational Church.

In most of the Churches there is no central pool from which the salaries could be paid more evenly, and every minister has to rely on his own devices to get a living. This offers, incidentally, an explanation of one of the most repugnant features of the Separatist Church movement. These organizations generally speaking are not evangelizing among the heathen. They rather tend to practise "sheep-stealing" from the folds of other, older Churches. One reason for this is the salary system, or rather the lack of such a system. Ministers refuse to work in new, heathen areas and prefer to expand their sphere of influence by inveigling established congregations to leave their old Churches and transfer their loyalty and resources to them.

This problem is bound up with another which constitutes one of the main weaknesses of these independent African Churches, the fact that *the great majority* of them *are over-staffed*. The urge, or rather the scramble, for African leadership in these Churches has produced a situation which could often be described as absurd. To take a few examples: the Holy Communion Church of five small congregations with 160 members in all has five ministers. Maphuza's Holy Apostolic Church in Zion, with a membership of 2500, has as office-bearers one Director-General, nine ministers, two assistant ministers, fifteen evangelists, and two deacons, which is an average of one church official for eighty-six members. The Christian Catholic Apostolic Church in Zion, with a membership of 1130, boasts of twelve ministers and two deacons, an average of one paid church officer for eighty-one members. The Ethiopian Church in Christ has, for its 2092 adult members, one presiding overseer for the Transvaal and Natal, one assistant overseer for the Cape Province, and one for the Transkei and Pondoland, plus fourteen priests, nine deacons, ten evangelists and "missionaries"; that is, an average of one church officer for every fifty-eight members.

As all these men expect to be supported by their congregations, we get in the case of the smaller and less successful Churches a situation which involves very heavy demands on the ordinary church members, and *in spite of this*, small salaries for the leaders. A mere pittance of £1 5s., £2 or £3 a month is the remuneration which ministers get in such Churches. This has, of course, to be made up by non-pastoral work with consequent loss of efficient working time for the Church. An interesting sidelight on authoritarian leadership in the independent Churches is provided by the fact that Bishop Limba, the wealthy chief of the Bantu Church of Christ (Port Elizabeth) pays his preachers some £7 to £10 per year! This system is only possible in an organization which exists for the leader, and where subleaders and members derive satisfaction from enhancing the power and prestige of the leader.

The best organized, as far as ministers' salaries are concerned, are the Churches which seceded from Congregational Missions. The Zulu Congregational Church with its 8000 members can afford to pay its twenty-seven ministers £12 to £25 per quarter. As a model of church financing, we single out the African Congregational Church, founded in 1917, which has had the good fortune to be under efficient leadership. In order to circumvent the difficulty of securing freehold plots for African churches and other purposes in town areas, this organization (which was eventually recognized by the Government in 1937) formed itself into a company in 1925 called the African Congregational Church Co. Ltd., the nominal capital being fifty shares of one shilling each. The company holds all property registered in its name in trust for the Church. By applying wise economy the Church has been able to buy a considerable number of farms and stands, and has erected hundreds of church buildings. In the latest available report, the total value of its property is estimated at more than £20,000.

It is instructive to study the yearly balance sheets of this Church, duly audited as they are by a chartered accountant, and arranged in a confidence-inspiring manner which should satisfy any reasonable standards of sound book-keeping. It is interesting to note that the Johannesburg minister's salary for one year was only £44 9s. 2d. As a matter of fact, it is usually some £100, but the leader renounced more than £50 in order to help in the completion of a church building in the strategically important Orlando Township. As to the corresponding item for the Durban congregation, it is pointed out by the accountant that the £92 for salaries shows a decrease over the preceding year, and is a result of a drastic reorganization of the Durban staff. In this case the superintendent has been strong enough not to permit a continuous overstaffing of the Church, but has reorganized and even reduced his staff in order to secure funds for buildings and extension of the work.

How different this is from the economic organization of certain churches of Zionist type, where the prophet by virtue of his semi-divine claims, assures himself an income and a fortune of very considerable dimensions. The most prominent example is Shembe's. About 1935 at the time of the prophet's death the value of his estate was estimated at some £25,000 to £30,000. According to information he owned thirteen farms, of which some were only ten acres, while others again of 800 and 1000 acres; and he had been given by Zulu chiefs a considerable number of "mission stations" in various parts of Zululand. All this money and all this land were, however, not the property of Shembe's Church but were in his own name. There can be no doubt that Shembe's European lawyer is right in thinking that the money with which Shembe had bought the land had been given to him personally as to a semi-divine being. He had of course no fixed salary, but his annual income was probably never less than £1000.

The Pietersburg prophet, Engenas B. Lekganyane, belongs to the same class. He has no difficulty in securing the cash for buying considerable farms where he can let hundreds of his followers settle down, forming Zionist colonies, owned by the prophet himself. In a much smaller degree, but working on the same principle, G. K—— has attained something of the same result. His Spookmill farm is worked by his faithful followers who have *surrendered* themselves, with all their personal belongings and all they earn, to the prophet. In his turn he is expected to feed and clothe his followers, just as the rich and generous king or tribal chief in Zululand of old was supposed to care for all the needs of his people.

(f) Attitude to property

Whether the property belongs to the leader himself, or is held in trust for the Church, it is unmistakable that both the leader and the members of a wealthy Church take a very considerable pride in the fact that they own property. James Weldon Johnson has recorded the instance of a prominent Negro Baptist preacher repeatedly taking "Buy Property" as the text of his sermons when addressing his Harlem congregations.[12] Not a few Bantu Independent Church leaders stress the same point in their sermons, in order to secure a firm economic foundation for their Churches. The Bantu Church cannot afford to cherish a Franciscan Il-Poverello ideal for the Church or for the individual. Poverty they always have among them. I know of only one case, a famous leader and prophet near Pretoria, to whom people referred with veneration saying: "He is as poor as Christ."

Whether the leader is of the chief or prophet type, the majority of the church people like to think of him as being rich, able to spend, and in so doing being able to represent their Church in the best manner. A typical case was a leader of a well-known Congregational Church. He told me in an interview that because his Church was recognized by the Government, many groups around sought contact with him with a view to joining it: "But then we put one question to them, 'Have you any property?' Because, you see, we will not accept any groups or churches who have no property. If they are going to join us, they must have property." His attitude and his frame of mind —at least so it seemed to me on this occasion—were less those of a pastor of souls than of a forceful and successful business executive. The Africans feel that the Whites, through wars and Land Acts, have deprived them of their land. The powerful church leader, as the king and chief of his flock, is intent on rectifying this injustice and secure for himself and his Church a foothold in the land of his fathers. This is why the acquiring of land and property becomes such an important concern.

(2) LEADER AND NUCLEUS

G. K. Chesterton, in a characteristic phrase, said of William Cobbett: "Cobbett was a demagogue in the literal sense; that is, he was a demagogue in the dignified sense. He was a mob-leader, but he was not merely a man mob-led."[13] The not-so-dignified mob-leader, on the other hand, in his attempt to lead, himself becomes mob-led. That happens among Europeans, and it happens among people of other races. It happens sometimes in the Bantu Independent Church, and this alters the very nature both of the leader and of the followers.

We shall here study leader, nucleus, and Church in the following relations: leader-nucleus, leader-Church, and leader-nucleus-Church. This division is, however, artificial and only dictated by the demands of clarity in the analysis. The ideal treatment of this subject would show the three forces as being in constant, dynamic interplay, and only so should we treat it realistically.

(a) Size and geographical spread

Before discussing the relationships between leader, nucleus, and church, we shall briefly analyse membership figures as to the size of representative churches and their geographical extension over a defined tribal area and beyond. Any attempts to compute the size of the Independent Bantu Churches must take into account the nature of their statistical returns. The material from which I have had to draw has probably been fairly unreliable. It consists chiefly of statements in applications for Government recognition, and in many cases the figures are obviously incorrect.

It is interesting that Mays and Nicholson admit that their primary material on American Negro Churches shows something like a 40 per cent. discrepancy when comparing the reported membership with the actual membership in the 106 Negro Churches investigated by them.[14] In spite of this, their book contains a number of statistical tables on church membership and related questions.

The main reasons why the statistical returns from the African Separatist Churches have to be taken with reservations are the following:

1. Churches which make any attempt at all to keep adequate records of their membership often lack a uniform basis on which to determine it. Within the same church, different standards are used by different pastors. Some country congregations consider as members all the people who have been on the roll from the start of the church, including the dead, and also those who have moved from the Reserve to the Rand, and are thus enrolled twice.

2. Many Churches of Zionist type have no adequate registration of membership. Any estimate for instance of membership in Shembe's Nazarite Church would remain sheer guess-work. Many occasional visitors to the Nazarite festivals count themselves as belonging to that Church for a while, but may tend to sink back into traditional heathenism after a period.

3. The constant flux of people from one locality to another, and the floating membership of people moving from one church to another make it impossible to get reliable statistics. I know of Zionist Churches which have actually given too low an estimate of their membership in a given district.

4. In many cases the figures have obviously been padded in order to make a good impression on the Native Affairs Commission and so secure Government recognition. When for instance a certain "Orthodox" Church, over and above the figure of five hundred for the whole of the Union and fifty-one in Bulawayo, claims a membership of 5000 in Uganda, it would frankly be more correct to locate those 5000 in Utopia rather

131

than in Uganda. A certain "National" Church which in 1941 claimed to have an overall membership of 5513, reduced this figure two years later to 3765, as at the latter date it had to give specific information of membership in each congregation.

After this note of caution as to the statistical material, it is fair to state that many churches do attempt to give as accurate a return as is possible in these circumstances. Some are small and insignificant, and the more highsounding the names, the more insignificant the Churches often are. Thus "Almighty God Church" claims twenty-four members; "Only Church of God" twenty to thirty; "The Holy Catholic Church of South Africa, King George Win the War, Native Anglican" has "already" forty full members and twenty-two leaders. The "already" seems to imply that the leader is looking forward to a great future for his new organization.

As for the somewhat older Churches, there are some which have been obviously unsuccessful and unattractive. Representative of this group are the statistical returns from an Ethiopian Church with Lutheran background. Though started in 1926, the church had in 1939 (the latest figures I have available) only 1463 members. The main reason for this slow growth was a serious split in the middle of the 'thirties, and this again was caused by certain defects in the President's ability to lead: he had become too embittered in his struggle against European missionaries and the Government to inspire over a longer period of time the confidence of his own people. It is also interesting that in this case the main bulk of his earlier membership in Johannesburg and Durban has fallen away, and those remaining faithful are to be found chiefly in farm areas.

There is an important correlation between the slow growth of this Church and the kind of embittered, self-centred leadership exercised by the President. The size of a particular independent Bantu Church is to be regarded as evidence of successful or unsuccessful leadership. The powerful chief or the supposedly inspired prophet attracts and retains an ever increasing mass of individuals. But this statement should be qualified. The Zionist following attracted to the famous prophet-type of leader nearly always expands faster than similar groups in Ethiopian Churches. Lekganyane, leader of Zion Christian Church, had in 1925 a following of 515 men and 411 women gathered at his Zion City near Pietersburg. In seventeen years this figure of 926 people had increased to 28,000 at fifty centres. Shembe's Nazarite Church, founded in

1911, had in 1935 grown to 30,000, and even if it is difficult to hazard a guess as to present numbers, one would probably not be far wrong in computing the figure of these now claiming to be Shembe-ites, as at least 50,000.

Most Ethiopian Churches by the very nature of the contact between leader and mass are unable to show such rapid growth. The Independent Methodist Church, for instance, had in 1940 only reached the number of 7800, of whom 1700 were juniors, whereas the United Native National Church of Christ arising as the result of a split in 1936 could report some 3765 members in 1943. The outstanding example of rapid and steady growth of a Church of Ethiopian type is the African Congregational Church, which begun in 1917, could report 28,000 members in 1937 and 45,000 in 1944. This result, achieved in spite of a series of threatening secessions (see p. 45), has been due to firm and far-sighted leadership of the three presidents.

The advance and growth of some Churches have been gained at the cost of a corresponding loss in others. Not all leaders are as adamant about their methods in this respect as the bishop of the African Zulu Johanni Baptist Church, who informed Government authorities of certain gains for his organization:

> SIR,—I have the honour of advising that department that early in January of the current year, I paid my missionary visits to my various Mission Stations within and abroad the Union.
>
> The first Mission Station I visited was at E—— of M—— being the surrounding of my kraal in Zululand, where I admitted in my church an Evangelist with his congregation formerly belonged to the American Board, consisted of 38 members.
>
> Thence I proceeded to B—— V—— Administrative Post over the border as far as C—— at Sh——, where I also admitted in my Church another congregation with its respective Minister, Rev. F. M.; total number of the congregation, 25.
>
> The last of my journey was at L—— M——. Also there I admitted 87 members of congregation with its three Evangelists, belonged to the Swiss Mission, that was on 16th June 1940.
>
> On the 4th August, I again received at that locality about 69 members of congregation.
>
> I then returned here on the 8th instant.
>
> I have the honour to be, Sir,
>
> Your most obedient servant,
>
> For the African Zulu Johanni Baptist Church,
>
> S—— M——
>
> (signed)[16]
>
> Bishop.

133

The size of a particular Separatist Church can only be appreciated in relation to its *geographical spread* within and without the Union. Even if we are chiefly concerned with Zulu Independent Churches, and therefore confine our investigation to conditions in Zululand, Natal and Johannesburg, it is nevertheless a fact that the more important Ethiopian or Zionist Churches, founded and led by Zulus, also reach over to other provinces and other language areas; and on the other hand Churches under Sotho or Xhosa leadership have established some of their outposts in the Zulu language area. The African Congregational Church may be taken as typical of an organization which is preponderantly Zulu in its geographical spread. Judging from its report for 1937, 28,000 members, distributed among thirty-five congregations, were from Natal and Zululand; 4000 were in thirteen Transvaal congregations, and of this number half belonged to Zulu congregations on the Rand. Two congregations of 400 and 100 members respectively, under Zulu pastors, were to be found in Swaziland and the Orange Free State, and two congregations with some 1800 members were under Zulu leadership in the Cape Province.

The Independent Methodist Church of South Africa (Ethiopian type), on the other hand, presents in its report for 1940 the picture of a Church more evenly spread over different provinces; 2800 members, chiefly Zulus, in Natal and Zululand; 1600 in Swaziland; 1000 in the Transvaal; and another 1800 in the Cape Province. On the fission of the Ethiopian Church of South Africa, the Zulu leader of this Church retained most of his Zulu followers, but his Xhosa opponent who founded the Ethiopian Church in Christ was nevertheless able to claim certain groups in Natal and Zululand, which for various reasons were dissatisfied with the Zulu leader.

In general these Churches are thinly spread over wide areas of the Union. The Ethiopian Church in Christ, for instance, has two priests in Natal, one residing in Ladysmith, the other in Estcourt. The former has under him five congregations with respective memberships of 12, 10, 8, 17 and 6. The latter has nine congregations, extending from Estcourt in the South to Mahlabatini in the North, the membership figures of his groups being 24, 62, 15, 31, 7, 14, 15, and 23. This case is no exception but rather the rule in the tribal Church which thrusts out its tentacles into other tribal areas. The chief reason for this kind of extension is the central role of the Rand.

The "Orthodox" Church which claims 5000 members in

134

Uganda was mentioned earlier. The extent to which some of these Churches influence areas far outside the borders of the Union is indeed startling. The Rhodesias and Portuguese East Africa have received special attention. Here they have followed the example of the American Negro mission organization, the African Methodist Episcopal Church. This Church has a special Zambezi Annual Conference which receives reports from the presiding elders of the following districts: Matebeleland, Mashonaland, Ndola, Wankie, Nyasaland, Lusaka, and Abercorn. So far this part of the work is under the jurisdiction of the (Negro) Bishop of South Africa, but the aim of procuring one bishop each for the Rhodesias and for Nyasaland is being envisaged.[16] Connexions between Nyasaland and South African Bantu Churches are kept up mainly by the labour migration from Nyasaland to the mines on the Rand. The visit of Bishop Alexander of the African Orthodox Church to Kenya and Uganda in 1930 was an attempt at extending such influence further North.

(b) Rank system within the nucleus

The leader's influence over his church is direct only in exceptional cases. It is usually transmitted through the nucleus of sub-leaders or staff who, as ordained ministers or lay helpers, men and women, represent their leader and their Church in their own locality. The nucleus is a small body of active and influential members with whom the main functions of the Church are locally identified, whilst possibly a large fringe of church members is comparatively inactive. The Independent Church thus presents an example of Cooley's nucleated type of group.[17]

One of the outstanding features of Protestant mission work in South Africa has been the emphasis on the *lay-element* of the Church as an evangelizing force. The programme of Protestant missions has, in general, been the founding of Churches of a distinct lay character, where the general priesthood of all believers might be realized and where the support and propagation of the Church would not be felt as the responsibility of a few leaders at the top, but of the common man in the Church.

In this respect, as in so many other matters, the strong Methodist Church has shown the way to other missions in South Africa. Conditions and tendencies within the mission work remind one of the struggle of the Methodist Church in Britain during the nineteenth century, with Jabez Bunting and his authoritarian tradition on the one side, and the growing, liberal demand from the laity for an effective share in Church government on the other.[18] This struggle led to secessions. The "Methodist New Connexion" and other groups left the main body over this issue. In the end, the "democratic" tendency prevailed.

The deepest cause was probably the Methodist class-organization, which more than anything else accounts for both the strong hold of the Methodist Church over its individual members, and the role of the laity within the Church. In the Protestant Church in Africa, sociologically speaking, this class-organization of the Methodist Church has been the most important and successful attempt to create an *in-group*, a close, personal relation between individuals within the greater organization of the Church.

In its mission work the Methodist Church in South Africa stressed the role of the laity and the lay preacher to a marked degree. After the gold-rush in 1885 and the concomitant influx of the British to the Rand, Methodism expanded its influence rapidly. The extent of this can be seen from the following statistics of Methodist missions in the Transvaal, chiefly on the Rand.[19]

	1880	*1902*	*1913*
European Missionaries	2	24	51
African Ministers	—	*17*	*36*
Local Preachers	5	*527*	*2091*
Churches	3	145	440
Other Preaching places	5	215	761
Fully accredited members	78	9300	21,300
Adherents	700	42,000	92,000

As the organization of African Methodist laity has had a far-reaching influence on most Protestant Missions in South Africa, and certainly on mission work among the Zulus, I shall describe how this organization works at the present time in Natal.[20]

(a) The smallest unit is the *class*, which ideally is supposed to be composed of only twelve members. Because of the difficulty in finding a sufficient number of suitable leaders, this number is often increased to twenty or more. The "class leader" is in Zulu called *umkhokheli*. Generally these class leaders are African men and women appointed as spiritual guides or helpers for a number of Christians either of older standing or recent converts from heathenism. The leader is also responsible for the collection of

136

the quarterly church subscription (2s. per quarter). Leaders are nominated by the Superintendent Minister at a Leaders' Meeting—*umhlangano wa6akhokheli*—and appointed by vote of the majority present.

(b) The Executive Officers of the Leaders' Meeting are called *society stewards (amagosa)*. They join with the ministers and leaders in everything that will promote the spiritual and material welfare of the church, and therefore are men of very considerable influence in the local circuit.

(c) *Exhorters*. Whilst class leaders and society stewards have to look after the organization of the smaller units of the church, the exhorters are men who feel the call to undertake preaching service among their people. They are beginners on the first rung of the ladder, but if they prove worthy they will be promoted to the position of preachers.

(d) *Preachers on trial* (Zulu: *a6alingwa*). These are men who desire to become Local or Lay Preachers. They are tested as to their spirituality, knowledge and general suitability before being advanced to the position of fully accredited Local Preachers. They must pass an examination in the Methodist Catechism and in the fluent reading of the Scriptures.

(e) *Local preachers (a6ashumayeli)* are appointed to preach in the various churches and out-stations of a circuit. To attain to this position a man must have been at least twelve months, often much longer, on probation and "have read the twelve of Wesley's Sermons now contained in the 'Marrow of Methodism' " (which is translated into Zulu and other Bantu languages). He must also pass a satisfactory examination in the catechism and effective knowledge of the Scriptures.

In Natal, the number of African exhorters in 1940 was 601, of preachers on trial 525, and of full local preachers 1068. The corresponding figures for the whole of Methodist mission work in South Africa for 1940 were, 2510; 3933; and 8915. The quarterly "Preaching Plans" of the various districts, such as the Rand or Natal, with hundreds of local preachers assigned to different churches each Sunday in the quarter, furnish a most impressive testimony to the splendid organization of Methodist mission work among the Zulus and other tribes. Other Mission Churches in South Africa, as for instance the Lutherans, have with certain modifications followed the Methodist scheme of lay organization, and now find themselves with a much stronger emphasis on lay work in the Bantu Church than is the case in the mother-Churches in Europe.

The Methodist tradition with its class leaders, stewards, and so on, is democratic in principle. It is characteristic that in the Bantu independent Churches these democratic principles are re-aligned and transformed into autocratic categories. The Nucleus of the Church—the office-bearers—becomes the *necessary intermediary in a hierarchic system of rank,* an intermediary agent of control by the Leader over his followers.

To appreciate this fact fully one must be present at a synod or other important meeting of leaders of an Ethiopian or Zionist Church. Resplendent garments are worn not only by the superintendent and the ministers, but the host of local subleaders also appear adorned with sashes and bands and badges, as insignia of their respective offices. There is a definite system for showing respect between these subleaders, and only after considerable study of the interrelations of the different ecclesiastical ranks held by the individuals is it possible to understand how this system works.

The order of rank includes at least the following officers: the Superintendent; the local ministers; the evangelists; the local preachers; the *amagosa* (stewards), men and women; and the class leaders, men and women; stewards of a poor fund; male and female leaders of the volunteers (or some such youth group). The rank system among the women leaders presents the following descending scale: the superintendent's wife; the ministers' wives; the stewards' wives; the prayer women. And these also have their particular uniforms of different colours and different shapes with a headgear of leopard skin.

This general pattern of rank shows certain *local and denominational variations.* The Independent Methodist Church of Africa, at its synod of 1940, protested against local tendencies within their congregation to create more than three classes of preachers (local preachers; local preachers on trial; and exhorters), and it was decided not to encourage such tendencies. Certain Zulu churches have developed a system of rank among those who pray for the sick; the Holy Apostolic Church in Zion has, for this purpose, divided the congregations among "twelve apostles" who have this all-important activity in their hands; the local congregation at Nqutu of the "Sabbath Church Messenger of God Zion South Africa in Zululand", defines the task of the *igosa* to be the examining of those who do not come to the service.

But whatever the local and denominational variations may be there is in this organization a definite system of rank, with well-defined tasks assigned to the subordinate in respect of his immediate superior, and of the higher ranks in the hierarchy. When discussing the question of the overstaffing of the independent Church, it was pointed out that many "ministers" have an average of less than a hundred people to look after; it is now necessary to add that even between each of these ministers and his little flock there stands a more or less elaborate system of office-bearers, who have to be controlled, and through whom the minister must control his flock. Here is the breeding ground for a host of new secessions.

I have already mentioned one Dubuzana, a heathen, who after a dream-visit to heaven, which was his call to become a prophet, turned out to be a successful healer. Although made an evangelist in recognition of his healing powers, he was however not quite content with this position and wanted to climb higher up the scale to more influential leadership. Here is, in embryo, the problem of the Nucleus. Any local preacher is a prospective superintendent.

But power has in it a tendency to expand. If it is not allowed to expand, its carrier becomes frustrated. Therefore Dubuzana wishes to become a more important *umholi*, a leader of men, of more men and women than he has hitherto had under him. In order to achieve this, he has to readjust his relations both to his superintendent and to his own flock. The main problem of authority in these independent Churches must therefore be studied in terms of the three-sided interplay between leader, nucleus and mass. But before taking up this question, I shall have to deal with the position of women as local leaders in the Zulu independent Churches.

(c) *Women as local leaders*

Within the nucleus, as the intermediary agent between leader and mass, women play an important role, and they are thereby given their share and position in the hierarchic system of rank in the Church. The influence of women leaders in the independent Churches is striking evidence of the rise in women's status in Zulu society at the present time.

The status of Zulu women under tribal conditions was certainly much higher than has been generally assumed. As *inkosikazi*, first wife of the kraal, a woman could within limits wield a very considerable influence and enjoyed a prestige which increased with her years.[21] It is true of course that in magic and in ritual generally, women had no place; they could seldom become war-doctors, rain-doctors or other types of magician. But on the other hand women and girls played an important role in the *Nomkhu6ulwana* cult (hoe-culture-ritual)[a] and above all, the large majority of possessed diviners (*izangoma*) were women. Through her activities as a diviner the woman could expand her personal influence beyond the narrow borders of the kraal, by which she would otherwise be limited, and as Gluckman says, it was the only way an outstanding woman could win general social prestige.

In the Mission Churches the influence of the African woman was enhanced, and she has responded in a way which shows that she has appreciated this side also of the work of the Church. In any Mission Church in Zululand the congregation is principally composed of women and girls, and African ministers often refer to their congregations (depleted of men by the labour emigration to the Rand), as an *i6andla la6esifazana*—"a women's church". As contrasted with conditions in Tanganyika, where the emancipation of the women has generally not gone so far as in South Africa, the proportion of girls in the schools (all run by missions) is higher than that of boys. The education statistics for Natal show that in 1935 the proportion was 58% girls, and in 1943 the proportion was 56% girls.

There are several reasons for this difference between the sexes in their response to the message of the Church. It is felt by the Zulu warrior that it is unmanly, not in accordance with his ideal of *u6udoda* (manliness), to wear European clothes and become a Christian.[b] Further, the polygamy issue is undoubtedly the great offence to the Zulu when he faces the possibility of joining the Church. Thirdly, cattle are the foremost source of prestige to the Zulus and only boys are supposed to look after the herds; this hinders them from going to the Christian school, whereas this obstacle does not exist for the girls.

A further step in the direction of emancipation of women has been taken in recent years on the Rand by the formation of voluntary associations or clubs, of the *Stokfel* and *Mahodisana* type.[22] The initiative behind these groups and their pattern springs from the activities of the Christian Church. These clubs are an important feature in the social life of the African woman in the towns, and their activities show how far she has advanced

[a] Cf. p. 20.

[b] "To be converted" is sometimes called in Zulu *ukulahla ibeshu*—to shed the buttock-covering—i.e. to put on European clothes.

in self-reliance and self-expression. The clubs help with loans, the paying of fines, burial collections and so on.

But the independent Church, much more than any other organization, gives to the Zulu woman a chance for self-display and assures her of a great measure of power and prestige. Actually this is also typical of certain sects in Europe and America: Mary Baker-Eddy, Ellen Gould White, Amie McPherson, are famous instances. What do their Zulu sisters look like?

The distinction made in this book between two types of Churches—Ethiopian and Zionist—and two corresponding main types of leaders—chief and prophet—is unmistakably reflected in the local leadership exercised by women.

1. In *Ethiopian* Churches women local leaders certainly play an indispensable part. I have already noted (p. 138) that among the female leaders there is the same system of rank as among the men. The position given to the superintendent's or the minister's wife is interesting. In the Presbyterian Church of Africa people feel that she should *not* be the official head of the Women's Meeting (*Unyamezelo*), because in such a position she might be criticized, but as the superintendent's wife she should be above all party strife. This is, however, an exception. In the Ethiopian Catholic Church in Zion, the "Archbishop's Lady" takes, *ex officio*, a prominent part in all deliberations of the Church, and above all in the work of the "Dorcas Women's Mite Missionary Society Fund".[23] The co-operation or otherwise of his wife will make or break the leader's career. A Lutheran evangelist seceded from his mission Church and started his own organization. His wife was against the secession, and refused to join the new sect. She would wait and see, she said, whether her husband's Church would become permanent and lasting. This proved his undoing. If his wife did not believe in his Church, who else could? And the venture came to nought.

In the Ethiopian Churches women's leadership runs on parallel lines to that of the men. This fact was borne out in a characteristic way by the arrangement at a recent annual synod of the Ethiopian Church of Africa. The President with his ministers, preceded by a standard-bearer, entered the meeting hall in procession, followed by the procession of the women office-bearers in their uniforms. After the close of the processional hymn, the President uttered an opening prayer and after another hymn the ladies left the hall in procession, to hold their conference in another room. At the end of the Synod, the findings and recommendations of the ladies were brought to the notice of the main (i.e. the men's) conference, through one of their secretaries.

As local leaders, especially in Zululand, women generally show more initiative and energy than men. They arrange prayer meetings, occasional collections as a special gift for the superintendent, and visits to other congregations. In these ways women wield a very great influence in their Church. A custom which is practised in Ethiopian organizations of the Bantu Methodist type is an example of this: to show their loyalty and affection to a minister, all the women will *in corpore* march up to the front of the church and congregate around him, kneeling in prayer and singing hymns. If the group of women for some reason does not appreciate the minister's work or person, this corporate demonstration of loyalty does not take place—and the omission may lead to serious consequences for the minister concerned.

2. The real power basis for women leaders is, however, the *Zionist* Church. The only Bantu Church with a female superintendent in South Africa, is a Zionist group called the Holy Apostle Mission Church of South Africa, led by "Sister Ministress" Lucy S. Mofokeng, and founded in 1943. She claims as followers seventy-four men and eighty-four women.

The increasing power of women leaders in Zionist organizations on the Rand is reflected in their "ordination". Bishop Gumede, of the Christian Catholic Apostolic Stone Church in Zion of South Africa, has issued an imposing Women's Ordination Certificate, which gives the women concerned "authority to Preach the Gospel of Jesus Christ, to pray for the sick, and to bury the dead, to Consecrate children, to Administer the Lord's Supper, to Baptize believers, to solemnize marriages".

It is significant that the "Sister Ministress" just mentioned is not a Zulu. However much power and prestige these Churches may be willing to give to women, it would be abhorrent to a Zulu to have a woman as superintendent; but as local leaders they have much scope. A typical example is Filipina Buthelezi Dlamini. She was baptized in a Lutheran Mission Church in 1910, but left it in 1928 "because the ministers fought against the Spirit". She then joined the Christian Apostolic Church in Zion for a while—the leading Zionist Church in North Zululand. She did not, however, get on well with the district leader of this Church. He had not the Holy Spirit, and he told her that "she was possessed by a demon". " 'Then', I said, 'I leave, if I have a demon, and I will establish my own church.' " In 1939, she joined the Holy Apostolic Gaza Church in Zion. Here she was unhampered by any restrictions, as the minister lived in Estcourt, and only visited the district once a year, if then. She virtually became the local leader of the Gaza Zion group. Filipina is an energetic, personable, and ambitious woman. In her Gaza group she has a following chiefly of women who have recently been converted from heathenism. With her education of two years in school and her ability to read the Bible, she regards herself as vastly superior to anybody else. In 1941 she even took up English Reading Charts together with one of her faithful, Bessie. In conversation with her one day, I suggested that Bessie might be quicker in learning English than she, and would possibly start a Church of her own. "No," was the reply. "I will always be quicker than she in learning things. So I will keep the congregation." Because of her superior standard of education, she never argues with women. "I only argue with men and I only compete with men about knowledge of Bible verses (*ukushayana ngamavesi*). I am myself a minister. The other women leaders are nothing but helpers."

Filipina's case is significant for the following reasons: (*a*) In the Reserve, depleted of men because of the exodus of labour to the Rand and the city, personable Bantu women exert a very wide influence through the Zionist churches. (*b*) Beginning in a Mission Church, Filipina has—so far—changed Churches twice, by a process which should be called *social separation* in the Wilsons' sense,[24] until at last she found a group where she could become prominent and which would serve her as a power-basis. In the Mission Church, her two years in school were regarded as only a mediocre attainment. In the Independent Church she was the constant object of the admiring gaze of the Gaza group. (*c*) Her claim to have the Holy Spirit and to be a healer gives her status in her Church.

In certain cases women leaders act as guardians of "Bethesda" colonies of the prophet in his absence (cf. p. 151). Shembe seems to have preferred women as treasurers in his congregations, because he had found them more honest than men in this capacity.[25] The most spectacular form of female leadership in the Zionist Church is seen when they act as media for a risen Bantu Christ (cf. p. 120). In Bantu organizations where the main requirement for rise to leadership is possession by the "Holy Spirit", women of a hysterical disposition may wield very considerable influence. In close relationship with the prophet himself, these women—who answer to fanciful names, such as

Umphefumulo, the Spirit; or *Ufakazi*, the Witness; or Maria Magdalene—exercise great power behind the scenes.

3. It has been pointed out here that female leadership in Ethiopian Churches is a part of the framework of the Church's hierarchic system of rank, whereas in the Zionist Church, the local prophetess may often become very self-reliant. It should, however, also be stressed that in many Ethiopian Churches, women acting as local leaders tend to employ more and more of Zionist methods, and in so doing prepare their flock for eventually breaking away from the Ethiopian group and joining some Zionist organization.

In an offshoot in Central Zululand, the grip of the old Ethiopian evangelist over the congregation was lost to a young girl who could speak with tongues and who claimed to be possessed by something which she called the "Holy Spirit". As the superintendent of the Church did not visit this group more than once biennially, the girl had many opportunities in which to prepare for the final transfer of the congregation from the Ethiopian to the Zionist camp. In this way leadership of women in the congregations is another factor making for constant flux within the independent Church movement.

(d) *Relation of leader and nucleus*

For both types of leaders, chief and prophet, the fundamental problems are the same: when the primary group expands and becomes a large-scale association, when the small circle of faithful in the neighbourhood develops into an ever-increasing Church of many congregations, the problem of control of the nucleus and of the mass of church people becomes pressing.

But there is a characteristic difference between, on the one hand, the Zionist prophet roving through Zululand with a trail of male and female subleaders behind him and instructing his followers as he walks along, and on the other, the "chief", the busy Ethiopian superintendent in his Johannesburg office, typing letters (adorned with the impressive rubber stamp of his Church) to his local ministers, and perhaps discussing with them the balance sheet of last year's accounts.

In each set of relations (prophet-nucleus; "chief"-nucleus) there are factors and forces which definitely strengthen the bond of authority and loyalty between leader and subleaders. But there are also in each set hidden forces which exercise a disrupting influence on the nucleus and thereby on the Church. The tremendous rate at which the fission of independent

Churches is going on has, in the mind of the leaders, made the secret of leadership and the technique of domination their great concern.

In practically all these Churches the leader has a decisive influence in so far as he is the one to choose the men for the ministry. In most instances where there is any "theological" instruction given at all, it is imparted by the president himself. The problem of ultimate control over staff and Church is possibly the reason for a lukewarm response to any suggestion for a United Theological College for the more respected independent Churches. I sometimes suggested that individual leaders should consider the possibility of sending their men to the A.M.E. Theological College at Evaton. But the reply was invariably that they themselves had to choose their men and observe their development in order to feel reassured that they would get the right kind of ministers for the congregations.

This training, privately given by the leader himself, is called "theological". In actual fact this may amount to a few weeks' refresher course of Bible reading and catechism once in a few years. The overseer of the Christian Catholic Church in Ethiopia claimed that he called his ministers together in Johannesburg three times a year, one month at a time, for theological instruction. Obviously this claim is more of a dream wish than a reality.

Shembe never chose a minister who applied of his own accord to be trained for that position. He insisted that "the Spirit remains, and speaks and chooses". He felt led by the Spirit to trust some particular man, and after having decided the matter, he would spend a week with the man in prayer. This minister usually accompanied Shembe on his journeys, the two walking through Zululand, staffs in their hands. The journey culminated in the ordination act on the holy mountain Nhlangakazi. The prophet anointed his ordinands with holy oil and told them to bring each a very heavy stone from the bottom of the mountain up to the place used for their Church gatherings: "These stones are your oath (*isifungo*) that you have surrendered yourselves to God. These stones will be a testimony before God."[26] The originality of the symbolism in this improvised act of ordination had a great influence on the men. And it is obvious that through symbols of this kind, and through the influence of his person, Shembe had from the very beginning a grip on his ministers unsurpassed by other Zulu church leaders.

In the Ethiopian Churches the choice and ordination of the

minister is not done in the same picturesque way. In principle, the Annual Conference chooses the men for positions in the Church. The leader of a Congregational offshoot observed to me that in this respect their organization showed a marked improvement on the American Board system. Whereas American Congregational missionaries claimed that the call to the ministry must in principle come from the congregation, the independent Zulu Church had delegated such powers to the Conference, he said. This was of course only half the truth: in actual fact the president himself had usurped this power and would retain it.

Also in Ethiopian Churches the ordination is often bound up with a solemn oath, a means through which the president seeks to exercise control over his staff. According to the form of "Oath of allegiance, taken by the ministers, and other officials on the day of their Admission to orders and offices of the Church", which is used in the Bantu Methodist Church, those concerned swear, *inter alia*: "I shall obey the Founder-President, and all those in authority over me, and perform all those duties assigned me to the best of my ability. The cause of this Organization shall come first to me in all my deliberations. Should I fail this cause, may the Almighty God fail me in the purpose of life."

It is characteristic of the situation that constitutions and ordination forms contain detailed instructions how the ordained should act if later excommunicated. In the Independent Methodist Church the ordained, on admission to the ministry, signs: ". . . Once I am excommunicated, I will hand to the officer concerned all documents and properties of the said church, repress myself and work no more with the name of the Independent Methodist Church of Africa."

Even more startling are the words in the constitution of the "National Swaziland Native Apostolic Church of Africa":

Any minister leaving the National Swaziland Native Apostolic Church shall return all certificates obtained by him *during his stay* (!) in the National Apostolic Church, and shall get a note from the National Apostolic Church stating what position he held and on what account he is leaving. No minister leaving this church shall form a branch of it, he may better join another church.

These quotations clearly show that anticipations and expectations of future secessions in themselves weaken the Church and make it unstable, a viewpoint to which we shall return later

146

(p. 170). The fact is, of course, that no such barrier of oaths and declarations can effectively stem the tide of sect formation. Not all Church leaders, by a long way, scrutinize their new ministers. I have come across men who, after only a few days of fleeting acquaintance with an overseer or archbishop, have been asked by the potentate in question to join the ministry and be ordained at once. In such circumstances the chances of a lasting loyalty are slighter than ever.

After "ordination" the minister is put in charge of a local congregation. The permanent contact with and control of the local ministers is the main preoccupation of the leader, and presents him with his central problem of domination technique.

Some leaders wish to preserve, in appearance at least, the delegation of power to subleaders. "Most Reverend Samuel James Brander, Archbishop Metropolitan and Primate for all Africa South of the Equator" has thus in his constitution expressedly stated that "no Bishop whatsoever, not even the Metropolitan, can interfere with any diocesan Bishop by exercising any Episcopal functions in the same without the consent of the Diocesan Bishop".[27]

Other leaders, however, have found that such delegation of power to diocesan bishops as envisaged by this archbishop, is frought with risks and dangers. One president of an important Church of Ethiopian type mentioned that some of his subleaders had suggested that he, the president, should have at his side a deputy who could be sent to various parts of the Union and there temporarily represent him: "But I am absolutely against such a plan. *I* am the head; I will never send anybody as a deputy to a local minister. I have no deputy; that would divide the loyalty of the local ministers [i.e. distract their loyalty from the supreme leader]. All power is concentrated in the Head, and that's *me*." "I have some fifty ministers under me, and they are all happy," he added with self-assurance. If trouble arose in one congregation, he would, therefore, always go himself and settle the matter there and then without having to rely on others. This man also asserted that he would never place two ministers in the same place as colleagues; that would only lead to trouble. "Place two bulls in the same cattle-kraal and they will fight each other," he said, quoting a well-known Zulu proverb. In view of the fact that Zulu Independent Churches as a rule are overstaffed, this attitude is easily understandable.

The main issues of conflict between the leader and his staff, or between individual ministers, which arise are whether the leadership of the Church should be hereditary or only for a period of years; whether the leader is radical enough or whether in some cases he is too radical, as in his criticism of the Government; or whether the leader has been right in his discipline of some minister. All these matters call for constant vigilance on the part of the leader and may quite unexpectedly cause the falling away of a certain number of congregations.

There is, it seems, a secret "something" which singles out some of these men as undisputed leaders who will as a rule have little trouble with their subordinates. Bishop Limba, of the Bantu Church of Christ, states in the Constitution of his Church:

> There is at present no Church discipline, no disciplinary council and no disciplinary code of conduct. The Bishop directs the policy of the Church and its entire discipline at his own discretion. The Bishop has the sole control and charge of the Church.

Quite a few Bantu leaders would, I believe, like to make the same claim, but very few could get away with it.

Whether the local or district leader is called bishop or priest or anything else, he is in most cases supposed to be allowed a certain latitude for freedom of action and initiative. I believe it is characteristic of the African outlook and of the emerging African Church that it does not identify strict unity of command with slavish uniformity of expression. So long as the local minister acclaims his archbishop as the leader, he may, within his sphere of authority, wield rather wide powers.

The independent Church is inherently African also in that it follows this principle. An example of this may be given: Rev. Mtabela, of a certain Zionist Church, had had revealed to him in a dream the Festival of the Tabernacles. That meant, of course, that he was by the Spirit led to introduce this festival in his congregation. In spite of the fact that his General Overseer in Johannesburg was not much given to innovations and would not accept such a festival for the rest of the church, nevertheless he benevolently let Mtabela have his way in his own local congregation, and they could put up their huts on some temporary Holy Mountain in accordance with Deut. 16. If the overseer in such a case had tried to hinder his man, the outcome might well have been a struggle, where Mtabela would have rationalized this struggle, fought essentially for power, by stating that the overseer did not follow the clear instructions of the Bible—and in so doing he would have made sure that at least one part of his own congregation would follow him, while probably the rest would, under some other subleader, be loyal to the general overseer.[28]

While the leader thus influences his subordinates, and in various ways maintains his control over them, it is of course at the same time true that the nucleus has a decided influence upon the leader. Especially is this the case when the leader is of the prophet type. As a prophet (as here described) he is more susceptible to outside influence than the chief. His authority rests on the claim that he has the Holy Spirit. But no less a claim is made by his subordinates. And moreover there is, as we shall see in a later chapter, a periodicity, a rhythm of rise and decline, in the prophetic claim to inspiration. After a time the prophet often says, not with regret but just stating it as a plain fact: *"Angisa hlushwa umoya"* ("I am no longer troubled by the Spirit"). Then and there is the chance of ascendancy for the young convert who has "git religion"—as the American Negroes would say—or who has "plenty of Spirit" (*umoya kakhulu*), as the Zulus would put it. To retain his influence the prophet has then to follow the dreams of his inspired subordinates, or to take the risk that they may establish a new Church without him. This may lead to renewed radicalism. So it was when Y inspired his leader X to enter into contact with the Holy Spirit by gazing at a holy stone; or when a bishop was persuaded by a local subleader that an expected eclipse of the sun would usher in the Day of Judgment, and all people in the neighbourhood were thereupon bidden to kill their pigs in order to be saved.

On the other hand as we have already seen in certain Ethiopian churches, subleaders may attempt to restrain the dangerous political radicalism of the president with a view to gaining certain advantages for their church. If he is too headstrong he may be ousted from his position, but the probability is that he will give way to the pressure in order to retain his leadership. In those independent Churches where a Methodist heritage still makes itself felt, the local church stewards have a power which may become quite embarrassing to the minister. The steward has the right to excommunicate those whom he regards as undesirable, and cases are known where a minister has unsuccessfully pleaded with a church steward on behalf of some unfortunate church member who has been excommunicated by him.

In any case it is true to say that there is a constant pressure on the leader, a surge and an urge from those below him who aspire to reach higher in the scale, and eventually to come to the top. Many a Bantu Church leader may well sigh as Bishop Khoza does in the Constitution of his Holy Catholic Apostolic Church in Zion: "Finally, we desire to carry out this Church's work unmolested by any would-be aspirants for the office of General Overseer."

(3) LEADER, NUCLEUS AND CHURCH

(a) The Leader's control over the Church

How far is it possible to measure the strength of leadership in its relation to the broad masses of Zulu church people? Or, to put the same question in another form: How far down in the mass does the leader's influence reach? At the outset a few general statements may be made. It is of course a fact that any Bantu Church shares the difficulty experienced by any association in the process of growth, the development from the local cell to the big organization. This experience is shared by the Mission Churches. There is a marked difference between the kind of bond that is created on the one hand between the missionary-patriarch and his initial group, assembled in his hut or house, meeting together for common menial tasks and for common prayer and instruction, and on the other hand the modern missionary superintendent whose relations with the broad masses are maintained by his Gestetner and his Ford. Of the 800 independent Churches, the majority are small-size, local cells, and in these the crucial leadership problem here discussed does not really arise. A case in point is that of some seventy people belonging to a Bethesda Church in a Native township in Johannesburg, where all the leaders, the bishop, a couple of evangelists, the drummer and the chorister, are of the same Malinga clan, and harmony prevails.

The problem does arise in the important large-size Churches of both Zionist and Ethiopian type. And there one can observe a characteristic difference in the strength of the relations between leader and Church.

In Ethiopian organizations such relations are generally *indirect*, solely mediated through the nucleus. The leader is that important man, somewhere in Johannesburg, who comes along about *"iGoodi"*-time (Good-Friday) every year or every second year. He is supposed to be very learned (*ufundile kakhulu*), and very clever, and to be constantly interceding on the Church's behalf with the Government in Pretoria. Some such leaders claim the privilege of performing at least confirmation themselves, a characteristic influence of Anglican episcopal pattern upon churches which have split away largely from Methodist or Baptist or Congregational missions. Through this solemn act they attempt to keep up some contact with the ever-increasing mass of church people.

In the case of the prophet as Church leader, the intensity of relations with the Church is much greater. In his case there are very direct forms of contact through his healing activities. Later we shall discuss the ritual and medical aspects of healing in the Zionist Church. In this chapter we are concerned with the sociological implications of church relationships. These are indeed far-reaching, if it can be shown—as I would claim—that the healing activities of the prophet and the corresponding congregational need have given rise to a unique kind of Church fellowship, *the "Bethesda" type of Church.*

I use the term "Bethesda" type to describe the fellowship of the prophet and his followers who, as patients, stay at his kraal for a considerable length of time with a view to being prayed for and going through purification rites. The name Bethesda is the word most commonly used by the Zulu prophet; the pool or the stream near his kraal is related by him to the healing Bethesda pool described in St. John, 5: 4–9. Bishop Morupa in Alexandra Township, Johannesburg, told me regretfully that on the crowded inhospitable Rand there was no place for such a community, centred round a healing pool. He therefore sent his patients to the Reserve away from Johannesburg and the Rand, and invited them to build their own temporary huts while staying at his place. The Bethesda Church belongs solely to the Reserves, and it is significant that prominent prophets do not stay in Johannesburg but have established themselves on big farms in the native-owned farm areas, or in the Reserves themselves: this is demanded by the very nature of their work. Only in the countryside has the prophet access to the holy mountain and the pool, the two essentials which his dream symbols have shown him to be the foundation of his church activities. In order to understand better the relation between the prophet and his Bethesda Church, I shall describe three such communities.

(i) Malko Shabalala is a minor Zulu prophet. He has a kraal in north Zululand just on the Natal border, and he claims to be the local minister of the Sabbath Holy Apostolic Zion Church of South Africa. To the usual lay-out of a Zulu kraal, have been added six small grass huts. These were put up by his followers past and present who have stayed at his kraal as patients for some three months at a time. At my last visit to the place only one male patient was staying there; the rest, thirteen in number, were women and girls.[a] From interviews with Shabalala and with those whom I knew to have been his patients, I gathered that the general routine of the day was as follows: At dawn prophet and patients go together to the waterfall close by. After the water has been prayed over by Shabalala they all drink from it repeatedly until they vomit, at the same time singing hymns and speaking with tongues. Some mornings Shabalala takes his flock with him to the top of the Enende mountain for prayers. During the day the women work in the prophet's fields. In the afternoon follow visits to kraals in the neighbourhood where they pray and sing, and Shabalala gives an evangelistic address.

Shabalala's group is, on a small scale, representative of the main characteristics of the Bethesda type of religious organization which from a sociological point of view is quite a new type of Church: "This is not a church, it is a hospital," one prophet exclaimed at a nightly meeting in Zululand. And it is important to observe that in these little communities the prophet eventually acquires an astounding personal influence over his followers. When he moves along, with his brass rod—"Moses' rod"—in his hand, and with a retinue of men and especially women following him, he is regarded with deep veneration by them, and his every word is law. It is a well-established fact that on one occasion a wedding party led by such a Zulu Moses, arriving at Blood River,[b] was told that the prophet would divide the waters with his rod, and that they would walk through dryshod, as did the children of Israel. This happened in November when Blood River was very high. The prophet himself was the only one who did not enter and he was the only survivor. The rest were drowned.

(ii) The next example is of two Nazarite colonies, a smaller cluster "X" in Central Zululand, and the central place of the Nazarite Church at Ekuphakameni.

At "X" the prophet has been allotted an extensive piece of ground by the tribal chief. Huts are built there in three groups:

(a) the woman's section (or *isigodlo*) of some forty to fifty huts;

[a] The women's complaint was barrenness; the girls were suffering from hysterical disorders.

[b] Blood River, a tributary of Tugela River, Natal.

(*b*) the men's section with less than half that number of huts;

(*c*) a stone house and *rondavels* built as an abode for the prophet on his occasional visits to the place.

Only a few of these huts are permanently occupied, but on the occasion of the prophet's visit they will be crowded with the owners (all belonging to the Nazarite Church) and their friends and relations. A local prophet is left in charge of the place. He prays for the women patients who come to stay there for a while. The women divide their time between work in the fields and preparations for the medico-religious ceremonies performed by the ministers. They have in particular to look after the holy grove, the place for worship, which always must be kept clean. There is an outside altar, and at the time of worship one of the women places a mat and a Zulu wooden headrest (*isicamelo*) near the altar: the Risen Servant is there present in spirit, if not in the flesh.

Ekuphakameni, the headquarters of the Nazarite Church, is situated on one of Shembe's farms, eighteen miles north of Durban. It is a big village, capable of accommodating more than 1500 people during the July festival month, when the followers of the prophet congregate there from all over Zululand and Natal and even from other parts of the Union.

Ekuphakameni village is planned on the same principle as village "X" but on a much larger scale: there is one section for unmarried men with at least 100 huts, the Jamengweni section for Natal women, and the Bhekuzulu section for the Zululand women; there are also sections for girls and other visitors. The central section is occupied by the prophet's private quarters, comprising some fifty huts and houses. Close by are the main places for worship—as for instance the "House of the Holy Vessels", which may only be entered by the most elect. I wanted to take a photograph of the house and arranged some prayer-women in the front of the picture. They objected, however, when I placed them so that their backs were turned (*ukufulathela*) upon the House, for this showed disrespect to such a holy place. Here is also the most holy shrine of all, the house built over Shembe's grave.

Most people who stay at Ekuphakameni do so only for the festivals, especially the great July festival. The main features of Church activity during this period, apart from preaching and testimonies, are the dancing carried out according to age-groups, and the prophet's praying for the sick. Isaiah Shembe built up his great influence on his reputation as a divinely inspired healer, and his reputation has been inherited by the son, the present leader. In the chapter on healing, I shall give an account of a healing service for 250 barren women at Ekuphakameni. The atmosphere of mystery and the feeling of tremendous expectation with which the prophet's healing activities were greeted, did indeed produce a unique experience. The prophet, praying with his holy black veil for the hundreds of frustrated women, became in this service the object of what one in psychoanalytical language would call a transference on a large scale, and by similar magico-religious services during the holy month of July, he established a bond of fellowship and dependence which easily surpassed in intensity all other leader-follower relations which I have witnessed in these churches.

As a complement to the annual July-festival at Ekuphakameni, the Nazarite Church celebrates an annual pilgrimage to their holy mountain, Nhlangakazi. This festival, with its dancing and sacrifices and singing and praying and healing, is another occasion when the bond between leader and followers is greatly strengthened and when there is created an intense and immediate contact between them.

(iii) The most typical example, in the collection of Zionist Churches, of what McIver calls a Utopian Community, is prophet X's Church at T———. The son of a village headman, X had for a while worked as a mine overseer in Johannesburg, when through his own and a friend's dreams he was led to start his "Salem Church". Beginning on a small scale he soon built up his reputation as a successful healer. The attractive power of his personality and message was *partly* built up round his healing activities: the large church building had as its centre a so-called "hospital", a cruciform part of the house where men and women were prayed for by X and his many "angels"; and *partly* round his teaching on marriage which was originally ascetic (the "Heavenly Marriage" implied, theoretically, celibacy for all church members), but which in practice developed into considerable licence. At the height of X's influence some 250 men and women lived in his colony.

It is difficult to ascertain how far a sexual element plays a part in the attractive power of the Bethesda colony type. Professed asceticism and actual licence are here often mingled inextricably. It is characteristic that in the cases already mentioned the majority of the prophet's followers were women.

Certain prophets insist on their Church establishing something called an "orphanage". In the case of one prophet, easily the most vile and vicious of them all, the records in a number of Natal magistrates' courts have established the fact that his orphanages for young girls, which he opened in every district wherever he went, were nothing but the prophet's temporary harems.

A psycho-analyst would probably have much to tell us about the significance in the Bethesda group life of the dream symbols which are most frequent in Zionist Churches. The most common of these are the pool or stream and the high mountain. Because these symbols have been seen both by prophet and followers, they are convinced that the Spirit directs them to perform daily purification rites in the neighbouring pool, and occasionally to congregate on the particular Mount Zion of the Church to which they belong. One does not need to be a Freudian to understand something of the hidden working of their minds, expressed in such symbols. Further, the prophet who is a successful healer of the mental and gynæcological diseases which usually bring these women to "Bethesda" becomes, as has already been said, the object of a collective transference. Through this sub-conscious process there are created very strong and lasting bonds between leader and flock.

In evaluating the sociological importance of the "Bethesda" type of church in Zulu Zionist Churches and the relationship it makes possible between leader and flock, two things should be borne in mind:

(1) The Bethesda type of Church is an adaptation to modern conditions of essential elements in two of the strongest institutions in the historical development of the Zulus.

(a) The temporary huts, grouped in sections according to status, recall to any Zulu's mind the *ikhanda*, Shaka's military kraal, where the king's followers of both sexes congregated, fulfilling different tasks assigned to them by the king. The followers' status was enhanced by their being in the King's presence.[29]

(b) The second traditional Zulu institution, on the pattern of which the Bethesda Church is evolving is the community of diviners (*izangoma*). I have shown above how the Zionist prophet's activities follow the Zulu diviner pattern in fairly minute detail. The routine of staying at the prophet's kraal for some considerable time, being prayed for, and going

155

through purification rites can be demonstrated to be very closely related to the group life of diviner and novices.

(2) The retroactive influence of the church on the leader is considerable and in the very nature of things much stronger than in the more formal relationship found in the Ethiopian Church. The dreams, visions, and auditions of the individual half-Christian members of the Bethesda colonies are highly respected by the prophet, because in the last resort he and his followers have one and the same authority—the "Spirit". The expectation of his people that he will be able to perform miracles, makes ever higher demands of the leader and propels him further along the marshy path of Bantu syncretism, specially through belief in witchcraft and sorcery with its corollary, divining.

It is important to notice that in this kind of relationship the nucleus does not play its essential part of intermediary between leader and mass. The influence from the numinous presence of the leader is direct and therefore the more effective. Further, the prophet does not dispense his influence through one pastoral visit here, another there. He is at the centre of his Church, which is Bethesda the Fount of Health, and Zion the Mount of Heaven.

This relationship is strengthened by the economic inter-dependence of leader and flock in Zionist colonies in Zululand. The Nazarite Church farms in Native farm areas or in tribal wards are examples of this development. In northern Zululand I came across an interesting Zionist colony that some years earlier had trekked from a farm in Natal, from which they had been evicted. The prophet succeeded in persuading the tribal headman to allot to his group a certain area of land, and there they built their kraals around the church. The leader was supported by contributions in labour, cash and agricultural produce from the land, and he repaid their efforts by praying for the sick, representing the community in legal matters, and through his increasing influence over more and more people, enhancing the status of his closest followers. Here, the leader as prophet of his Bethesda Church and as "chief" (on the kingship pattern) of his colony represents and embodies his flock in the most effective manner. Large-scale examples of these religious colonies in other than Zulu areas are Lekganyane's farms in the Pietersburg district and Bishop Limba's progressive agricultural and industrial community in Port Elizabeth.

(b) Finance of the Church

The question of the financial support of the Separatist Church should not be discussed independently of other problems of central importance to the life of these Churches. I suggest that the best angle from which to approach it is as an element in the relation of the leader to the led. The stronger and the more intimate the leader's influence, the better will he be able to secure financial assistance and induce his people to make economic sacrifices which a weaker leader would be incapable of doing.

Money and property are problems which play a very considerable role in the life of the Independent Churches. In certain cases these have appeared as prominent issues in secession from White Mission Churches. The most famous example is the crisis in the Methodist Church on the Rand in 1932, when the Bantu Methodist Church was formed. The reason given in this case was the increase of quarterly Church dues from 2s. to 2s. 6d. Leaving aside for the moment the probability that in this case the money issue was in part a rationalization of a deeper, racial issue, it is nevertheless true that in many cases discontent with financial obligations in the "White" Church is one of the causes leading to secession. It is of some interest to observe that ministers in the (American Negro) African Methodist Episcopal Church in Natal, when discussing the income of their church, stress the fact that from their Church dues "nothing was sent to America". One of the main planks in the platform of secession propaganda in certain churches has been a promise that the followers of the Independent Church will not have to pay any church dues. Such a generous promise is, however, difficult to keep. As a matter of fact church dues in the Independent Churches are decidedly higher than those in the Mission Churches.

Most Ethiopian groups follow the ordinary methods used in the mother Churches: church support is given in cash through Sunday collections, in a special annual fee, and in offerings at baptism, confirmation, and Holy Communion. Reliable statistics about such Church offerings cannot be given, but they seem to range from 4s. or 5s. per annum (which seems to be the general figure officially quoted by most churches) to 11s. per annum in the Christian New Salem Church, or 9s. per quarter (36s. per annum) in Lekganyane's Zion Christian Church. Some churches impose higher church dues on men than on women, and may differentiate between urban and rural areas, a higher cash offering being expected from the former.

These routine channels for Church income are, however, not particularly characteristic of the independent Churches. A popular way of getting cash income for the Church is the so-called "*auction-concert*". This device seems to emanate from certain Methodist practices in South Africa. It is a kind of amateur concert, where anybody in the audience may call upon anybody else in the hall to sing a certain song by making a contribution such as 6*d*. The performance will very soon be interrupted by someone else putting down a slightly higher contribution, 9*d*. for instance, to make the singer stop and induce another in the audience to sing. This method seems to be regarded as of high entertainment value. I have seen Ethiopian crowds in Dundee (Natal) or Durban or Johannesburg enjoy concerts of this kind immensely. The Ethiopian Church in Christ states in its constitution: "All pastors are allowed one successful quarterly concert within the circuit to make up for any shortage in the quarterly stipend."

If special methods like these are tried in urban areas in order to secure cash, the rural areas are noted for gifts and *contributions in kind*. The Harvest Festival, sometimes called "*uHona*", is an important feature. Offerings such as mealies and pumpkins are given to the minister. Extra efforts may be made in times of special financial difficulty. The Independent Methodist Church, at its Annual Conference in 1940, attempted to overcome its difficulties by an *ad hoc* decision: "As it has been reported by all our ministers that our congregations suffered and still suffer from starvation, and as cash is very scarce in these days, the conference passed the resolution that all kraal heads on behalf of their Christian family should sacrifice a beast in order to uplift our church once for all to have funds." ("To sacrifice a beast" in this context does not, of course, mean slaughter.) In certain Churches of Zionist type the giving of cattle to the leader is common. It is interesting to hear such people at the same time criticize Mission Churches for *their* exorbitant church dues of perhaps 2*s*. per quarter. Members of many rural Churches are expected to give support by helping the minister during ploughing and harvest.

The difficulty in assessing the amount of the individual's actual contribution to his Church is largely due to the fact that in many churches, certainly in most of the Zionist type, over and above the fixed annual contributions occasional collections are taken from time to time. Not a few members complain of this: they have discovered that demands on their financial resources have become a burden, they may be called upon at any time to give for any purpose such as a minister's house on the Rand or a stand (for a church) in Vryheid, and in conversation with Mission people they mention this, pointing out that the well-defined system of contributions in the Mission Church is better as "you know exactly where you are"

The promise by some leaders, in crisis of secession from the White Church, that in the Independent Church there will be lower church dues or even none at all, cannot of course be honoured. Actually, church dues are bound to become higher in the independent organization than they were in the Mission Church. Weak leaders have difficulties over this, and I know both of individuals and of groups who have felt deceived and have returned to the mission fold. But these are exceptions. The one great cleavage in South African society is the line of colour; the Zulu's conviction that he is contributing to his own Church, his very own, and not to the White Man's organization, makes up for all other shortcomings. This must not be misunderstood; the Zulu is as little enthusiastic about getting rid of his money or other possessions as anybody else. The financial support of the Independent Church does not happen as a matter of course, just as it does not in the Mission Church. It presupposes propaganda or *pressure*. It should not be overlooked here that Independent Church leaders are well aware that some of their colleagues have inherited a legacy of poverty, because the mother Church from which they separated has not taught Christian stewardship sufficiently well. The president of a leading Congregational Independent Church, who had started his career in a Lutheran Mission, compared his own financial situation with that of the superintendent of another Independent Church: "X cannot get a living out of his church, because he was a Lutheran. Lutherans, Anglicans, and Romans are not strict enough when it comes to this money matter, and they demand much too little from their church people. Methodists and American Board (Congregational) have taught their congregations to give, and Independent Churches separating from such missions have no financial difficulties." But whatever the ecclesiastical ancestry, it depends chiefly on the leader and his staff if the financial support in the Independent Church is to be strong.

Most successful in this respect is undoubtedly the prophet; above all, the prophet who is regarded as a Black Christ. As a type we select Isaiah Shembe. I should, however, point out

K   159

that when Dr. Dube said in his biography of Shembe that he "was very clever in extracting money from people", this evoked a protest from the heir of the Church, Johannes Galilee Shembe. The latter, in a sort of foreword to Dube's book, declared that nobody had any right to refer to his father in such terms:

> Here it is said that my Father was very clever in extracting money from people—further it is said that his churchwardens in asking people to give their offerings frighten them by stating that they will not enter heaven if they do not obey Shembe's command. My Father has never said that a man who does not pay his Church dues will perish, when coming to heaven. Anybody who makes such a claim is lying—he is abusive against us.

It is characteristic, not only of the Nazarites but of many other churches of Zionist type, that a considerable part of the church money is paid in connexion with Church festivals. In Shembe's Church this is organized with great care. On the fourteenth of each month the married women give 1s. each, on the twenty-third of each month it is the men's turn, and on the twenty-fifth the girls' day. At the great festivals of "January" and "July", thousands of people are expected to give 5s. each, after which the dancing before the Lord can begin. When contributing their gifts the people advance in procession, singing and dancing, heaping the money in front of the prophet himself. This act is described as "shaking hands with" the prophet (*ukuxhawula*). There is no doubt that ministers point out to the people that those who can afford it and do not pay will be condemned in the next life, and consequently there are few outstanding debts. The "Lantern Fund" falls into the same "pressure" category. Each member is supposed to pay 1s. a month. If he fails to do so, the light of his spirit will not remain burning (hence the name), and he will not go to Heaven. The names of the contributors are written in the "Book of Life", in order, it is said, to let God see the names of those really faithful. Because of his great influence over his followers Shembe, whenever he was in need of money, could ask each of his more wealthy followers to give him a pound. Before going on a journey he would also, as a matter of course, receive donations.

G. K——, when starting his Salem Church at N—— told the community that "*Izwi*", the Word of God, had in a dream directed that every kraal should deliver one beast to the Church. K—— would enter the cattle-kraal and point out the beast required and the contribution was the more readily given as the prophet promised that any kraal that gave him a beast would never lack meat.

In the Ethiopian Churches exhortation to give is chiefly founded on Biblical teaching about stewardship. In certain cases it is linked up with severe threats to the disobedient. In the printed programme of invitation for "The Final 30th Conference of the Christian Brethren Assembly", 1941, it is stressed that ministers and evangelists have to come to the Conference with the Annual payments of £1, 10s., 8s., and 2s. 6d. due from members. Defaulters are referred to a study of Deut. 16: 16; Matt. 21: 19; and Heb. 6: 8. The last of these Bible references has it: "If [the land] beareth thorns and thistles, it is rejected and nigh unto a curse; whose end is to be burned."

(c) Integrating and disintegrating forces in the relationship between leader, nucleus and Church

A systematic exposition of the factors which integrate the Church, be it of Ethiopian or Zionist type, should begin with the secession crisis, seeking to discover what serves as a cohering cement in the new group when it first appears. The wider problems arising out of such a situation have been thoroughly discussed in American social psychology, and in passing I remind the reader of the arguments involved. Sumner has shown that peace within the "we-group" and hostility against the "others-group" seem to be correlated factors.[30] Dollard makes an important contribution when, qualifying Sumner's statement, he demonstrates that aggressive responses are often merely displaced from "in-group" members and find substitute targets in the "out-group".[31] But in colour-obsessed South Africa the dividing line between White "out-group" and Black "in-group" will, ad hoc, be felt as too sharp and distinct for any Bantu "in-group" frustration to be acutely felt in the actual secession crisis.

Thus, in the memorable crisis in the Transvaal Methodist Church of 1932–33, the outcome of which was the Bantu Methodist Church, anti-European feeling was certainly the deciding factor which integrated the new group into a more or less united group (see p. 172). Another element which may integrate the group at the beginning is the apocalyptic emphasis in the message of the leader. The end of the world is at hand, and only those who join his flock are safe. The prophet enumerates certain visions which he has seen: blood, epidemics, wars, on the pattern of the Book of Revelation. In many cases the apocalyptic message is correlated with the advice not to plough the fields, or work any more—as, for instance, before the eclipse of the sun in 1940—because with the end immediately approaching such effort would be in vain. Utopian references to some dreamland-Ethiopia into which the sons of Cush will be privileged to enter are of the same nature. The leader refers to himself in this case as the Moses or Nehemiah who will bring God's elect to their peace.

Apart from these elements in the content of the message, there is one formal element which must characterize the leader's approach in order to secure his initial success: he must place before his group a *clear-cut issue*. A local example will explain what I mean. A mission congregation in northern Zululand was hit by a serious crisis. Two evangelists, Titos and Luka, leaders of important neighbouring local groups of some 200 to 300 members each, had responded to rather underhand feelers from a seceding minister. The initial chances of carrying the whole of their groups with them were similar for both at the outset, and both were reported to be strong personalities.

Titos, the older of the two, a leader of the *chief*-type, called the whole of his congregation to an important meeting on urgent business. He reported to them that he had just come from the mission station where he had been told that the Africans and the Whites must keep apart and that the former must look after themselves. (This was a distorted version of the missionary's appeal to develop self-support and self-government!) Therefore, those who wanted to worship with the Africans should vote by a show of hands. He, Titos, would, he emphasized, take that course. Those who wished to follow the Europeans could show that by raising their hands. The result was overwhelming: only three were for the "White" side. The rest, between 250 and 300, were told to sign their names immediately in a new book. This clinched the matter. Before, their names had all been registered in the old congregational record of the mission; from this day they had all signed in a new book. The sudden appeal, the clear-cut issue, the fact that all went at the same time, and that their trusted leader Titos took care of their common responsibility made it easy to decide.

Luka, like Titos, was an energetic and respected leader.[a] But he was not as resolute as Titos; he did not call a big meeting to

[a] I met, fifteen years later, people in this congregation who called themselves "Luka's people", in spite of the fact that he had deserted them many years earlier.

have the matter decided. The matter was complicated by his child's illness (in Bantu Churches, as elsewhere, personal matters play their part). His wife more or less openly resorted to Zionist healing devices for her child's sake, but there was no doubt in Luka's mind that he wished to join the same Ethiopian Church as his colleague, Titos. When one Sunday he rather casually announced that he had left the Mission Church and wished to join the Ethiopian organization, violent opposition met him from the church stewards. "We do not want Zionist tricks." All the same some seventy-five people followed him into the Ethiopian fold, but when three months later he followed his wife's example and joined the Zionists, his group felt they had been deceived and returned to the Mission Church.

The comparison between these two men, the matter-of-fact leader who puts before his people a decision of "Yes" or "No" and carries them all with him, and the hesitant leader, *ad utrumque paratus*, who in the end is left alone, is a clear picture in miniature of the secret of group integration in the crisis of secession.

It is an experience common to all independent Bantu Churches, that as communities they need distinct *codes*, which every member has to obey and follow. Everybody in the same Zionist sect has to wear the same uniform in colours prescribed in detail by the prophet according to revelations in his dreams. Ethiopian Churches tend to be the more lax in this respect the more their organization grows. But as a general rule every Church uses its own distinct formulæ in worship, in the "free" prayer, and in sermons. The Israelites greet one another with a holy kiss and call one another "Saint" So-and-So. Customs about cutting or not cutting the hair; eating or not eating pork; the Day of Rest being celebrated on Saturday or Sunday; entering church with or without shoes; all these are rules which distinguish one's own particular Church and thereby integrate it as a group. Shembe introduced circumcision for men as a rule for his Nazarite Church, thereby reviving a custom which had been abolished amongst the Zulu by Shaka. Shembe-ites often refuse to shake hands with other people, stating that they cannot be friends with the unclean and the uncircumcised. Actually, the same codes are followed by scores of Churches, but the particular leaders and members are convinced that the code in question is *only* followed by them. The fact that the Methodist and Congregationalist hymnbooks are used by most of these Churches might indeed work against exclusiveness, but

163

to counteract this possibility the particular Churches generally choose only a few hymns which are then sung by them Sunday after Sunday, thus becoming their very own spiritual property. By such a restricted selection they distinguish themselves from others who use a few different hymns from the same hymnbook.

Further, these hymns are supplemented by occasional home-made local songs. These are not seldom full of contempt for other Churches, and they therefore strengthen the integrating "we-group" feeling of the Church concerned. I have come across Israelites who sing:

> Hold fast in prayer to your God,
> Do not pray to Shembe,
> But pray to Christ himself.

I was amused by the following Zionist ditty, sung in the district where I used to work as a Lutheran missionary:

> Lutherans, Lutherans,
> You do not know anything.[a]
> The Romans and the Lutherans,
> They are afraid of going to the pool.
> I haven't got time any longer
> to sit in darkness.
> John the Baptist,
> He baptized in the river.
> Amen, Amen, Amen, Hallelujah.

Lastly, in this question of codes and sanctions, it is their very naïveté which makes them really binding and profoundly integrating. The *studied* approach by the Young Intellectual, inventing certain devices as a sort of political plank for his campaign, is doomed to failure. He may have learned in America that African prestige is something noble and he may broadcast slogans to that effect. But if this approach is com-bined with an intellectual contempt of the uneducated, he cannot retain his following. The history of the Independent Churches offers many instances in proof of this. The half-educated Zionist charlatan who boldly displays his green prayer-rope by wearing it round his waist when he is together with his own flock, but who slyly and shamefacedly tucks this church emblem into his pocket when other people come along, lacks that naïveté without which an Independent Church leader cannot for long keep his hold over his people.

The function of the detailed codes, of the uniforms and the

[a] Play on the Zulu word *"ukulutheka"*, "to be a fool".

petty laws and taboos about behaviour, is on the one hand to provide a standard with which to measure the loyalty of the members and to make sure whether they conform to the group or no, and on the other to ensure that all members of the group do feel at home in the Church.

While the codes and forms of group expression are manifold and varied, the *sanctions* behind these codes can indeed be reduced to very few. The strongest sanction of all in South Africa—colour—operates against everybody who, once he has left a Mission Church and joined an Independent body, might feel inclined for one reason or another to return to the mission fold. One Separatist Church leader told me in an interview: "If my church people saw me speak to you, a White man! My goodness, they would hate me." This sanction, of course, applies to both leader, nucleus and the broad mass of church people.

The leader's will is another sanction of great importance. When the leader, as in certain Churches of Zionist type, is revered as a divine being, he is believed to be omnipresent. His photograph displayed on the wall is a constant reminder of the church's behaviour pattern. Of at least one famous prophet it is believed that he can see in his sleep; he has eyes on his feet, and through these extra eyes he watches, even in his slumber, the thoughts and deeds of his followers.

The Ethiopian leader attempts to enforce his will in other ways, as for instance by requiring all members on entering the Church to swear an oath of loyalty to him. Other sanctions include the fear of ostracism from the group, the fear of sorcery, and the fear of ridicule through not conforming to what the others do.

The various attempts made by the leader towards integrating the church are felt by him to be imperative in face of the strong forces which pull in the opposite direction. The strength of the Church is the result of the loyal interplay between leader, nucleus and the mass of the church people. The tragic fact about the situation in almost any Independent Church is of course that it presents the picture of constant expectation, or even threats, of secession on the part of the nucleus, and these anticipations in their turn perplex and *disintegrate* the mass.

This is intensified by the fact that the leader himself may be a prospective seceder from his own Church! X, who broke away from an Ethiopian Church of Congregational origin, started a Church in the 'thirties, but seceded from his own organization two years later in order to found a new one. He does not stand alone. A list of those Johannesburg super-intendents and metropolitans who have changed Church allegiances three or four times would, indeed, be a fairly long one.

Then there is the ever-changing factor of the nucleus. I give a local example, chosen from H—— farm district in Natal, where a Presbyterian mission has worked for a long time. In this particular locality an African minister, A—— of that mission, started an Ethiopian organization called the Independent Presbyterian Church of South Africa. The wife of one of A's evangelists, B, had some eye-trouble and was prayed for by Zionists; Mrs. B persuaded B to leave A's Church and join C's local group of Holy Catholic Apostolic Church in Zion, with a Zionist bishop in Johannesburg as leader. B did so and co-operated with C practising Zionist healing. C had become a church leader without having received any teaching at all, did not even know how to read or write, and relied entirely on the inspiration of what he described as the 'Holy Spirit' for his pronouncements on the Christian faith. C had, besides B, two evangelists D and E; D however decided to leave C's church because of a personal quarrel with C and was presently received by the president of the Christian Zionist Apostolic Church as a leader for that locality. E, originally a member of the Anglican Church, had been seriously ill; C prayed for him and he "became better". Because of his past in a Mission Church and his knowledge of the three R's, he was marked out for a position in C's Church where he was made an evangelist. After some time, however, E was at loggerheads with C over some question of money ("after all, I was much more learned than C").

I have known a man who went through the whole series of Church cleavages, starting in a Mission Church, and then via an Ethiopian Church of Methodist origin joined another Ethiopian group which called itself African Seventh Day Adventists, and in the end turned up as an archbishop of a Zionist group, with lightning magic as a speciality. The result of these ever-changing constellations of the local leaders is seen in the sense of *spiritual vagrancy* among the ordinary church people. I have known Zulus who in a period of ten to fifteen years, have changed Churches some six or seven times, and who only with great difficulty could tell me who their present superintendent was.

The most pathetic by-product of this church vagrancy is the emergence of *leaderless groups* that float around, as it were, temporarily lacking connexion with any Church and in search of some leader to whom to give allegiance. One Zionist group of some fifty people at E—— were led by Mngcube for a while. The heathen chief made Mngcube a headman, and as his new job took all his time he ignored his church work. 'His' Zionist group is in the process of dissolving into fragments of which some are attracted to heathenism, others to some other form of Zionism. X was another Zionist group leader. He had broken away from the Methodist Church; but he was a successful farmer, and "as he no longer had any need of the support from his church" he left his group to its own devices. As it happened, one Zwana of an Ethiopian Church passed through the district and he incorporated this group into his own organization. At N—— most Independent Churches had to discontinue their activities in 1940 as a result of the Magistrate's order. Some groups then tried to join Government-recognized Churches, but others were for the time being left without any particular allegiance. At D—— farm Sithole, the leader of a small Independent Church, had died. His followers were for a whole year undecided, discussing whether as a group they should join some other Church, or whether they should dissolve and go their different ways.

The result of such a development is what one could best describe as a *floating membership* in Churches of this kind. In fact this is not confined only to the little "leaderless" groups to which I have just referred. "Floating" membership is an apt description of the church relationships of a considerable outer fringe of Zionist organizations. They may join one particular group when staying in the Reserve, but find their way into some other Zionist fold when moving to the Rand. Upon their return to Zululand they may discover that their first Zionist group has been dissolved and they may become more or less fervent crusaders for the new light they have seen in Johannesburg.

Disregarding for the present secessions from Mission Churches and taking into account only those factors which lead groups to split off from Ethiopian and Zionist Churches, we find that they fall into three categories: (1) Disputes over money and property and struggles for power and prestige; (2) Sex questions; (3) Tribal issues.

(1) Litigation over Church money and Church property is common on the Rand. In many cases these immediate issues are only rationalizations of a deeper one, the struggle for power. Almost invariably they lead to the formation of new Churches.

(2) The question of polygamy often leads to a splitting of the

Church. A Zionist leader may tell his congregation that the Spirit in a dream has shown him two beds, and that this proves that he ought to take a second wife. In one instance where this happened one third of the congregation declined to follow his lead, and some minor prophet in the group formed a new sect with monogamy as its central demand.

(3) One of the most powerful disintegrating forces with which the leader has to grapple is tribal differences. From Johannesburg many Zulu Churches have extended their influence among other tribes, and the Zulu leader may for a while try to keep these foreign sections within the common fold, by such methods as putting a Sotho minister in charge of the Sotho section. These attempts, however, are for the most part doomed to failure. The breach between the Rev. Hlongwane (a Zulu) and the Rev. T. M. Ramushu (a Sotho) after only one year's joint work in the Bantu Methodist Church, was caused partly by a matter of tribal prestige; the latter is reported to have said: "Such an honour [that is, occupying the leading position in the Church in Johannesburg] should not fall upon a Zulu boy in my country."

The leading Ethiopian Church of South Africa was split over the same issue, Xhosa and Zulu members pulling in opposite directions. This issue has also played an important role in the struggles of such Churches as Tile's Tembu Church, and Mzimba's African Presbyterian Church. In the same connexion, one should point out that the Bantu custom of kraal splitting is evidently also a disintegrating factor in Independent Bantu Churches. This custom, which in regard to the Zulus has been admirably analysed by J. F. Holleman, involved that after a certain time the sons of a Zulu kraal left it and built new homes away from the father's place.[32] Of course in the patrilineal Zulu society certain definite bonds with the clan were still maintained despite this kraal splitting (*ukukhipha ikhanda*). But time and again the Zulu church leader of to-day, when tackling a threatening crisis of secession in some part of his Church, is told by the would-be seceders that they are simply following the time-honoured custom of splitting off from the father's kraal.

(d) *The dynamics of fission and fusion in the leader-nucleus-Church relationship*

By interpreting the leader-nucleus-mass-relationship in terms of social dynamics we find that, as far as Bantu society and the independent Churches are concerned, there is nothing to suggest any state of equilibrium.[33] Instead there is a state of constant flux and perpetual change, and as we shall presently see initial changes, inherent in the first secession crisis of a Church, set in movement a whole system of mutually interdependent social variables. And, furthermore, the problem of the dynamics of church integration and fission, which is central in the leadership issue in these Churches, can only be understood when it is realized that not only are the Independent Churches for ever changing, but they are moving within a politico-social environment that, in itself, is in a state of change. The problem of leadership and Church cohesion must be understood in relation to at least two enveloping systems, themselves both in movement:

(1) On the circumference there are the political and economic conditions of the Bantu in South Africa. The whole complex of increasing economic discrimination, which has hit the African with particular force from the Native Land Act of 1913 onwards, is made more acute at a time when education for Africans is advancing and therefore such discrimination is felt all the more keenly. It is important for our discussion to realize that this politico-economic circumference of the sect problem is not stable but appears to the Bantu gradually to deprive him more and more of outlets for leadership and organization.

(2) Within this system there is moving another constellation of forces: the increasing *caste* oppositions between Black and White, which influence also the relations within missions and within the Christian Church. We have to realize that this caste opposition in the Church is felt by Africans to be on the increase, an observation which is objectively correct. The early close relations and the practice of common worship between Christian members of the two races has been increasingly superseded by social distance which is spreading to ever wider circles of Europeans, and ever-widening circles of Africans.

These restrictions intensify among the Bantu the search for some outlet for their leadership urge, and influence the Africans' attitudes and valuations in regard to religious group allegiance. They have also introduced, in the individual and in the group, a state of mind which is burdened with *expectation* of ever-changing conditions.

Having thus attempted to define the dynamic character of the state of society, of which the ever-emerging Bantu Churches are an inherent part, I shall now proceed to describe in some detail the interplay of the forces which make for fission or integration. This can most simply be done by analysing the effects of the secession, forwards and backwards, in three stages:

Stage I—The initial secession, breaking away from a Mission Church, or from some Ethiopian or Zionist Church. This is the crucial point where all the forces shaping the following development are overtly or covertly present.

Stage II—Integration of the New Church, characterized by a trend of centripetal rigidity and occasional social separation in order to increase the integration of the main group.

Stage III—New crisis and new secession.

This is of course an over-simplification of the actual happenings, and it should be used with two qualifications:

(*a*) None of these "stages" is in itself a complete whole, and there is no necessity for Stage I for instance to be followed by Stage II. There are other possible developments from Stage I than Stages II and III.

(*b*) Stage III is of course not a *terminus ad quem*, but a transition point for development towards further possibilities.

Stage I—The initial secession

The *length of the secession crisis* is an important point. To the outsider the crisis appears as a sudden surprise, while it may in fact have been in preparation deliberately or non-deliberately for a comparatively long time. I call the non-deliberate preparation for the crisis *expectations*, and, taking a long view of the whole problem, it is obvious that expectations are of the greatest importance in leading up to a crisis.

There are at least three component factors which make up the expectations of further secession; of these the two first are latent and hidden, while the third may be more overt. They are:

(1) The tradition of Bantu kraal-splitting, referred to on p. 168. This forms, as far as the African is concerned, an indigenous thought pattern which acts both as a stimulus toward secession and as a rationalization of the split when it has come about.

(2) The general state of unrest and uprooting brought about by the impact of Western civilization on African society.

(3) The Protestant outlook on (*a*) the inevitability of secessions, which is reflected in an African sect-leader's retort: "We do as Luther did on October 31, 1517"; (*b*) the aim of missionary policy, as expressed in the oft-repeated slogan: "A self-supporting, self-governing, self-propagating church." Two quotations

from the speakers at the General Missionary Conference at Bloemfontein in 1909 are revealing—E. Jacottet: "Give gradual freedom to the Native Church, and it will eventually work out its own salvation"; S. S. Dornan: Ethiopianism "arose even where Churches had allowed the utmost freedom to the Natives".[34] It is easy to be wise after the event, and back in 1909 they could not see the paradox that the more there is of "working out of one's own salvation" and "utmost freedom", the more secessions will there be, *because* the accent is misplaced: the accent is placed on *self*-governing church, not on the *Church*.

When studying the life histories of independent church leaders one is struck by the fact that expectations of secession play a great part, as when the African minister is time and again asked: "Aha, I think you want to break away and start your own church, don't you?" Such a question does not appear in a healthy church system, but is itself a symptom that something is wrong. For a number of years I knew personally one Zulu minister who repeatedly was asked this very question, and who as often would reply that the thought had never entered his mind. In the end—and in a sense just because of this very fact that he was part of a system where apprehensions and expectations of schism were ever-present—he did break away.

It should be pointed out that expectations as to the future of a particular leader may be completely wrong. I know one African church leader in a South African city, pastor Z, of a Mission Church of the "Holiness" type (under European supervision), who is a great leader of men. As a preacher he is able to play on the feelings and moods of his followers as Yehudi Menuhin can sway an audience with his violin. His people, when giving their religious testimonies in a church service, copy his every gesture. More than any Bantu church leader I have met, he is a man who holds his people in the hollow of his hand. I knew that he was not happy in his relationship with the White superintendent of his Church. Z said: "There is no constitution, no policy, no place for the black man in that church. I want my right. But I was treated as a little dog, sitting in a corner, barking, and barked at." The expectations were of course that Z would walk out and start a church of his own, and most of his followers, probably, thought the same. But that did not happen. He left together with some 4000 to 5000 followers, but not to found a new African church. Instead he joined another European mission, of the same denominational type, where he was called "Assistant Superintendent" and where he was given more voice in the affairs of the Church.

Expectations, here described as non-deliberate preparation for the secession, later become overt in the *deliberate* preparation stretching over a shorter or longer period of time.

Generally speaking, we find that the leaders who after the break prove to be exceptionally successful, have prepared with more care than others for leaving the parent Church. They build up a following amongst the nucleus and masses of the parent Church and this may take a considerable time. Of great interest from this point of view is the crisis that preceded the formation of the Bantu Methodist Church in 1932–33, because it shows the consequences of an attempt to draw out the secession crisis over a long period of time. Cutting through the jungle of conflicting statements about that crisis I venture to reconstruct it in this way.

R., one of the leading African Methodist ministers on the Rand, had for a long time been working behind the scenes for the formation of an independent Church. The economic world crisis, unemployment and the simultaneous raising of the church fees in the mission church became the stimulus which set a hitherto unwelded mass of discontented people moving.

Certain group leaders within this discontented mass were sent to R. to ask him to accept the leadership, an appeal to which "he replied in the most sympathetic manner". But, as he expressed it, he "had to resign first from his Mother Church", which really meant that he was hesitant whether (a) he should at all leave his old Church where he had an assured position and great authority, and (b) whether, if he were to break away, that was the right moment, or whether he would not gain more followers for his future Church by biding his time. With R. hesitating, the popular movement in the warmth of its enthusiasm could not wait for him, and early in 1933 the Rev. H. was called in to act on its behalf. It seems to have been the case, however, that apart from H.'s special followers most people wanted R. and hoped that, when he did come out, he would assume the leadership.

H. with a great deal of flair for stage management—*inter alia* using a donkey as the symbol of the Church, hence the nickname "Donkey Church"—led the masses until, more than half a year later, R. gave a hint that he was available. He was then, in October 1933, elected President. H., however, refused to surrender the reins of power, and the outcome of this long drawn-out crisis—with its hesitation on the part of the popular leader, rash acceptance of responsibility by another man, and a general state of bewilderment in the masses—was the formation of two competing Churches, the "Bantu Methodist Church" (under H.) starting early in 1933, and the "Bantu Methodist Church of South Africa" (under R.) starting in October of the same year. Both are comparatively strong to-day.

The crisis of secession works both ways, resulting not only in a new organization, but also producing after-effects on the parent Church. One is apt to forget these latter; they are, however, important. Often the secession is temporarily felt by the parent Church as a *catharsis*.[35] "The lions went, and the nice little lambs were left", one missionary mused when looking back on a serious crisis within his Church.

The rationalizations of the schism which the seceding leader has nailed to his mast during the crisis have also an interesting after-effect on the parent Church. When the real cause for the break-away is rationalized in the form of complaints about too great financial demands, for instance, from the leaders of the parent Church, there may appear in the older organization a new willingness to carry financial responsibility for the self-support of their Church. If the real cause for secession is rationalized by means of anti-White propaganda, the after-effect on the members of the parent Church may be increased appreciation of the dignified order of service, the comparatively well-prepared sermons, and the unambiguous presentation of the annual financial reports in the "White" Church.

A serious and regrettable after-effect is an increased fear, on the part of African leaders and common people in the Mission Church, of any mission-guided attempts towards an intelligent *interpretatio Africana*. An Anglican priest from Zululand told me that when he suggested the use of drums in festival processions, many of his people objected in that it savoured of the Zionist's beating of drums: "Music, yes—but no drums, for the Zionists use drums"! Or again, if one Ethiopian leader, X, leaves another, Y, in the hope of gaining certain advantages by an accommodating attitude to Governmental authorities, it will produce as an after-effect on Y's church increased bitterness against the Whites—a typical example of what *Dollard* calls "displaced aggression" (that is, when "out-groups are blamed for the frustrations which are actually incident to group life").[36] Obviously, the general after-effect of secession on the parent

Church is increased rigidity and increased expectation or apprehension of possible new crises.

Not only are the reasons for establishing one particular Church different from those for the emergence of another group, but within the *same* seceding body there are, in the crisis of secession, different stimuli in different sections. The young intelligentsia within the seceding crowd may be dominated by nationalist aspirations, while the broad mass of the people may be carried away by some slogan or other. Apart from these sectional differences there are regional differences between groups in the City, on the farms, and in the Reserve, one responding one way and one another.

Stage II—*The period of integration and growth of the new Church*

The crisis of secession is the crucial period not only for the parent Church but also for the new Church and for what will happen in Stage II. In the secession there are inherent expectations which could not be solved in Stage I but will be dragged over to Stage II and present the main problem to be solved there.

The period of integration and growth of the new Church presents the leader first of all with problems of control and domination over his subleaders and common followers. The fact that in Stage I, we could refer to certain rationalizations of the secession as *displaced* aggression, shows that there are still conflicts left over. One successful superintendent quoted a Zulu proverb about the two bulls in the same cattle-kraal that fight one another. Among his subleaders the bishop may soon find that he has individuals with whom he is actually incompatible. This incompatibility was not felt in Stage I because for a time all aggression was displaced on to some common adversary, the European for instance. In Stage II these conflicts become overt.

Stage II of the new Church becomes above all a *conformative* period. The group is consolidated by becoming modelled on a *type*, through imitating the leader's inspired snort, or inspired speaking with tongues, or, when witnessing, moving one's hand just as he does, and so on. Here belong all those activities referred to earlier as symbols of a liturgical or taboo character.

But as some will not conform to the type, they will, through occasional casting out of non-assimilable individuals or groups, be cut off from the new Church (see the Genealogical Table, pp. 44 ff.), and may then either return to the parent Church or form a new body. Thus Soqhothile followed the others into a new Israelite sect which with gusto practised the New Testament custom of the holy kiss. He was grieved, however, when he was ostracized because, they said, he did not shave and did not blow his nose. And this, they alleged, led to certain difficulties in following the new custom as far as he was concerned. So he returned to his old Church, which apparently was not so refined as the new group.

The effect of these tendencies to increasing conformity as part of church integration is increasing rigidity—the hallmark of the sect. The trend towards rigidity, however, may only be followed up to a certain point.

One of the most interesting factors in the relationship between leader and mass is that in most of these Churches time and convention act as conservative forces, and eventually bring the leader to modify his radicalism. A constant struggle is fought for a re-adaptation of the ideologies which once were sufficient to integrate the masses but which soon become antiquated because of their very radicalism.

At the beginning of its short history the Holy Catholic Apostolic Church in Zion boldly proclaimed that to use coffins for burials was un-Biblical and only an invention of the Whites; the only Biblical and at the same time African method was to shroud the corpse in a sheet. After five or six years this group abandoned their speciality and conformed to the common usage of most Churches. At the outset of his activities Khambule was against the practice of Holy Communion, which, he said, was only the custom of the Whites. It took him almost ten years to conform to the custom followed by other Churches. He also taught in the first year of enthusiasm that, as the end was imminent, nobody should plough the fields. For economic reasons this appeal was outmoded in a year's time. Ntshayi-ntshayi was applauded by some when he started his Church on a programme of considerably controversial nature: churches should not only abstain from beer (*utshwala*) but also from *amahewu* (a soft, non-alcoholic drink or fermented porridge). Years of wandering in hot Zululand in the end convinced him that *amahewu* was after all quite Biblical. He retained most of his followers by adopting the less radical attitude. The necessity for one leader to accommodate his programme in order to win Government recognition or face the alternative of being ousted from his position, has already been referred to.

L   175

The man who persists in rigid radicalism and is perchance ousted from the leadership of his Church, thereupon starts a new Church and his sense of frustration finds an outlet in even more bitter attacks on the Whites than before. The aggression is in this case partly direct, motivated by his general attitude of frustration against the Whites, partly displaced, finding in the White "out-group" a scapegoat for frustrations which virtually emanate from the Bantu "in-group".

Stage III—New crisis and new secession

While the fundamental causes for subsequent separations are the same as before, there is in many cases a characteristic change in the rationalizations covering the causes. We have just seen how in Stage II the leader was faced with the problem of having gradually to retreat from eccentricity and to modify his radicalism. In the new secessions between Stages II and III the new leader will often naïvely appear as the protagonist for a return to *orthodoxy*. Thus when the Bantu Free Methodist Church broke away from the Bantu Methodist Church of South Africa in 1936, three years after Stage I in this case, the seceders complained that in the parent Church "a donkey is revered and leads its procession; this is repugnant to this new church body". When leaving the New Church of Christ, the leader of the even newer African Catholic Church of Christ accused the parent Church of teaching that Christ was born in November, and added with dignity that the new sect "follows the usually accepted date". Another Church may declare that the hymn-book of the parent Church was "never sanctioned" and had even been forbidden (the latter allegation is of course not true). Or moral reasons may be referred to: they leave the parent Church "because there people dance and sing whole night through". Another seceding leader may declare that the present office-holder of the parent Church has betrayed the intentions with which the founder of that Church started his work. The new Church is in such circumstances described as a return to the good old ways of the first Church leader. So, for instance, when the leader of the new "Gardiner Mvuyana African Congregational Church" (seceding in 1934 from the African Congregational Church) exclaimed in his Manifesto: "Gardiner Mvuyana is risen from the dead. Hurrah!"[a]

In Stage III the anticipations of change, "expectations" as we have called them, the complexes of multifarious aggressions,

[a] Cf. p. 96.

176

the formation of new sects at a pace and on a scale of geometrical progression, have reached dimensions which can no
longer be controlled. New stages IV, V, to the nth degree follow
one another with accelerating speed. This leads to ever-increasing rigidity in the Church formed in Stage II, while new
secessions with their resulting groups stimulate union schemes—
some abortive, some successful—to cope with the situation. A
few of the best leaders succeed in building up strong organizations in spite of these difficulties, but for the great majority of
the Churches Stage III is also the period of decline, atrophy
and apathy.

In Stage III the relation of the leader to the nucleus and to
the mass of church people becomes an ever-increasing problem.
We have already studied these relations in their more or less
static form: the leader's control over his staff, or the prophet's
direct connexion with the mass in the Bethesda type of Church
(cf. p. 155). The dynamics of the situation could perhaps best
be studied in a series of diagrams. Simplifying a complex of an
indefinite number of variables into a comparison between
leadership problems in the Ethiopian and the Zionist groups,
one could express the relation between leader (L), nucleus (N),
and mass or Church (M) thus:

(a) In the Ethiopian Church:

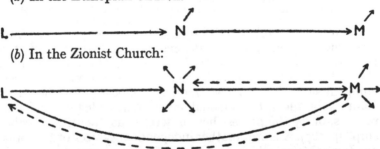

(b) In the Zionist Church:

In (a) the relationship is fairly simple, as the influence of the
leader over the Church passes mainly through the intermediary
of the nucleus. For various reasons, however, members of the
nucleus may revolt and start their own Churches.

In (b) the situation is much more complex, as the influence
of the leader is transmitted not only through the nucleus or
staff, but also directly to the individual members of the mass in
the "Bethesda" Church through healing and other means of
fairly personal contact. Here also the mutual influence between

leader and Church and between nucleus and Church is much more intense. This makes the organization gradually more difficult to control, and eventually a number of new secessions will follow.

But the full extent of the dynamics of the situation is only realized when this diagram is combined with the following picture of the situation:

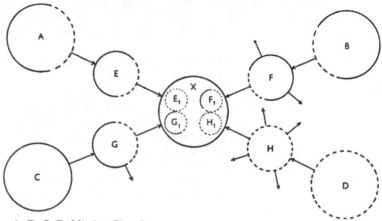

A, B, C, D: Mission Churches.
E, F, G, H: Independent Churches.
X: New Independent Church, formed by fragments of E, F, G, and H.

A, B, C, D are mission Churches with a sliding scale of inner cohesion and integration, dependent on varying Western traditions of church authority. E, F, G, and H are Independent Bantu Churches in different stages of integration and threatening fission. The arrows indicate opposition either from Bantu subleaders, for personal, tribal, nationalistic or religious reasons, or by the process here described as "floating membership" (p. 167). X is still another independent Church of Ethiopian or Zionist type which functions as the reception group for malcontents from the other four independent Churches. One important Ethiopian Church in a report to Government states that it consists of various Ethiopian groups which have amalgamated, *plus* "our portion of the Intercommunion church". This latter is an Anglican offshoot (in the diagram it would be G, for instance). The phrase "our portion of" such and such a Church is remarkable. It reveals rather better than any other explanation the "free-for-all" attitude general in these Churches, with constant expectations of fission, fusion, and—confusion.

In a segregated and "chlorocratic" society, as that of South Africa, the Separatist Church becomes an outlet for pent-up frustrations of the dominated group and tends to develop into a means of "reaction to conquest". Leadership problems become of primary importance, and the more so within a people, the ethos and "pattern" of which are characterized by a stress on the system of rank. Comparative studies—perhaps especially in terms of the "typological" school—of corresponding conditions among other African peoples may possibly reveal that leadership issues do not play such a fundamental role there, because the social structure and the contents of culture are different. In the leadership struggles within Zulu Independent Churches, however, the structure of the Zulu rank system shows its distinct features. Zulu kingship and chieftainship patterns as well as Zulu traditions about inheritance, rapidly supersede the democratic ideals professed in the constitution of most Mission Churches, or form a substitute for the patriarchal or hierarchical system prevailing in other Mission Churches. The study of Independent Churches provides— probably more than any other aspect of Bantu life—the opportunity for an insight into the role of personality and the characteristic trends of modern leadership among South African Bantus.

Bantu Independent Churches are an outcome of the political, social and denominational situation in South Africa. Without deep-going changes in these fields we must expect that the strong inherent leadership qualities of the Bantu will express themselves in terms of Utopian movements such as those described here. But when we Europeans lament the appalling strife and friction among leaders and followers in the Bantu's own churches, we should be careful to take our share of responsibility for the situation.

CHAPTER VI

WORSHIP AND HEALING

(1) WORSHIP

(i) *General Features*

Some of the most influential Protestant Mission Churches with which the Zulus came into contact were, in principle and in practice, anti-ritualistic. Theirs was a Church without an altar. The preacher's pulpit and the teacher's desk were all that was needed. And then there was the font. But the missionary was careful to explain about the font: what really mattered was not the water—because it was just ordinary water after all—but the word of God which alone made the holy act of the font acceptable in God's sight. But quite soon the font also became a problem. Other white men arrived from across the sea. They discarded the font and claimed that the river was much more efficient.

The African who left the Mission Church in order to build something of his own did not intend to make his new temple anything but a replica of that house of God where he had hitherto worshipped. "We do just as in Zion City, Illinois", one prominent Zionist leader told me when I interviewed him about the ritual life of his Church. The reasons for secession were of another order than liturgical. Separations occurred because of racial and tribal problems, matters of prestige and so forth.

(a) *Ritualistic trend*

Especially in the case of certain leading Ethiopian Churches there is an ambition to preserve the liturgical standards and forms of expression of the Mission Church from which they have seceded. The Sunday service follows largely the same order as that evolved in any Methodist or Congregational Mission Church—which in its turn is a copy of White Nonconformist services. There is a similar black gown, Charles Wesley's hymns are sung in the vernacular, and the collection plate is very much the same in Dundee, Scotland, and Dundee, Natal. It is not surprising, therefore, that the Tambaram Report, discussing forms of worship in the Younger Churches, endorses a South African statement on this similarity: "African ministers are ... very rigid in following European forms, and Christianity is

180

sometimes thought to be the White man's religion that must be carried out in the White man's way. Even the Separatist churches have not, so far as we know, contributed anything African to the form of Christian worship."[1]

This statement, however, needs very definite qualification. The ritual *interpretatio Africana* in some independent Churches has been brought to a considerable pitch of achievement. Left to themselves both Ethiopians and Zionists change their services into something which is very different from the worship life of the Mission Churches from which they once sprang. The African heritage shows itself in the fact that the anti-ritualistic programme of the mission is replaced by a tendency to move to the other extreme, to lay *a strong emphasis on the importance of ritual*. We observe here a tendency parallel to that taking place in the matter of leadership. In church leadership, the influence of the Zulu system of rank was strong enough to replace the mission's democratic Congregationalist pattern by a well-defined hierarchical system. There is a correspondence and interdependence between rank and ritual. Protestant Missions brought the Zulus into contact with a form of Christianity which was centred round a Book. The independent Church changed the stress and evolved a form of religion centred round a set of rites.

One of the archbishops of the Ethiopian Catholic Church of Africa who left the Wesleyan Church because of "strong desire to evolve an African system of religion, thus rescuing some of the Bantu customs and adopting the polity of the Anglican church", obviously had in mind that a richer and more colourful form of worship was more compatible with African conditions. The Archbishop of the Ethiopian Catholic Church in Zion, S. J. Brander, states that "he really missed the grandeur and solemnity of the Divine Services of the Catholic Church, during his whole life in the Wesleyan Church".[2] That is why he, as "Most Revd. Archbishop" of his new organization, stresses the "catholic" character of his Church in its liturgy and why he insists that each church building must have "vestments enough for the use of the sacred ministers during all Divine services, viz. cassocks, albs, chasubles, dalmatics, tunicles, stoles, girdles, amices".[3]

While the Ethiopians thus have a tendency to develop their ritualistic urge on lines which they are pleased to call "Catholic", the Zionists find outlets for this same tendency in more nativistic forms, above all in highly developed purification rites which I shall here bring together under the common denominator "Worship in Bethesda". They stress the importance of the correct ritual action, the correct ritual formula, and the correct ritual dress much more than the Ethiopians. But in their case the motive for this is not "catholicity" but the dictates of dreams and visions.

Whilst this differentiation is apposite in its broad outlines, there is in actual fact a mutual interaction between ritual tendencies in the two types of Churches.

My account of ritual life of these Churches is largely a study of the development within Zionist groups. Certainly one reason for this is that in collecting my material I naturally was more struck by the extraordinary in Zionist practice and found this more "interesting" than Ethiopian Church life which largely follows the pattern of the Mission Churches. But I should add, as a statement of a plain, obvious fact, that Zionist ritualistic practices exercise a very distinct pull on leaders and followers in Ethiopian organizations. The dream and the taboo are two of the most powerful influences through which many Ethiopians eventually succumb to Zionist practices. And in concentrating our interest on the latter we shall at the same time be able to study certain important liturgical problems in the Ethiopian Church and visualize what the future of the independent Church movement is likely to be.

Before discussing the nature of the different ceremonials that emerge at the present time in independent Churches, we give a few short *accounts of Sunday services*, snapshots which attempt to place the particular ritual elements in their general setting.

(b) Examples of Church services

(1) A Sunday morning service of the Ethiopian Church of South Africa, in one of the locations of Johannesburg: there is a din of church bells of various shapes and sounds all over the location. The minister whom we have chosen to visit has not been very successful in his work. Some years ago, he used to have big crowds flocking to his church. To-day there are seven men and four women and a few children in the tiny, dark room. There are no decorations of any kind on the walls. The preacher, a fanatical little man in a long black gown, stands behind a table. Two women, one of them the minister's wife, have hymnbooks and lead the singing. They continue to sing even during the sermon, which forces the minister to shout. The

preacher works himself up to a high pitch of excitement, addressing his congregation with a word from Gen. 24. He explains about Isaac and Laban and Bethuel and Rebekah. The question put to Rebekah gives him his clue: again and again he repeats with increasing strength and in a crying voice: "Wilt thou go with this man?" This question is explained as referring to the need for a leader, a man on whom you can rely, a man who can bring the Africans out of slavery: "Ye children of Cush, you people whose food is distress and whose drink is tears, you will not always be slaves. [Then with a sudden shout:] *Wilt thou go with this man?* You the despised children of Ham, you and I are going to build the city of Ethiopia in Egypt." The preacher fights with both arms in the air, sobbing, crying, shouting, and groaning, and the others—while singing—listen to this message of the glorious future which is in store for true Ethiopians. After a hymn one of the men in the congregation "leads in prayer", using the thoughts expressed in the sermon. After a unison "Our Father" there is a closing hymn. There is no healing service.

(2) From this Ethiopian church in the City, we move to the service of Christian Zion Sabbath Apostolic Church, in northern Zululand. We enter a kraal which has three grass huts and two sod houses. It is a hot day, and some of the Zionists who have walked for two to three hours in order to attend the service look rather exhausted. The prophet—let us call him Enoch Butelezi—rings the bell, a ploughshare, and the service begins. On the door of the sod house used as a church there is painted a green and white cross. The room, about 20 x 12 feet, is faced with daub. Mats and suitcases are piled up in one corner. There are no windows and the door is closed during prayers. One wall is decorated with a big placard, a picture in bright yellow of "Plymouth 1940" model, and on another is painted the name of the leader: ENOK BUTELEZI. Preacher and congregation sit on the floor, which has recently been smeared with cowdung to make the surface smooth.

There are sixteen women and three men and some ten children in the congregation. The majority of them wear white robes, some of the women have white veils on the head, and sashes of green or blue material or sackcloth round the waist. The leader has a long blue coat over his white shirt and carries a brass staff in his right hand. Only two people have brought hymnbooks but this does not seem to cause any difficulty, for when Enoch intones the opening hymn all join in with gusto to a rhythm beaten on a drum. Many of those present seem to know at least the first verse by heart for the simple reason that Enoch chooses the same few hymns every Sabbath.

The prophet intones the Jerusalem hymn:

Yek' iJerusalema
Umuzi okhanyayo.
(See Jerusalem, the shining City.)

Singing naturally in parts, they are carried away by the hymn, away from the difficulties and hardships of this earth, up to the heavenly Jerusalem. They begin to move their bodies in rhythm with the hymn, as if dancing. Two or three women "get the Spirit". They throw themselves about on the ground, speaking with tongues for a couple of minutes. The majority, however, restrict themselves to a few heavy yawns or snorts—"*ooh, hho hho hho*"—as minor signs of the presence of the Holy Spirit, reserving their more explicit display of inspiration till later. Anna and Othaniel are newcomers, they do not even know the Jerusalem hymn but sing their own little stave, "Amen, Amen, Amen" or "Halleluya ——". Enoch brings the hymn to a close by leading the congregation in the singing of Amen for a few minutes. Then he gets up on his feet: "Peace in the Church! (*ukuthula e6andleni*)." The congregation answers: "Amen." Enoch again: "Peace be in Zion!—Amen." This is the introduction to the *confession part* of the service (*ukuhlambulula*, to purify). Enoch: "I am thankful that the Almighty has allowed me to see this day. I have nothing to say to the Church to-day, but I am glad to see this day, and to see you all. The day before yesterday I was not well. I had a cold. I did not even think that I would be able to be here to-day—[with sudden rise of his voice]: Peace in the Church!—(Amen!) We ought to thank the God of Meshach, Shadrach and Abednego, that He has given us this day. My youngest son is ill to-day. He lies down. He has vomited near the river many days now, and we pray to God of Meshach, Shadrach and Abednego, that he will be fit again soon. Peace in the Church!—(Amen!) Last Thursday I had a letter from Abelina [a member of the congregation]. She says she is better now. They have prayed for her in Sophiatown [Johannesburg], and she is much better. She asks me to say 'Peace in the Church' on her behalf. Peace in the Church!—(Amen!) Amen. I have nothing else to say. May the Lord forgive me for that. Amen (Amen)." A woman in white robes continues the "purification": "Peace in the Church! Yes, saints of God!

Thakathile [another wife of her pagan husband] stole snuff from me. I was very angry and uttered bad words against her. But the anger in my heart soon disappeared. I threatened to mention her sin to Khumalo [their husband], but I did not do it. May the Lord forgive me for that. Amen! (Amen!)" Another woman: "Peace in Zion. Amen. (Amen!) A few days ago there was a terrible row in our kraal. One of my husband's wives hates me because he loves me more than her. She beat me with a stick, just here, on the forehead. And I bit her on the ear. May the Lord forgive me for that. Amen. (Amen!)" A girl, thirteen to fourteen years of age, very shy, said a few words, but was completely inaudible, with the exception of the opening and closing formula: "Peace in the Church. Amen", and "May the Lord forgive me for that".

As nobody else seems inclined to speak, the prophet goes on: "Let us pray." All kneel in prayer. After a few seconds the room, which during the Confession has been comparatively quiet, is filled with the most astounding volume of sound. All are praying at the same time, attempting to shout louder than their neighbours, as if in an effort to reach God's throne in heaven by the very power of the human voice. Add to this considerable din the clash of brightly coloured uniforms and the heavy atmosphere charged with sweat, urine and the cowdung of this dark room with its closed door and windows, and the very intensity of the sense impressions can be pictured. Then is the time for the Spirit to be shed abroad in real earnest. Enoch himself and six or seven of the women begin to speak with tongues, all at the same time. Some beat the ground with their fists. One woman keeps rolling on the ground. Another woman who has not yet received the Spirit cries loudly: "*Woza, Moya, woza* [Come, Spirit, come]! Thou Eagle of Judah, thou who art great in Jerusalem, thou Almighty, thou source of the power that flows out from Zion—*woza, woza, woza!*"

This goes on for ten minutes. One after another begins to quieten down. Suddenly one woman, the drummer, intones "Our Father". The others join in the singing of the prayer, followed by "Amen, Amen" for another three minutes.

Enoch orders: "Present arms! (*Mayihlome izikhali*)!" A man in a long green coat takes a bundle of wooden crosses from a corner. Placing himself in the middle of the room, he intones a hymn: "Carry your cross . . .". All get up on their feet and begin to walk round the man in the centre. After a while he hands a cross to each one of the people. Even the little tottering children receive their crosses and during the whole performance they continue singing the hymn about the Cross. For the rest of the service each one holds his cross with his right hand. Enoch himself does not enter the procession. He is in a class apart, because he has a brass cross.

This leads on to the sermon. After the Arms ceremony there is a pause of a few minutes while Enoch is searching in his Bible for a suitable text for his preaching. The prophet fumbles with the pages of the Old and then the New Testament and then back to the Old again. The women are feeding their babies, and one of the men, for lack of anything else to do, yawns heavily, just to let off Spirit: *"hho-hho, hhooo"*.

At last the preacher is satisfied with his choice of a text, and he announces *"uMateu* five"—the well-worn *pièce-de-résistance* for this kind of preacher. He reads with some difficulty and much emphasis verses 13–16, "Ye are the salt, Ye are the light". Apart from one or two introductory remarks, the preacher does not further refer to his text. He is soon struggling with his favourite theme: "The time is short. You will soon stand before your grave (*uzokuma phambi kwethuna lakho*). Are you prepared to die to-morrow?" From time to time he interrupts himself with the formula "Peace in the Church"—(Amen). Twice he is himself interrupted by the drummer who intones a hymn. The congregation joins in the singing, and the preacher gets a much needed opportunity of finding out what he should say next. Suddenly the sermon comes to an end, and Enoch announces a hymn.

Everything so far, however, has only been a preparation for the real business that follows, the *healing service*. The prophet announces: "The sick, come forward!" One man and eight women, three of them carrying children on their backs, move to the centre of the room. Enoch approaches the little group of patients, while the others walk in procession round the healer and the patients, singing and shouting. The prophet shuts his eyes and begins to pray. He seizes one old woman by her arms and begins to shake her violently, beating her with his fists on arms and shoulders and shouting: "Depart, thou demon (*phuma dimone*)!" He now "prophesies" to the patient: "You are possessed by a demon, like a snake which first entered your womb and then went into the stomach and then to the head, causing a terrible headache." The old woman admits with an *"Ehhe"* (yes) that his prophetic diagnosis is correct in every detail. Enoch hands over the woman to the drummer who by feeling with her hands all over her body apparently attempts to press the blessings of the Spirit into her being. Still another prayer-woman takes charge of the old patient, praying for her in the same drastic way as the prophet and the drummer. Enoch the while busies himself with the other patients, sometimes chiding them with his brass rod while crying: *"Phuma dimone!"* Children are treated with rather more gentle methods. The prophet takes one in his arms and lifts it up to the grass roof, shaking the child to right and left. He cries a prayer to the God of Meshach and Shadrach and Abednego on behalf of the little patient who sobs in terror, while the child's mother stands beside him swaying her body to the rhythm of the hymn and singing happily "Amen, Amen, Amen".

(3) *Shembe's amaNazaretha Church.* Sabbath service at Ekuphakameni, the Mecca of the Church.

For weeks the Nazarites—some 1500 of them—have been living together at this place, coming from all over Natal, Zululand and even Swaziland and Pondoland, to take part in the annual "July" festival. The climax of the festival is from Thursday to Sunday in the last week. On Thursday evening there is the Washing of the Feet and the Passover. On Friday and Sunday dances are held. On Saturday all congregate in the "Paradise", an open space in the centre of Ekuphakameni. The Paradise is divided into two parts, the upper for men and the lower for women. All are dressed in white, only a few of the priests wear long blue vestments. When "The Servant" himself —Johannes Galilee Shembe—arrives in the middle of the service he is all in black, wearing his father's black veil round his head. There reigns a dignified quietness throughout the service, contrasting with the vivid gaiety of the dancing on Friday and Sunday. The Sabbath service—with its lengthy exhortations on the keeping of the Sabbath and the observance of the *hlonipha* (rules of the Zulus)—is read by priests and congregation. Free prayer follows with all taking part at the same time, but there is no hysterical shouting.

Then some testimonies by various people. The first man starts off by putting a rhetorical question: "Who is going to open the Gate? There is only one who can open the Gate for us Zulus. Therefore, ye Senzangakhona's people, come to Ekuphakameni. There is nobody whom the Lord of Ekuphakameni loves as much as you, Nazarites. Do not waste your money on medicines. Come here and you will be healed for nothing."

No. 2: "My spirit is small (*umoya wami umncane*). I shiver

when I speak here to-day. Because the God of Ekuphakameni is great, and nothing can be compared with Him. I was a cripple once. I lost everything. My five children died. I lost all my children, all my cattle, all my money. Then I saw the God of Ekuphakameni, the Lord of the Sabbath, with my own eyes. Here I am standing at the Gates of Ekuphakameni. And trembling, I ask myself: Am I written in the Book of Life?"

No. 3: "We must all search for the Key with which to open the Gate. Whoever you are, remember there is only one Key. I had a dream. A voice told me: You are called.—By whom? You are called by the Man of God [meaning Isaiah Shembe]. I saw the Man of God. He looked very sad. But he gave me the Key. We are here to buy the Key, so that we will be able to enter. If you have not the Key, you cannot enter." After this follows the Servant himself, Johannes Galilee Shembe. His testimony lasts one solid hour. He refers to the hardship their church has passed through, how "their enemies had prophesied that, ha ha ha, that church will soon come to an end." (This is a quotation from his father's hymn No. 160, where these same words appear.) The preacher shows the value of their message which presents God as a living and real God, "a God with arms and legs, and love and compassion". He is himself a proof of the value of healing by faith: "As a teacher I was of poor health. I had difficulties in standing the whole day at the blackboard. But one night my father revealed himself to me in a dream. I told him: Father, I am ill. Then he put a shirt on my body. And at once all my illness disappeared. Now I can dance from morn to night, and I do not feel tired" ("a-A-A-men" from the crowd).

(4) *"Church of God and Saints of Christ", alias the Israelites,* in the coastbelt of Zululand. Ethiopian type.

The service starts at 3.30 in the morning. My watch says 9.30, but that is because I do not belong to this Church, whose members are Biblical and therefore observe Jewish time. The attendance is good, some sixty to seventy people are gathered. The women wear black shirts and black ties and white coats, and the men frock-coats. The Israelites are deservedly famous for their fine singing; the choir has a prominent place in the church. After a hymn the minister gives a short address: "The right day on which to worship God is the Sabbath, as it is written in the Book. To worship God on Sunday is not written in the Book. People who worship God on Sunday are hypocrites, for if they study the Scriptures they would find that they ought to worship on Saturday. The calendars show that this is true, because there the first day is Sunday and the seventh is Saturday. Our church is the Church of God and Saints of Christ. We do as the first Church of Christ did." After an anthem by the choir, the minister reads a Bible text and "Our Father" is sung by all. After that the kissing ceremony follows. The members of the congregation pass in procession by the minister who kisses them all on their cheeks. All those present kiss each other.

A deacon addresses the congregation with a few thoughts about the creed of their Church: "I thank God who has sent us the Prophet William T. Crowdy, who came with the plan of salvation, the ten commandments and the seven keys." (*Amen.*) He deals above all with "Grandfather Abraham", and the blessings they have received through him (this grandfather is a Negro bishop, H. Z. Plummer). The main thought in his address is the necessity of worshipping on Saturday. No less than twenty-one people follow him with short testimonies, all beginning with the formula of their Creed: "I thank God who has sent the Prophet William T. Crowdy, who came, etc." The choir, led by a young boy carrying a banner, passes in procession out of the church and round the building. They return again into the church, kneeling before the minister. The healing service follows. The sick are placed on chairs in the middle of the room. The minister lays hands on them, reciting Jas. 5: 14 over and over again. The service which has lasted three and a half hours, ends at seven o'clock (Jewish time).

(5) A "hot Gospel" church in Durban. A Wednesday evening service, 7–10 p.m.

At least half of the audience, 150 in number, are men—house boys, garage mechanics, office clerks, etc. Loud singing welcomes the visitor. The people in the congregation when singing mark time with rhythmic handclapping and, although seated on benches, move their bodies as if dancing.

The minister announces that the time has come for testimonies to be given: "And we will have a service of joy and happiness. Those who criticize are of Satan and have no business to be here." After the hymn "Count your many blessings", sung with gusto and more handclapping, the testimonies begin.

About thirty men and women come forward to testify. They remain standing for the rest of the service facing the audience. One of the leaders stands behind the speakers, telling them to

speak louder or to be short and concise. All testimonies refer
to miraculous healing. The sermon delivered by the leading
minister is bristling with stories and allegories, and is one of
the liveliest and most original sermons in Zulu I have heard.
I could now see that the mannerisms of previous speakers were
copied from the leader himself: the movement of his right hand,
and the tone of his voice. After the sermon some fifty men and
women come forward to be prayed for by the leaders. This part
of the service, lasting forty-five minutes, is trying for one's ears.
All these hundred and fifty men and women shouting their
prayers to God, banging chairs and floor with their fists, rolling
to and fro, speaking with tongues, and screaming, "Come, Holy
Spirit! Jesus, Jesus, Jesus!", must be seen and heard to be
imagined.

Obviously the pattern of Protestant revival meetings shows
through in some of the services here described. The influence
from Mission Churches of "Apostolic" or "Pentecostal" type is
evident in Nos. 2 and 5. But on the other hand the African
imprint on the whole is unmistakable. Let us, however, not
simply analyse these rituals with a view to putting the various
elements into different categories (Western Church *or* African
religion). These ceremonials *are* something new and unique,
they exist in their own right.

We shall here analyse some of the more important elements of
the services, in order to study recent developments and possible
trends, concentrating on the preaching, the praying and the
singing, and connected ritual forms, as integral parts of Ethiopian and Zionist ceremonials, and finally the problem of
so-called emotionalism in the service.

(c) *Preaching and testimonies*

In the Ethiopian church service *the sermon* still plays the
central role. It is difficult to characterize it in a short formula,
as the whole series of Protestant homiletic traditions—and lack
of tradition—is reflected in the new Zulu interpretation. In
1945 I listened to a prominent independent Wesleyan minister
deliver a "charge" to his fellow ministers in English. Both
thought and phraseology were a faithful replica of some English
Presidential sermon of eighty to a hundred years earlier: "I
warn every minister not to leave the study room for the pulpit
without having prayed first. . . . I beseech you not to preach
false science, but Christ, and Him crucified. . . . Our venerable

DANCING BEFORE THE LORD.

Isaiah Shembe, in sun-helmet and umbrella, leading the men's section dancing through the Ekuphakameni village.

THE PROPHET WITH WOMEN FOLLOWERS.

Isaiah Shembe paying a visit to the women's section at Ekuphakameni, the headquarters of the Nazarite Church.

ON HOLY GROUND.

Most Zionists carefully observe details from Mosaic legalism such as putting off their shoes before entering the church. Freedom from European footwear also makes it easier to take part in sacred dance.

father J. Wesley says 'Do not hate anything but sin'. *Skokiaan* queens are the very recruits of heaven."[a]

A short résumé of a sermon in an African Methodist Episcopal church may be quoted from a church report:

"The preacher took for his text the Gospel according to St. Matthew 10: 22, 'He that endureth to the end shall be saved.' The preacher told the audience how men fail to endure to the end. Paul and Christ were placed before the gathering as examples of endurance. Obstacles, he said, lie between us and the goal. He stressed the importance of endurance and heroism in the battle against sin. The preacher's whole deportment was serious, solemn and weighty. The house being thrilled, many came forth and knelt before the altar. Rev. M—— concurred encouragingly. Offering was raised and amounted to £3 2s. 7d."[4]

Even in Ethiopian sermons the role of the Bible is, however, rather precarious. Many local preachers are not able to read and they therefore rely on knowing by heart a few well-worn Bible passages to which they invariably return. The example of an Ethiopian sermon (p. 183) shows how the racial emphasis gives a peculiar bias to the interpretation of the text, which is often chosen from the Old Testament. Respectable Ethiopian Churches follow the pericope system of their (Anglican, Lutheran, Presbyterian, and so on) parent Churches. In this way a more varied choice of homiletical texts is assured. One of my Zulu evangelists told me that "the sects fancy all the holy books of the Lutherans, especially the Almanac," the reason for this predilection being that the yearly almanac of that Church contains a pericope system.

A characteristic *formal* element is that *shouting* is regarded as a vital requisite of good preaching. In all too many cases absence of sermon preparation is compensated for by a deafening volume of sound which is supposed to show the presence of the Holy Spirit. Upper-class Africans in the cities are however repelled by these empty shouting sermons, and are therefore becoming attracted to the African Methodist Episcopal Church with its better trained ministry, or to European Mission Churches.

An important development is taking place *within the Zionist church* as far as preaching is concerned. *The sermon is being superseded and replaced by testimonies.* This development is closely connected with the present emergence of one important

---

[a] *Skokiaan*, the Zulu name for a strong alcoholic concoction, cf. Hellmann, "Beer-Brewing in an Urban Yard", *Bantu Studies*, 1934, p. 55.

ritual element in the Zionist service: *the confession*. Being in fact only another aspect of Zionist purification rites, the confession as a means of homiletic expression is now accepted in most Zionist church services, and is also gradually entering the Ethiopian Church. In these confessions or testimonies a large number of the members of the congregation take part, publicly confessing some sin or distress and testifying to victories over sin and sickness on the pattern which has been drawn in the examples quoted above. There is obviously a tendency to substitute these testimonies for Biblical teaching.

But it is also in keeping with the general character of Zionist religious life that these testimonies have become *set in certain fixed formulæ*, differing in different sections of the Zionist movement, but all being similar in essence. A typical example is the following, by a young woman in a Sabbatarian sect:

Peace be with you, Amen! (Amen!)
Yes, my friends in the Lord!
When I rise, I have nothing to say,
But I rise to bring thanks
because I have been healed.
I am of good health now.
I have been revigorated by my Lord. Amen! (Amen!)
And His Spirit is living within me.
It is said: The one who is neither cold nor warm but lukewarm,
The Lord will spit him out of his mouth.
I thank the Lord, my friends,
because I don't even take enema or emetics.
I have been healed by the Lord!
Peace be in the Church. (Amen!)
Peace be in Zion. Amen. (Amen!)

The testimony has here been arranged in versified form. The reason for this is that the confessions and the testimonies of the Zionists have already become definite liturgical formulæ, uttered in a half-singing, half-speaking tone, which invariably has to be followed by all the faithful. In the name of the freedom of the Spirit, the serfdom of the formula is being definitely established.

(d) Prayer

Zionist public prayer is "free" prayer. The Zionist prophets speak with scorn of the Anglican, Roman or Lutheran Mission Churches which have to use prayers printed in a book. Ethiopians are also criticized because some of them take over these printed prayers invented by the Europeans. And as with "spiritual" preaching, so also with public prayer: it is in the Zionist Churches—as elsewhere!—turned into certain stale supplication formulæ, repeated over and over again, Sunday after Sunday (or Saturday after Saturday): "Thou, God of Meshach, Shadrach and Abednego", "Thou Eagle of Judah", "Thou with the wounded side (*nhlangothi zinamanxeba*)", may be formulæ used repeatedly in one Church. In another Zionist Church they may be somewhat different.

The most characteristic thing about Zionist common prayer is the fact that all take part in it at the same time, everyone seemingly attempting to outdo his or her neighbour in shouted supplications to God. Here is another important point where Zionist influence is gradually seeping through into Ethiopian Churches. While the Superintendent of one particular Ethiopian Church may be against such Zionist practices, a local leader may be in favour of emotional display of the outpouring of the Holy Spirit over the flock. In certain cases such conflicts have led to minor secessions.

(e) Hymns

The hymns as far as both the Ethiopian and the Zionist groups are concerned, have been largely taken over from the parent Mission Churches. The hymnbooks used are those published by the American Board (which is by far the most popular in these Churches), and by the Methodist, the Anglican and the Lutheran Churches. Some of these independent Churches use the Methodist hymnbook in predominantly Methodist areas, and that of the American Board in areas mainly Congregationalist. I have not taken a poll of the frequency of the hymns selected, but judging from my experience of these meetings I think it is correct to say that passion hymns and hymns about the heavenly Jerusalem are those most commonly sung.

The hymns, although translated into Zulu, are however only translations, and the tunes are all European, from Bach to Sankey. One of the most striking—and disconcerting—examples of the White man's dominance even in spiritual matters over his Zulu co-religionists is this fact that Zulu Christians have not felt led to express their new faith in the composing of songs and hymns of their own, whereas this is quite common in certain Mission Churches in East Africa. Dr. B. W. Vilakazi has well pointed to the important contributions of P. J. Gumede and N. Luthuli in the *"Amagama okuhla6elela"* (*American Board Hymnbook*). But their influence was limited. "After these two there is a great break, up to now. The field of hymns seems to be dead."[5]

For want of their own original African hymns, the "Israelites" extensively practise the singing of Bible verses to some well-known Zulu tune. The leader intones the first words and the members of the congregation follow suit, all at the same time moving their bodies to the dancing rhythm of the tune. The words from the Bible are, of course, not always quoted very carefully. They are more often improvised for the occasion.

So, for instance:

> On the Mount of Zion, I saw the Lamb
> And with it were the forty-four thousand.
> On their foreheads they had the names
> of the Father and the Son and the Spirit.

or

> Rejoice and jubilate, ye Israelites,
> for rich is your reward in heaven.
> For this is the way in which the prophets
> Who went before you, were persecuted.
> I thank the Lord who sent us William S. Crowdy,
> and the ten Commandments and life and salvation.

The verse is brought to an end by a few minutes' hearty singing of Halleluya's and Amen's to the same Zulu tune.

Dr. Vilakazi's statement in 1938, that "the field of hymns seems to be dead", was more or less true so far as the orthodox Churches were concerned. But at the same time there appeared collections of some of the most remarkable hymns ever published in Zulu, Isaiah Shembe's *Izihla6elelo*. Some were printed in John L. Dube's biography of Shembe in 1937, and the whole of his output, 222 hymns in all, in the *Izihla6elelo zama Nazaretha*, published in 1940.

Shembe was deeply conscious that his hymns were inspired. Shembe Jr. explained to me that his father sometimes had auditions of a girl's voice singing the hymn, and immediately after the audition he would write it down. (Shembe Jr., who also writes hymns—see Nos. 223–26 in the *Nazarite Hymnbook* —says that the inspiration of his hymns comes through visions: in his dreams he sees a blackboard being lowered before his eyes. On this blackboard the hymn is inscribed, and the visionary has only to copy it from memory.)

194

Shembe's hymns deserve our close attention, both because of their formal qualities, and because of the contents. "The field of hymns among the Zulus seems to be dead." This decline I believe, is largely caused by the foreign prefabricated stuff with its cheap verse-making (and its horrid tendency to over-work certain rhymes such as *"sonke-nonke"*, *"lami-6ami"*, *"mina-thina"*, various personal and possessive pronouns). Shembe's hymns have a freshness and immediacy born out of deep religious experience. Often there is a chorus following each verse. The prophet as a precentor sings the verse and the illiter-ate mass of the church respond by joining in the easily learned chorus—a formal element of great importance in a Church of this kind:

> Our Father, who art in heaven!
> I am in Thy kingdom.
> May Thy name
> be kept holy!
>
> *Chorus:* May Thy spirit come, O King
> And give life to Thy people.

One oft-repeated key-word gives its peculiar character to each verse in certain hymns:

> *Tha6ani Tha6ani,*
> Bufikile u6uNazaretha.
> (No. 208)

Some of the hymns expressly describe themselves as dance hymns:

> Ngo sina nginethemba
> Ngiyintombi yomNazaretha,
> Angiyikwesa6a lutho
> Ngo6a mina ngiphelele.[a]

And some are in their whole structure nothing but Zulu dancing songs:

> Wo kusile!
> Wo kusile Zulu!
> Wena Uthi makahlome!
> U Simakade!

[a] Literal translation:
> I shall dance, I have hope
> I am a Nazarite girl.
> I do not fear anything,
> because I am perfect.

From the point of view of the contents of the hymns, Shembe's production is easily the most important source-book that we have for the study of the emergence of Bantu syncretism in the independent Churches. There is, of course, a strong Zulu nationalistic note in the hymns.

> Africa, rise!
> And seek thy Saviour.
> Today our sons and daughters
> are slaves.
>
> (No. 46)

The meaning of the term "Saviour" in this particular setting is certainly not Biblical. As we shall see in Chapter VII (Black Christ)—where the syncretistic message of Shembe's hymns will be evaluated more fully—these hymns contain remarkable evidence of a "Black Christ" ideology. It is characteristic that the three last hymns, attributed to Isaiah Shembe, are stated in black and white to have been written by him "after his resurrection from the dead" (emva kokuvuka kwakhe kwa6afileyo.)[a]

While other independent Zulu Churches so far retain the heritage of Western hymns which they have taken over from the missions, they may still within these limits find means of expression which make their worship genuinely African.

Herskovits relates a remarkable example from the West Indies of how the "process of injecting legally tabooed Africanisms into approved Christian procedure is condensed in a recording, made in Trinidad, of the singing of the 'Sankey': 'Jesus Lover of my Soul'. The song begins in its conventional form. After two or three repetitions, however, the tempo quickens, the rhythm changes, and the tune is converted into a song typically African in its accompaniment of clapping hands and foot-patting, and in its singing style."[6]

Zulu Zionist Churches could produce examples of a similar nature, adapting Western hymns to African forms of expression. The hymn is not first of all a versified statement about certain religious facts. The hymn is sacred rhythm. And the rhythm is naturally accentuated by the swinging to and fro of their bodies, by loud hand-clapping and by beating of the drum. The Western form of worship practised in the Mission Church is felt as an unnatural straitjacket. Quite logically, the Zionists regard shoes as taboo. With a quotation from Exod. 3: 5 they

[a] Nos. 220, 221, 222. In an interview, Shembe Jr. explained this to mean that the Risen Prophet had revealed the hymns through visions (izi6onakaliso) to some of his followers.

forbid their followers to enter the holy ground of the church with shoes. The actual reason for this avoidance is, of course, that shoes would hinder the faithful from moving to the dance-like rhythm of the drum.[a]

The wooden *drum* (*isigubu*) has, it seems, only recently been introduced among the Zulus,[7] but its use is felt by the Zionists as a definite nativistic means of self-expression. Its wide popularity among the Zionists has made the drum a symbol of their form of worship, and it is therefore rather looked down upon by Christians in Mission or Ethiopian Churches.

(f) Sacred dance

The sacred rhythm of the hymn craves to express itself in sacred dance. In this respect Isaiah Shembe has been a great innovator. At the festivals of his church there are certain days set aside for dancing. Different groups (old men, young men, married women, and girls) dance separately. The old women appear in long white skirts, the girls in short scarlet or black skirts, but are naked from above the waist, except for necklaces, and girdles of beads. The men wear kilts. Just as at the Feast of the First-fruits of old, a quiet stately dance with accompanying songs was performed,[8] so to-day the Nazarites dance at their "July" festival and on similar occasions in a dignified and quiet manner. The prophet himself, in kilt and white helmet, heads the dancing groups.

The significance of the Nazarite sacred dance has been expressed by Shembe in various hymns, as for instance:

Great is, O King
our happiness
in Thy Kingdom
Thou, our King.

We dance before Thee,
our King.
By the strength
of Thy Kingdom.

May our feet
be made strong;
Let us dance before Thee,
Eternal.

[a] Interviewed about the points on which his church differed from other churches, Shembe Jr. replied: "We do not take medicine, we do not drink beer, we do not wear shoes in church, and we celebrate Holy Communion during the night." In fact, most Zionist Churches claim to adhere to the same rules.

Give ye praise,
all Angels
to Him alone
who is worthy of praise.
(No. 112)

Through Shembe's influence, the practice of the sacred dance is rapidly spreading among Zionist Churches. It also is an integrating part of "Bethesda" purification rites: when prophet and novices proceed to the Bethesda pool in the morning, they do so dancing, and they transmit spiritual power to their patients by dancing in procession round them. R. R. Marett's phrase about primitive religion being "not so much thought out as danced out", has its bearing also on the Nazarite form of Church.[9]

Praying and singing, drumming, dancing and shouting are intensified during the special services that are held from time to time in both Zionist and Ethiopian churches, the so-called "watch" (umlindelo). These nightly services are very popular and have a remarkable tendency to make people forget their denominational differences, for all in the vicinity come together. Here also is one of the channels through which Zionist practices flow into the Ethiopian groups and, incidentally, sometimes also into the Mission Churches. The service may last from nine or ten o'clock in the evening, usually on Saturday night, until dawn the following morning. All pray at the same time, and the Spirit is mightily shed abroad in the tense and thick atmosphere. There is speaking with tongues, and the sick are prayed for. The flickering light from a small kerosene lamp is reflected in the white and blue and green colours of the sacred dresses of those taking part. Hymns about the Heavenly Jerusalem are sung to the rhythm of the drum, and swaying their bodies to this tune the faithful are lifted above the frustrations and hardships of this bitter world.

(g) Religious festivals

The ideal setting for the hymns, dances and other ritual elements here described is the religious festival. The Nazarite church year oscillates between two great festivals, the "July festival", at the Mecca of the Church, Ekuphakameni, eighteen miles north of Durban; and the "January festival" on the Nazarites' holy mountain, Nhlangakazi (also in southern Natal).[a]

[a] The "July festival", lasting some three weeks, is very elaborate, comprising healing services, and leading up to the final days with dancing, preaching, and the passover (with the "Washing of the Feet" as a central rite). The "July" rites have been referred to in some detail, pp. 228 ff.

In 1916 Isaiah Shembe received a revelation that he, like Moses of old, would meet God on a holy mountain. The yearly, two-weeks' festival on the Nhlangakazi mountain, as distinct from other rites and festivals of the Church, is surrounded by an atmosphere of great secrecy.[10] When on the fifteenth of January the long procession of white-clad Nazarites—anything from 500 to 1000 in number—has reached the top of the mountain, the prophet offers a prayer to God: "Listen, O God, I bring Thee Thy children, the followers of the Nazaretha Church." Grass huts are built half way up the mountain with separate huts for men and for women. It is a "Festival of the Tabernacles" (*umkhosi wamadokodo*), Lev. 23: 39–43. At the prophet's order the rhythm of the drum calls people together. Some of the leading men run along the edge of the krantz of the mountain, calling upon all the peoples of the earth to join the Nazaretha Church. Facing in turn to the east, the west, the north, and the south, they call out: "Come to us, all ye people, let the Spirit come and send you to us!" This continues for a long time, until the sun sets. The two weeks on the mountain are fully occupied with prayers, healing services, sacrifices of various kinds (Exod. 27), dancing and singing.

Before leaving the mountain, everybody gathers *impepho*-flowers. These are put together in two big heaps, one for the men's section, the other for the women's. The heaps of *impepho* are set alight and while the drum beats its suggestive rhythm, all pass the fire dancing in solemn procession, and inhaling the fragrant smoke—thus also in this respect combining Old Testament and Zulu religion. The *izangoma*-diviners used to inhale the smoke from the *impepho*-plant in order to increase their divining powers, and the Scriptures give instructions to the leader of the church "to make an altar to burn incense upon" (Exod. 30). The whole *ensemble*—the offering, the sacrifices, the hymns, the rhythm of the drums, the dancing, and above all the presence of the healing prophet himself on that high and holy mountain—creates an atmosphere which surpasses anything else in Nazarite ritual. The service on the mountain brings them very near to heaven, they feel.

Other Zionist Churches also have their Festival of the Tabernacles on their particular Zions, that is, some Zulu hilltop in the vicinity or far off, as shown by the directions given them in dreams. These are "Zion-festivals" *par préférence*. They vary in their individual forms, but as a rule include sacrifices of goats or beasts for healing and are generally one of the strongest agents for the increased nativistic tendency of Zionist ritual life.

(h) Emotionalism and possession

I have already used the term "emotionalism" to characterize the atmosphere of Zionist ritual. That word must, however, be carefully qualified lest it be misleading.

There are some influences of American sawdust-trail technique in the emotionalism of the independent Church. In the "hot Gospel" service, described on page 189, one of the leaders stands behind the row of thirty confessing men and women, directing their activities—an arrangement copied from the White Church of the same denominational name. In certain Churches, like the *A6azalwane* (Brethren), the faithful readily resort to shedding tears, especially when praying for the sick. This relation between religious feeling and the lachrymal glands is definitely a European influence. It is, however, of very limited importance and it does not appear in the great majority of Zulu independent Churches.

Anticipating here subsequent conclusion, we should point out that what to the European appears as religious emotionalism, is actually a variety of stages of Christianized *possession*. Certain conditions are especially favourable for producing these effects: night-time services, dancing, immersion in a pool or under a waterfall, praying for the sick. On these occasions the hidden depths of repressed African possession come to the surface in the form of speaking with tongues, and shouting in the Spirit. From the Zionist's point of view it is all part of his mighty effort to drive out demons. But they are driven out with the finger of traditional Zulu religion.

(ii) Worship "in Bethesda"

The student of the Negro Church in the New World is impressed by the great strength of the Baptist movement. Various explanations of the attractive power which this religious group exercises on the Negro's mind have been given, apart from the important role of the Baptists for the liberation of Negro slaves. The most common argument is this:

> The Negro fastened at once upon the Baptist precedent as giving him his best pattern on which to organize his own churches. The independence of the local congregation, and the absence of any elaborate ritual or involved theology, and dependence upon the Bible as seat of religious authority—these and other kindred characteristics fitted the Negro's temperament and needs.[11]

This argument is insufficient when applied to similar phenomena in Bantu Independent church life. As a matter of fact the tendency is the very opposite of the one here cited: what we see is a strong propensity to form, ritual, liturgy. In the name of the freedom of the Holy Spirit an elaborate and minutely detailed ritual system makes its entry into the church life of the African.

The American anthropologist M. F. Herskovits has introduced a new viewpoint into the discussion by the stress which he has laid on the role of the vital African past in the Negro's social and religious life. He has suggested that the Negroes were attracted to a rite of purification because it "tended to reinforce an initial predisposition of these Africans toward a cult which, in emphasizing baptism by total immersion, made possible the worship of the new supernatural powers in ways that at least contained elements not entirely unfamiliar".[12] The suggested importance of West African river cults as a background to this liking for purification rites is a somewhat startling argument which nevertheless deserves our attention, not least when we are concerned with the "Bethesda" cults of the Zionist Church.

Herskovits refers only to West African material. River cults are known, however, "throughout Bantu Africa, from the Cape to the Sahara indeed", as Willoughby asserts (*Nature-Worship and Taboo*, p. 2). It is the thesis of this section on "Worship in Bethesda" that the propensity of the Zulu Zionist to total immersion is intimately linked up with traditional Zulu ritual practices in streams and pools. These tendencies have been strengthened by the Biblical teaching of the Zionist churches on baptism. Zionist baptismal practices do, in fact, show the confluence of different streams of myth and rite, heathen and Biblical. The Zulu Jordan is, as it were, the River of Life which like an artesian well springs to the surface in the various purification rites of the Zionist Church.

(a) Baptism and purification rites

Worship in the Zulu Bethesda is not a fortuitous conglomeration of disparate ritual elements, but a well-knit system in which myths and rites fit of necessity together, and where beliefs and liturgical actions are organized around a single centre. That centre is the pool—the Bethesda or the Jordan. The Zionist Church is a syncretistic movement of baptizers.

Baptism and purification are their main rites, of which other activities are more or less dependent corollaries.

"Believers' baptism by triune immersion" as propounded by Zion City, Chicago, Ill., was taken over by Zulu prophets and their followers. But while claiming that "we are exactly as in Zion City, America"—as one leader told me—they have made baptism into a purification rite which cleanses from magical pollution, and thus it can and should be repeated in order to accumulate its healing and redeeming power.

Why are these purification rites regarded as desirable and necessary? Because according to traditional Zulu outlook (shared by the Zionists) there exists something called *imikhokha* —"a train of ugly, unpleasant consequences which a person brings along with him, e.g. from committal of some crime, or hot-bed of contagious disease".[13] The usual Zulu term for "unclean" is *uku6a nesinyama*—"to have blackness on".[14] This refers to people passing through critical periods of life as for example menstruating women, people who have recently handled a dead body, and so forth. The Zionists prefer the term *imikhokha*. Some forms of sickness, as we shall show in the chapter on healing, are regarded by the Zionists as demon possession. Both *imikhokha* and demons have to be washed away by a definite system of ritual purification.

In order to show Zionist purification rites *in situ*, I shall here describe one such service in some detail.

The chief character in the story is a prophetess, Dolosina Mchunu Hlangothi, living on a European farm near the Zulu-land border. She was baptized in a Lutheran Mission church, but when she married Hlangothi, who already possessed two wives, she was excommunicated. Some years after this she got visual and auditory hallucinations; she heard voices and thought she saw people or snakes. She was brought to a herbal-ist who cured her by making her an *indawe*, i.e. substituting for her earlier hallucinations *indawe*-possession. She also became a famous doctor herself, knowing how to cure hysteria by in-ducing *indawe*-possession in its place. After some time she met a Zionist prophet, Mateu Mthethwa, who prayed for her and overcame her possession by purification rites (*u6undawe 6ami 6aphela emanzini*). Following this she was possessed by the Holy Spirit, which she defines as distinct in its symptoms from her earlier form of possession. Through the Spirit she heard a voice telling her from time to time: "There will be a serious illness and wounds among the children". She paid no heed to the voice, but was very perturbed when another prophetess, Angelina, told her through prophecy that she, Dolosina, was called to purify children with water. Dolosina resisted the call and in 1939 went to a neighbouring town, Vryheid, to escape the responsibility that the call involved. There she was constantly haunted by a recurring dream in which a number of small coffins appeared. In the dream she would ask what the coffins meant, and would receive the reply: "Coffins of little children, and it is your fault that they have died, for you were not willing to obey the Voice." (Dolosina herself has had two children, the first died in infancy and the second is a weakling.) At that she could resist no longer. She started to purify with water, and her clients were chiefly children. At a night service which I attended it was explained by a Zionist prophet that in the past Dolosina had worshipped the *indawe*-goat (a sacrificial goat offered the ancestors on behalf of the person initiated), but that as a Christian she wished to know the blood of Jesus alone.

The purification service which was held in the month of February was preceded by a prayer meeting in Hlangothi's kraal the night before, starting at 10 p.m. Dolosina's minister, prophet Mthethwa, led the service. Short addresses were given by the prophet himself who, possibly for my benefit, spoke in particular about Dolosina's life and visions. The prophetess also gave an address. Recalling her early studies of Luther's Catechism she stressed that the water, in order to be efficacious, must be united with the Word of God. She said, she felt the work of purification to be a heavy burden, but she had to carry on. Others had tried to do this work for her but had failed as they had not the right power. Other Zionists who spoke on the same occasion pointed out that the pool which was to be used the following morning was teeming with dangerous reptiles, having many and hideous heads. Prayers were offered that Satan might be driven away and the water made clean and holy.

The "rope service" (*inkonzo yezi6opho*) followed. Each mother had a grass rope, about two yards long. These were given to Dolosina, who in her turn presented them to Mthethwa. The prophet held the ropes high in the air and, shaking his arms, prayed: "Lord, may this which I hold in my hand, be blessed by Thee. When I bind a person with it, may his illness leave him." After this followed the *isiguqho* (kneeling). All the mothers knelt, holding their children before them, while

Mthethwa, Dolosina and two other women prayed for the little ones, shaking them violently during the performance.

The following morning at 5.30 a.m. the purification service took place in a most beautiful setting. The pool was situated among mighty rocks and just below a waterfall. On the rocks the leaders met clad in their picturesque robes with coloured sashes, and a mass of some 200 heathen and Christian Zulus of all ages came together. After a hymn, Mthethwa preached a sermon quoting as his Bible references the Bethesda text, John 5, three passages from the Psalms (29, 77, 104) which speak of Jehovah as reigning over the water, and the healing of Naaman (2 Kings 5). "Some might say that we should baptize in some other Zululand stream, just as Naaman claimed that they had two rivers in Syria with better water than in all the streams of Israel. Ehem!—well—I shall tell you the names of these two rivers some other day. [My presence as a listener made the preacher self-conscious, and as he was not sure of the names, he preferred to tell them on some other occasion when the European was absent. I asked him about the names after the ceremony, and he called them 'Abana' and 'Farpara']. But no! people of the Lord, it was in Jordan that Naaman was immersed seven times. And the Angel has shown me this our Jordan in a dream. Here we are to baptize and purify in order to let all your sins flow away."

He especially stressed how dangerous the pool was, full of snakes and crocodiles and all the works of Satan. But in the name of the Lord, he, Mthethwa, would enter the water and through prayer and ashes make it pure and holy and give it healing power. He would go into the water before the prophetess Hlangothi, because, he said, he was her head. Carrying a bucket of ashes he cautiously entered the water, feeling his way into the pool with his brass staff. One woman standing on a rock exclaimed: "We shall all die to-day. There are dangerous beasts in the water." Mthethwa prayed in the water: "Lord of Light and Glory, thou who reignest in the midst of the water, help us to kill all dangerous beasts that hide in this pool." With his staff he chased away the imaginary creatures, saying: "May there be peace in this water." He spread ashes over the water, praying: "We pray thee, Angel of the Waters, come with power and purity to this pool. Hasten, thou Angel of the Waters, and stir up this water, so that all dangers be removed."

Mthethwa then planted his staff in the middle of the pool so as to have his hands free to fill bottles with holy water for the mothers. About this time Dolosina also entered the pool. She took charge of the children, and no less than ninety-six children aged from one to seven years, were *hlambulula*'d. She received them from the mothers who were standing on the rocks, and holding them in one or both arms, without much ado she plunged each child in the water three times. Most of the children were terrified and cried in fear, the adults meanwhile singing hymns. Some of the older boys of six or seven years of age tried to show a more heroic temper and appeared to enjoy themselves. This display of early pride was, however, promptly extinguished. Dolosina forced these youngsters under water seven times—like Naaman of old—and at the end of this ordeal most of their arrogance had gone. Some of the children gasped for breath, which caused Dolosina to scold the mothers, saying that they had not confessed their sins. The gasping for breath among the children was the proof that the parents had not confessed. When all the children had gone through the purifications, it was the turn of the adult patients. The service came to an end at about 9 a.m.

The pool is the centre of this service in more than just the local sense. One Zionist bishop very aptly referred to his own organization as a "Water-Church" (*i6andla lamanzi*). A striking feature of these rites is the view held by all those present that the water teams with mysterious monsters which the prophet—another St. George in shining white armour—has to defeat in order to be able to do his work. This is one of the fundamental elements of baptismal theology in the Bethesda Church. Johannes Mlangeni, Shembe's right-hand man, told me of his experiences at one baptism where thirty-seven people were baptized; the pool was very deep and the water appeared at times extremely cold, at other times almost unbearably hot: "The two last baptizees slipped out of my hands, drawn into the depths by tremendous snakes. But with God's help I overcame those snakes." In the same way, he said, Shembe himself had had to struggle with river monsters on the occasion of a baptism at Nhlangakazi. Nor is this belief restricted to the backward areas of the Reserves. In 1943 it happened at Orlando (Johannesburg) that a Zionist bishop, after having prayed for and blessed the pool, threw himself into the water lifting his pastoral staff as a spear, resolved to kill Satan who hid deep in the baptismal pool in the appearance of a fearful monster. His followers now tell that their bishop fought valiantly with Satan but was caught under a rock in the pool and was drowned—

overcome by the snake.[15] It is characteristic that the entering of the pool is always supposed to be a dangerous and awe-inspiring act. In a hymn quoted above (p. 164) I have pointed out that Zionists in northern Zululand sing of Lutherans and Romans as *being afraid* of entering the water. This fear is said to be not an aversion from water as such but the terror of lurking river monsters. Obviously these monsters are identical with those known by traditional Zulu folklore: *isiququmadevu* or *ugungqukubantwana* or *usilosimaphundu* or *isitshakamana* or *umnyama*.[16] The prophet's struggle with the monster can be seen to be related to the diviner's search for white earth which he finds under the *inhlwati*-snake in the pool. But we should also remember that the pool and the snake are extremely common stereotyped symbols in Zionist dream life. To the student of Freud's pyscho-analysis it seems evident that the water symbolism in the Bethesda Church, where women stay at the prophet's kraal to be cured principally of barrenness, has a hidden but very real sexual meaning.

Whether it is a matter of baptism or of other purification rites, the water must be prepared by prayer in order to make it efficacious. This prayer is referred to by a technical term meaning "prayer for the water" (*umkhuleko wamanzi*) or the blessing of the pool, which, as a matter of course, includes exorcism of the demoniac monsters in the water. In many cases the purifying power of the water is increased by the fact that the prophet, as a preparation, walks round the pool pointing at it with his specially purified white-coloured holy sticks or "weapons" (*izikhali*).

The prophet implores the "Angel of the Waters" to help him in his struggle against the monsters of the pool. The idea of an Angel of the Waters reminds one of a verse in the Bethesda-text, John 5: 4, where it is mentioned that "an angel went down at a certain season into the pool, and troubled the water". It is, however, not at all certain that prophet Mthethwa had received his idea from this Bible passage. As a matter of fact, this verse does not appear in the Zulu translation of the Bible. Mthethwa did not know a word of English so that he can hardly have got it from the Authorized Version.

Anticipating the discussion of the relation between angel and ancestral spirit in Chapter VII, I should infer that the water-angel in this case is the Christianized version of the ancestor-spirit in its function as a guardian of the pool. Dr. E. W. Smith has shown that among the Ba-ila the ghost of the

MRS. NKU.

Mrs. Nku, or Ma Nku, is the head of St. John's Apostolic Faith Mission.

BAPTISM IN ZULU JORDAN.

The bundle of palm leaves stresses the River Jordan connotations.

THE HEALING TOUCH.

Rev. J. J. Magangane used to be cleaner in a Johannesburg garage. Here he is seen praying for some of his flock, in a Sunday afternoon open-air service, just off Pretoria road, near Johannesburg.

ancestors is regarded as the guardian of the pool.[17] The Zionists claim that the Spirit can nowhere be experienced so effectively as in the pool: "If a person is not filled with the Spirit any longer, we just bring him to the pool. There the Spirit (*uMoya*) will re-enter him, and with new force." "Spirit" and "angel" are here used indiscriminately; essentially the latter concept is evolved out of the former. Willoughby was able to fix "the exact point at which an ancestral spirit evolves into a Nature Spirit".[18] In the Bethesda-cult of the Zionist Church this development is brought one step further: the complex of ancestor spirit and nature spirit evolves into the "Angel of the Waters".

The pool used in the example just referred to was ideal, according to Zionist standards, because it was situated below a waterfall, and because it was deep. The terms employed in Zionist theology to denote the right kind of Bethesda-pool or Jordan-stream are "living water" (*amanzi aphilayo*) and "much water", that is, of sufficient depth (*amanzi amaningi*). The pool must be *deep* so that the baptizee can be totally immersed in the water. Baptism as explained by St. Paul in Rom. 6—a re-enactment of the Christian death and resurrection drama—is very real to the Zionist Church. The whole of the man must be immersed. This is why the prophets are so scornful about most Mission Churches where only sprinkling is practised. They point out that in most Mission Churches only the forehead is washed and purified, whereas sin and pollution cling to all the rest of the body. Such baptism is the "Mark of the Beast" (*uphawu lwesilo*), the beast being the White missionary. Their Book of Revelation tells them that the beast "came up out of the sea" (Rev. 13: 1), and whoever could that be if not the missionary who was brought to their land from the other side of the sea (*phesheya*).

But the pool must also be in a river, with *rapidly flowing water*, preferably below a waterfall. In this way one is assured that the water is efficacious in washing and rapidly removing sin, sickness and pollution.[a] The stagnant, dead water in the font or the dish (*endishini*) of the Mission Church is not efficacious. The "living water" gives the Spirit. Bishop M—— told me

---

[a] The question of the "living water" is a matter of constant theological discourse between the Churches. One of our Lutheran evangelists was totally against the baptism in a river: "Because, you see, if you throw a bundle of dry grass in the stream, it is soon removed and brought further down. The Zionist prophet prays into the water, but as the baptizee enters it, the blessing has already been removed downstream. It is much better with our Lutheran font. The priest prays into the water, and the water becomes really blessed."

that if a man feels that there is no Spirit in him, he is brought to a Jordan-stream. In more difficult cases he will be brought under a waterfall. There he will unfailingly be filled with the Spirit, which shows itself in ability to speak with tongues.[19]

Having thus reviewed the main elements which are common to both baptism and purification rites, we can now proceed to analyse some of the distinctive features of each.

The central role of *baptism in Zionist syncretism* is underlined already in their constitutions. The Rev. M. K. S——, bishop and founder of the National Church of God of South Africa, in Section I of the "Beliefs" of his Church lays down that he "believes the Old and the New Testament by the interpretation in the river". The most succinct and true-to-fact description of Zionist baptismal rites is presented in the Constitution of the Christian Apostolic Faith Assembly in Zion of South Africa: "We baptize the people by dipping them thrice in the water and let them confess their sins; after that we give them white uniforms and teach them the word of God and let them understand Amen". The "triune" immersion is imported from Zion City, Ill. Churches deriving from Pentecostal and Baptist groups are content with one immersion. Others again practise the seven-fold immersion, following Naaman's example. One prophet told me that he had himself insisted upon being immersed nine times, "for I was *very* ill, and three or seven times would not have been enough to drive away my illness".

In his work, the baptizing prophet is effectively assisted by the congregation. Some of the subleaders listen to confessions which precede the baptism, and others help by dressing the neophyte in white clothes after he has completed the "crossing of Jordan" (*ukuwela iJordan*—a technical term for baptism). During the whole of the ceremony the other members sing and speak with tongues. Only at the moment of the immersion(s) is there a period of numinous silence.

It is because of the central role of the rite of Baptism that John the Baptist becomes the most important Biblical personality in the Zionist Church. "We do everything which was done by John the Baptist" they constantly claim. When baptizing in a Zulu Jordan or going through purifying and vomiting rites in a Zulu Bethesda, when fasting on the hilltop of a Zulu Zion or putting on a sash of sacking (reminding them of the clothing of hair-cloth of the Baptist), they feel that they mould their behaviour on that of John the Baptist who is to them the ideal Christian prophet.

It is characteristic that in the quotation from the constitution of the Christian Apostolic Faith Assembly in Zion of South Africa it is stated that the threefold immersion comes first and the instruction follows later (p. 208). No organized Biblical instruction is given to the neophyte other than what he can pick up from listening to testimonies. The condition for baptism is not an intellectual preparation, as it is in the Mission Church where some knowledge of the Catechism is one of the main prerequisites, but the ritual act of confessing sins. This is also the reason why in certain Zionist Churches children are excluded from baptism: not because they have not attained a certain intellectual or spiritual maturity, but because "they do not understand to confess sins." They are consecrated or "blessed" instead. But the rite takes its revenge on this Baptist dogma: in the Holy Catholic Apostolic Church in Zion, the child is brought to the Bethesda pool on the eighth day if a boy, and on the fifteenth day if a girl, and it is there and then, not "baptized" (because the dogma is against baptism), but "purified" (*ukuhlambulula*) by immersion, just as in the purification service described on p. 205. Thirty-three days later, if a boy (or sixty-six if a girl), the rite is concluded as the minister "blesses" the child: "I bless thee in the name of the Father and the Son and the Holy Ghost." Two doves are presented to the Church, all in accordance with Lev. 12.

Baptism can be repeated, although no strict rule is followed here. If the individual believer or the prophet has it revealed to him in a dream that he should be baptized a second, or third, or ninth time, this is considered as being quite in order and does not necessarily constitute a precedent for the others. In one interesting case the prophet opposed the repetition of the baptism of a certain woman. She had had such a strong dream-revelation, however, that she should go through the sacrament once again that she would not be deterred, and for want of a baptizing priest finally baptized herself.

With this development we have left the domain of baptism and should speak of *purification rites*. The repeated baptism is the transition stage from baptism as a sacrament over to lustral ablutions. Or seen from the other angle: daily or weekly purification rites are the constant repetition and re-enactment of the death-and-resurrection drama in the baptism. It is important to study the technical terms used for purification. The pagan term *ukuphothula* referred to washing the body in water or anointing with grease, medicated with charms, and was connected with a complicated magical mechanism through which "black medicine" was replaced by "white medicine".[20] The aversion of the Zionist prophet from anything connected with medicine (*umuthi*) is reflected in his reaction to *ukuphothula*-rites, which he regards as demoniac. Zionist purification is called either *ukuhlambulula* or *ukusefa*. As a derivative of *ukuhlamba*, "to wash", *ukuhlambulula* means to "make thin", "to make a person free, loose, unbound", and in pagan Zulu religion denoted rites through which a person was made "free and refined of dross and imperfection, as an *um-ngoma* (diviner) from the process of initiation."[21] It is, of course, no coincidence that this term used of *isangoma*-initiation is employed as *terminus technicus* for Zionist purification rites, as the latter are dependent on the pattern of the former. But in this new connotation the term takes on a somewhat different meaning. The fact that the Zionist regards his purification rites as radically different from those of the heathen diviner is expressed in the frequent use of the other synonym for Zionist purification, namely *ukusefa*, a term actually formed from the Afrikaans verb "te sif". By using this foreign term, the distance from the pagan *ukuphotula* is indicated.

At dawn on Sunday (or Saturday) morning the Zionist prophet and his followers proceed to their Jordan-stream. After prayers and speaking with tongues, the prophet asks those who are filled with the Spirit: "What do you see?" They reply: "We have been shown by the Angel that So-and-so's robes are unclean. His heart is bad. We see that he committed adultery yesterday, or that he drank beer. His robes are soiled with red, the red colour of sin."

The sinner is promptly caught by those standing by and the actual *ukusefa*-ceremony begins. His white stick is taken from him, not to be returned for seven days. He is forced into the water, and while some beat him all over his body, especially on the shoulders to drive out his demon, others take a firm grip on his throat. After having been dipped in this fashion, three or seven or nine times he is dragged up on the shore. The grip on his throat is released and he vomits on the rocks, thus allowing the "bad spirit" (*umoya omuɓi*) to leave him. All the while there is a deafening din of singing and shouting and speaking with tongues from the faithful.

This procedure may be repeated with the same individual for one or several weeks. While the details may vary in different

Churches, the basic structure is the same in most Zionist groups, and appears in all purification rites practised by prophets and neophytes in their Zulu Bethesda. In driving out the "demons" from a person, by beating and vomiting, they attempt to wash away the complex of sin *and* sickness caused by this demon. Ritual and medical considerations are combined in the performance. The "living water" of the stream carries away all defilement.

(b) Confessions and purification

Around the pool, so to speak, around the baptismal and purification rites as the centre, the Zionist Church arranges its other rites, all being essentially purgative. Baptism or purification rites cannot take place without being preceded by confession of sins. The objection to infant baptism is that "children cannot confess sins". The confession must be complete, nothing may be hidden. If some sins are left out in the confession, the omission will invariably be detected because in such case the baptizee will, during the immersion, gasp for breath, and even be choked and drowned. This was the reason why Dolosina (p. 205) told the mothers in the case of *ukuhlambulula*-rites for children, that they had to suffer for this. The confessions are made in public, just before the immersion is going to take place, and are addressed to the leading prophet. No confession is regarded as complete until sexual transgressions are mentioned by the baptizee. Assistant prophets standing by, prepared to help with the immersion, will continue speaking with tongues or at least grunting and belching up wind (*ukubodla*) in the Spirit, until "the real thing" has been disclosed.

Confession is also connected with medical cure. To get rid of the bad spirit through ritual vomiting or *isiwasho*-enema will only be effective if preceded by a total clearing of the system of the person through the exhibiting of hidden sins. H. Webster has pointed out that among primitive people generally "confession acts as a real purgation, an elimination of evil matter in the patient's body", and this explains the appreciation of the efficacy of confessions in the Zionist Church.[22] The role of Zionist dream-life in regard to confessions is naturally very great. The confession made is probably in most cases thought to be dictated by an angel or the Black Christ himself whom the neophyte has seen in a dream-visit to heaven.

Isiwasho is the wider Zionist name for the various kinds of *purgatives and enemas* (water mixed with ashes or soap) used in connexion with ritual purification. The use of ashes, vomiting and purgatives, technically of course belongs to the chapter on healing. But they have also a very considerable ritual importance in Zionist religion. Ashes are connected with most purification rites of the Zionists, as indeed was the case in traditional pagan Zulu purification rites. The holy grove (*isiguqo*) in the prophet's kraal where the faithful meet for prayers is cleansed and encircled by being demarcated with ashes. The Bethesda-pool must also be cleansed with ashes. Vomiting is procured by forcing a mixture of water and ashes down the throat of the sinner or the patient, the ashes in this case combining a desired nauseating and cleansing effect. When the Zionist neophyte realizes that he has received heavenly inspiration for the first time, he will in many cases ask his Zionist friends to cover his body with ashes, "because I have been filled with the Holy Spirit". Any self-respecting Zionist congregation now has a special holy "Vessel of Ashes" (*isitsha somlotha*) set aside in the church house as a receptacle for its holy ashes. The role of vomiting in connexion with purification rites (*ukuhlanza*) has been discussed already. Zionists are convinced that by the process of vomiting they not only get rid of physical illness, but of spiritual defilement as well. The prophet, in order to meet the new day as a holy and pure man, begins at dawn by vomiting in a stream near his kraal.

In many Zionist Churches the use of purgatives plays a very prominent role. The European may regard a name like "The African Castor Oil Dead Church" as an inadmissible joke. When visiting the founder and leader of the Church in question in his house in Sophiatown, Johannesburg, I discovered, however, that the prophet was an enthusiastic crusader for the use of this purgative. The name "castor oil" stood for hope and new life—not unnaturally in a socio-economic setting where malnutrition and little variety of food (mostly starches) is causing indigestion and constipation. On the same level is the use of blue soap and blue stone which together with water are used as an enema or for washing the body of the patient. It is a matter of argument whether these practices should be discussed in a chapter on worship or under healing. Our difficulty of deciding into which epistemological department phenomena of this kind should be placed reveals a very important fact in the religious outlook of the Zionist prophet. He does not make the same clear-cut distinction between the sacred and the profane as the European. Obviously, his borrowing from the Europeans is selective. We would like to know what makes his selection as preferential as it appears in the choice of these medicaments. Why does he choose castor oil, Epsom salts, blue stone and blue soap, borrowed from the material culture of the Whites but not used in any of the ritual systems of these same Whites?

The use of soap in Zionist medico-religious practices is connected with the fact that the heathen *isangoma* (diviner) used froth (*u6ulawu*) in her purification rites, and something of the same effect of froth is obtained by using these European articles. But that does not give a satisfactory explanation of the matter which can probably be reached only by a psycho-analytic approach to the subject. In my opinion it is probable that in this preferential selection from the culture of the Whites is expressed something of the Zionist prophet's ambivalent attitude (aversion *and* admiration) towards the European. The soap probably represents White-ness both in a cultural and religious sense. Soap is also believed by the Zionists to be effective as a means of washing off one's sins in much the same way as confession of sins is thought of as a purgation and elimination of evil matter in the patient's body.

(c) Sacred dress

The dictates of dreams decide also the sacred dress of the Zionist. The close relation between dream and dress in these Churches makes this subject somewhat difficult. I do not doubt that an analysis on Freudian lines of Zionist dream-stereotypes about sacred attire and colour symbols would reveal very important secrets of Zionist psychology. For various reasons I shall, however, leave it to those of my readers who are trained psychoanalysts to draw their own conclusions from the material, and I shall here content myself with a more superficial registration of these phenomena in so far as they affect the purification rites of the Zionist Church.

As in pagan dreams, *Nomkhu6ulwana*—the goddess of fertility —appeared dressed in white, which is also the colour of the possessed-diviner's robe,[23] so in the Zionist prophet's dream the angel or the Christ mostly appears in white. For this reason also the Zionist neophyte must put on a white dress. Sometimes other colours such as green, yellow, or the buff of sackcloth are revealed, and will then invariably have to be worn by the one who is initiated. A local leader in the Christian Zion Apostolic Church stated that the colours of uniforms, sashes, and holy sticks were revealed by the angel according to the particular illness which the neophyte wished to overcome: "A particular illness requires a particular uniform and a particular colour." Prophet Mhletshwa told one woman in a service that the Spirit had shown him that she must wear a green dress with white crosses on the shoulders. She had complained of rheumatic pains in her back. In another Church green sashes may be claimed to be effective against sores. A person with many different illnesses will be purified from the magical defilement which brings sin and sickness by wearing perhaps three different robes of various colours, one above the other.

White is an active and effective colour: it carries with it purity and purification and acts as a guarantee that the *imikhokha*, the magical defilement, has been washed away. Therefore the neophyte is given a white dress after the "crossing of Jordan", i.e. after the immersion, and the sick put on a white veil which through its very whiteness will attract a host of healing angels. For similar reasons the prophet hoists a white flag on a pole in order to drive away lightning by this magical influence.

Green clothes are referred to as the dress of the Spirit, (*izingubo zika Moya*). Two colours are taboo, red and black. The Biblical reason given for the aversion from anything red in their dress is that "Jesus was given a red dress by the Jews". Linked with this aversion from the colour red, is the fact that blood according to Zionists is taboo. Black is the colour of death. The wearing of anything black is a sufficient cause for excommunication from most Zionist Churches. It is, however, a mysterious and unexplained fact that the holy veil which Shembe Jr. inherited from his father and which he uses in his healing services is black. The colour symbols in the dreams are of course later supported by an impressive array of Bible verses, especially from the Book of Revelation.

The holy sticks are also a common symbol in Zionist dreams. In a service the prophet will "prophesy" to a neophyte, that is, give him a detailed description of the length, colour and shape of the stick he is expected to carry. When a certain time has elapsed after baptism, the newly initiated is given his holy sticks, to which Zionists refer as their "weapons" (*izikhali*), their armour of light. Wherever the prophet or any ordinary Zionist goes, he will carry them with him. Generally three or more sticks are tied together in a bundle. More than one will be needed because each stick has a different function; thus one may be used for warding off lightning, another to drive out demons from the sick. The most precious is the stick with the cross. It embodies the veritable spiritual power of the Zionist Christian. Before every Sunday service it has to be white-washed anew—a ceremony reminding one of the washing of the spears (*ukuhlamba imikhonto*) which followed the conclusion of the month of mourning in heathen Zulu society.[24] We have already seen their use in the Sunday service. The holy sticks are very definitely connected with the confession element in the purification rites. If one leading Zionist "prophesies" that in a dream he has seen red spots of sin on the white stick of one of the members, and the person concerned admits having committed some of the grave sins (adultery, beer-drinking, eating pork), this may result in excommunication for a certain period. The excommunication is symbolized in the breaking of the stick. This is a dreaded punishment, for it signifies taking away from him his spiritual power, and it therefore acts as a strong sanction against immoral behaviour.

(d) Purification and Holy Communion

I have tried to show how baptism, the one rite of the Christian Church, which can be most easily related to the heathen past with its lustral ablutions and purification rites, tends to become the central act in the Zionist Church, and how other ritual ideas and actions are brought into relation with baptism and purification in one way or another. The preponderance of the purification motif is shown also by the fact that even *Holy Communion* is turned into *a purification rite*. That is, the Zionist prophet proves that the most important thing about Communion is—the Washing of the Feet.

The reason for this development is not difficult to find. Some of the Protestant Mission Churches from which the independent Churches broke away, presented to the African the pattern of an altar-less Christianity where Holy Communion was only infrequently practised. This is reflected in the development of most independent Churches. Communion is at the very most held three times a year, at the "Passover", Pentecost, and Christmas. In other organizations again, it may not be celebrated over a matter of years. Zululand Zionists, asked by me when they received Communion, replied that they did so when going to their central church in Johannesburg, where their president lives, but many of them may never make that pilgrimage to the Rand. The difficulty about procuring wine for

215

sacramental purposes—a question connected with the recognition of Churches by Government—also makes for very infrequent practice of this Christian sacrament.

In the cases where Communion is held, strict rules of taboo guard the purity of the sacrament. Menstruating women are not allowed to take part. If the priest for some reason has been aroused to anger that day, his choler may bring *imikhokha* in contact with the sacrament, and the Communion is therefore postponed. In one exceptional case a prophet expressed drastic criticism of the practice of Holy Communion, as being only a filthy invention of the Whites who wanted to deceive the Africans. He introduced instead the Passover to be eaten once every seven years: a lamb is slaughtered and eaten, and instead of wine water is consumed.

In this situation the Washing of the Feet comes to be much more stressed than the Communion itself. It is found in the Bible—I have heard Gen. 18: 4 quoted in support of the praxis as well as John 13. The practice has this extra value: that White Churches generally have neglected it. But above all, it is regarded as a purification rite, and thus is to be understood as still another means of removing the *imikhokha* which threaten man wherever he goes.

(e) Ritual avoidance

Are the taboos of the Zionist Church a consequence and function of their purification rites, or is it vice versa? Whatever the answer to that question, it is sufficiently obvious that there is a connexion between the two, and it is evident that *ritual avoidances*, or taboos, play a fundamental role in the religious outlook and ritual life of these Churches. On this point also the influence of Zionist tendencies on the practices of the Ethiopian Church is very considerable. The dream and the taboo are the two back doors through which the African past enters the Church. The Ethiopians have gallantly attempted—and, so far, fairly well succeeded—in keeping the door of dreams under control. But strong pressure has thrown the second door open. To the seceding Zionist, the careful keeping of taboos appears, of course, as the very opposite of syncretistic adaptation to his own African past. One local Zionist leader told me that he had left the Anglican Church "because they mix Christianity and heathenism by allowing tobacco, beer, and pork". It is very important in this connexion to remember the initial influence from Zion City, Ill., U.S.A. One of the Europeans who had taken a leading part in the work of that organization on the Witwatersrand in the years before World War I, told me in an interview: "Zion said, Zion does not allow beer, medicine, tobacco and pork. Dowie was against pork. We felt sick if we ate it. And as you know it is forbidden in the Bible."

The authority of Zion City, Ill., together with that of the Mosaic law, was cemented with Zulu tradition into one of the cornerstones of the new Church. The printed constitutions of these Churches abound in taboo rules. As a matter of fact, many constitutions are nothing but just a set of such rules.

Food taboos are strongest regarding *pork*. Zionists cannot combine forces with certain Ethiopians because of this (p. 52). Bishop M—— told me in 1941 that the Germans would lose World War II because they were such great pork eaters. Before the eclipse of the sun in South Africa in 1940, Zionist prophets proclaimed that the kraals where pigs were to be found would be utterly destroyed in the apocalyptic catastrophe which would overtake the world. The Constitution of the Ethiopian Holy Baptist Church in Zion has the following paragraph on the matter:

> Meat of Pork—Lev. 11: 4, 5, 6, 7, 8. How to leave such a beautiful smoke and Swine's flesh? Jesus the King said, I am sought of them that have asked not of me, that provoked me to anger, which they have eating the Swine's flesh, who have been saying this is the smoke in my nose, a fire that burneth all day. Isa. 65: 1, 3, 4, 5; Job 41: 19, 20, 21.

Apart from the fact that pork was taboo to certain sections of pagan Zulu society,[25] this aversion among the Zionists seems to have at least two other roots.

One of the incidents which led up to the Zulu Rebellion of 1906 was the so-called "pig-and-white-fowl-killing-order" given by leading Zulus. Stuart, in his history of the Rebellion, sees in this order a symptom of general anti-white reaction: "Pigs . . . had been introduced by the white race, and were regarded by natives as creatures whose flesh 'smells'." The underlying intention of the order "was that the natives of Natal and Zululand should rise against the White man."[26] Whilst of course no such rebellious connotations are to be attributed to the taboo in the Zionist Church to-day, it nevertheless is very probably part of the general aversion and reaction against the White man. It is also a reaction against the Zulu *izangoma*-diviners. While the diviners had mutton as their most important

217

food taboo, ("sheep will make the ancestral spirit dumb"), they rather cherished the fat of pork which would let the ancestral spirit move easily in the being of the diviner. That is the very reason why Zionists abhor pork: it conveys the *isangoma*-demon. And had not Jesus himself sent the demons into the pigs, *vide* Mark 5! To the same class of Zionist food taboos belong fowls, which are regarded as unclean. There is of course a Bible quotation against them: "Did not the cock crow in the night when Jesus was betrayed"? A prophet of an Apostolic Church told me that if a cock or hen happened to come into his kraal, he had to slaughter a goat in order to clean the place. The fact that fowls have been introduced by Europeans is a further reason for regarding them as taboo. Of less significance, but always carefully enumerated by the Zionists, are the other taboos mentioned in Lev. 11, a Bible passage of central import-ance in the Zionist Church.

Related to the *ukusefa*-ceremonies mentioned above, are *taboos against blood*. Meat of an animal that has died, i.e. not been slaughtered (*ingcuba*), and blood of slaughtered animals (*u6u6ende*), both relished by pagan Zulus, are abhorred by the Zionists, and generally also in Ethiopian Churches where local leaders are anxious to point out that they will have nothing to do with such meat.[a]

Connected with food taboos are rules about fasts (*inzilo*) followed in both Ethiopian (though not all) and Zionist organ-izations. Certain prophets take their faithful with them to a Zion hilltop for a four days' fast, all being clothed in sacking and covered with ashes "as Jonah in Nineveh". The length of the fast varies in different Churches. Some only practise it as preparation for Holy Communion. The Constitution of the Ethiopian Catholic Church in Zion (p. 86) energetically under-lines the necessity of this practice: "Christians shall not at all, at all, at all, and yet again at all, *eat, drink, smoke* or be engaged in *unnecessary conversation*, until the Mass is over, this being quite an *irreverent and unbecoming habit*."

The taboos against *medicines* will be discussed in the chapter on healing. Here I anticipate by merely stating that just as the

---

[a] While fish was generally not eaten by pagan Zulus, there exists one little Church calling itself the Church of the Fish (*ibandla lenhlanzi*), an interesting ichthyological parallel to the history of the Early Church of the martyrs! The members of this organization, which is remarkably nativistic in other respects, must regularly go through purification rites in the Tugela river, and must consume fish in order to be sure of salvation. Here again the fundamental symbol of the Church—the fish—has been shown to the prophet in his dreams.

swine-taboo is partly a reaction against the "demon" of the heathen diviner, so the medicine-taboo is a reaction against the heathen leech, whose medicines are reputed to instil *amandawe-demons* in the patients.

I have earlier (p. 167) pointed out that polygamy has in certain cases been the reason for new secessions. One sect leader, the husband of nine wives, told me that on this point he only differed from other Churches in one respect: "We are not hypocrites!" This attitude does not of course in any way exclude the existence of very definite *sexual taboos* within the same organization. The prophet's wife (or wives) may not prepare his food if incapacitated. Menstruating women may not take part in the Holy Communion.[27] The most remarkable example of sexual taboos as a central message of the Church was the activities of prophet X (p. 112). His prophetic calling included his dream-angel's commandment that all ministers should "go down from their beds". The core of the Church membership consisted of the *isigodlo*, two hundred young men and girls who had "married the Lamb" or contracted the "Heavenly Marriage", and were to remain virgin. This soon led to the downfall of the Church as the colony was dissolved by the authorities.

Special prophets are usually set aside by the Zionist Church to guard the chastity of their young people. The method used is "prophesying": the prophet is shown by the Spirit that there is red or black on the robe or the holy stick of some of the young members, and this is taken as an unfailing indication that they have succumbed to sexual temptations.

There are also *burial taboos*. The corpse contains in concentrated form the *imikhokha*, the pollution and defilement which are a danger to the kraal and to the whole of the community. A Zionist prophet expressed to me his horror at the thought of people dying in the mission hospital far away from their own kraal, for when the corpse had to be carried all the way from the hospital back home the *imikhokha* would destroy the harvest in the fields wherever the mourning procession passed. Shembe insisted that those who had touched a corpse would not be permitted to attend a church service for seven days. After this period the mourners had to visit the Nazarite priest, bringing an offering of flowers or money. The priest would purify their hands with water contained in a special vessel kept in the House of the Holy Vessels.[28] In other Zionist Churches the mourners have to go through *ukusefa*-rites (cf. p. 210), which for example include re-cleansing their holy sticks.

Prophet X (p. 112) proclaimed that true brides of the Lamb do not touch a corpse at all. Jesus had said: "Let the dead bury their dead." This meant that the saints of X's Salem Church should not be engaged in such unclean activities, and the burial of their dead was therefore to be left to the mercies of heathen or of Christians of other Churches. Sometimes, from four to seven days would elapse before the relatives heard of the fate of their dead and were called to the prophet's Bethesda to attend to the matter—no pleasant situation in a subtropical climate.

The Zionists are buried in their white Church garments, as a promise of the whiteness and holiness of heaven. And there the two poles between which Zionist syncretistic religion moves and oscillates are brought together, the dream and Heaven. The dream, which once inspired him to put on the white sacred garment as a guarantee of health and life, and the heavenly Zion, where he will wear white robes day and night, without spot or blemish.

(2) HEALING

While the Roman Church is an Institute of Grace through its sacraments, and the Protestant Church in Africa appears as an Institute of the Word through teaching and preaching, the Independent Church, Zionist type, is an Institute of Healing. The Healing Message is the pivot of all Church activity. "This is not a church, it is a hospital", one prophet told his congregation. The usual answer to the question as to why a person has joined a Zionist church is: "I was ill. They prayed for me. Now I am well."

The fact that the Christian message carries with it healing effects and blessings is of course not a Zionist discovery. In my work in the service of Lutheran Mission Churches, both in South and Central Africa, I have been strongly impressed by the role that the Christian hospital is playing in the evangelization of the African. I should say that at least one-third, probably many more, of the first generation in both areas where I have been working, have been won for the Christian faith either generally in crises of illness, or more specifically through the influence of a hospital. The mediæval monastery was at the same time a hospital. The mission station in Africa in our time—with church, hospital, school and farm in one unit—functions in the same way and with much the same result, being maintained by the conviction that the Gospel is for the whole of man.

Zionist Churches among the Zulu stress the element of healing in the Christian message to an extent and in a way which is unique. Already the names of some Churches show this predominant interest in healing. The members of "The Jerusalem Apostolic Kuphiliswa Church in Zion" have put in the Zulu word *"Kuphiliswa"* ("to be healed") to show their chief aim.

I think that in order to understand these activities of the Zionist Zulu, one has to regard them as a result of two converging lines—traditional Zulu ideas of illness and healing, and the faith healing message of various radical American sects, notably from Zion City, Ill. But the result is not just a combination of these two influences. It appears as a unique system in its own right, the nature of which is interpreted in the following pages.

(a) *Illness and health among the Zulus*

W. H. R. Rivers has shown that in primitive culture, medicine, magic and religion are closely related and that their domains overlap in many respects. I was interested to find, among the Bahaya in Central Africa, that their verb "to heal", *okutamba*, also means "to sacrifice". This shows, I believe, that originally the priest and the leech or herbalist had a similar function and that religion and medicine in this particular tribe have sprung from a common root.

Generally speaking this is true of all Bantu. At least according to Zulu concepts there is a definite connexion between medicine on the one hand and religion and magic on the other, constituting the warp and woof of the whole pattern of Zulu belief. Witchcraft and the whims of the ancestors are the two main causes of illness. The diviner and the herbalist depend on the ancestors for their calling, but they use magically-charged medicines or ward off the influence of such medicines. The word for herbal medicine, *umuthi*, also means poison.

The belief in the *inyanga* still persists strongly among the heathen, less so among Christians. This old profession has lately been somewhat modernized and has changed character through the patent-medicines racket which floods the market from Rand to Reserve. At exorbitant prices, anything from 15s. to £3 10s. or more, various Native "Chemist" shops sell, not only remedies for all kinds of diseases but also love-charms and charms for obtaining higher wages, and means of getting work. A missionary in Africa has to be a *bonne-à-tout-faire*, and in my capacity of Postal Agent of a mission district in northern Zululand I was impressed by the fact that by far the most important item sent through the parcel post to the district was these patent medicines.

The pursuit of health is the gravest concern of the Zulu today. Problems of diagnosis and of medical treatment arouse a tremendous interest among them. The reason for this is of course the low standard of health, caused chiefly by malnutrition, which prevails among the Zulu in these times. This causes folk to be constantly on the move from one medical practitioner to another in the search for health. One example will show this clearly. Melika belonged to a group of women who would appear rather intermittently in the Lutheran church at Z——, and at intervals she would join some Zionist group. Her case history in the hospital was as follows: Age 32. Examined September 18, 1939. Had been ill for many months with abdominal troubles, and ulcer on the right hip. Diagnosis: Syphilis and gonorrhœa. In hospital September 19 to November 8, 1939. Was treated for syphilis. Developed pneumonia and pleurisy, and the treatment for syphilis had to be postponed for a while, but was later resumed. Further diagnosis showed also bilharzia, but not treated for this, as it was felt that she should rest between the treatments. Next stay in hospital February 15 to March 11, 1940. She was then pregnant, sixth to seventh month. Treated for threatening abortion, gonorrhœa and bilharzia. Delivery May 1, 1940, normal. Some time after birth the child came out in a rash, Melika brought him regularly to hospital for injections. He recovered, but when some eight months old was brought to the hospital with a big abscess on the arm. He had been cut by his father when trying to cure the infant of some ailment. The mother now refused to stay at the hospital, and the child was treated as an outpatient. The abscess healed, but a few days later the child got conjunctivitis. Treated at the hospital service, with marked results. One day the father reported that they could not bring the child, as it had got diarrhœa. He asked for medicine and was instructed to bring the child to the hospital. It was too late, however, for it died the same day. February 19–25, 1941, Melika was treated after abortion. After that she disappeared from the hospital for a long time.

We discovered that while visiting the mission hospital Melika had also sought the following treatments:

(1) She visited another European doctor living some twenty miles away, who was believed to possess specially effective medicines; she procured a bottle from him for 5s. 6d.

(2) She was treated by an *inyanga* for three weeks, and paid one beast and one goat for this.

(3) She stayed two months at prophet Ntshangase's Bethesda, where she went through an intense vomiting-cure, to get rid of demons and internal snakes.

(4) She was being prayed for daily during that whole period by the Sangweni Zionists, the method used being chiefly pummelling with holy sticks.

And all this over a period of seventeen months! If one wishes to understand the appeal of the Zionist Healing Message at the present time, one has to remember cases of this kind. Melika's case is of course no exception. It would be an exaggeration to call it typical of the Zulu society as a whole, but that it is typical of a growing mass of under-nourished, infected, desperate Bantu in South Africa, nobody with any knowledge of the medical situation among those Africans would deny. Under the pressure of this need Melika and many others receive the Zionist Healing Message as a gospel for the poor.

(b) Illinois and illness

On the bookshelves of Zionist leaders in Johannesburg and Zululand I have sometimes found dilapidated copies of *Leaves of Healing*, the church paper of G. W. Voliva's Zion Church, Ill., U.S.A. Usually they date from about 1910–15, the period when the Zionist movement received its initial impetus in South Africa. In this magazine you may see for example a photo of an American family, parents and children, with the caption *"God's Witnesses to Divine Healing"* and the record presented:

> Father healed of Rheumatism, Delivered from the Liquor Habit and Secret Societies; Mother Healed of Consumption, Erysipelas, Healed Breast and La Grippe. Children Healed of Scarlet Fever, Measles, Cholera Infantum, Rupture and Spasms; Entire Family Brought into Zion and Blessed in Tithing (*Leaves of Healing*, June 3, 1916).

Another number may be almost completely filled with healing testimonies delivered one Sunday morning service at Zion City, Ill.:

O   223

Miss Reninger, Zion City, Illinois: I have not words enough to thank God this morning for His wonderful blessings to me. A little over a year ago, I took sick, and I was very bad. I had such terrible pain in my shoulder blades that I thought they would meet, it drew me so. I do thank God that He healed me; and I am stronger now than I have been ever since living in ZION CITY; Miss Erickson, Zion City, Ill.: I want to praise God this morning for delivering me from doctors and drugs. It is eighteen years ago since God delivered me from these things (*Leaves of Healing*, January 16, 1915).

Missionaries from such a Church would naturally expect the same thing to happen in Africa. Sister Verna B. Barnard, who arrived in 1908 in South Africa, found that "mighty miracles were performed in the name of Jesus. Many mighty healings took place" (*Comforter-Trooster*, Johannesburg, August–September, 1940). One of the main initiators of the Zionist movement among the Bantu on the Rand, the Rev. J. G. Phillipps, a Nyasaland Native, belonged to those who were healed:

He had a very sick chest, and he suffered much at intervals. No medicine did him any good, and the ministers of the Church of England did their very best for him. He had read some religious papers which taught Divine Healing, and when sick here in Johannesburg he went to Pastors Tome and Lake, of the A—— F—— Mission. These brethren prayed for him, with the Laying on of Hands, and he got wonderfully healed and delivered from his sickness (from *Constitution of the Holy Catholic Apostolic Church in Zion*).

After such happy experiences, and following the custom of Zion City, Ill., it became a rule to regard Divine Healing as one of the tenets of faith of the Zionist Churches which sprang up on the Rand. Sweeping promises of healing are generally made in the constitution of these Churches, and this is, of course, still more the case in the Sunday service testimonies where references to successful healing abound.

It is interesting to find that the link, however weak, with some sort of European Church (apart from the Zion City, Ill.,) tends to damp the enthusiasm for healing practices. The African Orthodox Church claims "Unction of the Sick" as a speciality, and teaches that such unction when given to someone seriously ill gives "health and strength to the soul, and *frequently* to the body". As a matter of fact, most Ethiopian Churches do not even mention faith healing in their constitutions. Therefore I need not stress again that this chapter on healing refers to Churches which I describe as Zionist, and not to those of Ethiopian type.

(c) Causes of illness

In order to understand the healing activities of the Zionist Churches it is necessary to define both traditional Zulu ideas and Zionist views of the causes of disease.[a] Generally speaking Zionists accept as a matter of fact the tribal outlook on causation of illness, but they also propound views on the subject which to some extent clash violently with traditional Zulu ideas.

(1) Zulus distinguish between *umkhuhlane-nje* (any slight illness) and *ukufa* or *ukufa kwa6antu* (lit. death, e.g. a serious or fatal illness). Zionists in common with other Zulus refer to headache or stomach ache as only *umkhuhlane*. I cannot say with certainty whether Zionists have in any way widened the idea of the natural causation of disease. I would suggest that they rather act as a conservative force within the Zulu community in this respect.

(2) I hope to make clear later the role of the ancestors within the syncretistic system of the Zionists. Following the traditional Zulu pattern, Zionists often refer to the ancestors as causing loss and mishap rather than serious illness or death. Most Zionists when divining point to the neglect of the ancestral spirit as a general cause of barrenness. General ill-health in a child is thought to be caused by the ancestors not having received the sacrifice to which they were entitled. A child may fall ill because of the fact that its parents remain heathen or insist on remaining Lutherans, Methodists or Anglicans, and do not become Zionists. Such parents are "unclean" (*6angcolile*), and only after they have undergone Zionist baptism and purification ceremonies will the child recover.

(3) Fatal disease (*ukufa kwa6antu*) according to the Zulu conception is caused by *u6uthakathi*. There are two forms of *u6uthakathi: Ukuphosa* (to throw) and *ukudlisa* (to bring somebody to eat, i.e. poison). This second is sorcery. Tuberculosis for example is by Zionists and others regarded as "thrown" through the agency of some witch-familiar. The great importance of Zionist prophets in their capacity as witch-finders is only possible in a community where most illnesses are believed

[a] On the causation of disease among other South African tribes, see Hunter, *Reaction to Conquest*, 1936, p. 272, and Krige, *Realm of a Rain-queen*, 1943, p. 222.

to have been caused by various kinds of *imithi*, or poisonous medicines, which the sorcerer has prepared in order to destroy his enemies.

(4) It is, however, not sufficient to state that Zionists' views on the causation of disease are merely copied from the general Zulu pattern. As a matter of fact this pattern has been modified by other elements which are regarded by the Zionists as specifically Christian, such as their views on the causes of hysterical possession, the "healing" of which plays a great role in Zionist Churches. The most important trait of possession for our purpose is that which has been induced by a herbalist through his manipulation of medicines. The patient may show some hysterical symptoms, caused by some ancestral spirit. The cure for this, according to heathen Zulu ideas, consists of introducing into the patient another spirit or group of spirits, called *amandiki* or *ama6utho*. The spirits will, when called upon, speak in various tongues.

In relation to these possession phenomena the Zionist finds himself in vehement opposition to heathen Zulu society. Whereas, by the latter, initiation is regarded as therapeutic and possession as a cure, the Zionist regards the *amandiki*-possession as demoniacal. This attitude, however, not only has a bearing on Zionist views of what we should call hysteria in particular, but has a much wider significance in relation to their views of the cause and cure of disease in general. I suggest that the Zionist's opposition to the use of medicine derives from his attitude to possession. The role of *umuthi* in inducing (mostly by inhaling) that which Zionists regard as demoniacal possession accounts for the total aversion to medicines that prevails in Zionist Churches. No doubt another factor contributing to this result has been the teaching of American sects of Zionist type to the effect that the Bible is opposed to the use of medicines.

From these considerations the Zionists draw the conclusion that *medicine is not a cure of disease, but the cause of demoniacal possession*. This is the most important reason for Zionist refusal to have anything to do with hospitals and all their works. In their testimonies they state that those who seek the help of hospitals and European doctors "get demons", i.e. will be possessed just as the *indiki*-possessed people are when doctored by a Zulu *inyanga*. That is why in Zionist testimonies one invariably hears that after conversion they have never used medicine. In the Sabbath liturgy of the Nazarites it is announced with great emphasis: "For you, who are a Christian, it

226

is a sin to touch medicine with your hand; [if you do,] you will verily die." When Othaniel was asked whether he intended to follow his wife who had left the Lutheran Church and become a Zionist, his reply was: "No, I won't do that, I still believe in medicine" (*Cha, ngisakholwa umuthi*). To depend on medicines is to worship Satan, as they often express it. Titus Msibi, of the Congregational Catholic Apostolic Church of Zion in South Africa, has taken over the views held by J. A. Dowie of Chicago when in a letter to Government he puts hospitals on a par with places rather lacking in respectability: "Remember, that in Zion God's Kingdom there are (1) no Breweries or Saloons, (2) no Gambling Halls, (3) no Houses of ill fame, (4) no Hog Raising, Selling or Handling, (5) no Hospital or Doctors' offices, (6) no Theatres or Dance Halls."

An interesting way of tackling this problem can be seen in the constitution of Bishop Richard S. Mhlanga's National Swazi Native Apostolic Church of Africa. As a Zionist he opposes hospitals and doctors with great energy, but he wishes to form a National Church of the Swazi tribe. This claim forces him to compromise and soften his radical views somewhat. He says: "All the sick shall receive the prayers' blessing in the name of the Lord. We don't forbid any person to go to a Doctor. He may on his own account. The one who does not want a Doctor, the great Doctor is there, Jesus Christ" (and then follow Bible references).

Zionist opposition to medicines has led to serious difficulties on the vaccination issue. Vaccination is regarded by most of these people as "the Mark of the Beast". Isaiah Shembe's stand on this point was inexorable. Since about 1926 the issue has been a grave concern to the Administration in Natal. Nazarites' refusal to allow vaccination of their church members has been a menace to the rest of the community. Shembe's attitude was that "they had taken a sacred oath not to resort to medicine in any shape or form nor submit their bodies to be cut". As Act No. 15 of 1928 provided for the exemption of conscientious objectors to vaccination, Shembe's case was not pursued by the Administration, and matters were allowed to drift. On various occasions the question was later discussed with his son, Johannes G. Shembe. He officially took the stand that his followers were not directly forbidden to use medicine. In the long run he has also, officially, given in to the representations of the Government. He has been able to compromise by deciding that vaccination is, after all, just cutting in the arm, and not connected with demon-inducing *umuthi*. In 1944 the Nazarites declared themselves ready for vaccination, Shembe Junior in this matter acting on the legal advice of Senator D. R. Shepstone, his lawyer.

Malarial assistants in the badly infected coastal belt of Zululand complain that Zionists of various descriptions refuse to take quinine. The toll of death by malaria is exceptionally high in such districts.

(5) The general Zulu pattern regarding causation of disease is being changed in still another direction by the Zionists. The religious interpretation of illness as being caused by sin is given on various occasions. The view that healing should normally be preceded by confession of sin implies a connexion between sickness and sin. The prophet, God's representative in the Church, can also cause illness. The curse (*isiqhalekiso*) of the prophet may cause madness or aimless wandering. Isaiah K—— had become weak of mind. The Salem Church considered this affliction to have been caused by the curse of the prophet. Isaiah had accused the prophet, a relative of his, of adultery, and the prophet was believed to have taken vengeance on him in this way.

(d) Healing activities

I have stressed repeatedly that prayer for the sick is not just a detail of Zionist church services, but is their most important feature.

In the Jamengweni hall at Ekuphakameni, eighteen miles north of Durban, a pathetic group of some 250 women had assembled for a service to be led by the Rev. J. G. Shembe, B.A., of the Nazarite Church. Some had been waiting for this occasion for months or even years. One could feel the urgency of their expectation. All other doctors had failed, and now, hoping against hope, they had come to the "Servant", to Shembe's holy Ekuphakameni, to be prayed for in order that the shame of barrenness should at last be removed and their suffering come to an end. On a Friday afternoon in the culminating week of the "July-festival" their hour had come. The Rev. J. G. Shembe had invited my wife and myself to attend as observers together with a Zulu theological student. We took off our shoes at the door, and waited for some time. When expectation had reached its highest pitch, a church official in a long blue garment entered and announced that only barren women were allowed to stay, the rest had to leave. Nobody moved, however; they had all come for the same reason.

Now the Servant appears. Dressed in a long black garment with golden embroidery round his neck and with a black veil round his head, he enters the hall. First he removes his shoes, and then courteously comes to me to explain that whenever we want to leave the service, we are at liberty to do so. Then the séance begins.

One or two of the women have begun a sort of continuous hiccough. The Servant stands before the mass of women, stretches out his right hand over the crowd from one side to the other, moving his long nervous fingers while he prays: "Lord, I pray, give them life in their wombs and in their spirits, so that they may bear children."

He unwinds his father's long black veil, which is thought to transmit hidden powers of life. To me the prophet of course explains that he has to use a veil in order to cope with the whole clientele in one afternoon. To lay hands on every individual would take far too long. He walks along the rows of seated women and flicks first one, then another with that veil, giving it a rapid jerk, as if cracking a whip.

The effect is astounding. Almost everybody starts, as though receiving a powerful electric shock. One woman, wearing a top-knot, who has been hiccoughing more and more loudly, is struck by the veil and starts to cry with a terrible loud, shrill voice, and continues crying long after the prophet has left her. Next to her is sitting another woman who also begins to cry. She throws herself to the ground. The prophet touches her, placing his finger-tips upon her shoulders. Then quite unexpectedly he signs for me to approach and explains the case as if he were a professor of gynæcology, but at the same time he is of course well conscious of the fact that in the eyes of these women he has supernatural powers. The case history of the woman, the prophet explains, is this: Three abortions, the third at the beginning of that same month; now she accuses herself of having murdered her children, her *indiki*-demon has told her so: "I ate my children" (*nga6adla a6antwana 6ami*), she cries in her terrifying voice. The prophet asks: "Whose children?"— No reply, only streaming tears and crying. "Whose children?" —"Yours, my Lord!" (In this case referring to the supposed fact that she had already once been healed by the prophet and that the snake inside had killed the child). She continues to cry, but the prophet moves on. And then, with a most pathetic effect, the crying of this desperate woman changes suddenly into a lullaby of four notes which are continually repeated.

229

Near her sits a heathen diviner in her characteristic attire. The prophet touches her shoulders with both his hands. Some in the vicinity start to cackle like hens and others throw themselves to the ground. One woman runs away when the prophet approaches. He allows her to do so and explains to me: "She will drop down in a moment"—which she does. Another woman kicks out when touched with the veil. The prophet touches her with his fingertips, first upon her shoulders, then in the region of the umbilicus, and at last allows his long veil to rest over her womb. He explains to me: "She cannot get children. I think that she has a snake in her womb."

Another woman becomes as if possessed when the prophet comes close to her. He invites me to listen to her crying. Out of her subconscious mind comes a stream of images and notions. She sees people who try to murder her: "You will bring me back by means of a white snake (*nizongibuyisa ngenyoka emhlophe*). But now I believe in X——. He will help me. I will take vengeance on you." At this point it appears that she is addressing her own people at home, who have scorned her because of her barrenness. Her voice becomes hard and harsh: "You hated me because I had no children. But I will return. The Servant will give me children, and I will triumph."

The prophet explains to me: "I remove demons. I am amazed to find that in the case of women, demons take their abode in the shoulders and in the womb. In the case of men, demons reside only in the stomach." Sometimes the prophet shouts, as he hits out with his veil: "Get out, demons! Depart immediately!" And as he moves along, the din of cackling, hiccoughing, crying, shrieking, singing, weeping, grows into a tremendous volume of sound. Bitter is their need—and here is their great hope, perhaps their last chance. Can this veil, can this man, can God give life?

One of the most important elements of this method of healing is the atmosphere of suspense and expectation that pervades the whole act. The service takes place on one of the last days of an important church festival, and has been preceded by much longing on the part of the patients and many eager testimonies given by the minor leaders, as to the healing powers of the Servant himself. Dube tells an instructive story about Isaiah Shembe, healing a woman who complained about some female disorder (*isilumo sasesinyeni*). In spite of the fact that she was very ill and seemed almost dying, Shembe did not seem to care about her, in fact he seemed to have forgotten her. She thought that this neglect was due to the fact that she was not a Nazarite, but belonged to the Congregationalists. However, she followed the members of the Nazarite Church when they went to the Holy Mountain, Nhlangakazi. There, one night, Shembe suddenly sent for her and told her when she came: "Woman, rejoice, for this is your day of healing. God has just told me that you will be healed." He then addressed the disease: "Oh, Disease of the Womb (*isifo sasesinyeni*), that possesseth this woman! Depart from her that she may become whole!" The woman fell to the ground as if dead, but her illness left her in the same moment, the testimony says. Here again is the same expectation, culminating at the festival on the Holy Mountain, together with the overwhelming influence of the prophet himself—and the patient feels instant relief.

In this process Shembe Senior and Junior and George Khambule and such prophets of great influence have displayed more intuitive psychology than the minor Zulu prophets who pray for the sick at every service. The constant praying for the same patient Sabbath after Sabbath—without results—deprives the service of that all important element of definiteness and efficacy that means so much to the patients.

As for the arrangement of the healing service, this is worked out in different ways by each individual Church. In prophet X's Salem Church of Saints the sick and the healers would stand or kneel in the form of a cross in the church room. If praying in the open air, a so-called *isigugqo* (a place where one kneels) is arranged. With a holy stick or ashes, used in order to drive away all black magic influences (*imikhokha*), the leader draws a wide circle on the ground, and the patients are assembled within it. The leaders then lay their hands upon them while the other members of the congregation go round the circle.

The official Zionist doctrine is of course that prayer as such is efficacious in the overcoming of illness. The whole argument against medicines and hospitals is built on the teaching that Jesus relied upon prayer alone for his service of healing. All the same, Zulu Zionists are not consistent on this point. It is admitted that ordinary prayer is sufficient for the healing of diseases which are brought about by "natural causes". But Zionists in the Mahlabatini district told me that they had never seen anybody who was suffering from a really grave illness healed by prayer alone. Something more was needed to increase the potency of the prayer.

Laying on of hands must in some way be part of the healing

activities, but it is thought by the great majority of Zionists that it must be strengthened by more tangible methods. The violent shaking of the patient while shouting *"Phuma, dimone!"* ("Depart, demon!") is common, often accompanied by beating the patient with holy sticks. At Bergville there existed for some time a sect which was called *"A6adu6uzi"*, the Pummelers, because of its outrageous methods of dealing with the patients. With furious energy they beat the sick ones as a means of exorcism. Then again, the prophet's holy veil is a more subtle method. He lets his cherished relic rest for a while on the diseased part of a patient's body. Its curative power is, I suppose, considered to be at least as strong as the X-ray equipment used in European hospitals. At one annual festival of a Church the priests used to touch the sick with the prophet's robes in order to heal them.

The use of robes, veils, sashes, in combating illness has a definite evangelistic aim also. A sick person may be told at first by the Zionist prophet that the Holy Spirit has ordained that he shall wear a white robe and a green sash; if he does not wear these, his illness will become fatal. When the patient has put on the uniform, he will be told that the Angel does not wish him to stay in a Mission Church. Because prayer women in some Mission Churches wear black skirts, one is warned that one's illness will turn into blackness and death if one is so conservative as to remain in such a Church. In the majority of cases the patients have been prepared for a miraculous result by a dream in which the sacred dress and holy stick to be worn by the patient have been pointed out to him.

The role of water as a medical remedy is of central importance in Zionist Churches. One of them lays down in the constitution of the Church: "We put our hands, water, and ashes on the patients and they are cured in the Lord's name, we work day and night, praying that the water be blessed to cure." But if such methods are not enough, more drastic ones may be required. The use of ashes has become very popular in these Churches. In heathen Zulu religion ashes were used for purification and also as a symbol of forgiveness and restitution (in the *ukutelelana-amanzi*-ceremony). Zionists use ashes in accordance with Biblical practice, they say, quoting Num. 19: 9 and pointing to the example of Jonah in Nineveh. A Zionist group in Kingsley put their ashes in a sacred vessel in the church. They explain that only by so doing will the healing power of the ashes be preserved. Some of my observers point to the connexion between ashes and the ancestor-cult. If ashes were not used, the ancestors would be angry and some illness would follow.

Although the traditional Zulu heritage is thus clearly discernable in these healing practices, Zionist prophets have also borrowed extensively from European culture for their medicaments. In actual fact Zionist prophets make use of a whole range of European hygienic and medical articles. Castor oil, Epsom salts, blue soap and blue stone are used as enemas. Zionist healing, which is only the other side of Zionist religious purification ritual, emphasizes the importance of emetics and enemas. The prophet with his cross and his enema syringe round his neck is a common sight on the Rand and in the Reserve.

(e) The place of healing in the Church

Healing activities in the Zionist Churches are not an end in themselves. The Message of Healing is in fact the strongest asset of Zionist evangelization. Heathens and Christians from Mission and Ethiopian Churches are attracted in various degrees by the sweeping promises made, and the more so as the Zionist belief in healing is supported by alluring testimonies which witness to the supposed fact that the cure has indeed brought with it positive results.

The healing of a patient who may have stayed at the prophet's Bethesda for a long time is greeted with jubilation, and it is used by leader and Church as propaganda for the religious group concerned. From this arises a new type of church service, the "bringing home of the convalescent" (ukum6uyisa osindileyo ekhaya). This custom very largely follows the isangoma pattern. The initiation of rites of the new diviner used to conclude with a ceremony in which she was taken back to her home. One example of a Zionist bringing-home festival is recorded here, and one notices the influences of traditional Zulu pattern in this supposedly Christian service.

Beselina had been suffering from tuberculosis for a long time. After having stayed at prophet Sibiya's Bethesda-kraal from April, 1944, to January, 1945, she showed signs of recovery. When she considered herself to have improved, she was brought home by Sibiya and his whole Zionist flock. All were attired in white robes and blue and green sashes. A two-day festival followed. On the first day only the prayer-women of the local congregation were present. They demanded of Beselina's

husband a beast for sacrifice, and he was quite willing to
"thank with blood" (uku6onga ngegazi), as it was expressed.
The beast was brought into the cattle-kraal, and all the Zionists
walked round it in procession, singing a hymn composed for
the occasion:

> Light, thou Angel of Light,
> Thou, mighty one of the road which cometh from Jerusalem!
> The shoulders get tired of carrying sins,
> Oh, help us with this thy lamb,
> So that it will be strong and fat,
> So that we shall succeed through it,
> The day when we bring back thy daughter.

One of the Zionist men hit the ox with his holy brass staff,
"blessing the ox", as this action was described. The actual
slaughter followed. On this occasion most of the Zionists
present spoke with tongues.

The sacrifice was only preparatory for the rites that followed
the next day. Prophet Sibiya and his Zionist flock circled the
cattle-kraal, singing with delight a hymn about Jerusalem,
accompanied by the words: "May peace reign in Zion. Amen,
Hallelujah!" The spirit was present, this being made apparent
by the energetic manner in which the prophet was sneezing. He
beat himself with his hands, speaking with tongues: "Hshiii"
or "Hmmmmmmmmmm", whereas the others replied with Amen
to the prophet's sneezing.

All entered Beselina's hut. One prayer woman gave a short
address speaking about the grave illness that had befallen their
friend and how she had been tied with the chains of Satan, but
now had completely recovered. Beselina kneeled in the middle
of the hut and the others laid their hands on her head, singing.
A collection was taken, and some ten shillings were given to the
prophet.

But the work of healing was not yet complete. Behind the
illness there was sorcery, and therefore Beselina's hut had to be
purified from sorcery-medicine. Suddenly a prayer woman
exclaimed: "There is an evil person among us! You have all to
admit that." She peered into the face of each one present and
found not one but four evil persons. (This is not surprising, for
she had picked out the four non-Zionists in the hut, three
Lutherans and one belonging to the American Board Mission.)

Prophet Sibiya exclaimed: "There is something hidden here",
and he pounded with his cross on a skin which was spread on

the ground. The others removed the skin and started to dig on the spot. But nothing was found. Esau M6atha, a Lutheran, one of those who had been pointed out as evildoers, could not restrain himself, and in a somewhat derogatory manner asked to be shown the evil thing which was hidden. The Zionists had, however, a standard reply ready: "The angel has refused to allow us to produce it now, because there are evildoers in our midst." A woman suggested that there might be something hidden high up in the wall. She took ashes and sprinkled a certain spot on the wall. But still nothing was found. Two others then saved the situation by going out alone and soon returning with a horn which they claimed to have found at that very spot in the wall, but on the outside. M6atha was still unrepentant and suspicious and said that he did not believe this claim. To this Beselina's husband, himself a heathen, angrily retorted: "Get out from here, you only want to find fault with the people of the Lord."

The festival concluded with a beef party, on which occasion Beselina herself gave a short address:

> Before I used to be a great sinner
> Specially I used to slander other people.
> But now the Lord has not only healed me
> But also freed me from many sins.
> I no longer drink beer.
> Peace in Zion!

Zionist friends shouting loudly:

> Amen!
> I don't use snuff.
> Peace be in Zion! (Amen.)

The testimony of healing often goes together with testimony to liberation from sin. I quote a specimen delivered in Zulu by a young man in a Full Gospel Church. His educational background was comparatively high (Standard VIII).

> I thank thee, righteous Jehovah
> Who hast freed me from Satan's might.
> I used to be ill, I used to have to lie on my bed all the time.
> But now I am kicking with my leg.
> I am not ill at all.
> I used to drink beer, but I don't do that any longer.
> Now I walk with the people of the Lord.

Some Churches are sufficiently modern to use the printed word for testimonies of healing. One Full Gospel Church

("Jerusalem Native Branch") in Durban used to publish a small four-page paper with testimonies. At the end of each short passage is given the exact home address of the particular person who has been miraculously healed, thus conveying the impression that facts, and not fiction, are being reported.

Zionist healing activities must not be understood to be just another kind of religious eccentricity of primitive people who do not grasp what Christianity means. The fact that this message attracts an ever increasing number of people from other Churches shows that it appeals to a very real and vital need. The Healing Message promises quick results and immediate relief. The African Presbyterian Bafolisi Church (chiefly Sotho) says in its Constitution: "Singing with Spirit by hands and feet, *at once* the sickness healed. Read Ps. 150; 2 Sam. 6: 15–16; Luke 10: 19. . . ."

One must acknowledge the zeal and the energy of the Zionists, and their personal interest in those who have fallen ill. This is strengthened of course by their belief in the possibilities of prophecy or divination. When Julia had left the Lutheran congregation at Ceza, Zionists were asked why she had done so. The reply was: "If you Lutherans had been able to divine (*ukubula*) you would have seen that she was ill. We discovered her illness even from a distance." The personal interest shown in the patient by prophesying and urgent prayer has a strong attraction. The physical contact between prophet and patient, the laying on of hands, the use of holy sticks, veils, and so on, all strengthen the bond between them.

We must also see healing against the background of the uncertainties and perplexities of modern times in Africa. It is not surprising that this message was first accepted on the Rand and brought from there to the Reserves. When the Zulu left the environment of the Reserve where relative safety was guaranteed by the religio-medical sanctions of his traditional beliefs, he was drawn into the whirlpool of modern civilization in the Golden City. Naturally he felt utterly foreign and experienced a loneliness that was overwhelming. His most pressing need was the promise of health and abundant life through methods he could understand. The Healing Message soon developed divining methods ("prophecy") which appealed to his inherited eagerness not simply to accept illness as such but to "understand" and interpret its causation. The constant praying and the violent methods gave him the feeling of being cared for, which was important to him in a bewildering and absolutely new situation.

The Zionist way of healing also points to a common factor shared by traditional Zulu views on illness and healing and the Biblical interpretation. Through divining and prayer they procure the religious sanctions without which a Zulu does not really believe that healing can be secured. In European medical treatment the wholeness of man is seldom recognized. The appeal from the Zionist message undoubtedly comes from their insistence that both the practice of medicine and religious experience spring from a common root. A mission doctor who used to call nurses, patient and relatives together for prayer before performing an operation was often referred to by Zionists as a real Christian in whom they had confidence.

The healing issue has also a definite bearing on the leadership question. Faith healing among the Zulu is intimately bound up with the personality of the prophet. His capacity as healer gives to the leader his greatest opportunity of asserting himself as an inspired prophet. In spite of his intellectual shortcomings the prophet can therefore well hold his own in comparison with the chief-type of leader. In fact the healing issue is the strongest influence in drawing people from Mission and Ethiopian Churches into the Zionist fold.

Melika's case-history was quoted on p. 222. The real clue to an understanding of the appeal of the Healing Message to South African Natives is to be found in a social setting where ill-health, malnutrition and child mortality take a terrible toll. One may say that in the changes and exigencies of modern times, the Zionist Church wishes its message to function as an adaptation of the Christian message to the social needs of African peoples. These healers are, however, a very definite threat to the progress of the African. Their rash promises are more high-sounding than they are sound. They cannot by their methods bring the Africans out of the vicious circle of malnutrition—ill health—low wages—low social status—race hatred, but only serve to accelerate the downward plunge.

CHAPTER VII

NEW WINE IN OLD WINESKINS

(I) BLEND OF OLD AND NEW

This chapter deals with syncretistic tendencies arising out of the Zionist prophet's and the Zionist Church's interpretation of the Christian message in terms of the Zulu religious heritage. I emphasize that my study is here directed upon independent Churches of Zionist type. Where and when these syncretistic Zionist practices and ideas exercise an influence upon Churches of Ethiopian type, this is as far as possible pointed out in the text.

(a) *Ancestral spirit and Holy Spirit*

> *Ehhe—ehhe—ehhe—ehhe ee ee*
> *Ngiyamazi uBa6a*
> *owangenzayo*
> *Ngiyalazi idlozi*
> *elangenzayo*
> *Ehhe—ehhe—ehhe—ee ee*[a]

It is dawn—there is still half an hour to go before the sun rises out of the Indian Ocean. Near Ekukhanyeni the diviner Dlakude approaches with her novices (*amathwasa*). The pupils dance around the leader as they come half-running down the slope to the Ihlekazi stream, chanting songs to the ancestral spirits.

They are not alone. On the opposite side of the stream another group approaches, some of them clad in white robes with green or yellow sashes. It is the prophet Elliot Butelezi of the Sabbath Zionist Church and his followers. Half-running, dancing in circles around the prophet as they move along, they sing with shrill voices:

> *Thixo, Ba6a, ngidukile,*
> *nasekhaya ngisukile.*[b]

[a] Ehhe—I know my father
who made me
I know the spirit
who made me.

[b] God Father, I have erred,
and have gone astray from home.

238

The diviner group arrives at the stream first. All the members of the group have brought their calabashes and when these have been filled with water, *ubulawu*-medicine is added and the concoction is stirred until froth is formed. The diviner gives each to drink from the frothy water, and they begin to vomit.

The Zionists look on silently for a while, but presently Elliot asks the *isangoma* leader: "When are you going to finish, preacher?" This joke produces laughter from the Zionists, whereas the diviner and her pupils remain silent, intent on their vomiting rites. To conclude the ceremony, Dlakude finds some white clay, which she smears upon herself and her followers. One of them starts the spirit-song:

> *Ehhe ehhe*
> *Ngiyamazi uBaba. . . .*

The whole group leaves the stream, returning to Dlakude's kraal. The leader dances round her group in joy, beating them with twigs as they run homewards.

Now comes the Zionists' turn. "The water has been defiled, because the diviners have entered it," complains one in the group. But Elliot replies: "Pay no heed to that, for this is running water, and the impurity has been removed by its flow." He intones a hymn. The older Zionists follow suit, but newcomers to the congregation follow with "Amen, Amen," to the same tune There follows blessing of the water. Elliot stirs in the stream with his index finger and looking up to heaven says a short prayer to the Lord of the Living Waters (*inkosi yamanzi aphilayo*) that the stream may be cleansed of vile things. One of the group is brought to Elliot by a prayer-woman. With both hands he scoops water into the mouth of the patient, at the same time shouting: "In the name of the Father and of the Son and of the Holy Ghost. This blessed water will take away illness from this sick person. Drink!"

Elliot then takes the patient with him in the middle of the stream and makes the woman stoop until the water goes over her head. He places his hands upon her head and in the same moment becomes filled with the Holy Spirit. His whole body shakes, and he shouts, first slowly, but soon faster and faster: "*Hhayi, hhayi, hhayi, hhe, hhe, hhe!*" The patient drinks repeatedly from the water, praying in the intervals: "Descend, Spirit, descend like a dove!" Soon she also gets the Spirit, begins to shake and to speak with tongues: "Di-di-di-di-didi." While this is happening, the faithful on the banks sing a hymn. The sick woman comes up from the stream and begins to vomit on the rocks.

Other patients follow her into the water and go through the same process ending with vomiting. One of Elliot's brothers, Philemon, an elder in the Church, is suddenly possessed by the Spirit. He dashes round the group in his long white gown, beating the air with a long white cross. He sings, shouts, and speaks with tongues. After the "water and vomiting" ceremony, Elliot takes white ashes and mixes them with water. He smears the patients' faces and shoulders with this mixture. To complete the cure, green sashes are tied around their shoulders.

The Zionists then return to Elliot's home. He leads the procession for a while, but when he is again possessed by the Spirit, he circles round the others in the group, singing and dancing. The older Zionists soon follow him, dancing round the remaining group of patients.

Watching this encounter at dawn, between the group of heathen diviners and the Zionist flock at a beautiful Zululand stream, gave me much food for thought. As a European churchman, thinking in terms of Church History, I was led to consider the significance of this transition: from modern Western "hot-Gospel" religion with its healing and speaking with tongues, to a shouting and vomiting Zulu Zionism, a development through which Western, supposedly spiritualized religion is eventually changed into African spiritism. The French saying, *"Plus ça change, plus c'est la même chose"*, sprang to my mind.

The distance between Elliot the Zionist prophet and Dlakude the witch-doctor, was not great. Anybody could jump over that stream—and many have done so. Elliot was not in a position to understand Christianity in any other way. He had to interpret it in the only terms he knew: the pattern of Zulu religion, the pattern of the *isangoma* system.

In this chapter I shall endeavour to show how in sects of Zionist type, Biblical and Christian ideas are merged into the old Zulu religion. It must be emphasized that in Churches of Ethiopian type responsible leaders are fighting against such tendencies as in their opinion degrade the Christian standard of their Church. But we emphasize also that in Ethiopian Churches —as no doubt in Mission Churches—the pull from this heathen heritage is very strong and constitutes an everpresent problem. One is reminded of Herskovits' view of the vitality of African culture and religion when one becomes acquainted with the Churches which are studied in this book. The parallel, drawn in Ch. V, p. 109, between heathen diviner and Zionist prophet is in fact very well exemplified by this encounter between Dlakude's novices and Elliot Butelezi's Sabbath Zionist group. It should, however, be pointed out that the Zionists, on having this parallel pointed out to them, feel it to be an awkward problem. On the one hand, if in a matter of healing the Zionist prophet's diagnosis is doubted by his client, he may establish some co-operation with his colleague in the Zulu "Harley Street" by advising the patient to consult a diviner. This latter will probably support the prophet's diagnosis with his own authority. But on the other hand, just as Elliot Butelezi's Sabbath Zionist group regarded their "Jordan-stream" as having been defiled by the diviners, so all Zionists agree in regarding the diviner as possessed by demons. One woman who had left the Lutheran Church at Ceza gave as her reason for leaving, the fact that for some time she had felt the *isangoma*-demon—in traditional Zulu language, the spirit (*idlozi*)—wanting to enter her. Therefore she rushed to the Zionists, who prayed for her and put her through purification rites. She believed they had saved her just in the nick of time. If this had not been done, she would have been completely possessed by the *isangoma*-spirit and all his works. The matter was urgent, because once a person has become a fully qualified diviner, his spirit is virtually thought to be stronger than all the powers which a prophet has at his command.

The more daring Zionists try to convert diviners. Tryfina Nthuli invited four groups of diviners to her kraal where they stayed for two weeks. She fed them, and every morning, when her guests had returned from the vomiting rites at the river, she would call them to prayer and explain the teaching of the Bible to them. It would seem that her visitors rather enjoyed themselves, but they would not become Zionists, much to Tryfina's disgust. Filipina Dlamini, a forceful and personable prophetess, rather hurt the feelings of her diviner friends when she sent them the following invitation: "Come and let me pray for you, so that your demon may leave you." Nevertheless they came, led by their "Father", a wise old woman. They were six in all, but the Zionists who received them in Filipina's hut were more numerous. Waiting for the tremendous encounter with the heathen diviners, the Zionist group had worked themselves up into a stage of religious hysteria—shouting, singing, speaking with tongues. But when the diviners quietly entered the hut, Filipina and her followers suddenly became completely silent. The demons had made them mute, they said. They were over-powered, and after a short while Filipina had to ask her heathen guests to leave because they could not worship with demons in the hut. Only when the diviners had departed and disappeared in the distance did Filipina regain her spiritual power, and they all started to sing and pray with renewed strength. I think it is interesting that the young diviner who related this instance to me states that when she goes to a Lutheran or Anglican church service, her ancestral spirit will keep quiet, but when she comes to a Zionist service, with its shouting and tongues, "her spirit wakes up with strength" (*idlozi lami liyavuka ngamandla*). Not even baptism can, according to Zionist theology, purify a diviner. All other hysterical illnesses can be washed away by holy and living water, but not this one. It is frequently said that if they tried to baptize a diviner, the ancestral spirit would kill him in the water.

While on the one hand the Zionists have formed their religion on the pattern of the *isangoma* system, yet on the other they are very careful to point out that of course they have nothing in common with such people. The prayer-woman Anna Khu-malo knew not how close to the truth she was when she once told me: "The diviners defile the Christian faith, claiming that they too have the Holy Spirit."

The basic pattern from which Zulu Zionism is copied is that of diviner and witch-finder activities rather than that of the historic Christian Church. We have already studied in some detail the sociological implications of the parallelism between heathen diviner and Zionist prophet—a parallel which is admitted by most Zulus and upon which they often comment. We shall reach a deeper understanding of the Zionist system as we become acquainted with the Zionist "theology" of *uMoya*, the Spirit. This reveals the existence of a distinct system of Zionist theology, the emergence of a Bantu syncretism.

UMoya-theology in Zionist Churches

The fundamental concept in Zionist ideology is *uMoya*, the Spirit, by them understood to be the Holy Spirit of whom the Book has spoken. Within modern Protestantism, especially in America, most of the secessions which have arisen from time to time have been caused by different interpretations of the Holy Spirit, and it is only to be expected that some of the same

difficulties will arise in such African Churches as are the outcome of missionary efforts from Western Churches of Pentecostal, Apostolic Faith and Zionist type. To give an idea of
what happens when this radical Holy-Spirit-message is conveyed to the Africans, we quote some passages from an
autobiographical tract written by a lady missionary:

> My real call was while attending the convocation of prayer at
> X Grounds not far from St. Louis, U.S.A. I had a wonderful vision
> of the whole map of Africa and natives coming towards me. After
> receiving the Holy Ghost, the Lord showed me that it was not the
> outward adorning but a meek and quiet spirit of the heart that
> pleased Him. At a Camp meeting in the summer of 1908 I received
> the baptism of the Holy Spirit and soon left for the shores of
> Africa. Arriving safely at Johannesburg I was met by a party of
> Missionaries who had just preceded me a few months and who
> were the first to carry the glorious Gospel of the Holy Ghost to that
> land [sic!]. God was pouring out His Spirit upon both black and
> White in a marvellous way. Natives were filled with the Holy
> Ghost and spoke in languages that they knew not. Sometimes also
> in English fulfilling the second chapter of Acts. We had separate
> meetings for the children where they were saved and filled with
> the Spirit by the score. . . . We went to Native compounds. Often
> we began to speak to them through an interpreter but soon the
> Holy Spirit spoke through us in their native language which we
> had never studied, and they recognized that it was the real voice
> of God, speaking to them. The result is that the Pentecost message
> is spreading throughout all parts of the country among the natives.
> (*Comforter-Trooster*, Johannesburg, August–September, 1940).

There started a fire which missionaries such as the lady just
quoted would probably describe as the fire of the Holy Spirit.
In Churches of Zionist type one nowadays wades through the
ashes resulting from such fires.

Churches of Zionist type point out in their constitutions the
importance of the baptism of the Holy Ghost. The Holy Catholic
Apostolic Church in Zion says that this spiritual baptism "was
the normal experience of all in the early Christian Church. This
experience is distinct from and subsequent to the new birth.
The Baptism of the believers in the Holy Ghost is indicated by
the initial physical signs of speaking with other tongues as the
Spirit of the God gives them utterance."

But when attempting to find out what *uMoya* really means
in Zionist Churches, one is of course not much helped by a
study of their constitutions, nor by official or private statements

of the leaders alone. Only through mass observation by means of a great number of interviews of leaders and followers, men and women, in the reserve and in the City, has it been possible to get some understanding of the root meaning of these religious ideas.

Any Zionist will admit that there are two distinct aspects of the *uMoya* concept. First, *uMoya* can be understood in general terms of piety and good Christian behaviour. Second, *uMoya* in its specific sense is the sum of supernatural gifts, among which speaking with tongues is the most coveted. It is with *uMoya* in this second specific sense that we are here concerned.

What are the conditions for becoming possessed by *uMoya*? Some leaders among the Zionists and the Nazarites are known to have *uMoya*, others are generally known *not* to have *uMoya*. Even Europeans can have *uMoya*, although this is supposed to be an exception. Zionists told me of a European missionary who must have had *uMoya*, because he had prophesied that one Amon Butelezi would die, and it happened just as he had said. Further, the missionary concerned had cursed a lapsed Christian who afterwards, true enough, became insane.

uMoya is recognized as being a power which is independent of most of the orthodox signs of Christian behaviour. Thus, one may have *uMoya* before being baptized. Isaiah Shembe, for instance, before being baptized was given power by the Holy Spirit to pray effectively for the sick.[1] *uMoya* is even morally neutral. I had a discussion with the prophetess Andelina Dlamini on this point. She told me of a prophet Shabalala who had ten wives and whose practice it was to take a new wife whenever he got tired of an earlier union. In spite of this, Andelina was very emphatic that he had the Holy Spirit. I tried to show that this was certainly not in accordance with Bible teaching on the Holy Spirit. Her reply was: "I know that there is no support in the Bible for my point of view. But one must believe one's own eyes. Both Shabalala and Sangweni [another prophet in the neighbourhood whose moral standard was about the same as Shabalala's] have the prophesying spirit. They can find a thing even if you hide it in your shoe. They *have* the Holy Spirit." "Rather Satan's spirit," I suggested. "No, the Holy Spirit. Even if they throw away all appearances of Christianity, yes, even their cloths and put on *ibeshu*—the heathen men's tail-cover—and eat earth, still they have the Holy Spirit."

People who otherwise are known to have *uMoya* would as a rule show no sign of it when attending a service in a Mission

Church. The Spirit is there blocked (*uyavinjwa*), it is explained. Usually, *uMoya* will be given to the faithful in a dream or during the night. I quote extensively from two cases. The first is that of a man who earlier was a helper in a Mission Church and who still claims to belong to that Church—as a matter of fact he has never joined the Zionists. His whole somatic type—thin, nervous, fanatic appearance, hair long in Zionist fashion—immediately leads one to feel that he belongs to the Zionist type. The second is that of a woman who during the last twenty years has three times vacillated between a Mission Church and two Zionist groups.

(1) Simon Xaba: "The missionary always used to bother me with reminders about my church dues. I become tired of it. I said to myself, it is much better to worship at home, and so I left church life for a long time. Then one day I had a dream. I saw a man seated on a great throne and surrounded by huge burning candles. A pain developed in my neck through my having to turn my eyes upwards in order to see him. Then a Voice asked me: 'Are you a preacher?' I replied: 'Yes, my King, but I am alone.' This question and the reply were repeated twice; then replying the third time, I said: 'I was never ordained for that work.' The Voice said: 'I will put *uMoya* into thee, because thou hast received a Heavenly Ordination.' I awoke. A sharp wind blew. I felt that I was full (*ngisuthile*), I was full indeed. I almost burst, yes, I was ready to burst. I fell down. I threw myself in all directions. My whole body was shaking, not for fear, but because I was filled with *uMoya*. I got up and ran from the door to *emsamo* in my hut (the inner, sacred part of the hut) and back again. I was perspiring and filled with *uMoya*. Next morning I went out on the hilltop. But even though it was morning, my eyes only saw darkness for I was ill, and I had to sit down. Presently I returned home. Two Zionist girls passed our place. I was lying on the floor. 'What is the matter with you?' they asked. 'I am sick.' 'Drink water and ashes and vomit,' they advised. But I could not. The girls said: 'That man is dying. We had better call others.' Some neighbours of ours came, and when they asked what was the matter with me, the girls replied: 'He is made sick by the *uMoya* (*uyaguliswa uMoya*). In your school [= Church] *uMoya* is hindered. He is going to die, if he doesn't join the Zionists.' [The conversation continued in the following manner]—(Simon): 'I am never going to be baptized a second time.' (Other Zionists): 'We have seen the vision of white clothes and sashes with

245

crosses upon them. You will have to accept that.' 'No, I am not going to leave my church.' 'If you persist, you will die.' 'Yes, but not because of that.' 'You must go through purification rites for then you will see other great things.' "

(2) Anna Khumalo: "When the Prince of Wales came to Eshowe[a] I got suddenly ill with severe headache so that I nearly died. My husband had planned to go to Eshowe, but was hindered by my illness. Then I had a dream. I was brought along a road, and had to pass through a narrow passage, as narrow as between two fingers. I managed to pass and came to a house. Outside there was fine short grass, just as in the mission garden. I saw a man in shining white clothes (but I cannot say who he was) together with the Native minister, A. M——. The man in white asked me: 'Do you see that man?' pointing to somebody sitting on a chair on the right side of the door. 'Do you see that it is your Zulu King.' *Hhawu*, then I saw that it was our king (Dinuzulu). And I saw processions of many people. Exactly so it was at Eshowe that day. That is how I got the Holy Spirit, and I was filled with joy, and with longing to lay hands upon the sick. I now often get *uMoya* when singing, always when praying for the sick."

Analysing these two *uMoya*-dreams, I think it is significant that in Simon's dream the inspiration is felt by him as if he was gorged—certainly a genuinely Bantu conception of well-being! Still more interesting is the remark by the Zionists: "*Uyaguliswa uMoya.*" When one remembers how often Zulus will refer to a person as having been *gulisa*'d, or made sick, by the ancestral spirit, or other hysterical illnesses, one is struck by this formula, as it reveals something of the to-be-possessed-character of the *uMoya*-state of mind. In Anna's dream there is a delightful reference to King Dinuzulu, sitting in heavenly glory and receiving the faithful among his own Zulu people into the Green Pastures. I venture to suggest that here the picture of the Zulu king (besides being reminiscent of the Eshowe festivals held for the Prince of Wales at which Dinuzulu's son, Chief Solomon, was present) is a dream symbol for that national supremacy also in religious affairs which Anna felt was needed to provide that full and free sway for her *uMoya*-religion denied her in the Mission Church. The Spirit does not come in dreams only. The singing of certain hymns, especially those about the heavenly

[a] The main place in Zululand; the royal visit to South Africa took place in 1925.

Jerusalem or about Ekuphakameni and Zion (in *ama*-Nazarita and Zion Churches) will so stir up feelings that *uMoya* appears. One of the more hysterical women in my Ceza congregation, Dolosina, told me that when certain hymns were announced by the evangelist she immediately had to leave the church and sit down for a while under a tree outside, because even during the singing of the first words she felt the *uMoya* in her shoulders, and her arms would begin to shake. During prayer, and especially prayer for the sick, the Spirit wakes up with irresistible power. That, by the way, is given as an excuse by certain young prophets—boys of sixteen or seventeen years of age—who while praying for sick or barren women will feel with their hands all over the body of the women concerned: *"uMoya* is too strong, it cannot be controlled by man."

An important observation should be made in this connexion: many informants stress that *uMoya* is most acutely felt at the outset, when first joining the Zionists. After that it reaches a climax and eventually fades away. There is no regret attached to this statement by my informants, sometimes expressed in Zulu *Angisa hlushwa inkolo* (I am no longer troubled by religion). It seems to them that to be possessed by *uMoya* was a certain stage through which they had to pass on entering the Church—much the same as the novice is more pestered by the *idlozi* than is the older diviner.

It is characteristic that Dolosina, mentioned earlier, felt the Spirit in her shoulders. Some specify this feeling as that of being burnt or as "the lighting of a match", but it is always located in the shoulders. Although thus focusing the Holy Spirit at the same point as the supposed abode of the ancestral spirit, Zionists who have earlier been diviners or have had *amandiki*-possession are anxious to emphasize that the *uMoya*-feeling is not the same as that in heathen hysteria. My friend Elias Mavundla, an earlier member of the Lutheran Church and now a follower of his wife's Zionist group, made the distinction from a more specifically phenomenological point of view: *"uMoya oyingcwele akasini. Amandiki namandawe ayasina"* (The Holy Spirit does not cause a person to dance in the way that the *amandawe* and *amandiki* spirits do.)

Speaking with Tongues

Pentecostal Churches, whether they are led by Europeans or Africans, are definite on the gift of speaking with tongues: "The Baptism of believers in the Holy Ghost is indicated by the initial physical sign of speaking with other tongues, as the Spirit of God gives them utterance.'' At a Zionist meeeting which I attended recently the congregation had just commenced a hymn, when one of the women suddenly started convulsive movements of the body and gesticulated with her arms in an up-and-down movement. With half-closed eyelids she spoke with tongues:

> Dji-dji-dji-dji-dji,-dji, Hallelujah, Hallelujah, Hallelujah,
> Do-do-do-do-d-do-do-do-zzzzzzzzzz. Amen.

This went on for just over two minutes. Then she was calm again and sat down on the floor, but did not sing. At a Zionist service one almost invariably experiences happenings of this kind. Failing more spectacular demonstrations of *uMoya*-presence, a Zionist prophet must at least produce the typical Zionist snort during a service to show that the Spirit is very near.

But singing and prayer, especially prayer for the sick, holy ablutions, especially if under a waterfall, are favourable conditions for the fuller appearance of tongues. Two examples from this language of the angels may be given, as one hears it at any service of Zionist or Full Gospel type:

> 1. De de de de de de de de . . .
>   Hlo hlo hlo hlo hlo hlo . . .
>   Blood river sign Blood river sign Blood river sign. Amen.
>
> 2. *Zzzzzzzzzzzzzzzzzzzzzz*
>   Hhayi hhayi hhayi hhayi
>   Sorry Jesu Sorry Jesu Sorry Jesu
>   Spy spy spy spy spy, Naughty boy naughty boy
>   Hhayi hhayi hhayi,—Hallelujah, Hallelujah, Amen.

This sort of thing is regarded in these circles as something super-Christian. A study of the different types of glossolaly among the Zulus would, however, make it difficult for the Zionists to maintain that these phenomena have any distinct Christian value. At least it would show that when the Zulu prophet follows his Corinthian colleague, rather against St. Paul's advice, he does so because it is an old heathen pattern.

The best parallel to tongues which people in northern Zululand know of is the so-called *izizwe* or *amaбutho*. When a person is ill the Zulu doctor (*inyanga*) may treat him in the following way:[a] He gives his patient a mixture to smoke which when

---

[a] As this form of treatment for hysteria has not been described by others I briefly mention it here.

248

inhaled will drive away the illness or rather replace the illness by something the Zulus call "soldiers" (ama6utho). The mixture to be inhaled consists of certain bones and herbs plus an ingredient which decides which language the "soldier" (or "demon" in New Testament language) is going to speak. If the doctor wants the "soldier" to speak as an Englishman and instil in the patient the physical and mental powers of an Englishman, his ingredient will be, for instance, a piece of hair of such a person or a piece from an Englishman's mat. If the doctor wants the person to get the powers of a railway engine, the ingredient will probably be some grease from an engine wheel. The result will be that in the first case the demons of the patient will speak English, for instance: "Naughty boy, naughty boy"; in the second case, the Railway language (which, by the way, is quite simple: "Tu-tu-tu-tu!").

Various forms of native speaking with tongues have been known since times immemorial among the Zulus. The outpouring of uMoya which results in tongues did not start among the Zulus when, in 1908, certain American missionaries were "the first to carry the glorious gospel of the Holy Spirit" to South Africa. It had started long before that. In fact, long before the first Zulu had ever heard the name of Christ.

Spirit and Angel

Spirit and Angel (*ingelosi*) are concepts which Zionists sometimes use rather indiscriminately. There is, however, a definite tendency among most to differentiate between them. Simplifying Zionist ideas on this particular point, I think it is safe to say that *uMoya* is thought to be a general state of being divinely possessed, whereas *ingelosi* and the Voice are channels by which *uMoya* reveals itself and makes its will known. Whereas the Spirit is the latent to-be-possessed-feeling, the Angel is always active, and active in two ways: critical of some misbehaviour and showing the way out of an impasse.

The Angel appears chiefly in dreams and during prayer, especially prayer for the sick, and here it tells the prophet how the patient should be healed (according to the formula: "The Angel says: You have to wear a green sash." *Ingelosi ithi, ufanele ukugqoka ibande eliluhlaza*). After special invitation a prophet may take his own special short-cut to inviting the Angel. One told me that when he put on a white veil, a host of angels would come with fluttering wings around him. This to him was a sure way of knowing that the patient for whom he was praying would recover. If the angels failed to appear, the patient would die. The Angel expresses itself according to a stale formula of two elements: *Ingelosi yathi* (the Angel said . . .), or *Ingerosi iyasora* (the Angel criticises—here the Zulu language is made angelic by changing "l" into "r"); and *Ingelosi iyafuna* (the Angel wants . . .).

A Zionist's wife was childless; his married sister also remained barren. Then his prophet was visited by an angel. The Angel said: "You are both without children because you have neglected your ancestral spirits and they are angry. The angel wants you to sacrifice a bull to them." So they did, and it is declared that they were blessed with children. The Angel's main reproach in Churches of Zionist type is that the ancestral spirits have been neglected. Othaniel, our garden boy at Ceza, brought his child to the Zionists to be prayed for. They would agree to this on one condition: "That you slaughter something, because your father's angel wishes a bull to be slaughtered." Or they may tell a person whose child is ill: "Your child has been made ill by the grandfather. His spirit wants a beast" (*Ingane yabulawa uyise, idlozi liyafuna inkomo*). This is exactly what occurs among the heathen diviners, who say that a bad omen (*ishwa*) has appeared because the ancestral spirit is angry and has to be pacified by a sacrifice. In these last two examples we reach the very root of the matter. The Angel not only brings a message from the ancestral spirit; the Angel *is* the spirit, the ancestral spirit.

The Angel's advice for bringing a person out of an impasse (*ingelosi iyafuna . . .*) is often to tell So-and-so to put on a white uniform or a green sash. But in a real crisis, the only way out is the sacrifice (*kuhlatshwe into* or *kushelezwe impahla*). This is carried out with support claimed from the Old Testament: "We do as Abraham did, when he wanted to sacrifice Isaac. And God told him: Your belief is great." A bull or a goat is killed. The Zionists eat and drink and pray and sing. The Angel is pacified. The patient recovers. (Sometimes, of course, he does not, but they soon forget about that.)

Isaiah Shembe, though reticent in speaking to Europeans on the subject of sacrifices, nevertheless insisted on the need of them: "They hold people together by blood. The Gate of Heaven is opened through sacrifices." The ancient custom was by him Christianized in an interesting way: one of the Nazarite ministers had to wash the head of each beast before it was speared.

This was explained by a prominent Nazarite woman: the beasts were baptized.[2]

It is particularly important to sacrifice a beast on the occasion of *uku6uyisa ofileyo* (bringing back of the deceased). This is an old Zulu custom: about a year after the death of the head of the kraal, people were invited to a ceremony (*ihlambo*) which included the sacrifice of a beast,.and which ceremony was supposed to localize the wandering spirit in the kraal, so that he would stay there and guard his descendants. Some Mission Churches in Zululand call people to a simple service or prayer-meeting at the kraal a certain time after the burial. Other missions are against this, and there may be good reasons for this attitude. An African Angelican priest told me that a Zulu churchwarden had arranged an *ihlambo*, or as the Christians call it *isi6usiso* (blessing), for his deceased mother. When he was asked why he did so, the reply was: "I bring my mother back" (*ngiyabuyisa umame*). The example is interesting because it is implied that the spirit of a woman can be "brought back". In olden times it was thought that only the spirits of men could be thus "brought back".

The Zionist prophet Meshak Mdletshe has evolved a distinct, new form of service for this occasion. When all the people have gathered he goes into the cattle-kraal clad in his white robe and carrying a dish of water. There he makes the sign of the cross over the water and sprinkles the beast before it is killed. When the blood flows out on the ground, he exclaims: "God will see by the blood that it is a well-pleasing sacrifice." After this he goes to the grave, takes a twig and exclaims when he has placed the twig on the grave:

> This is So-and-so's twig,
> He will rise by it.
>
> (*Isihlahla sakhe, uzokhuphuka ngaso.*)

It is thought that after such a sacrifice the spirit of the deceased will come and, as an Angel, take up its abode in the kraal and guard it against all dangers.[a]

A further development of this idea is the differentiation of function among the Angels which is taking place in Zulu Zionist Churches at the present time. Thus there is an Angel of Wrath,

---

a Many Churches of Zionist type do not practise this sacrifice for the deceased. The reason why Nyembe of the Full Gospel Church of Spookmill is against *isi6usiso*, is interesting: "We do not celebrate *isi6usiso*, because that is to give the deceased food, just as the Europeans do at their burials".

and an Angel of the Waters, or more specifically an Angel of a certain pool where baptisms and purification rites are performed. The local congregation may get its particular Angel as a guardian, this (so the Zionists say) being in accordance with the Book of Revelation (e.g. "the angel of the church in Laodicea"). When visiting an outstation where church attendance was particularly weak, one Emtulwa prophet exclaimed: "I should like to curse this place, but the Angel of this place does not permit me to do it" (*ingelosi ya lapha ayivumi*).

Through the commands of the Angel the faithful will be led in the way of righteousness. However, certain difficulties appear when the one *uMoya* makes its will known through two or more persons' individual Angels. I was present at a purification ceremony which was led by the prophet Mthethwa, though the actual purifying act was conducted by the prophetess Dolosina Hlangoti.ᵃ Before going to the pool there was to be a prayer meeting. There were many people present, and when Mthethwa said that the Angel wanted us all to congregate in a little hut for prayers, I grew somewhat hesitant in view of the crowd there would be in so small a space. I cautiously suggested that we might sit outside. To my delight Dolosina then proclaimed that *her* Angel insisted on our remaining outside. But when the purification started Dolosina mentioned that the Angel wanted the following order: first the bottles which people had brought should be filled with blessed water, and only after that the immersion of children and adults could begin. Mthethwa, however, had got other light: his Angel had shown him that if he, Mthethwa, took care of the bottles and Dolosina of the actual immersion, the act would sooner come to an end—and in this case his Angel won.

It is not surprising then that this same Spirit, by the Zionists interpreted as the Holy Spirit, can be cited as the authority for any subjective fancy or predilection which the particular prophet may have. A typical quotation is one from a letter written by the leader of the Jerusalem Apostolic Church of Africa: "By the permission of the Holy Ghost we marry two or three wives. O, Sirs, we are not doing this on our own, but we are empowered by the Holy Ghost and God. If the Holy Ghost comes to me, I shall also marry two or more wives, according to these laws I have just mentioned."

Through the whimsicalities arising out of these subjective visions and auditions, called Spirit and Angel, a tremendous

ᵃ Cf. pp. 202 ff.

uncertainty is brought into all church matters, leading to disputes and strife. In many cases the *uMoya*-theology has been the real cause of the constant division and breaking-up in these Churches.

There is a reason for this. Churches should be built upon the Rock. They should not be built upon sand.

(b) *Magic and Divining*

Witchcraft and Sorcery. Frank Melland has done African missions and administration a great service in analysing the status of the so-called witch-doctor in African society. He has shown how misleading the term "witch-doctor" is: "He is no more a witch than an Inspector of the C.I.D. is a burglar."[3] In discussing the place of magic in the Zionist Churches we must divest ourselves of the all-too-common connotation of the word "witch-doctor" and realize that according to pagan African standards and ideas the "witch-doctor", or to use a better term the diviner, is more than anyone else engaged in stamping out witchcraft. Thereby, according to their logic, he is a wholesome and necessary element in society. Audrey Richards has introduced the term "witch-finder", and this term very aptly describes the nature of the diviner's work.[4]

It is against different forms of magic that the Zionist prophet, as a diviner, directs his energies. In order to understand Zionist divining it is necessary to know traditional Zulu ideas on the cause of ill-luck and illness, because pagan Zulu logic about the magical causation of sickness and death is the pattern on which Zionist divining activities are based.

As shown above, *u6uthakathi* can be either witchcraft (*ukuphosa*) or sorcery (*ukudlisa*). This means that illness or death or some other calamity is either sent or "thrown" by a witch-familiar during the night, or else transmitted by some poisonous substance which after having been duly treated is brought into connexion with the would-be victim. This thought-pattern is adopted and adapted by the Zionist prophet and his followers. An Israelite minister whom I used to know suffered from tuberculosis. His wife was convinced that it had been "thrown" by night by some of their enemies. When asked what kind of witch-familiar she thought had done it, she would not explain. But she was certainly unshaken in her belief that the illness had actually been thrown.

E. J. and J. D. Krige have shown the role of the internal snake in Lovedu belief. It is obvious that the Zulu share this belief and attribute to a snake the same functions as do the Lovedu, especially with regard to fecundity and childbirth. Among the Lovedu "everyone is said to have a snake in his stomach. . . . It is believed that semen comes from a man's snake. If his snake is 'no good', a child will not be born. The snake of a woman is sometimes identified with the womb and for conception it is necessary that this snake should accept the semen."[5] This belief is shared by Zionists. They explain barrenness thus: witches (a6athakathi) send a snake which penetrates the body and gets into the womb, where it kills the fœtus. I have referred to an experience from a Nazarite healing service for barren women which I observed in July, 1941. One of the most pathetic sights was a Nazarite woman who kept on crying the whole time nga6adla a6antwana 6ami ("I ate my children"). Undoubtedly this referred to her conviction that her internal snake had caused the many abortions from which she had suffered. The prophet, himself a B.A., explained to me that the reason for barrenness of another woman was that she had a snake in her stomach.

Still more important than the belief in witchcraft is the Zulu belief in sorcery (ukudlisa), which as a matter of course Zionists share to the full. The Zionist prophet explains various illnesses as having been caused by medicines hidden in the hut of the patient. One woman, whose children used to become blind a short time after birth, was brought to Isaiah Shembe for treatment. His advice was that she should go home and remove all medicines from the hut and sweep the house well. This may refer to Shembe's aversion to medicines in general (see p. 227), but in this particular case it probably reflects the Nazarite belief in the hidden magical poisons which cause sickness and death.[6] In the Ceza area, Zionists claimed that an umkhokheli (prayer-woman) must be very careful about the water in which she has washed. If a sorcerer obtained some drops of the dirty water, he might mix it with poison and thereby do harm to the prayer-woman herself and to the whole congregation. One evening I met a Zionist prophet who had returned from ploughing his fields. I discovered that he had been very careful to hide his plough lest some evil-doer should find it, scrape off the sweat that had adhered to the handle and mix it with some of his medicines. A Zionist has to be specially careful about locking away his Bible if it is old and torn. A sorcerer may tear a piece from a page, mix it with poison, and put it into the owner's food. At Makitika a Zionist flock told me that an old heathen had suddenly recited the whole book of Jonah. He had never read or heard this story himself, but some *inyanga* had taken a page from the Old Testament, and had mixed it with his medicines—and that was the result!

The changes and upheavals in modern Zulu society—be it in the reserve, on the farms, or in the city—have brought with them uncertainty and its corollary of the ever increasing search for security against all threatening dangers from ill-omens to death. Some Zionist prophets in this situation form, as it were, a modern movement of witch-finders, who assist and in many ways replace the heathen witch-finder or diviner. The pattern of heathen divining is closely followed, but it has been reshaped to suit modern conditions.

I quote an instance of Zionist "prophesying" in action. Amos Qwabe, belonging to a Mission Church, had built a new hut in his kraal, and when the work was finished he invited his friends who had given him a hand. His wife had prepared large quantities of *amahewu* (fermented porridge) for the guests. Unfortunately all those present at the party became ill, including Amos' wife; the only exception was a woman, Anelina, who did not suffer any ill-effects. Now it was obvious to all that somebody was an *umthakathi* (evil-doer), and had put poison in the porridge. But who was the culprit? Amos' father was a Zionist. He knew an unfailing method of discovering the truth of the matter. He called the most famous specialist on prophesying in the whole district, A. Dlamini. One day Dlamini came with his Zionist flock, and the whole village congregated in Amos' kraal. After two hymns and a prayer, Dlamini, as is his custom, started with the preliminary business side of the matter: "You will have to show me a beast or put £5 on the table." The latter was done. "You all have to sign a statement that if any of you personally is pointed out as being the evil-doer, he will not report the matter to court." This was done. Dlamini then called before him Amos' wife and the woman who had not been affected. The Zionists started a song with many Amens, and the inquiry itself took place to the pious accompaniment of a hymn.

Dlamini to Amos' wife: "Did you brew the *amahewu*?"
She: "Yes."
D.: "Did the guests feel well after drinking it?"
She: "No."
D.: "They became sick?"
She: "Yes."

D.: "How did people become sick?"
She: "I don't know."
D. (to other woman): "Do you know anything about this *amahewu* matter?"
She: "Yes."
D. "Do you know how the people became sick?"
She: "No."
D. (with emphasis): "*You* did it!"
She: "*Cha!* (No!)"
D.: "I prayed to the Lord and He pointed you out to me."

The prophet lifted his hand to tell the congregation to stop singing, called the local Zionist evangelist and told him: "Here is the woman who has done it. The Lord pointed her out to me." (Then to the woman) "You tell us now where you have hidden the medicine!" Anelina: "I did not do it!" Dlamini, addressing the congregation, made the final pronouncement: "This is the woman who put poison in your porridge. Even if she denies it, the Lord has shown me the truth." The Zionist faithful started to sing again with jubilant Hallelujahs and Amens. Dlamini put the £5 in his pocket, and the woman left the hut crying.

Prophesying with its pointing out of the evil-doer should, according to the rules, take a more roundabout and less direct way than the one shown in this example. But Dlamini's undisputed authority among heathen and Christians of various Churches freed him from concern with regard to such details and detours that a lesser man would have had to observe. Apart from this, however, I think the example is representative of what Zionists mean by prophesying.

Prophesying is divining, in a supposedly Christian form. The pattern of *isangoma* divining (*ukubula*) is followed very closely. The general idea about heathen divining is of course that the *isangoma* by asking leading questions eliminates various possibilities and reaches a conclusion (about the illness of a certain person, about the place where poison has been hidden and so on). The people who ask for advice assist in this process of elimination by shouting in chorus: "*Yizwa*" (Hear!), or hitting the ground with sticks (*ukubula*). If the diviner's guesses are incorrect, the *yizwa*'s and the smiting are quiet, but when his guesses are correct, *yizwa* is shouted with force.[7]

In Zionist prophesying *yizwa* is replaced by Amen, and to divine is called to prophesy. Further, the ceremony is accompanied by hymns and prayers. But otherwise, and essentially, it is the same thing. This is felt to be a problem by some prophets: they do not want to be mixed up with demon-possessed diviners. The difficulty can, however, be overcome with the help of the Bible. For, to be sure, you are told to *ukubula*, or divine, in the Bible!

Abisayi's child died suddenly. Prophet Ndlovu was called to divine the reason. He was to point out where the sorcerer's medicine had been hidden. As a prophet he knew his Bible. He read (Micah 4: 13): "*Vuka, ubule ndodakazi kaZioni!*" The Authorized Version has: "Rise and thresh, daughter of Zion." The whole context of Micah 4 uses images from Israelite harvesting: Rise and thresh—the corn. The Zulu translation has here the verb *ukubula*, the original meaning of which is "to smite". But from the custom of smiting the ground at the heathen divining, this ceremony as a whole is also called *ukubula*. Our Ndlovu, however, did not bother overmuch about exegetical technicalities; he read in his Bible: "Rise and *ukubula*", i.e. divine in *isangoma* fashion. He preached for a while on this text. Then he climbed to the top of the thatched hut, and after fumbling in the grass produced a bottle which contained the magical medicine responsible for the death of Abisayi's child.

The role of anti-lightning magic in pagan Zulu society is reflected and deflected in the methods which Zionist prophets use. I have already written of lightning as one medium of the heavenly call to the would-be prophet. It is significant that "the thing above all others which had interested Isaiah Shembe was lightning", as his son testifies, and he spent much time speculating about it.[8] The prophet, being filled with heavenly powers transmitted by lightning, is particularly fitted to help the community in warding off lightning from the kraals. Whereas the pagan heaven-doctor used charms (*intelezi*) in order to prevent lightning striking the kraal,[9] the Zionist prophet modernizes the precautionary measures. The most effective method is the display of white flags on flagpoles. A prophet, J. N. of northern Zululand, had erected two flagpoles with white flags in his own kraal. At the foot of each flagpole a small wooden cross had been fastened with strings. This device was by the Zionist and pagan inhabitants of the kraal regarded as a means of making the prophet's lightning magic both Christian and much more effective than the charms hitherto known.

In conversation with me the prophet was reticent on the subject of the flags, and cheerfully suggested that he had put them up so that people would recognize his kraal and know that "here lives J. N." When I suggested that his wife and the other people of his Church had a more specific interpretation of the flags—namely to avert lightning—J. N. retorted that this was caused by their insufficient knowledge of the Bible. Nthuli, of an Apostolic Church in R——, Central Natal, was more outspoken on the subject. He had no less than seven white flags flying over his kraal. They were the seals of the seven angels in the Book of Revelation, he confided to me, and while all the flags had not the same function, some were waving prayers to God day and night, thereby warding off lightning from the kraal.

On a certain occasion in 1944, in V——, some Zionist prophets murdered a Zionist woman by forcibly pressing ashes down her throat. This they did in order to cleanse her from sins which she had not confessed. When struggling for her life, she implored her sister to help her, and her last words were a threat to her sister (I quote from the minutes of the court): "You are also looking on while people are killing me! God will strike you with lightning!" In view of such threats, the prophets of course have every need to be well prepared to combat any lurking danger.

The more important functions of prophetic divining in Churches of the Zionist type are the following:

(1) Diagnosing illness: A girl was ill with some disorder; the heathen diviner's diagnosis was: "She is full with blood." But prophetess Dolosina was not satisfied with this. When observing the patient, Dolosina felt her own womb being filled (*isisu sami sakhuluphala*). She then "prophesied" that the girl was pregnant—and this proved to be correct. Prophesying about causes of barrenness is extremely frequent. In all healing activities there will be some prophesying about the colour of sash or cord that the patient should wear to get rid of the illness.

(2) An example of pointing out the evil-doer (*umthakathi*) has already been given in some detail. This power of discernment is supposed to emanate from *uMoya*. In a dramatic struggle for supremacy between a famous Zionist Church-leader and the inspired female medium of the deceased prophet, the church was given to understand by the prophet that the medium had attempted to use *ubuthakathi*-medicine against her rival power. On this charge she was excommunicated from the Church.

258

(3) Revealing hidden sin in the Church and prophesying about general calamities in the world. *uMoya* gives the prophet power to see through a person. As Philemon Mthembu of Damaseku Zion Church told me: "The heart of man can be read (*inhliziyo yomuntu iyafundeka*); nobody can hide his innermost feelings from a prophet. Before a Communion service I can feel if there is a stone in the congregation, that is; a person with unconfessed sins. I prophesy to him that he is, for instance, a thief. And he will reply: 'Yes, man of God. I cannot go against God's spirit, which is in you.'" In this way prophesying also becomes the means of watching over and safeguarding the chastity of young and old in the congregation. Vague reminiscences from the Book of Revelation of St. John give some Christian colour to prophecies about general calamities, wars, epidemics. One Velemina told me that she had for the last eight years wandered about Zululand and Natal, proclaiming what *uMoya* had shown her in a prophecy, namely the imminent appearance of wounds, sicknesses, harlotry and *amandawe*-hysteria. These various forms of prophesying keep the faithful in a state of constant expectancy, and if slackening threatens, *uMoya* can be counted upon to reveal something else through prophesying.

(4) *uMoya*-inspired prophesying dictates new action and behaviour in the Church. A prophet explained the existence of the Feast of Tabernacles in his congregation (Lev. 23) as having been given by his prophesying about this particular festival.

(c) The element of change

We return to the encounter at the Ihlekazi stream between Dlakude the heathen diviner and Elliot Butelezi the Zionist prophet (p. 238). It served to exemplify an important development in which—if we look at it through the glasses of the church historian—Western spiritualized religion was eventually changed and overcome by African spiritism. And we quoted the French saying to the effect that the more things change, the more they remain as they were before. That quotation might lead us along the wrong track, however. The decisive question is of course: Has there been any real change at all, and if so, in what direction? The church historian who, because Elliot happened to call himself a Sabbatarian Zionist, thinks of him in terms of the development of modern American Protestantism, will not be able to understand the meeting at dawn between the pagan diviner and Zionist prophet at the Ihlekazi stream. I have attempted to show that Elliot was bound to think and

act in the categories and according to the patterns with which
he was familiar—namely, the categories and the pattern of
the Zulu diviner. But something new and very decisive had
changed his outlook: his Zionist conviction and what he would
call the inspiration of the Holy Spirit had led him to a conviction and a life which was undoubtedly different from that of
the heathen diviner. Can we measure that difference?

In a synoptic chart of "African Heritage in Zulu Zionist
Churches" (pp. 262–3), I have attempted to demonstrate suc-
cinctly the dynamic forces at work in the religious change
taking place at the present time within the Zionist movement.
In focusing the interest on three important aspects—ancestor-
worship, magic, and healing—and in analysing those elements
and patterns of heathen religion which have proved sufficiently
vital to survive in the new Christian form, we try to evaluate
the change from the heathen outlook to that of the Zionist
prophet and his followers.

(1) The two pillars of functioning Zulu religion—ancestor-
cult and magic—still stand in the very chancel of the Zionist
Church. The ancestor-cult and its corollary, sacrifice, form the
pattern on which Zionist Spirit-religion, cult of angels and
sacrifices, is built. The pattern of the heathen *isangoma* is
closely followed in the Zionist prophet's calling and activities.
Perhaps the most important point is that inspiration by the
Holy Spirit, *uMoya*, is interpreted in terms of possession, as a
state of mind. We came across the significant expressions
ukuguliswa uMoya, to be "made sick by the Spirit", and
angisahlushwa uMoya, "I am no longer troubled by the Spirit".

But an important change has taken place: whereas the
heathen knew two classes of sacrifice, thanksgiving to the
spirits (*ukubonga*) when the general life of the kraal developed
well, and scolding the spirits (*ukuthetha*) when things in the
kraal went wrong, the Zionist prophet—in relation to his Angel
—only knows the former kind of sacrifice, the thanksgiving.
There are other changes also: A heathen would never admit that
he felt well for fear that such pride on his part might bring down
the wrath of his ancestors. The Zionist counterpart to-day will,
when once initiated, never admit that there is anything wrong
with him: "Long ago I was sick. But the Zionist prayed for me.
Now I am well", is the formula ever to be used. It is quite
obvious that in the Zionist there is a spirit of optimism and of
joy which marks him off from the heathen with his more gloomy
outlook: the *amadlozi*, the Spirits, have been baptized. There is

also a difference in scale.[10] While the effective beneficial influence of the ancestors did not reach beyond the narrow boundaries of the kraal and the kin, the Angel may extend his sphere to a whole congregation or Church.

(2) The belief in magic survives in the Zionist Church. The reason for the vitality of African magic in modern times has been admirably stated by Audrey Richards in her study of "A Modern Movement of Witch-Finders" in Northern Rhodesia (*Africa*, 1935):

> Missionaries all over Africa are teaching a religion which casts out fear, but economic and social changes have so shattered tribal institutions and moral codes that the result of white contact is in many cases an actual increase in the dread of witchcraft, and therefore in the whole incidence of magic throughout the group.

Compare the fate of ancestor cult and magic in the Zulu society! The ancestral spirits and their cult have dwindled away in the City, driven out by the new spirits of secularism, industrialism, and western individualism. Only in the Reserve, where the ancestral graves are found, do they still retain an influence in the shining disguise of benevolent angels. Magic, on the other hand, does not give away to the pressure of modernism. It is driven underground, but by this very fact—by being forbidden and driven underground—it is revitalized and it reappears in the Zionist Church.

The Zionist prophet, who looks upon himself as a martyr and who more or less deliberately stresses the nationalistic and nativistic return to the olden times, uses the belief in magic as the foundation for his witch-finding activities. Perhaps "uses" is not the right word. The Zionist diviner-prophet does not—at least that is my contention from what I have experienced of them—"use" the belief in magic, as if it were a deliberate, clever technique on his part.[11] He practises witch-finding or "prophesying" because he shares to the full with his Zionist followers and his pagan friends their dread of witchcraft and their belief in its terrible reality. The social, economic, and religious upheavals of modern times have created an emotional crisis in their hearts, and even if the Zionists call their divining "prophesying", it is easy to see, with Malinowski, that "under the stress of emotional crisis the indigenous belief becomes stronger than the alien creed".[12]

I have not studied sufficiently the correlation between the morphology of Zionist magic and the various types of

SYNOPTIC CHART OF AFRICAN HERITAGE

	(*A.*) *European Influences*		(*B.*) *Process of Culture Change.*
I.		Missions.	
European Government and White Population.			
European scepticism against *Ancestor-worship*.	(1*a*) Puritan and sweeping condemnation of ancestor "cult", because involving sacrifices and divination.	1. City-ward trend of the Zulus leading to breakdown of the family.	
	(1*b*) Catholic (Roman Catholic and Anglo-Catholic) reinterpretation of the concept as integral part of belief in saints. Protestant Church: emphasis on the High-God *uNkulunkulu*, in place of the Ancient Spirits. Widening scale from the kinship protection by the spirits to the One Family of God.		
II.			
(2*a*) Common desire to exterminate belief in *witchcraft*		(2*a*) Resentment of Africans against European pressure to eradicate the belief in witchcraft itself. Intertribal suspicion among newly urbanized population on the Rand.	
(2*b*) Legislation against witchcraft and diviners, not realizing that the diviner claims to be opposed to witch-craft.	(2*b*) Common cause with Government and educated Africans, against "witch-doctors", because they conserve belief in witchcraft.	(2*b*) Ill-health, perplexity caused by impact of Western civilization. Diviners driven underground; rapid increase in number of diviners in the Reserve and in the City.	
(2*c*) Educational measures in schools, taking for granted that the very belief in witchcraft is absurd.			
III.			
(3*a*) *Health* propaganda by medical, educational, agricultural officers.	(3*a*) Scientific explanation of causation of disease in mission hospitals. "Divine Healing", as per Zion City, Ill., U.S.A.	(3*a*) Land shortage—urbanization — malnutrition — ill-health.	
(3*b*) Government Hospitals: Scientific diagnosis and treatment	(3*b*) Mission Hospitals: Scientific diagnosis and treatment, together with positive Christian teaching on illness and health.	(3*b*) African orderlies and nurses as assistants to European doctors and nurses. African doctors now being trained at University of Witwatersrand. European and African charlatans selling useless medicines and charms at exorbitant prices.	

IN ZULU ZIONIST CHURCHES

(C) *Surviving Forms of Zulu Culture*	*(D)* *New Expressions in Zionist Churches*
1. Neglect of ancestors felt by Africans as logical explanation of various forms of misfortune, particularly barrenness. Ancestor-worship in newly adapted forms of possession: *amandiki*-possession.	1a. "Ancestral Spirit" interpreted as "Holy Spirit" or "Angel". Being "religious" is being "possessed", although no longer by ancestral spirit, but by *uMoya*, the "Holy Spirit". *Ukuthetha*-attitude towards the spirits abandoned, and replaced by sacrifice of thanksgiving, p. 260. (1b) Hunger for revelation leading to a Black-Christ-theology.
(2a) Anxiety to be rid of witchcraft and sorcery. Witchcraft and sorcery regarded as cause of ill-health and misfortune.	(2a) Conserving the belief in witchcraft. Driven underground by the Whites, magic is revitalized by the Zionist Church.
(2b) Role of diviner as strong in the Zionist Church as in traditional Zulu culture.	(2b) Zionist churches acting as a "movement of witch-finders". Resorting to diviner-pattern in order to build up effective anti-witchcraft protection.
(2c) Anti-lightning magic and forms of healing magic.	(2c) Scientific explanations of causation of disease or misfortune believed to apply only to Europeans. Africans needing stronger, i.e. magical, protection.
(3a) Traditional Zulu ideas of magical causation of disease.	(3a) Sharing belief in magical causation of disease. Because of supposed demon-inducing properties of medicines opposing hospitals, medicines, doctors. Also influence from Pentecostal "divine healing".
(3b) Activities of *izinyanga* and increasing number of diviners. Glut of African medicines in both Reserve and the City.	(3b) Zionist prophets diagnosing disease on pattern of traditional divining. Healing through removing ritual uncleanness: purification rites.

community (rural and urban) in which it develops, to be able to confirm, in the case of the independent Churches, Evans-Pritchard's important suggestion about a correlation between magic and the type of political system.[18] But the material I have published certainly supports the general contention that the actual belief in witchcraft is vital in the Zionist Church. Both Zionist prophesying and Zionist healing are built on such a belief. No healing is complete until the prophet has found and removed from the patient's hut some horn or bottle, supposed to contain *ubuthakathi*-poison. In the Johannesburg areas I have come across a few examples of soil from a grave used as an anti-magical charm, but my evidence here is too scanty for the drawing of definite conclusions.

The importance of divining and prophesying for social behaviour in the Church and on the society should also be stressed. Accusations of witchcraft against those who do not conform to the accepted standard and type of the Church are common. In this way the belief in magic is another method of securing a rigid conformity within the religious group. And on the other hand, those who are accused of being the instigators of magic do form new sects after being ostracized: once again, in the history of religion, rigidity and secession are found side by side.

(3) And finally, I would draw attention to the role of lightning magic in the Zionist Church. So far, the full implications of lightning as the conveyor of the prophetic call to some of the foremost Zionist leaders, and the great incidence of anti-lightning magic measures are not quite clear to me. Broadly speaking, these beliefs are in line with the heaven-herds and the heaven-bird of pagan Zulu religion. Cattle killed by lightning may not be eaten by the ordinary members of the Church, as this is the prerogative of the prophet himself. One may be able to offer rough-and-ready explanations of such phenomena. But the very stability and strength of these notions leads one to suggest that possibly Zionist lightning magic throws light upon the very nature of certain primitive notions of God among the Zulus. It is possible that this shows that the Zulu idea of *uNkulunkulu* is only a recent layer of belief, under which lies the older idea of God as "The Lord of Heaven" and the god of thunder. Possibly it is in the dream world of the Zionist prophet that the Lightning-God of old reappears and reveals himself in his shining splendour.

(2) DREAMS AS MEANS OF REVELATION

"Please, sir, one day I was asleep, I dreamt of this church. 24 September 1933, I was dreaming about this church." In these terms, the Rev. J. M—— informs the Native Affairs Department in Pretoria of the beginning of a new religious organization under his leadership, the African Baptized Apostle Church. The place of dreams in independent Churches, especially those of Zionist type, is very considerable. In order to understand the religious life of leaders and followers in these organizations a study of their dream life is essential.

It is no easy subject, and I approach it with a considerable amount of diffidence. The reason for my diffidence is not lack of relevant material. My conclusions are drawn from some fifty dreams which I myself and my assistants have recorded. Apart from these I have listened to hundreds of Zionist dreams in my contacts with various people. The difficulty begins when it comes to the evaluation and understanding of the dreams. I should state from the outset that when recording the dreams I was not interested in them from a psycho-analytical angle, though I am fully conscious of the fact that my material could lend itself to such an analysis, if one were to get to know the personal conflicts of the dreamers concerned. It may even be that a study of these dreams, in psycho-analytical terms, would lead to a much fuller and more penetrating understanding of the frustrations and longings of which the religious forms of the independent Church are a symptom.

Freud has taught us to distinguish between the manifest and the latent content of a dream: the deep and hidden conflicts which form the latent content are, according to Freud, during the process of the "dream-work", distorted and transformed into that which appears as the manifest content of the same dream. It is only this latter manifest content of Zionist dreams which we are studying here. More particularly we are concerned with the process of standardization of dreams, which is so characteristic of the Zionist Church, and indeed of primitive dream life in general. The manifest dream content in its standardized, stereotyped form influences the Zionist Church leaders and their followers in all important matters pertaining to the life of the Church.

(1) Zionist dream life can only be understood against the background of *the pattern of dream activity in heathen Zulu morality*. Zulus differentiate between three kinds of dreams:

those sent by ancestors, those sent by wizards, and ordinary spontaneous dreams.[14] Callaway has made a special study of the third group, and he has shown that such dreams are generally interpreted by their contraries: if a person dreams of death, this is taken as a proof that he will get well.[15] But although discussed and commented upon by the people, such ordinary dreams are regarded as being of much less importance than those sent by ancestors and wizards.

Malinowski has investigated dreams among the Trobriand natives. His conclusions are far-reaching and will here be applied to Zulu dream-life. Malinowski makes an important distinction between "free" or "ordinary" dreams on the one hand, that is "spontaneous visions arising in sleep, in response to physiological stimuli, to moods and emotional experience, to memories of the day and of the past", and on the other hand dreams "prescribed and defined by custom".[16] Such stereotyped or standardized dreams, the author explains, "are expected, hoped for, and awaited". Of these two kinds the stereotyped dreams, because of the fact that they are believed to have been induced by ancestors or magic, are alone regarded as true and prophetic dreams.

One finds this distinction also among the Zulus. The ancestral spirit communicates with his people through their dreams, especially in times of crises, illness, or death in the family. Above all, dreams are the channel through which the ancestors extend the call to their elect to become herbalists and diviners (*izinyanga* and *izangoma*). Saula Mthembu related his call dream to me: He saw an old herbalist, standing at the side of a river, dipping one foot in water. He observed that the great toe was especially long. Saula went to a herbalist living some twenty miles away, and he found that he corresponded to the dream-picture. This was both by the dreamer and the old herbalist interpreted as an evident intimation that Saula should become a herbalist himself.

Ndlulangaye Ngcobo, a famous diviner in northern Zululand, told me about his call: He saw in a dream the spirits of his father and of an old diviner. They told him to go to Polela river where he would become initiated. He walked for two days, and arriving on the third day, he recognized the diviner who had been pointed out to him. There and then his initiation started. In the case of the diviner, dreams play a central role. Not only must his call be extended by the ancestors through a dream, but he has to go on dreaming in order to assert himself as a real diviner. To receive clear dreams, he avoids certain food and he smears himself with white earth. It is characteristic of the diviner that, as in Ndlulangaye's case, rivers and pools and water seem to form an integral part of his dream.[17] This is obviously related to his daily visits to a river where he performs purification rites.

(2) The relative importance and the real nature of dream activities in the Zionist Church must also be studied against the background of the role of dreams *in Mission Churches*.

The importance of dreams in the crisis of conversion is well established from the experience of missions in Africa. Allier has demonstrated this in a convincing way, drawing chiefly on material from mission work among the Sotho. The material of dreams from Mission Churches, would probably have been even more extensive than it now is, Allier argues, if it had not been for the fact that some missionaries have felt humiliated and even scandalized because of the stress laid upon dreams by Africans. Missionaries are almost shocked that such an important spiritual revolution as conversion would seem to be due in many cases to some absurd dream rather than the conscious decision of the will. He quotes Coillard as having observed that Christian converts, on being asked by heathen: "What can we do to become like you?" reply: "To be converted, one must see visions."[18]

The most striking symbols recurring in the dreams quoted by Allier are: light, shining cloths, group of Christians on the other side of the river calling the dreamer to pass over.[19] E. W. Smith has recorded the following dream from the Ba-ila: A young man stood on a high mountain and saw the villages and people below. Coming down he found a crowd collected at a river. There was a missionary who lifted up his hand, with something in it, and immediately water flowed from it. The people fell to the ground amazed, thinking that the end of the world had come. He, the dreamer, stood with folded hands praying. Suddenly the scene changed. Now he was in the river fishing and heard a voice saying, "Follow me and I will make you fishers of men". Then he woke up.[20]

I have been struck by the fact that in dreams collected by me from among Christians in Mission Churches in Zululand and in Hayaland (Tanganyika) largely these same symbols appear. The importance attached to dreams, both among Zulu Christians and Haya Christians, is great. A deacon in the Haya area showed me an impressive dream-diary where he had entered short records of his dreams from 1930 to 1944. The general character of these were Joseph-dreams, referring to the important role he wanted to play in the Church. As a type of dream from a Mission Church in Zululand, the following may be related: Asiyena Zulu lived not far from the mission station. She heard of people being baptized and becoming Christians. All in her kraal were heathen, and so was she herself. One night she had a dream: "I saw many Christian women in white baptismal robes in a room. I was standing outside a hut. One woman took me by the hand and led me into the room. Then she said: Your name is Anna. I was stupified, but all the others laughed for joy." The dream showed Asiyena that she had to go to the mission station and attend the baptismal class. When, at the end of the baptismal instruction, she was asked by the minister what name she had chosen she called out, against her will, the name she had heard in the dream.

(3) As we shall show presently, the characteristic thing about *Zionist dream activities* is the stereotyped symbolism and interpretation. The interesting part of it is that in the Zionist dreams largely the same symbols appear as those quoted from heathen dreams and the Mission Church. At the outset I record fairly fully two typical Zionist dreams.

(*a*) J. N., a farm labourer from Central Natal, age about thirty, belonged to the (Lutheran) Norwegian Missionary Society. "In the dream I saw two mountains in front of me. Then there appeared a man in white clothes, coming between those two mountains, and he held a cross in his hand. The man pointed out to me two pools below the two mountains, and he said: One of these belongs to the Lutherans and the other to the Zionists. As I am a Lutheran I went to the Lutheran pool and prayed there. After the prayer, the man in white stirred with his finger in the Lutheran pool and sprinkled me with water. Then the man in white disappeared."

When J. N. told this dream to the Zionists (to which Church his father belonged), they tried to show him that the dream was an indication that he should become a Zionist. They also "prophesied" saying that the man in white was Jesus. After a while J. N.'s fiancée became ill and was brought to the Zionist church and baptized there. She had a dream, and said that she had been shown that J. N. loved another girl. The *umkhokheli* (woman leader in the church) scolded her saying that she had prophesied things of the flesh and not of the Spirit. She had better dream something else. The Zionists said that J. N.'s dream showed that he had the Holy Spirit and they in their turn had in their dreams been shown that he ought to put on a green sash with a white cross and some stars. J. N. eventually left the Lutherans and joined the Zionist Church.

(b) Lazarus M., earlier a Methodist, now a Zionist Sabbath Church member. Age about fifty. "I came to a beautiful place with green grass. I first passed a small stream, and then came to a wide river. I saw many people on this side of the river, and another group on the other side. When those people saw me coming they laughed and said: 'We would like to see how that one is going to cross the river.' But when I arrived at the river, I suddenly saw myself already on the other side. There I saw a very steep mountain (which is called Zion) and people climbing the mountain. At the foot of the mountain I saw an old woman praying. When I started to climb people laughed saying: 'We would like to see how that one is going to climb that steep mountain.' When I tried the second time I was quite surprised that—whip!—I was on the top of the mountain. There I saw a big city, so big that one could not see where it ended, and right through that city there passed a road. Over the city were morning mist and rays of the dawn. When I came near, there arose three men in white clothes. Two of them were half-hidden, but the third spoke to me and said: 'It is not permitted to enter here without repenting.' I heard a fine choir singing, and they were all in lovely white robes (but I don't remember what song it was). Then the man in white said: 'I will send you to evangelist Makhaye, you must ask him why he has turned the day of the Lord into a working day. If they do not repent and honour the Sabbath [Saturday], the Lord will send cold winds and hail and storm, to destroy all that they have planted.' " He awoke.

The following Sunday, when he came to the mission church, he remembered the dream and the choir whose song he had listened to. He started to cry on remembering this. People were startled and asked what was the matter. When he had narrated his dream some people made a laughing stock of him, saying: "Why do you see *Nomkhu6ulwana's* veils of mist in your dreams and why do you point to her day as the day for church service?" And they did not care for what he said. Lazarus then began to pray for himself in the bush. One day a Zionist came along, saying that he had in a dream been shown to come to pray with Lazarus. When Lazarus was brought to the Zionist church, he at once recognized the white garments and the song from the dream he had had.

In the Zionist dream pattern there are certain elements which always recur. The warp and woof of this pattern are the formal and the content elements which appear in the great majority of dreams.

(i) Of the *formal elements*, I mention the most important dream symbols: A river or a pool (sometimes these are, as in the dreams just related, duplicated); people standing near a stream; baptism in a stream. Of the colours, resplendent white is predominant, appearing as a luminous figure or luminous group of people. Next comes green or blue, appearing especially as the green grass or the blue of water. Sometimes yellow appears, often attached to a sash on a robe which the dreamer is advised to wear. Red is very rare and when appearing is interpreted as symbolizing the fire of hell.[21] Snakes appear frequently in the dreams. Or the dreamer sees his own corpse on earth, this accompanied by the sensation of a bad smell.

Characteristic are the clear and distinct impressions as recorded by the dreamer. The length, or rather shortness, of the green grass as seen in heaven is always commented upon. Minute detail in dress and outfit (for instance the shape of the staff which a person is carrying, whether adorned by a star or a cross) is often pointed out. One prominent prophet—a university graduate—would in his dreams receive a revelation of the church hymns he afterwards wrote: he saw a blackboard being brought down from heaven and the hymn, verse by verse, clearly written on the board. Prophet X (p. 112), in the dream through which he was called to become a prophet, saw a huge, slowly rotating wheel, and the seven prayers of "Our Father" engraved on the wheel. Prophet Y (p. 112) saw a geometrical plan of heaven. In a report to the Magistrate of his district he copied the whole of his apocalyptic vision as shown to him in his dream.

(ii) As to the *manifest contents* of the dream, it is important that in the cases of both J.N. and Lazarus there is a dual element, the choice between two alternatives, symbolized by two rivers, two mountains, two groups of people. As a matter of fact ethical conflicts seem to appear more often in these dreams than one would expect from a study of sermons and testimonies. A sexual-ethical problem plays a prominent role in one of Isaiah Shembe's call-dreams.[22]

Typical in these dreams of prophetic call is the dreamer

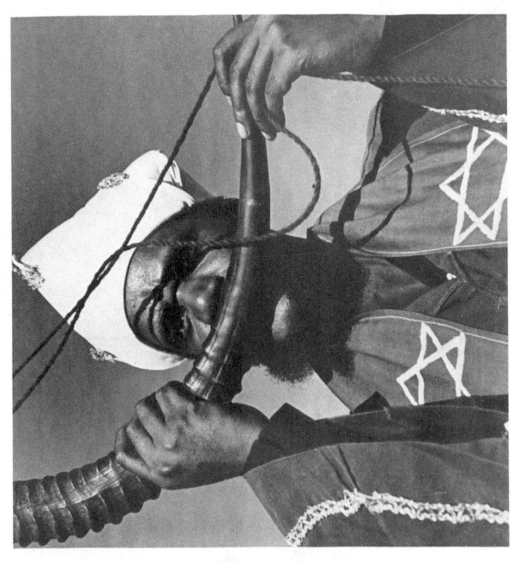

PROPHET WITH MITRE AND RAM'S HORN.

Typical of the blend of Bantu religion and Christian ideas, to be found in certain Bantu churches. Dressed in blue vestments with the star of David, which symbol has a mysterious fascination for some prophets; it has been revealed to them in dreams, they say.

SHEMBE WASHING HIS DISCIPLES' FEET.
Some of the older men have the Zulu headring (*isicoco*) on.

INHERITOR OF A CHURCH.
Rev. J. G. Shembe, son of the famous prophet, inherited the leadership of the Nazarite Church.

offering resistance to the call, and only yielding after energetic pressure from a Heavenly Messenger. Shembe, when called through a dream to preach the Word, attempted to evade the issue by various excuses. Eventually he yielded. There are examples of actual struggles in the dream with the calling angel (i.e. Jacob-dreams). There are also many typical Joseph-dreams. A. M. of the Holy Catholic Apostolic Church in Zion at H—— says: "I was brought by a policeman to a holy place where I saw three men in white with green sashes and with long hair. One of them said to me: 'That one is going to be a heavenly doctor, pray to him.' And the three men in white, together with the police, knelt before me."

Interpretation of dreams

No mere recording of the couple of Zionist dreams can give a true impression of the stereotyped character of the symbols perceived by the dreamer. Allier points out that the material of recorded dreams in Mission Churches would have been much more voluminous if it had not been for the missionaries' apprehension of repeating over and over again the same thing.[23] In the same way Zionist dreams appear as an endless series of the same recurring dreams, which however are experienced by the individual dreamer as fresh and unique. The stereotyped dreams have as their corollary stereotyped and standardized interpretations.

In J. N.'s case, the dreamer himself thought that one pool represented his Lutheran Church and the other pool the Zionist Church. This interpretation, however, met with criticism from the Zionists. Through an interesting development they have actually succeeded in monopolizing for themselves any dreams referring to water, rivers and pools. J. N. saw himself being sprinkled (ukufafaza), and not immersed, in his heavenly baptism. But this argument was not accepted as valid in comparison with the overwhelming fact that he had seen pools: that was sufficient proof that he should join the "Water-Church" of the Zionists. Through the same monopolizing process, it is now generally agreed among Zulu sects that shining white clothes refer to Zionists, and that on seeing such symbols in a dream a man should join a Zionist Church.

In the same way other Churches may monopolize other dream symbols. Azariah's wife—herself belonging to a Mission Church—had a tumour in her stomach. In a dream she heard a choir of angels singing a hymn. In her dream she recognized

R   271

the hymn as one of the Israelite Church (Church of God and Saints of Christ) to which her husband belonged. She saw an angel putting a hand on the tumour. As she woke up, she realized that the tumour had burst, and she soon recovered. After this happy experience, she left her Mission Church and joined the Israelite Church, "because her dream angels had sung one of the Israelite hymns, not a mission hymn". She had, in fact, been visited by the angels of that particular Church. In this case the dream also produced a longed-for solution of a domestic-denominational conflict: the woman had long opposed her Israelite husband's advice that she should abandon her Mission Church and join his particular Church. The angels themselves in the end had to overcome her resistance.

Some Zionists know of what they refer to as the "gift of dreams" (isiphiwo sokuphupha), just as St. Paul in 1 Cor. 12 enumerates other gifts of the Spirit. Others again have to be trained and schooled in dreaming in order to achieve the right stereotyped dream. In J. N.'s case the church steward tells J. N.'s fiancée not to dream things of the flesh but of the Spirit; thus she ought to try once again and dream again, dream something else. In order to see clear and correct dreams, the Zionist prophet sometimes smears himself with a mixture of ashes and water, just as the heathen diviner used to do. Prophet X (p. 112) attached much value to the dreams of his neophytes. After an initial general confession of sins, he would tell them to go home for three days and later return to relate to him all they had dreamed during that time. They would not fail to have very significant dreams, he assured them.

The one great thing waited for and expected in the dreamer is the revelation of Jehovah, or the Angel, or Jesus, always appearing in shining white robes. In the dream Jehovah gives the dreamer orders as to action in various situations. Examples of these are: (a) When leaving one Church or choosing to join another religious organization, the prophet and his followers are sure to be shown their way by dreams. (b) The Holy Spirit or the Angel shows the patient through a dream what kind of uniform or robe he should wear in order to become cured.

Zionist dreams present important material for the study of the stereotyping of dreams among primitive peoples, and from a general sociological point of view, I suggest, an additional item of interest is that in the case of Zionist dreams the historical or time element can be controlled. One can within the limit of so many months or years show how the stereotype has evolved.

I referred earlier to Malinowski's study of Trobriand dream life which showed that the stereotyped and not the "free" or spontaneous dreams are regarded as true and prophetic. This same holds true for Zulu Zionists. *They dream what their church expects them to dream.* That is, only those dream elements which fit in with the accepted dream pattern of the Church are remembered. They are remembered because they have a function in the Church, which expects from its members that they should in the Sunday's church service produce testimonies about dreams. People are prepared to listen for hours to detailed descriptions of dream after dream, because they know that Jehovah has revealed Himself through this channel.

On this point there is of course a characteristic difference between the role ascribed to dreams in Mission Churches and in the independent Churches. Zionists complain that when a dreamer comes to his mission congregation and relates a dream, he is not seldom scorned and made a laughing-stock. In Mission Churches, they feel, the mighty waters of primitive dream life are in various ways subdued and repressed. In Zionist Churches the sluices have been opened to the full. Here is definitely one reason why some people have left certain Mission Churches and joined organizations of the Zionist type. Mafuzula, a Presbyterian, saw in his dream an angel. The angel, looking eastwards, beat his hands as if applauding and told Mafuzula: "You, too, must testify about Jesus." Mafuzula wanted to relate his dream in his Presbyterian Church, "but as they don't witness in that church" he joined the F—— G—— Church, where he was not only permitted but expected to do so.

Dreaming in accordance with pattern becomes in the Zionist Church a group-integrating force of surprising strength. The stereotyped dream is also the true and prophetic dream in the Zionist Church. To dream rightly reveals a right attitude to the Church, it is a declaration of loyalty to the group. In the name of the "freedom of the Holy Spirit" the sect thus exercises a totalitarian control over the individual, which does not even shun the hidden depths of the person's subconscious mind. The individual is malleable and the sect is moulding him into a standard type.

Some people fail in the test. Their dreams do not fit into the pattern. Philisina Mkhize, 24 years of age, belonging to a Mission Church, had *"isipholiyana"* (hysterical illness). In vain she had tried doctors and herbalists. In a dream she saw a group of people in white garments, with white veils on their heads.

273

Each carried a long stick in his hand. She had not heard of Zionists before, but after this dream she joined one of their groups and related her dream to them. After a while she discovered, however, that the sticks carried by this group of Zionists did not correspond to the sticks she had seen in her dream. She was fortunate in finding in the neighbourhood another Zionist Church that used the right kind of stick.

As far as I can make out, Zulu Zionists definitely differ on this point from the rather easy-going ways of the Tikopia. Professor Firth has demonstrated that there is no rigidity of dream interpretation in Tikopia society but considerable flexibility and elasticity, "stock attributions of meaning are few" [24] Zulu Zionists do not show such flexibility in their dream interpretation. The outcome of their rigid stereotyping of dream interpretation leads instead to social flexibility of a sort. Those individuals who do not dream according to pattern are forced by social separation to join, or themselves form, another Church where their dreaming activities are more appreciated.

Because of his prominent role in the Church, the leader's own dreams are of particular importance as a pattern for the dreams of the members of his group. If, however, his dreams should be extraordinary and revolutionary, they may be liable to question and scrutiny. Prophet Mthethwa of the Jerusalem Zion Church had no children. He told the congregation that he had seen in a dream two beds, on one he himself was lying and on the other a young girl from the congregation. The Spirit, he said, obviously wanted him to take this girl as a second wife. The dream created a problem in the congregation. They all believed, of course, that dreams were the very channel for the revelation of Jehovah. But some thought that perhaps the prophet was mistaken. After a stormy church meeting, Mthethwa was told that his dream would only be accepted as true and prophetic, if it were corroborated by an identical dream, dreamed by his first wife. When Mthethwa did not want to submit to so drastic a test, the greater part of his flock left him, and Mthethwa carried on with a smaller group, henceforth preaching that Jehovah had in the Bible revealed his approval of polygamy to Abraham and Solomon.

Experiences of this kind lead to much theological argument in the life of some Zionist Churches. Bishop Mgwena's attitude is representative of those who have felt the problem and tried to find some solution as far as it goes: "If a person has a dream which is in contradiction to the Bible, then that dream has been inspired by the angels of Satan. If a man dreams something which is not in contradiction to the Bible, then he has received that dream from Jehovah's own righteous angels."

This bishop felt the need for some standard by which to measure and evaluate the revelation transmitted to the Church through the channel of his own and his followers' dreams. And well do they need such standards. Lazarus M——, when describing his dream (p. 269), mentioned specially that he had seen the morning mist and the rays of dawn on the Green Pastures of Heaven. When he mentioned this in his Mission Church, people at once thought those symbols were connected with *Nomkhu6ulwana*, the Princess of Heaven, the goddess of fecundity of heathen Zulu religion. Their intuition was right. They understood that through Zionist dream life a back door is opened for traditional Zulu heathenism to enter the Church. *Naturam furca expellas . . .*

(3) REVELATION

(a) Revelation through the Book

Not a few Christian Zulus, when asked why they have left the parent Church, reply: "I left because of the Book" (*nga-khishwa incwadi*). In many cases this is probably a rationalization of some other cause, but even admitting so much, it remains true that the interpretation of the Bible and its use as a source of revelation, are important and ever-present problems within the independent Churches. We focus our attention on the problem only in so far as it affects Churches among the Zulus.

In many well-established Ethiopian Churches, the faithful bring their Bibles with them to the service and during the sermon follow with interest various references made by the preacher. I do not doubt that there are Ethiopian Churches where the general standard of Bible knowledge can stand comparison not unfavourably with that in certain Mission Churches. On the other hand one comes across Churches where the standard in this respect is appalling. We know of scores of congregations where the only owner of a Bible is the preacher himself—and he perhaps is not even able to read! In spite of this handicap the prophet may impress his more simple-minded followers with his knowledge of the Book. He manages with the help of a small notebook from which one of his more educated assistants reads chapter and verse to him. Bible knowledge, according to these prophets, is knowledge of verses. Some of

275

them have an amazing command of chapter and verse on the legalistic specialities in which they are interested (healing, the Spirit, food taboos, baptism). A theological discussion in Zululand often becomes a competition in knowledge of such verses. Zulu Zionists now have a term for it: *"ukushayana ngamavesi"* (to compete about verses). Prophet Zwana, near N., could rattle off by heart all the passages in the Old Testament referring to the Nazires who, to him, were his own Nazarites. Because of this mastery, he told me, he in fact knew the Bible better than anybody else in the world. Other leaders again, Sunday after Sunday, hold tenaciously to their "uMateu five" (Matt. 5). One can well believe bishop T. M——, when in a letter to his Magistrate he states: "T. M—— explains the Bible from the following chapters Amen: Jer. 1: 4–5, Proverbs 8: 22–26. Amen." Pathetic is the continuously recurrent choice of John 14: 2 as a text: "In my Father's house are many mansions; if it were not so, I would have told you; for I go to prepare a place for you." It is pathetic because in the South Africa of racial discrimination this verse is by the Zulus taken as a charter and a guarantee that there will be, possibly, a separate mansion for them. The poster *"Net Vir Blankes*—For Europeans Only" is written with such bold letters on the religious life of the country that the African feels the need for a scriptural guarantee about the fate of his race.

Brookes says, that "to some extent 'Ethiopianism' is due to the shibboleth of the 'open Bible' ", and does, no doubt, put his finger on an important point.[25] The difficulty is felt also by the Ethiopian and Zionist leaders. At a meeting of Zionist prophets where I discussed the question, one of them said that "the Bible is a forest" and it is not easy to find the path through it. He had discovered, he said, within his narrow sphere, that the Bible was a dangerous book because it had led some of his people to become Sabbatarians.

In this situation what is the main authority by which to judge the interpretation of Bible verses? The Zionist Church, just as any other in the West, of course claims that it is a Biblical Church. And when this statement has been made by more than one Church, there arises in Zululand, as in Europe and America, rivalry between those who wish to prove that they are more Biblical than the others. In Zululand as elsewhere everybody finds in his Bible just what he wishes to find. I have come across one example of "modern" criticism of the Bible, provided, as one would expect, by the theological expert of the African

Methodist Episcopal Church. In a lecture on "The Life of our Lord Jesus Christ" he tackles in his way the problem of an eschatological interpretation of the Gospels:

> The Gospel at first was an oral proclamation to the Gentiles, it was taught amongst them over 30 years, as an oral proclamation, as the people thought that the time is near. At last it was made into a Book form now called the Bible. The idea of putting it to a Book form was to keep the true Gospel for the generation to come. Secondly, to witness that Christ's coming was not so soon.[26]

Obviously the Old Testament forms the foundation of the belief of these Churches. A common argument in all *materia theologica* is: The truth is to be found in *"uDutelonom"* or *"uLevi"* (Deuteronomy or Leviticus). Moses is the central figure in their Bible; Moses, leader, liberator, lawgiver; Moses overcoming the dangerous waters of the Red Sea; Moses fixing detailed prescriptions or taboos (food and sex). In some quarters, the differences between the Old and New Testament standards are felt as a problem, and where this is so the Old Testament standard is generally accepted.[27] Prominent leaders do not even hesitate to launch radical criticism against St. Paul publicly. Isaiah Shembe declared that European monogamy was only St. Paul's invention: it was Paul's legislation but not God's. Had not God said: *Zalani nande* (Be fruitful and multiply . . .)[28] In the same way, the Israelites (Church of God and Saints of Christ) as early as 1910 declared that "the Whites distort the scriptures: they have instituted marriage, although Adam and Eve were never married, just to get money from you" (i.e. from the Africans). One could of course multiply examples of this to show that conformity with the Bantu heritage is really taken as the standard by which to judge of Bible interpretation. This explains the central role of John the Baptist in the New Testament. As has already been shown (p. 208) John the Baptist becomes the prominent figure of the New Covenant, because he personifies, in the eyes of the Zionist, much that is valuable in the old order of African life: purification rites, ancestral cult ("He is himself Elijah, who was to come", Matt. 11: 14). The ascetic on the threshold between the Old and New Covenants is interpreted as the ideal Christian diviner-prophet. It is because this Bantu standard for testing Bible interpretation is accepted as self-evident that it is possible for the Zionists to quote Micah 4: 13 in support of *isangoma*-divination (p. 257).

The most tragic sidelight on the colour-obsession in the independent Church is perhaps the insidious rumour that the Bible has been distorted by the Whites. The Bible which the Bantu now have is the wrong book. There exists, they say, another Bible, hidden away from the Bantu by the Whites, a book containing the real truth, whilst the "old Bible"—as the Bible is called in such circles—was written only to cheat the Black man. One source of this propaganda seems to be the Afro-Athlican Constructive Church, of Negro origin. At least, they are the only ones bold enough to claim that they know and possess "another" Bible, the right, Ethiopian Bible, called "The Holy Piby". According to them, the "old Bible" was given to the children of the house of Israel, whereas the Holy Piby has been given to the children of the house of Ethiopia.

The problem of the nativistic interpretation of the Bible can be seen in a wider and more important perspective, namely that of the life of myth and rite. In another connexion we have shown that, with the acceptance of Christianity, the pagan myths were readily abandoned, but the rites have persisted tenaciously and in the nativistic Zionist movement have provided the main outlines of the ritual pattern followed in the new groups. Instead of the myth, handed down through generations by oral tradition, the Book was given to them by the Mission. The important thing is that in the Zionist Church the African myth has been revitalized and modernized, and as we have seen, even penetrates its new opponent, the Book. It is also evident that when the Book is interpreted in this way, the main responsibility for its interpretation will come to lie with the prophet, that is, with the Black Christ.

(b) Revelation through the Black Christ

Some fifteen hundred of the faithful had come for the big festival of the year. All were in their white robes, and the "Servant", the young prophet who had recently inherited the leadership from his deceased father, preached to them. In his sermon, which lasted for more than one hour, nothing struck me more forcibly than this passage:

"You, my people, were once told of a God who has neither arms nor legs, who cannot see, who has neither love nor pity. But Isaiah Shembe showed you a God who walks on feet and who heals with his hands, and who can be known by men, a God who loves and who has compassion."

There was no doubt, in the preacher's mind or in the minds of his listeners, to whom these words referred. The important thing to me, the missionary, one listener among those fifteen hundred, was the attitude behind the words, the hunger it revealed and expressed in such tangible terms: a God with real legs and real hands, a *real* God. There was *hunger for revelation*, that God should be revealed in such a fashion that the African could touch him and exclaim: *"My* Lord and *my* God" . . . As I listened, two very different verses sprang to my mind: one, the observation of scepticism, as old as Xenophanes:

> The Ethiop's Gods have dusky cheeks,
> Thick lips, and woolly hair;
> The Grecian Gods are like the Greeks,
> As tall, bright-eyed, and fair.

But the missionary in me reminded me of that passage in Browning's "Saul":

'Tis the weakness in strength, that I cry for! my flesh, that I seek
In the Godhead! I seek and I find it. O Saul, it shall be
A Face like my face that receives thee; a Man like to me,
Thou shalt love and be loved by, for ever; a Hand like this hand
Shall throw open the gates of new life to thee! See the Christ stand!

I remember another example from a place distant only some twenty miles from the mission station where I lived in northern Zululand. For weeks people in the vicinity were troubled by the nightly visits of a little group of men and women. They called themselves the "people of the Spirit" (*a6antu 6aka Moya*). In moonlight one could see them on a hill, arms outstretched towards heaven, and singing over and over again the same few words night after night:

> *Jesu, woza noyihlo,*
> *A6antu 6ayafa*
> *lapha emhla6eni.*[a]

Here is the same hunger for revelation. But Jesus, the White God, seemed so mute and so remote and all the while people are dying here on earth.

The study of modern African ideas and expectations of a Black Messiah or a Black Christ could of course easily be extended from a short chapter into a big book. I shall, however, resist the temptation to draw upon the rich comparative

[a] Jesu, come with Thy Father.
People are dying, here on earth.

material from other parts of Africa, and limit myself to phenomena of this kind among the Zulus. One disadvantage of such a limitation is that it rules out any comparison between tribal ideas of God and the modern notions now emerging of the Black Christ. I believe that a comparison on this point between Zionist Churches among the Zulus and the Sotho for example would be of great value.

Although to some extent Black Christs appear in other parts of Africa also, it is only logical that they play their leading role in chlorocratic South Africa. A passage in the book *I Am Black* shows how the reaction of the African against the colour bar influences his attitude to Jesus Christ. A former Christian, Shabala by name, is explaining why he follows the old ways of his own people:

> Do you not understand that Jesus is not the God of the Black men? I found that out when I came to this Big City of the White people. At home there was one White man, the Preacher, and many Black people, but there was no talk of Black people or of White people. The writings spoke only of men. . . . Here [in the city] are many White men, and Jesus is their God only. Here there are great houses built for Him. . . . but I cannot go into these houses of the White man's God.[29]

I remember being present at a Bantu Sunday School Conference in Dundee, Natal, where a display of religious pictures was given, chiefly from the life of Jesus. One Zulu teacher then put the question: "Was Our Lord black or white? What was His colour?" The question was just as characteristic as the European's reply: "Oh, you know, there are Arabs for instance, who are not really white but rather darkish. And Jesus, being a Semite, was probably somewhat more brownish than ordinary Europeans." A perplexing question and—well, an attempt at a nicely accommodating reply! This is the same problem as that of Black Hamlet:

> John loved the statue of Christ. He even referred to him as the Great Healer. Was he perhaps, he wondered, the great-great-great-grandfather of all the *ngangas*? He knew that Christ was born in Africa, and wished that he could have proved that Christ was a real African, black as all Africans. But he knew from the Bible that Christ was a Jew, and he had not seen a black Jew.[30]

Black Hamlet discovers that his salvation is not to be found through the White Christ, because Jesus is only the Christ of the Whites.

The question whether Jesus is the Christ also for the African is a theological and religious problem of great importance in Zionist Churches in Johannesburg and Zululand. Dr. J. L. Dube told me in an interview that he had come across Zulu prophets who claimed that "another God had born another Son in heaven, and that Jesus, the White Christ, had been driven out of heaven because of his jealousy"—a modern Bantu Lucifer-legend! A Nazarite woman, on my asking what she thought of Jesus, replied: "Jesus! Him we have only seen in photos! But I know Shembe, and I believe in him. He is the one who created heaven and earth; he is God for us black people." In this respect, the purely Zulu Church is of course in a stronger position than the American Negro Mission Churches in Zululand who may claim that one of their saints is a Negro prophet. The Church of God and Saints of Christ sing in their services as response between minister and congregation:

Minister: "There are many prophets, but who preached the truth?"

Congregation: "Prophet Crowdy, the founder of the Church of God."

But however interesting this American Negro church leader may be, he cannot of course appeal to the imagination of the Zulus as a Zulu prophet of their own can do.

From time to time there appear in Zululand prophets who claim: "I am Jesus." Philemon Butelezi of the Sabbath Jerusalem Church, a brother of the earlier mentioned Elliot Butelezi, is an example. He supports his Messianic claim with a ritual in which he claims to follow the example of John the Baptist in the New Testament. On various occasions he retreats to a hilltop, fasting and praying there for four days and four nights. After this he returns to his congregation which has been waiting for him in prayer during this time. On reappearing before his flock he hands out palm leaves to each one, with the words: "Jesus has come to-day!" The receiver exclaims: "There is Jesus. Amen, praise the Lord!" Philemon's influence is, however, very limited.

Much more important is the Black Christ ideology that has grown up within the Nazarite Church around the personality of Isaiah Shembe. For various reasons we confine our study of the Black Christ in Zulu Zionist Churches to Isaiah Shembe. The Nazarite hymn-book offers the careful reader a mine of information about it. The fact that the hymn-book is printed and edited by the Nazarite Church also gives the investigator somewhat more liberty in drawing and publishing conclusions from such material than if it had been otherwise collected. The Black Christ dogma, as applied to Shembe, is the outcome of an interplay of two factors: on the one hand the self-testimony of the leader as to his being the prophet, the Servant, the Promised One; and on the other, the vision-inspired declarations by media and the need of the mass to worship and to believe in a Man of Miracles.

According to the Nazarite hymn-book there appear to be two stages in Shembe's self-testimony. The first is his official claim to be a prophet to the Zulus; the second is expressed by statements which show that he claimed to be something more than a prophet, to be "The Promised One" (*uThumekile*). And though the first claim would always be officially announced as being the exact expression of what Shembe regarded himself to be, the second claim would always be there in the background to be appreciated to the full only by the initiated. It is also of course easier to the Bantu than it is to the more analytical Western mind, to combine and intertwine these two sets of dogma without feeling the contradiction. Shembe as a prophet to the Zulus describes himself first of all as a Liberator, a Moses:

> Our Liberator,
> We Dingaan's people
> We have heard him,
> He has come.
> The Liberator has arrived,
> You, Zulus, we have heard him.
> (No. 214)

Because of the arrival of the Liberator the needs of the people of Sendzangakhona and Dingaan have been fulfilled, and this is the ground of their praise:

> Praise Jehovah
> Because he is righteous
> Because he is benevolent for evermore.
> He remembered his people,
> He sent them Isaiah, his Servant,
> Because he is righteous.
> (No. 60)

Shembe, the Servant of the Lord, will wipe the tears of his people.
> (No. 134)

But Shembe is something more than a mere prophet or a national liberator:

How do you do, my friends,
The Lord bless you.
The peace from the Lord
Be with you.

But I alone,
I come from afar.
I am sent by the King
Amongst you.

(No. 77)

The Lord called Shembe in his mother's womb (197), yes, "my Lord loved me before the mountains hardened, from time immemorial he anointed me. I am the first of Thy way." (No. 71). In a sermon in 1932 Isaiah Shembe testifies about himself: "Scrutinize the writ. We are not surprised at Shembe who has been sent to-day, because the writ testifies about him. . . . He said [referring to Jesus Christ of the New Testament]: They who believe in his works, they will do greater things than these. John 14: 10–13. And great are the things that are now done, in the name of the God of our fathers, through this Shembe, who is with us to-day." According to the same sermon,[31] John 7: 15 ("How knoweth this man letters, having never learned") refers to Shembe. The servant also has power to forgive sins (No. 217).

In Shembe's hymn-book there are very few references to "Jesu Krestu", and he is chiefly spoken of as the one "who promised to send us the Spirit" (No. 58). Still more significant is the omission of the name of Jesus or of the Son in formulae where one would expect to find it. An important hymn (No. 154) gives the *summa fidei* and *credo* of the Nazarites:

I believe in the Father
and in the Holy Spirit
and in the communion of saints
of the Nazarites.

Here there is no room for the Son in the creed and life of the believers. His place has been usurped by another. The few references to the life of Jesus that there are in the hymn-book are interpreted as being repeated and re-enacted through— Shembe.

They came, the wise men
arriving from the East,
Saying: Where is He,
Who is the King of the Jews

Chorus: So it is also to-day
    On the hill-tops of Ohlange
        (No. 34)

And the "hill-tops of Ohlange" are Ekuphakameni, the holy place of the Nazarites.
  The hymn ends:

> In no wise art thou least
> among the princes of Judah,
> For out of thee
> prophets shall come forth,
> who will save
> the city of Ohlange.
> *Chorus:* So it is also to-day
>   On the hill-tops of Ohlange.

This is an important and significant hymn. Its meaning is: What once happened through Jesus, among the Jews and for their salvation, is now being re-enacted through Shembe, among the Zulus and for their own salvation. Through this repeated revelation—which is the secret of all syncretism—Shembe is represented as the Christ of the Zulus.

And the proof of such claims? "The Ngema-girl from Empangeni was bitten by an *ihobosha*-snake, in her seventh finger (and was dangerously ill). And people said: 'She will die.' But the servant said: 'In the name of Jehovah the God of our fathers she will not die', and in fact she did not die."[32] The Healer is the Christ. Just as Jesus healed the blind and the deaf among the Jews, so also to-day, "on the hill-tops of Ohlange", Shembe heals and gives life among the Zulus.

These claims by the leader, in order to become the living faith of the Church, must be endorsed by the belief of the medium and the mass. In an interview in 1941 with Shembe Junior, I expressed my amazement at the fact that three of the hymns in the printed Nazarite hymn-book are there described as having been written by Isaiah Shembe "after his resurrection from the dead". The Rev. J. G. Shembe explained that the hymns were thus described because they had been revealed in visions and auditions to some women. I call such people media. In their hymns the claims show Shembe's status still further enhanced:

> The springtime of the earth has come
> The time is here
> Be afraid, you hartebeests,
> You are called to Ekuphakameni.

The Star of Heaven
Rose in the East
Until it entered
In the holy city.

Let your testimony echo widely,
There he is, Jehovah,
Now he has come,
You people of Dingaan.

(No. 221)

The media edify the Church by relating their visions of heaven and how in dream-visits to heavenly places they have met the Risen Prophet.

The status claimed by the leader, enhanced through the visions of the medium, is raised to yet further heights by the will to believe of the mass. There are obvious elements of "tremendum" and "fascinosum" in the awe-feeling with which Shembe was acclaimed by his followers. At the burial of Shembe the deceased prophet was hailed by the acclamation: *"Uying-cwele!"* (He is holy.) When describing Shembe as Christ, some of his followers qualify their statement: "Jesus came first as a White man. But now he has come as a Black man, in the flesh, through Shembe." Shembe is omnipresent and omniscient. One must not try to take medicine even secretly, because the Risen Shembe will see it. (When I discussed this with the Rev. J. G. Shembe, he corrected this attitude of his followers, saying: "That is wrong. They ought to put it: God sees it.") One Nazarite told me he had heard Shembe's voice speaking to him soon after the prophet's death. Shembe asked: "Have you eaten pork? Where were you when you ate pork?"—"I was at Khumalo's kraal." "You will all die if you eat pork."—"And, *Mfundisi*, it was his very voice, and nobody else's. What do you think of that?" The Nazarite hymn-book has become a best-seller; among its attractions is a photo of Isaiah Shembe; if the sick only look at the picture, the very look will have healing effects. In the belief of his followers Shembe becomes co-creator with God, and he is the mediator in heaven: if he turns his head away from a person, the unfortunate will not inherit life eternal. Because of the opposition which these dogmatic statements call forth among other Christians, Nazarites are sometimes careful not to call him God. "It is this way," one informant told me; "he *is* God, but in *inhlonipho*-language we call him prophet."[a]

The two main qualifications required for a Black Christ to be acknowledged as such are the power of healing and resurrection from the dead. Isaiah Shembe, after his death in 1935, is supposed to have risen from the dead; *vide* the hymns which, it is claimed, have been written by him after his resurrection. But the death-resurrection drama can also be staged in the lifetime, so to speak, of the prophet. I could mention the names of numerous prophets of Zulu and other South African tribes who are rumoured to have "died" and "risen" after this event. With Mark Twain one might perhaps point out that these rumours are gross exaggerations of the fact: the "death" and "resurrection" refer to visions in a dream-visit to heaven during the crisis of a serious illness, but the sensations as reported by the dreaming prophets are no less vivid because of this. George Khambule in his heaven-vision after his "death" claimed to have seen the heavenly Jesus, who appeared to him as half-white, half-black. In certain cases this death-resurrection drama is conscious charlatanism: one prophet in the northern Transvaal suddenly disappeared from his village and on reappearing two years later was acclaimed as having died and risen. It is characteristic that the Nazarites' Black Christ dogma is corroborated by conscious nativistic tendencies: thus when dancing before Jehovah they must not wear European clothes, but should as true Zulus appear in *ibeshu* and *isidwaba*. In 1942 I came across a still more nativistic sect in northern Zululand, the Mfibinga (Zulu for the Job's Tears seed), the members of which little sect wore long strings of this plant instead of clothes. Their leader claimed to be *uMvelingqangi* himself, and said he had come directly from heaven to Zululand. Some of Shembe's followers make a similar claim that their prophet is identical with *uMvelingqangi*. It is interesting that the Black Christ in these definitely nativistic movements is identified, not with *uNkulunkulu* or *uThixo*—the names for God used by the missions—but with the more pronounced pagan name for God. In this respect the anti-White tendency is stressed once again. While the Black Christ is in one sense envisaged on a distinctly New Testament pattern in the re-enactment of the

[a] In order to show respect to male relatives, Zulu women have evolved certain terms of their own, in order to avoid the use of the name of a relative or any word containing the radical of such a name. "Another word must be used instead, and so the speech of the women differs considerably from that of the men." This is *ukuhlonipha*. Krige, *Social System*, p. 30.

BOYS BEATING THE DRUM.

Drums are popular, indispensable for keeping the rhythm. The old gentleman in the centre, attired in clerical collar and vestments, follows, more than leads, the rhythm with his stick.

GEORGE KHAMBULE, A ZULU MESSIAH.

Together with the General of the Lord and the General's Clack of the Lord.

death-resurrection drama and in the Christ as healer, never-theless, the nativistic strands of the pattern show through very clearly in the sacrifices, in the cult of the spirit of the deceased leader, and once again in the stress on the healing activities of the Black Christ.

The Black Christ dogma, finally, leads one to suggest that there is revealed in the Zionist church to-day a tendency in the Zulu tribe which once was driven underground but now is given a new lease of life. Gustav Asmus has recently, after thirty years' missionary experience in Natal and Zululand, given—as far as I can see—the finest interpretation of Zulu life and belief that we possess.[33] His views on the role of Shaka are of special interest in this connexion. I translate from Asmus' book:

> Shaka was the original and the ideal Zulu, the embodiment of the whole tribe. And just as the *Izulu* (heaven) is the heaven of Zululand and the Zulu people, so Shaka was *izulu eliphezulu*, heavens above, embracing all. As long as the Zulu people feels itself and knows itself to be '*Uzulu*', so long the soul of this people cries out for Shaka, who in his person embodies and realizes the unity of them all. Only when the Bantu are no longer Bantu, will there be no more Shakas. . . . In the Zulu tradition there existed definite attempts towards a Shaka myth. When one hears expres-sions like: '*Latsho izulu lika Mjokwane kaNda6a*' (the heaven of Mjokwane of Ndaba thunders), an expression which only can refer to Shaka and his lightning and the striking of lightning, then one realizes to what extent the appearance of Shaka dominates the Zulu mind and that the deification of Shaka had already begun for the Zulus. In the circumstances of to-day these tendencies become only attempts. Shaka will never become the God of the Zulus. . . . The myth working on his person can no more be brought to realization.

I feel sure that Asmus is right when he thus claims that Shaka, in the minds of the Zulus, was well on his way to become a Zulu deity, "the God of the Zulus", just as in Central Africa deceased kings were incorporated in the Bantu pantheon (so, for instance, in the Hima area round the Central African lakes).

But this trend was cut short by the conquest of Shaka's kingdom through the Whites. The young Zulu myth was violently destroyed by them. The deepest root of Zulu aversion from the White man is possibly to be found in this cold fact: In crushing their political hegemony, the Whites also snatched away from this people their proudest aspiration and their most cherished myth.

S

And here it is that the Zionist and the Nazarite dogma of a Black Christ comes in. On the Zion hill-tops of Zululand and at Ekuphakameni, the High Place, this Zulu myth is reborn, and this same aspiration comes to life. The myth of the Zulu prophet borrowed, as we have seen, some of its contents from the Zulu kingship pattern. In the Zionist church, this royal myth is Christianized, and one might say, baptized in the living waters of the Zulu Jordan. As once the deified African king was acclaimed as the saviour of his people, so in certain churches of Zionist type to-day, the prophet is regarded as Saviour and Christ.

It is because this pattern is revitalized to-day that the Zionists tell the missionary: "Before, we did not know that Jehovah was ours. But now we see that Jehovah is ours, our very own." This is the reason why Shembe sings in a hymn:

> We are the first fruit
> of that root.
> We do not want.
> We have Sendzangakhona.[a]
> Yes, my King.
>
> From time immemorial
> We used to drink
> from the spring,
> Sendzangakhona's spring,
> Yes, my King.
>
> (No. 216)

As a logical consequence of this repeated revelation in Shembe or some other Black Christ follows that the image of God is changed. It becomes something else than that of the traditional Zulu *uMvelingqangi* or the God professed by the orthodox churches, *uNkulunkulu* or *uThixo*. L. Mqotsi and N. Mkele have recently in a valuable study of J. N. Limba's Xhosa church, *"I6andla lika Krestu"*, shown that in this church God is referred to as *"uThixo ka Tata"* (the Father's God).[34] The Bishop is *"uTata"*, the Father, and the God whom Limba's followers know and to whom they address their supplications is *Tata's* God. The mystical role of the Bantu mediator in relation to this God can be seen by the fact that *"Tata's* God" can even withhold or bring about rain "in order to bring humanity to the realization of the abundance of its sins". In this church one can hear the following remark: *"uThixo ka Tata uqumbile"*, *Tata's*

---

[a] Sendzangakhona was Shaka's father.

288

(or bishop Limba's) God is wrathful (and withholds rain). In the same way the Zulu Nazarites refer to God as *uNkulunkulu ka Shembe*, "Shembe's God". In their prayers they refer to him in such terms, thus proving that the God they know is the God revealed by the risen Zulu prophet, the Black Christ.

In his search for "a God with hands and feet and love and compassion" the Zionist prophet, in his reaction against the spiritual conquest by the Whites, returns to the past. In his creed there is no longer a place for the pale White Christ. His place has been usurped by somebody else. In this case, as elsewhere, the refusal to accept White Christ leads men back to the ancestors, to the "blood and soil" of the tribe.

(4) THE GREEN PASTURES—ZULU VERSION

(a) The Gate

> And I saw the Holy City, the new Jerusalem, coming down out of heaven from God—, having twelve gates, and at the gates twelve angels.—Rev. 21: 2, 12.

When the apostle visualizes heaven and the new Jerusalem he naturally sees it according to the pattern of the Old Testament: the twelve gates are the twelve tribes of Israel. When the Zulu prophet lifts up his eyes to the mountains he sees *his* new Jerusalem. There are gates and angels in the picture. But the numbers and the colours are different. Heaven is different—in Zululand. . . .

The idea of the Gate of Heaven plays a fundamental role in Zionist theological thought and discussions. There is no conformity about the supposed number of the gates. Prophet J. N., attempting to reconcile the Book of Revelation with the actual social situation in South Africa, thought there were 12 + 1 gates, twelve for the Whites, and the thirteenth for the Africans. Others again claim that the number is three, called after the angels standing as guardians: Meshach's gate "for Europeans only", Shadrach's for the Africans, and Abednego's gate for the Indians. Whatever the numbers—and the variations on the theme are many—the all-pervading colour-complex follows them right to the Gate of Heaven. The African's gate is, in accordance with the "mythical charter" of the Church, sometimes called "the Gate of Cush" when the supposed Old Testament foundation of the Ethiopian attitude is to be stressed; or "Malandela's Gate" with a direct nativistic connotation, as Malandela is believed to be the ancestor of all Zulus.

The name of the gate is all-important, as it defines who is the mediator and guardian standing at it. "We enter by the help of others" (*singena nga6anye*) as it is said in one of Shembe's hymns (No. 164). The need for a mediator is taken for granted. In the Nazarite Church the mediator is of course Shembe himself. In their dreams his faithful followers have seen him standing at the gate. In this capacity Shembe is referred to by a term which has ancient ecclesiastical tradition behind it but which in this case expresses an idea that is evidently formed by Zulu dream-life: "The Holder of the Keys" (*uyena ophethe izihlutulelo*). In Nazarite sermons and testimonies "to find the key" has become a formula meaning to find one's way to the Nazarite Church and thereby secure salvation. This idea re-appears in various ways. "The Sabbath is the Key, so that the gates may be opened", we read in the *Nazarite Hymnbook*, No. 212. In Nazarite sermons I have time and again heard the expressions: "We have come here to buy the key in order to enter Heaven"; or, "Let us seek the key with which to open the gate." The proof of the existence of such a key is the united testimony of "those who have returned from heaven", that is, who by visions or dreams have seen the Zulu Holder of the Keys at the Gate. For this reason when dancing at religious festivals they often sing a hymn with the words:

> May the King open the Gate,
> open it for the children of Dingaan.

(b) The reversed colour-bar in Heaven

The Black Christ at the gate has the power to open and to shut. The faithful themselves may, on their arrival at the gate, for certain reasons, be turned away. One well-known prophet told his followers that if they did not fulfil the "fourteen", that is pay the monthly Church contributions, due on the 14th of each month, he, the prophet standing at the gate, would turn his head away and they would not be allowed to enter but be thrown into hell. The function of the Zulu Holder of the Keys is, however, still more specific. The colour problem accompanies the African up to the Gate of Heaven. The Gate of Heaven idea is in the Zionist Church a product of reaction against the colour-bar in South Africa. In a country where some irresponsible Whites tell the African that Jesus is only for the White man, the African takes his revenge by projecting the colour-bar right into heavenly places. The colour-complex has painted their very heaven black, and the Black Christ at the gate has to see to that. Shembe at the gate turns away the Whites, because they, as the rich man, have already in their lifetime received their good things, and he opens the gate only to his faithful followers. The fate of the Africans who belonged to White Mission Churches is lamentable: "One race cannot enter by the gate of another race", and on their arrival at the White people's gate, they are turned away. (One observes that in this ideology of the reversed colour-bar in heaven it is sometimes stated that there is only a single gate, at which of course the Black Christ has control; sometimes there are two gates: the number depends on the need of the argument.) The colour-complex takes the parables of Jesus into its service. Here is one to which I have heard references in some Zionist churches: "There were ten virgins. And five of them were White, and five were Black. The five Whites were foolish, but the five Blacks were wise, they had oil in their lamps. All ten came to the gate. But the five White virgins received the same answer as the rich man received [in the parable of Lazarus and the rich man, Luke 16]: Because the Whites rule on earth, the Blacks do so in Heaven. The Whites will go a-begging to dip the tip of their finger in cool water. But they will get as a reply: '*Hhayyi* (no)—nobody can rule twice.'"[35]

(c) *Zulu Canaan and the New Jerusalem*

I have pointed out in another connexion that the high-sounding names of these Churches are not simply ornamental but reveal a deeper-lying ideology. They are connected with that "repeated revelation" to which we have just referred. To be purified and baptized in a Zululand stream is "to cross Jordan". The pools are Bethesda-pools and the hill-top is the Zion of the Zulus. One Zion congregation called itself Jerusalem, and the outstation three miles away was Cæsarea. The kraals of the faithful are called by Biblical names: Bethlehem, Gaza, Judæa. This name practice is even used as an argument to prove the quality of the Church concerned.[a] In the same way, the name can be used in denouncing another Church. One Nazarite local leader told me that the Zionists could not enter heaven "because they worship and work for a mountain" (*6ayase6enzela enta6eni*).

The name Zion or Ekuphakameni or Nazareth has a double meaning. The earthly Zion is only the mirror of the heavenly, and the church service on earth is but the court of the heavenly

[a] P. 59.

worship. This ideology in its most pronounced form has been expressed in Shembe's hymns: Ekuphakameni (the head-quarters of the church, eighteen miles north of Durban) and heaven are in these identified in a way which may appear to the outsider and the onlooker confusing and confused but which to the faithful is evidently a perfect expression of their faith. The exultations in the hymns over the beauty and splendour of Ekuphakameni are, without warning, transposed into a higher key and suddenly you find yourself, not eighteen miles north of Durban, but in heaven and Eden and Paradise (Hymns 49, 50, 74, 102, 221). With evident allusion to Ps. 137 the prophet sings:

> I remember Ekuphakameni
> Where there is gathered
> The holy church
> of the Nazarites.

> I remember Ekuphakameni
> Where the springs are
> Springs of living water,
> lasting for ever.

> I remember Ekuphakameni;
> a loudly falling cascade
> is the response of the saints
> of the Nazarites.

> Ye all who thirst
> Come ye to Ekuphakameni
> Ye will drink freely
> From the springs of water.
> (No. 102)

The Zulu word for Ekuphakameni means "the high and elevated place", and the name can easily be given its double meaning, so that the faithful will realize that Ekuphakameni is indeed heaven itself. In a processional hymn the Nazarites sing:

> We are all standing before thee,
> Gates of Ekuphakameni.
> All the generations of Heaven
> jubilate because of thee, Ekuphakameni.

In a similar way Zionists regard their Zion Church as the court of heaven. The positions in the church house at T—— of prophet X's Salem Church show clearly how the church is a replica of the heavenly temple: at the altar is sitting prophet X himself, "the Judge" (*uMahluli*) in episcopal vestments and his episcopal-cum-Mosaic brass staff. He is not always present, however, in his episcopal chair at the altar. If he is absent it is owing to higher duties: he has gone to the vestry where he is speaking to God through his "Heavenly Telephone". Near the altar are also the twelve prophets and the twelve apostles, the former in purple, the latter in white. In front of these are seated the Brides and Bridegrooms of the Lamb, some eighty to a hundred young men and girls, all in white. In the four corners of the nave of the church four men in white vestments stand silently: they are the four cardinal points, North and South, East and West. The "Hospital" is—logically—in the middle of the church: here are gathered the sick and those who are especially set aside to pray for them.

The Zionists feel remarkably at home in heaven—*sit venia verbo*. Their collective experience has provided a consistent "dream-geography of heaven" (corroborated by the denominational stereotypes of the dream-life in the various Churches), with its rivers and pools and its delightful lawns with short green grass. At a religious dance at Ekuphakameni, when the girls of the Church had given a good performance, I heard an old woman address them: "May it be that, also in heaven, you will dance like that."

The Book of Revelation has kindled in the heart of the Zionist prophet a longing to enter the heavenly Jerusalem. The Book of the Law of the State, with its *"geen gelijkstelling"* (no equality), has led him to modify, as far as he is concerned, the number of the heavenly gates from the Israelite holy number twelve to the figure "two" of racial segregation, or even to the exclusive nationalistic standpoint that only accepts one race, one gate. But there is yet another pattern which also determines his outlook on heaven, a pattern not found in the one or the other of these two books. Shembe has expressed this latter influence, in what is, in my opinion, his most beautiful hymn.

Shembe, who according to his son was more interested in lightning, than in any other subject, knew well the folk-lore of his Zulu people about the heaven-bird, or the lightning-bird.[36] In this hymn, heaven is likened both to a mountain eagle and to a hen:

> O Mountain Eagle
> lift thy mighty wing
> we need thy shelter,
> Thou rock of our fathers.

We have no fortress
other than thee
In which to find shelter,
We thy wayward creatures.

We stand before thee
O, beautiful hen.
Thou dost not love
Jerusalem alone.

O love us and hatch us
Wondrous Hen!
We dwell in thy kingdom,
Our Hen of Heaven.

O Lord, bring it forth,
this Ekuphakameni,
Just as a hen
loveth her chickens.

O Jerusalem, Jerusalem!
How great was my longing
to gather thy children
under my wing.
But they would not.
Thus art thou left desolate.
(No. 101)

In that light the Zulu prophet sees his heaven and his church. To him, these two focusing points in life are the refuge from a bitter and cold world; mighty and warming wings; "shelter in de time of storm".

CONCLUSIONS

Causes

Those who have hitherto given any attention to the problem of "Native Separatist Churches"—such as the (South African) "Native Affairs Commission", 1925, or Allen Lea, W. H. G. Shepherd, G. R. Norton, or Dom M. Peleman—have almost exclusively limited themselves to a discussion of the causes of the rise of the movement.

In this book an attempt has been made first and foremost to find out what leaders and followers of these churches do and believe, and it is claimed that only on the foundation of such an insight—locally and tribally defined—is it at all worth our while to put the question about the causes of these phenomena. We should also bear in mind the observation made in this book that Independent Church leaders nowadays do not so much secede from White Missions as from other Bantu leaders, and the "causes" in each case are quite different.

The two main reasons for secession from Mission churches are the colour-bar of White South Africa and Protestant denominationalism. The sign *"Net vir Blankes*—For Europeans only"* stares every African in the face wherever he moves. Figuratively speaking, this sign is also affixed to many, nay, most Christian institutions of the country, and the "Separatist" church is, on the part of the African, his logical reply to the Whites' policy of segregation and separation.

Claims that "political" reasons are behind the Separatist Church movement miss the mark. The few instances of radical party affiliations of certain Ethiopian or Zionist groups do not offer a sufficient proof of any definite political trend; and even admitting the existence of much outspoken anti-White propaganda in most Independent Churches, one should not forget that the attitude of the leaders and masses of these Ethiopians and Zionists has on the whole been loyal, not least during the trying experiences of war. A different question altogether is that the Separatist Church movement—both in its Ethiopian and Zionist form—is often nationalistic. The term "Ethiopian" has definite nationalistic connotations.

We have also shown the fissiparous influence on Bantu church life of Protestant denominationalism. The eight hundred Bantu Independent churches in South Africa are, as it were, the arithmetical progression of sectarian divisions in the West. In the chapter on "Dynamics of Fission and Fusion", we used the term *"expectations"* of further secessions. In all too many missionary organizations in Africa such expectations exercise a great influence, preparing the minds of both European and African for the seemingly inevitable consequence of division. Not only African "Separatist" Churches, but also many European missionary organizations bring to mind Coleridge's phrase: "I belong to that universal and invisible church, of which I actually am the only member." Bishop Gore's warning at the Edinburgh Conference in 1910, that "continuous life depends on continuous principles" had been forgotten by some of those who had taken upon themselves the immensely responsible and difficult task of building Christ's Church in Africa.

Borrowing an expression of the late Professor Malinowski one might say that the missionary approach, against which the African reacts by secession, has been characterized by *"selective giving"*. Malinowski has shown that in the culture contact between White and Black in Africa there is not only "selective conservatism" on the part of the African—who accepts and adopts mainly those elements of the new culture which fit into his old system—but also a selective giving on the part of the European. This is the case also in Mission work. Each denomination and missionary organization from overseas brought its characteristic denominational one-sidedness, its own particular kind of Christianity. Generally speaking, the Christian Church was by these organizations presented as a preaching and teaching institution only, whereas the rich devotional heritage of the Church Universal was not transmitted to the young African Church in the same degree. Our analysis of the activities and ideology of Independent Zulu Churches has *inter alia* revealed an *emphasis on ritual* as characteristic of these organizations, which is an important intimation of the true *interpretatio Africana* of the Christian message.

To these general causes should be added conflicts in relation to Church discipline in Mission churches, and personal incompatibility between the African minister, or catechist, and the European missionary.

The fact that Bantu leaders secede from their own African churches shows however that there are other causes at work besides those already enumerated. In our analysis of leadership problems (Chapter V), we have demonstrated how the Africans urge for leadership and his desire for prestige and power express themselves in these church conflicts, leading to new secessions. The Bantu Independent Church affords the only legitimate outlet for this leadership urge, and, in a society of racial discriminations directed against the African, it turns out to be one of the few psychological safety valves. Perhaps more than any other comparable institution, the Independent Bantu Church offers an opportunity of studying Bantu leadership emerging under modern conditions. In a segregated society this church leadership is characteristically copied on the Bantu systems of *rank*, of authority and leadership, namely, the kingship tradition and that of the Zulu diviner.

Apart from the nationalistic and tribal connotations of the kingship pattern, we would here point out that in this leadership pattern there is also expressed some of the fundamental economic causes of the Independent Bantu Church movement. Any Native problem in South Africa must be seen as a corollary of the land problem, and of the Natives Land Act of 1913. The Independent Bantu Church, in its attempt to secure its own land or church colony, is an outcome of the Bantu's search for a place of their own, where under modern conditions they can form a church-tribe, the leader of which borrows his traits from the kingship pattern of old.

The behaviour and activities of the Zionist prophet and his church reveal that, in certain cases, the deepest cause of the emergence of Independent churches is a nativistic-syncretistic interpretation of the Christian religion. In the latter part of the book we have paid special attention to this problem of an emerging Bantu syncretism. The more a particular separatist organization in the process of secession loses its effective contact with the Christian traditions and teaching of the Church, the more marked does this Zulu nativistic trend become. One example. On the diagram, p. 44, we showed that, as an outcome of the Zulu Congregational Church there appeared among other organizations a "Zulu Shaka Church". It is significant that here the pagan Zulu king turns into a Bantu Church Father. *The syncretistic sect becomes the bridge over which Africans are brought back to heathenism*—a viewpoint which stresses the seriousness of the whole situation. It can be shown how individuals and groups have passed step by step from a Mission church to an Ethiopian church, and from the Ethiopians to the Zionists, and how at last via the bridge of nativistic Zionism they have returned to the African animism from where they once started.

The desire of the Zulus or the Fingos or the Sothos for a tribal church was at the outset not necessarily caused by these nativistic tendencies. The phenomenon of the tribal church is rather a symptom of awakening Bantu race-consciousness and nationalism, the African's reply to the colour-bar of the Whites. But an overwhelming evidence from South Africa shows that the Independent church, tribal and nationalistic, and isolated from effective Christian teaching, is in the long run defenceless against the forces of old African heritage.

Trends for the Future

The trend of the Bantu Independent Church movement depends upon the political and social conditions of the Africans in the future. If African leadership is given a wider scope in political and civic affairs, then the energy, which now flows into sectarian squabbles and secessionist struggles, will be directed to constructive and worth-while problems. If, on the other hand, the restrictive policy hitherto followed with regard to Native affairs is continued, simultaneously with the educational advance of the Africans and the rise of their social and economic demands, then the pressure within Bantu society will result in an increase of Utopian movements. Judging from the situation at the time of writing, it seems that the latter of these two alternatives will be followed for a considerable period in the future. In such circumstances one of the following alternative trends seems probable.

1. Some of the prominent Ethiopian leaders, especially those whose churches are recognized by the Government, may succeed in amalgamating a considerable number of other Ethiopian and Zionist churches. With the success of such attempts, the demand for a Union or Federation of many churches under a few recognized Church leaders, will be raised and may result in a nation-wide organization. The Bantu press is interested in such a solution, and the bulk of the African intelligentsia may decide for these ventures in the hope of consolidating the African Church and thereby strengthening the influence of the Africans.

2. The rapid rise to prominence and power of prophets such as Shembe, Lekganyane and Solomon Lion, shows that South Africa may yet, and perhaps soon, see the day of some outstanding prophet who will succeed in calling to life a religious movement of overwhelming strength. Isaiah Shembe among the Zulus was well on his way to a far-reaching influence of this

nature, but his death, in 1935, cut short his chances, and his son and successor has not carried the same weight.

3. It may be that the fissiparous tendencies of to-day will continue to exercise their influence, dividing the Bantu Independent churches into still smaller fragments, and nibbling at the outer fringes of the Mission churches. In such a case, no dramatic or spectacular development will follow, but the movement will continue to cause, as it does to-day, difficulties both to Missions and to other, older independent Churches.

4. The future of the movement will to a certain degree also depend upon the attitude of the Mission churches, and what kind of Missions in the near future are likely to be most influential in Africa. Because, to be sure, there are missions *and* missions.

Professor K. S. Latourette, writing on the post-war situation in the Church in the Anglo-American world, has pointed to "a major shift in the complexion of the Church which is following the decay of Western Europe, the tribulation of Great Britain and the augmented position of the United States". This shift in the complexion of the Church is, according to Latourette, caused by the growing importance of what he calls "the left wing of Protestantism" in America.[1] This forecast, if in the future proved to be correct, is very much the concern of Africa as being one of the main spheres of interest of the evangelizing churches in the West. The emerging Prophet movement among the Bantu in South Africa and in other parts of Africa owes much of its initial inspiration and impetus to radical Protestant sects of the "hot-Gospel" type.

There was, also in Zululand, a change in the complexion of the Church when, via the syncretistic bridge of Zulu Zionism, radical spiritualized Christianity from the West was changed into African spiritism. The complexion changed, and took on a darker hue. Obviously, certain radical types of Western Protestantism has been more susceptible to this "change of complexion" than churches of older standing with a more balanced and more "universal" message and organization. This is the reason why some Bantu leaders warn their people against the influence of left-wing Protestantism from the West. Their revolt may very well lead them in the direction of Mission churches of assured stability and strength. As far as I can see, leaders and masses of the Independent Bantu Churches will be attracted by Mission churches with episcopal authority, prestige of liturgical tradition, and a liberal attitude in racial questions, as was the case, one generation ago, when Dwane founded the "Order of Ethiopia".

Recommendations

There is obviously a whole set of problems of a political, economic, social and ecclesiastical nature which should be tackled in order to clear the ground for a settlement of the problems presented by the Independent Churches of the Bantu. I have in this book stressed how seriously the fundamental cleavages in South African life affect the Separatist Church situation. On this point, however, my presentation of the case does in itself imply certain indications for a long-range policy, which here need not be made specific. I confine myself to a few points which call for practical action now.

I. *Research*. 1. The S. African Council for Educational, Sociological and Humanistic Research and or the Christian Council of South Africa to sponsor planned and co-ordinated research into the conditions of the Bantu Independent Church movement in various tribal areas, such as among the Sotho, Xhosa and Chwana. It is quite possible that a comparative study would reveal, much more consistently than has even been attempted in this book, a morphological correspondence between the "pattern" of a tribal culture and the type, or types, of Christianized prophetic movement which it tends to produce.

2. Similar research to be undertaken in West Africa and the Congo region. The West Central Africa Regional Conference, 1946, explicitly recommended the setting up of a "permanent commission" to study the separatist prophet movements.[2]

II. *Administration*. 1. The recommendations of the Native Churches Commission (Union Government Report, 39, 1925) to be revised in the light of twenty years' experience. The actual praxis of Government recognition (or rather *non*-recognition) of Separatist Churches has obviously rendered the recommendations of the Commission obsolete.

2. For any such recognition the conditions regarding educational qualifications or the ministers to be particularly considered, and the whole question of theological training to be thoroughly investigated.

3. If the machinery of Government recognition is to have any real significance, the five-miles-radius rule (p. 78) should be

applied consistently. The situation to-day is, both from an administrative and from the point of view of the Christian Church, far from satisfactory.

4. The Native Affairs Commission to open certain channels of consultation with the Native Representative Council and the Christian Council of South Africa with a view to securing advice in regard to applications for Government recognition of Native Separatist Churches.

III. *Missions.* 1. The Western Churches *have* a responsibility for the Christian development and future of the groups and individuals in this movement. Many of these Bantu leaders feel the need for a renewal of the contact with the Older, Western Churches. But they want to be met, and should be met, not primarily as problems, but as persons, not in a spirit of patronage and condescension, but in the mind "which was also in Christ Jesus" (Phil. 2: 5), the mind of the Good Shepherd. I have already expressed my personal conviction that churches with real authoritative leadership are best fit for meeting this opportunity. The all-important issue of strengthening the hand of African leadership within the Mission churches through theological education of high standard should constantly be kept in view.

2. Any such attempt, however, presupposes bold and constructive measures in regard to co-operation and union of the missionary forces themselves. The great South African, Dr. J. du Plessis, said a generation ago: [South Africa] "has a right to enter the fellowship of the Christian Churches unencumbered by the unhappy entail of sixteenth and seventeenth century divisions". So far, this has been only a *pium desiderium.*

The fact remains that divided Christian forces cannot ever expect to tackle the challenge which this movement presents to the conscience of the Christian Church. Is it too much to hope that the near future will bring a solution of these problems, a solution in keeping with the vision which the Tambaram International Missionary Conference of 1938 holds as one of "the future functions of the Missionary":

"To embody and transmit the experience of the Universal Church."

DEVELOPMENTS 1945-60

(I) THE SEPARATIST CHURCH IN THE AGE OF APARTHEID

Church as Bridge

The Bantu Separatist Church—a bridge to a religion of the past, a bridge leading people back to "African spiritism", was our concluding note when writing on the subject in 1945–46. Looking at the situation some fifteen years later, we have had to ask ourselves whether this viewpoint was not, in fact, too foreign, too Western, perhaps.

The European observer of these phenomena is apt to think of these groups mainly as syncretistic, shading off more and more into Bantu religion. In the 1950's, not least among the Zulu and Swazi, this tendency was of course continued and emphasized. There appeared groups such as the Amakhehlane under John Nthusi, where the Christian element was submerged in a blend of ancestor-worship and dreams, magic and a modernized cult of "luck". The few, but important, Messianic groups functioned mainly in a similar direction—we must point out here that we are now speaking of *a third, a Messianic type* as distinguished from the Ethiopian and Zionist types of Churches (cf. pp. 53–9).

Another aspect of the great majority of the Separatists— Ethiopians and Zionists—must also be emphasized, more clearly than has been done hitherto. To the African masses in Reserve or City, their Churches appeared as definitely Christian organizations, adapted to their own real needs, and as bridges to a new and richer experience of life. In the city, with its rapidly industrialized civilization, they functioned as "adaptive structures".[1] In Zululand and Swaziland they were, relatively speaking, bridging the difficult transition period from traditional religion to new structures and a new ideology. Above all, the religion of the White Christ was there represented in a vital and generous form which appealed to and attracted the mind of the Bantu. No longer was it foreign. It had become their very own.

---

1. Using Talcott Parsons' term, cf. his *Family, Socialization and Interaction Process* (1955), p. 130, and Bengt G. Rundblad, 'Family and Urbanization', in *Studies of the Family*, p. 225 (ed. Nels Anderson).

Church Apart

The issue between White mission and independent Bantu Church was settled before the Second World War. It was in the period 1913–39 that the tensions between Western missionary and African pastor in a number of dramatic cases led to separation from the missions and the founding of Ethiopian and Zionist organizations. In 1913 there were some thirty Separatist Churches. By 1948 the figure had risen to 800. In 1960 there were 2,200. This multiplication after 1945 was no longer a result of racial tension within the missions, but was due rather to fission among the Bantu Independent Churches themselves. We are dealing with a development and growth in a religious world *apart*, distinct from the rest of South African church history.

The Western missions were no longer concerned to repair the broken bridges over to the Separatists. The 1950's in South African church history were a period of fundamental debate. The Dutch Reformed Church in 1950 took a radical step in asking for absolute territorial segregation, "based not on inferiority but on diversity",[1] and was engaged—in South Africa and on the world scene—in important ecumenical discussions on Church and race. The ideal of a multi-racial Church was strongly emphasized by some of the leading Anglican bishops, while some of the most noted missionary leaders in the English-speaking Churches questioned the idea. Dr. R. H. W. Shepherd of Lovedale pointed to the example of the Bantu Presbyterian Church. Besides, did the existence of Separatist sects, he asked, "point to needs and opportunities unmet in multi-racial Churches".[2]

It was largely taken for granted by the missions also that the needs of Separatist Churches were somehow met by these Churches themselves. Generally speaking, the missions did not regard these needs as an opportunity for establishing contacts. There were some exceptions. In November 1959 Bishop Reeves called for "unity among all African Church sects in South Africa".[3] Another was the initiative taken by the Sweetwaters Bible Institute, Natal, where some Ethiopian and Zionist

1. Cf. Ben J. Marais, "Is there a practical alternative to apartheid in religion"? *Optima* (Johannesburg), 1958, p. 149–58.

2. R. H. W. Shepherd, in *S.A. Outlook*, February 1, 1958; *Chr. Century* (N.Y.) Jan. 28, 1959. Cf. *Christian Recorder* (Standerton) Jan.–Feb., 1958, and *Die Kerkbode*, Febr. 19, 1958.

3. *The World* (Johannesburg) 7 November, 1959.

preachers were given Bible courses lasting some two to three years. The effort was significant as an experiment in theological bridge-building.

Pushed, or having been placed, aside, the "Native Separatist Churches" observed from their own particular standpoint the change of the political climate in South Africa in the 1950's. To them, the apartheid policy of the Nationalist Government did not appear as a new invention but was accepted as a logical consequence of the age-old caste structure of South African society as a whole. "Accepted" is the word. In the harsh world of realities, influential groups of Africans had decided that apartheid was, perhaps, not a bad solution after all.

The rising commercial group—African business men, bus-drivers—belong to this category. The most important exponents were the leaders of the Bantu Churches. To a great many among them, apartheid was their opportunity. They felt that they implemented Government policy. That this was in fact so could be gathered from certain semi-official communications passing between leaders of Bantu Churches. In the field of religion the official attitude was to favour—in principle—independence of Bantu Churches from European, *or* from American-Negro, control when the administrative ability of Church officers had been established.

Adaptation to this policy—at least, so it appears on the surface—has been rapid in Bantu Churches. The astute African politician in Durban who acts as a legal advisor to a number of Zulu Church leaders asked himself in 1958 if apartheid was not "possibly a blessing in disguise". The Ethiopian Church leader from Queenstown, now on the Rand, and who had studied sociology in the States, was prepared to accept the new dogma: "As a sociologist I have found that Africans are retarded by relying on the Whites." The head of the Government-recognized African Congregational Church, a big impressive executive type of leader, was sure of his position: "Of course, the Group Areas Act affects me. Think of all the property we own! But I like this Nationalist government. And I tell my people, don't take any interest in this colour bar. Forget about it, forget about politics!" And many Zionist prophets and the few Bantu Messiahs agreed with this. For their emotional Utopia thrived in the world apart.

One should therefore not expect to find radicals or even the politically conscious in these groups. There are, of course, exceptions. We think of one or two Churches of an "Ethiopian" type to which the politically aggressive intelligentsia on the Rand and in Durban is attracted. But broadly speaking, the politically awake and active, if subscribing still to "Christianity" at all, are found in other Churches, and not among "the Native Separatists". The Separatists go out of their way to state that they take no part in politics. The Zulu leader in Orlando of the Pilgrims Apostolic Sabbath Church of Christ in Zion is emphatic on this point. "I testify and promise to the Secretary [of Native Affairs Department] never to be found among the politicians except only when I am preaching the Gospel of the Lord Jesus Christ." The restrictive clause in this sentence is obviously occasioned by grammatical difficulties rather than by other considerations. In relation to further aspects of White power, the Church leader could feel that he served the interests of the powerful. Saula N., an educated man with a Junior Certificate, had served as a mine clerk from 1918 to 1956. In 1943 he was ordained and made president of his Church. He liked to preach to the mine labourer, he said. "The mine is always interested to have church services in order to tame the boys."

But the Church Apart had to find a foothold not only in corners of "Bantustan" but also in the world of the Whites, however restrictive the administrative Acts of apartheid were to become. Government recognition for the Church became the one burning issue for these Churches. One example from a coal-mining town in Natal seems to me to epitomize this problem as it presents itself to the Church Apart.

In a meeting I had in 1958 with the four local leaders of the Separatists—three Zionists, one Ethiopian—the various privileges following upon State recognition of the Church were discussed. The permit for sacramental wine was mentioned. The Ethiopian Church president—once a clerk in a magistrate's office, now an ex-Lutheran pastor whom I know very well—snorted at his naïve comrades: "But why bother about alcoholic wine! I get around the whole problem by using only non-alcoholic wine. You can get it easily from Durban." The most vocal of the Zionists answered literally—in Zulu: "But the magistrate doesn't know me without wine. My regular twice-yearly representation in court for a wine permit is my only chance of being known to Government. If we were to use non-alcoholic wine, I would remain unknown to the Government. If we apply for wine, then we are known. I want to be near the Government."

This discussion is of great significance: once all the traditional bridges between the races had been pulled down, the Bantu Separatist Church had to find some makeshift over which to contact the White world. The Ethiopian who knew the Whites only too well also knew that he could and would manage without them. The illiterate Zionists were of course much further away from the White world than he, in culture, in ideology. But the further away they were, the more prepared they were somehow to come closer to the White world and its ways. Red Communion wine, once a symbol of sacrifice in the service of unity, had in a split culture become a symbol of group status, of being noted by the powers of the Whites' State.

In February 1959, these expectations came to a sudden end. Government clamped down upon the Separatists; instructions were issued to the effect that by December 31 1960, church sites occupied by unrecognized Churches in urban locations had to be vacated. The reaction in the Bantu Churches was one of consternation and dismay.

In this situation two different solutions were tried. Some of the Churches associated themselves with already recognized Mission Churches or Ethiopian groups. An example is the amalgamation of the Ethiopian Catholic Church in Zion, under Archbishop Brander, having some 30,000 followers, and Rev. Mooki's (Swedenborgian) New Church Mission, of some 10,000 members. This particular union is interesting chiefly because it shows that in a major crisis the supposedly theological traditions of a Separatist Church are cast aside in favour of more solid realities. Archbishop Brander's father—coming from an Anglican background—maintained the claims to represent a "purely Catholic Mission". Recognized Ethiopian groups became another centre of gravitation in this crisis. President L. M. Makhoba, of the influential, Government-recognized African Congregational Church, told us in 1958: "Without recognition you are just playing." He has a strong position to-day. Others again advocated strong federations of as many as possible of the Bantu Churches, sometimes with the hope of forming one big united African Church—an ideal which, for political reasons, had been recommended in 1949 by Dr. J. S. Moroka. A number of attempts at such federations, of Ethiopian and Zionist types, were made in the 1950's. The Bantu Church union movement became a matter of particular urgency after February, 1959. The Federation of Bantu Churches in South Africa, under the spectacular Bishop Walter M. Dimba, caught the imagination in the first few months of the new situation.

The result of these individual and concerted efforts was meagre. While in 1948 the number of recognized Bantu Churches was 8, out of 800 applying, the ratio in 1960 was 10 out of 2,030.[1]

Accommodating the Church

During the period 1913-45 the prophet's theme was protest: against the Natives' Land Act of 1913; against the domination of the missions; against the cultural patterns of the Whites in education and preservation of life. The interesting aspect of the development after 19(45)-48 is a tendency towards accommodation even in a culture dominated by the laws of apartheid. This accommodation can be seen in the fields of private business enterprise, education, and care of the sick.

Some of the greatest leaders of Zionist and Messianic groups established themselves as successful business men. The Church colonies of Shembe, Nzuza, Limba, Lekganyane became not only religious centres but also headquarters for flourishing enterprise in the leader's name: village store, tea-room, bus-station. In the case of Shembe the business is in the hands of a dynamic executive who by telephone settles deals all over Zululand and Natal with great determination. In other cases, the prophet increasingly devotes his time to business interests.

Local Zionist leaders in Zululand and Swaziland establish themselves in retail business and above all in building. I was impressed by the fact that in a number of villages in Zululand the neatest buildings were those put up by skilled local Zionist prophets—builders. In Swaziland, Zionist leaders have also, of late, taken a determined lead in modern agriculture. They have been the first to adopt Government-sponsored schemes for irrigation, contouring, and the introduction of new crops, such as rice. There was a spirit of independence and energy—a modern Nguni parallel to the combination of Methodist revival and business enterprise in eighteenth-century England.

The motives behind this enterprise may differ. The Shona leader, John Masowe, at Korsten, Port Elizabeth, insisted that

1. The latter figure should be rightly understood. For while 2030 was the number of Bantu Churches officially known to the Government, it should be understood that part of these did in fact no longer exist as actual social groups. At least 250-300 of these, perhaps many more, were already defunct, "dormant and deady", as one ex-member said. In 1958 we made a special study, not only of the rise of the movement but also of the no less interesting aspect—the decline and downfall of these Churches. The perspective must properly include this aspect of life-span.

all men of his Church must be independent tradesmen—basket-weavers and plate-smiths and so forth: "You are Israelites and should not work as slaves for non-Israelites." Here was a spirit of enterprise and collective energy born out of protest against the White caste. Something of the same drive lies behind the various economic activities of the Zulu Messiahs. Among the Zionists, on the other hand, I found the motive rather in the tendency towards accommodation to modern conditions. Success in business and building confers status on the hitherto despised Zionist leaders among the Bantu educated class. Not all Church leaders were able to unite their two interests. Sometimes the grocery shop became the dominating interest and, perhaps, the cause of the decline and fall of the Church.

Attitudes towards *education* have changed in the same way, for two reasons. First, economic pressure in an increasingly industrialized community made it necessary for the Zionists, to overcome their earlier negative attitude to education as being worldly or of the Devil, and so to send the children to school. Secondly, the Bantu Education Act of 1953 removed apprehensions which these segregated Churches had had. "No longer need we fear that our children will be taken by the missionaries," was the reply in one of the Natal districts. The result is plainly to be seen in the school attendance of children from Separatist Churches. Through the assistance of the Regional Director of Bantu Education for Natal and Zululand we were able to make an inquiry into Church membership of Bantu children in all schools in 1958. Replies were received from 186 schools, representing 60,585 children from Substandard A to B through Standards I-VI in the Primary school up to Forms I-III in the Secondary. These Zulu school children claim membership in no less than 116 different denominations.

For our particular purpose we arranged three groups: Lower Primary: Substandards A to B through Standard II (i.e. the first four school years); Primary: Standard III-VI; and Secondary: Forms I-III.

School attendance for the four leading mission Churches ("leading", in terms of number of children in school):

	Lower Primary	Primary	Secondary
Methodists	5,572	3,567	808
Lutherans	4,319	2,925	609
Anglicans	4,149	2,472	528
Roman Catholics	3,298	1,951	301

Attendance by children from all Bantu Separatist Churches:

Ethiopians	5,596	3,020	525
Zionists	6,897	1,962	208

The result of this inquiry is revealing and probably important. The total for these children from the Separatist Churches— 18,208—shows that they form almost one-third of the total. With regard to the Zionists, we take for granted that this is a recent development. Some ten or fifteen years ago, the number of children from the Zionists was very low, owing to the initial aversion of prophets and parents to Western schooling. To-day they represent the highest number in the lower primary, while characteristically their low figure in the Secondary forms seems to indicate that as a group they are still satisfied with the three R's. They have not yet discovered the values of higher education; they even fear that the acids of sophistication will have a harmful effect on the faith of the future generation in their Church. This attitude may possibly change in the next few years. The Ethiopian groups more nearly follow the trend prevailing in the missions.

The Zionist child still fights against certain odds; Zionist parents are less inclined than those in other Churches to encourage the child to continue school after Standard IV. There is still a certain stigma in belonging to a Zionist Church. An Anglican boy in Form II, age about sixteen, in a High School in Zululand, when asked in class about his church allegiance, said with a broad smile, "I am a Zionist." This was the big joke of the day in that school. There is a tendency for Zionist youngsters who go on to secondary education to join other, more "respectable", Churches. In 1958, we saw letters written to Zulu pastors in certain influential mission Churches by young Zionists applying for entry to institutes of higher education. The request was for a certificate to show that the applicant was a member of the mission Church in question.

Further signs of accommodation are seen in the recent changes in Zionist attitudes to the *hospital* and to medicine. Not that the role of the Zionist Church as an "Institute of Healing" was in any way weakened: rather the opposite. The prophets, in city and reserve, seemed to outbid one another in providing facilities for ritual ablutions, ensuring health and happiness.

But the Zionist Bethesda can no longer fully convince the ailing. In Zululand, therefore, certain prophets allow their people to visit the hospitals—whether run by missions or by the Government—to be operated on and to receive medical treatment—a course hitherto regarded by the Zionists as a mortal sin. When the patient is about to be discharged as healed, the prophet and his helpers arrive at the exit of the hospital in order to counteract the effect of the medical care: they lather their fellow believer all over with water and blue soap and pray in tongues. Here is a fair compromise that secures the best of both worlds. Among the student nurses, a certain number are now daughters of Zionist preachers, and these told me with a smile that "doctors and nurses have the spirit of Christ".

In view of the hold that the beliefs in Zionist healing has on the masses, these signs of recent compromise are interesting.

(2) TRIBE, CHIEF AND CHURCH

Zululand

The "wind of change" in present-day Africa is not blowing in the direction of the chiefs—unless it be to sweep them away. The role of the chiefs in modern African democracies outside South Africa is becoming increasingly precarious.[1] In South Africa attempts have been made recently to strengthen the hand of the chiefs. The Tomlinson Commission of 1955 found that previous governments had "tended to break down the powers of tribal Chiefs" (p. 94), and the policy of the Nationalist Government is "to build up and strengthen the powers of the Chiefs in accordance with their capabilities and traditions".[2] The blueprint of this development was drawn up in the Bantu Authorities Act, 1951, the fundamental idea of which was defined by Dr. Verwoerd as being "Bantu control over Bantu areas".[3] In 1957, Paramount Chief Cyprian accepted Bantu Authorities; his example was followed by a number of Zulu chiefs in Zululand and Natal.

It is here that the role of the Bantu prophet becomes of particular interest and, indeed, importance. Between local chief and local prophet there was in the 1950's a marked rapprochement. The cause of this tendency is obvious. For while in the South Africa of apartheid the chiefs become, in Dr. Lucy Mair's phrase, "symbols of difference", as figureheads of a culture distinct from Western ideas and ideals—their position *apart* is

1. Cf. L. P. Mair, "African Chiefs Today", *Africa*, 1958, pp. 195–205.
2. Summary of the (Tomlinson) Report. U.G. 61/1955, p. 66.
3. *House of Assembly Debates*, Second reading, June 18, 1951, col. 9808.

buttressed by the leaders of the purely Bantu Churches, particularly those of Zionist and Messianic type.

Chiefs have now become members of some of the leading Separatist Churches, and there is a certain amount of competition among these Independent groups for the patronage of the chief. President Makhoba knew of five belonging to his African Congregational Church. Two chiefs in the traditionalist Nkandla and Nqutu districts were known to be Zionists. One of them was of the same lineage as the great nationalist leader Bambata Zondi, the instigator of the Zulu Rebellion of 1906.

Zionist leaders compete in paying homage to the Paramount Chief. As Paramount Chief, Cyprian will automatically be regarded as the patron of the most influential Churches, just as the local chief gives his support to the leading Churches in his particular area, or ward. A public function, such as the opening of the Paramount Chief's new court house at Nongoma, cannot fail to attract a number of these worthies, who take the opportunity of paying their respects and declaring their loyalty to the first of Zulus. This will be done by those Church leaders whose constituencies are mainly Zulu; it is even more true of leaders of Churches whose membership is multi-tribal and whose position in Zulu society is therefore rather precarious.

The prophet—chief relationship must ultimately be understood on the deeper level of the dream-life of the Church and its leaders. The role of Zulu royalty in the dream-world of the Zulu prophets is important, and not only in the more deliberately nativistic groups, although the tendency is of course particularly marked here. John Ntusi was visited in a dream by the late Paramount chiefs Solomon and Mshiyeni together, the former in military uniform, the latter in a European suit. They had a message for him: "You must be our Induna," they declared.

The problem of tribal tension can perhaps best be approached on the dream level. To Josiah Mlangeni, as Zulu representative of the Zion Apostolic Swaziland Church of South Africa, the relationship between Zulu and Swazi is an ever-present dilemma. This Zulu prophet feels his employment in a Swazi Church to be a problem, because it compromises his loyalty to his own tribal group. Since 1956 he has often experienced this dream: "In my dream I come to Zululand. I am asking for a place to live there. They tell me! 'Enter there. Whom do you want?' 'I am looking for Dinuzulu, the King.' Then as I enter, he [now referring to the king himself] says, 'Whom do you want?' 'I see

you, my King.' Then he says, 'I am going to give you those
people,'—and it is the Zion group at Kingsley which he hands
over to me. I can never forget that I saw this Dinuzulu who died
so long ago." Difficult as this personal problem may be in broad
daylight, it is somehow capable of solution in the realm of
dreams, where the old Zulu king is a real king.

Whatever administrative arrangements may be made to
strengthen the hand of the chiefs, it must be admitted that in
the modern world their influence is fast dwindling. Here, then,
is the prophet's opportunity, brought about not by calculating
opportunism but by the logic of events. When the chieftainship
is weakened, there follows a vacuum of power and authority,
which is soon to be filled by the Separatist Church leader. This
has been especially true of Shembe.

The significant trend is not so much the trek of the prophets
to the royal kraal, but rather the pilgrimage of the chiefs to
the prophet's temple. At the great church festivals at
Ekuphakameni and at Nhlangakazi an astonishing number of
Zulu chiefs congregate: fifteen prominent Zulu chiefs are
members of the movement. The prophet has lands, and kraals
and cattle—and maybe wives—farmed out in their wards, just
as did the Zulu king in times past. When a new school is to be
built in a ward, it is the chief who puts up the school, under the
Bantu Education Act, but with financial support from the
prophet, and on the understanding that special privileges will
go to the African Church which has in fact taken the initiative.
The chief will probably be commended in the books of the
Government for his enlightened initiative, and everyone is
happy.

Whenever possible, a special day in the July Festival at
Ekuphakameni is set aside for a private conference between the
chiefs and the prophet. There are pressing questions to be
discussed on these occasions: the attitude of the chiefs to the
Bantu Authorities Act, to Bantu Education, and to the whole
net of legislative enactments that descends upon chief and
people. One would misunderstand the whole trend of this
movement if one were to suppose that the prophet-king was
inclined to give radical and revolutionary directives to the
chiefs who ask for his advice. All the evidence goes to show that
prophet and chief tend to agree over the essential issue—a
Bantustan *apart*, a Church *apart*.

Of considerable sociological significance is the fact that the
chiefs' clans claiming seniority to the royal, *Zulu*, clan are

prominent members of Shembe's Church; thus the Mtetwa and Qwabe.[1] The membership of the Qwabe clan in the Nazarite Church is linked with one of the most dramatic occasions in the history of Zulu nationalism. Messen Qwabe was one of the chief supporters of Bambata Zondi and a leader of the Zulu Rebellion of 1906. He was deported to St. Helena where he saw a vision of a prophet dressed in white. Six years after his death, his widows recognized Isaiah Shembe as this very prophet. When Shembe came to Messen's grave, they exclaimed: "There is Jehova dressed in white." The prophet arranged a great remembrance feast in Messen Qwabe's honour and announced: "I am going to revive the bones of Messen and of the people who were killed in Bambata's Rebellion." The great Messen had five sons, all of whom became members of the Church which their revered father had thus posthumously joined. It is here taken for granted that any Qwabe, illiterate or literate, should become a member of this Church. Since a missiological problem of great urgency in Africa is that of "individualism v. collectivism", the Church membership of the Qwabe clan provides an interesting, if unorthodox, approach to the problem!

Swaziland

To the north of Natal and Zululand lies Swaziland, a tiny British Protectorate with some 230,000 inhabitants. Broadly speaking, the history and cultural backgrounds of Zulus and Swazi are similar, the Swazi language being only slightly different from Zulu. But there are very significant differences between the two peoples. In Zululand, the power of the chiefs has to a large extent been superseded by other authorities. Swaziland is partly surrounded by the Union of South Africa. The possibility of a transfer of the British Protectorates to the Union hangs like the sword of Damocles over the territory. Under this threat the people are brought together into one solid block, centred around one central fact and one personality, that of the king, Sobhuza II, who represents the nation and its survival. Here the ecclesiastical situation plays its part. For Swaziland, a small country with a great king, has a divided Church. And modern Swazi nationalism declares it is a divisive Church.

That is the strong and growing criticism against the White

---

1. On Messen Qwabe's place in the line of descent, see A. T. Bryant, *Olden Times in Zululand and Natal* (1929), pp. 184-186.

missions, expressed both by vociferous Swazi intellectuals and by the chiefs. One of the most prominent in the leading clique of Swazi politicians told us in 1958: "I am no longer a member of any Church. I am against the White missions and Churches. Missions were given large tracts of land by us but have destroyed our valuable Swazi customs, led to an individualistic breaking up of our family life and have let us down over education." One of his colleagues, now a national councillor at the King's court, was no less emphatic: "The Churches should remember that Christ said, 'Every kingdom divided against itself is laid waste.' The missions divide us. If I were Sobhuza, I would chase away all the Churches and the missionaries. Only the Zionists and their great leader Bishop Nkonyane respect our customs."

There is not space here for even the barest outline of a history of missions in the territory. It must suffice to note that English Methodists began work in the South about 1880, after an unsuccessful attempt in 1847; they were joined in the South by South African and Scandinavian Holiness groups, and about 1909 by the American Nazarenes. Anglicans, through contact with King Bunu, father of the present Paramount Chief, were granted land in 1881 in the central part of the country; German Lutherans established themselves in the North about 1887. In 1914 a Roman Catholic mission appeared. The 1936 census, which estimated the Swazi population as slightly more than 150,000, reported some 25,000 members of the six main mission Churches. But there were at the same time over 20,000 members of "Native Separatist Churches", organized in more than twenty different groups.[1] A Missionary Conference had been formed in 1911, but conditions in the First World War made effective co-operation impossible, so that the Conference did not meet between 1914 and 1929. When in 1931 African pastors were invited to the Conference for the first time, they expressed glad surprise at the fellowship and unity apparent among the White representatives of different missions. In the local congregations they seem to have been led to think that such unity did not exist.

Though Methodists were the first to establish themselves as a mission in Swaziland, they were also the first to lose part of their membership to new Separatist groups. One of these, the African Methodist Episcopal Church, erected its first Church

1. H. Kuper, *The Uniform of Colour* (1947), pp. 113–14 and 122.

at Makosini in 1904. Only two years later a new development took place. It was then that the forceful Methodist pastor at Mahamba, Joel Msimang, decided to launch out on his own. He formed the Independent Methodist Church.

Yet, while the Ethiopian line seemed to be asserting itself in Swaziland, it was the Zionists who became the determination influence. Swazi Zionism is closely linked with that known in the Union. Le Roux's disciple Daniel Nkonyane (p. 49) came from a Swazi clan, and Daniel authorized his own brother Andreas to represent him in Swaziland; they are now regarded as the Church Fathers of Swazi Christianity. The statement that "all churches were started by Nkonyane" is heard in all these groups, irrespective of whether they belong to Nkonyane's line of Zion Churches, or to some other.

The remarkably strong influence of Nkonyane Zionism depends on two factors: 1. Daniel Nkonyane's first convert was Johanna Nxumalo (d. about 1930), who followed the Nkonyane family over to Charlestown and served there as a teacher, about 1910–15. She belonged to one of the most influential and gifted families in modern Swaziland. Her brother Benjamin Nxumalo became the founder of the Swaziland Progressive Association in 1929, and in 1942 he represented his Church, the African Methodist Episcopal Church, at a conference in the United States. But even more important was the fact that Johanna had two famous sisters; Queen Lomawa Nxumalo (d. 1933), Sobhuza's mother, and Nukwase Nxumalo (d. 1958), Sobhuza's aunt, were successively Queen Mother. This was a relationship of the greatest importance for the development of Nkonyane Zionism in Swaziland, since it forged a strong personal link between Zion and King. 2. Another link, between Zion and Swazi custom, was established through Daniel Nkonyane's son Stephen, the present bishop. When Daniel died in 1935, Stephen was called from his menial work in Johannesburg to succeed to the leadership of the Church, and in 1937 he was invited by the Paramount Chief to attend the *Incwala*, the dominant national Swazi festival. This was a great challenge. All the missions forbade their people to attend these ceremonies. Nkonyane saw his great opportunity. His decision to be present is interesting also from another point of view. His own grandfather had lived in Swaziland and taken part in the national festivals, although he and his father had done their work away from Swaziland. His positive reaction to the King's invitation thus also meant a return home in a more personal way: the cosmopolitan's return from the Golden City to the home of his tribal ancestors and to the values of the past.[1]

It was in 1938 that Nkonyane attended the *Incwala* for the first time. By the 1950's his attendance, not only at the *Incwala* in December, but also at the *Mhlanga* (Reed-festival) in July, had become an established institution. Bishop Stephen and his wife appear in their blue-and-white Cadillac, followed by colourful local priests in full force, to look on at the national drama from their place as honoured guests in the front row near the King and [British] Resident. Immediately after the two national festivals, the Church calls its own religious conferences at the central Zionist Church at Lobamba. Here the local pastors report to Nkonyane, honouring him as a great chief.

But this is not all. Another great national ceremony, invented by the Zionists, emerged about 1944, and here again Bishop Nkonyane's connexion with the Queen Mother was of special importance. The actual initiative was taken by another prophet, Stephen Mavimbela, who had by then seceded from Nkonyane. Mavimbela was a great personality, whose position as the greatest Zionist witch-finder in the realm made him *persona gratissima* with the old Queen Mother. When he died in 1949, the real leadership of this movement was taken over by Bishop Nkonyane's personal representative in Swaziland, Meshak Sithole-Masangane (d. 1960), who lived at Lobamba, the royal kraal. The new move had started as an ordinary Good Friday church meeting. Referred to as the "*iGoodi*", it soon developed into a festival of national importance, graced by the presence of the Paramount Chief and successive Queen Mothers, who have taken a strong personal interest in this ceremony. Thousands of people from all over Swaziland, from Transvaal and far-away Johannesburg assemble for the occasion. Sermons are preached at Lozitahlezi—the King's residence—by the leading ministers. Sobhuza sometimes comments upon the homiletic performances.

It was in this context that a far-reaching initiative was taken by the late Queen Mother Nukwase herself: the building of a national cathedral at Lobamba, to be dedicated to the memory of her predecessor, Queen Mother Lomawa, and built to overlook her grave at Lobamba. By 1958 nearly £3,000 had been collected for this purpose, mainly among the Zionists, and the

1. The Nkonyane clan is one of the *Bombdzabuko*, or true Swazi clans. Cf. H. Kuper, *An African Aristocracy*, p. 233.

Swazi weekly, *Izwi lama Swathi*, had become actively engaged in pushing the idea. The foundation having now been laid, both intellectuals and Zionists regard it as a matter of national urgency that this cathedral, as a symbol of Swazi religious and national unity, should be completed.

The successive Queen Mothers, *Indlovukathi*, have without fail been very sympathetic towards Zionist activities. In the Swazi culture, where the female line (*gogo* line) is so important, contact with their sister, Johanna Nxumalo, formed the personal link. The first act of healing was performed as early as about 1911, when the then Queen Mother, who had been temporarily blinded, was prayed for by Daniel Nkonyane, and had her sight restored. "Never shall I abandon a Church that has helped me thus," was her promise, to which she adhered loyally and royally. However, both Lomawa and Nukwase were anxious to be impartial and to encourage all the African Churches, a task made easier by the fact that in the Swazi setting, the distinctions between Ethiopian and Zionist types of Church were more blurred than in the Union of South Africa. It became the rule for local prophets and pastors to hold regular prayer-meetings on Sunday afternoons in the Queen Mother's residence. With all these many Churches around, wise old Nukwase took a step that endeared her greatly to all. She had a vision of a bird building a nest with mud of different colours. The significance of this was obvious to her: for Church services she was to wear a stole of different colours, characteristic of the various Churches. Three prominent pastors' wives bought the relevant strips of material, and the pieces were stitched together into one whole, the symbol of unity and concord. Worn for religious services, the multi-coloured stole carried its silent message.

The Paramount Chief himself—although not a member of any Church—takes an active interest in the affairs of the Swazi Churches. This interest dates from the end of the 1930's, the period when the influence of the European missions came to a standstill and when that of Nkonyane and of the other Zion leaders was rising on the crest of emerging Swazi nationalism. Sobhuza called both Ethiopian and Zionist leaders to his residence. In 1939, on his suggestion, the former founded a National Swazi Church, the name of which in 1944 was changed to the United Church of Africa. This change was again Sobhuza's doing. Their Church ought to branch out and associate with people of other tribes and its name should therefore not

317

be restricted to the Swazi. This organization found a remarkable secretary in one of the close associates of the Paramount Chief, Mr. J. J. Nquku, a Zulu by birth, who as an African nationalist has made a bid to out-Swazi the Swazi.

When in 1937 the Zionist groups, consisting mainly of nationalist break-aways from Nkonyane, formed a Federation of Zion Churches of Africa, the Paramount Chief took great interest in their work. The Federation became the cradle of the Good Friday movement which we have already mentioned. As a Priest-king and Defender of the Faith, the Paramount Chief resolves urgent church matters. For example, on Easter Eve 1958 he had to adjudicate between the two claimants to the leadership of the Mavimbela off-shoot.

The prophets *in corpore* thus meet the King at Easter time, though those related to the King by family ties can see him much more often. Nkonyane's Swazi representative, Rev. M. Sithole-Masangane, had married a Dlamini of the royal clan. Members of the royal household told me that the royal family regard Masangane as *"liso lenkosi"*, the king's eye, and Masangane himself said, clearly referring to the relation of the English Sovereign to the Church of England—"All in our Church are Dlamini's. This Church is their *England.*" On the wall of the manse Mrs. Masangane has displayed her own impressive royal genealogy, proving her close family bonds with the Paramount Chief. The late Luka Ziyane, perhaps the most gifted and progressive among Swazi Zionist leaders, also took his wife from the royal Dlamini clan. Other prophets, particularly those representing new arrivals among the Churches, try other means and outbid the others by their adulation of the King. Bishop Masango from Germiston of Ma Nku's St. John's Apostolic Faith Church, comes only on occasional episcopal visits to Swaziland. In 1958, travelling from the Rand in his impressive blue-and-white car, he managed to get an audience with the King and later in the day, preaching at a purification service in the Usutshwana river, he expressed his temporary Swazi royalism in glowing terms: "We have come to the land of the Lion, holding our baptism in this Jordan. We shall see to it that the Law of the Waters shall fulfil the Law of the Kings."

Local chiefs in Swaziland were at first antagonistic to the new Zionist groups with their close-knit social coherence symbolized by modern taboos. These were sometimes very different from traditional Swazi taboos. The Zionist local prophets therefore at first appeared as centres of anti-social forces. But Zionist acceptance of the national festivals changed the attitude of the local chiefs as well, and the Zionists now count about ten out of some 150 local chiefs as full members.[1]

Sobhuza's influence over the Bantu Churches is in the last resort a function of his position as a modern priest-king. In the Swazi weekly *Izwi lama Swazi* (December 8, 1956) Bishop J. S. Mncinah—the present leader of a Zionist splinter group— wrote an article under the heading: *"May God bless our Croco- dile (Ingwenyama) Sobhuza II. Sobhuza II! I will compare him with Solomon of old so far as wisdom is concerned."* One of the most important ladies of the realm told us: "Sobhuza is the imitation of God or of Jesus." The "drama of kingship", played yearly in the *Incwala* festival, ensures the unity of the people at a time when the powers of both king and people are threatened, and the Zionists' presence is appreciated as an act of loyalty to king and people.[2]

Here again, Swaziland is characteristically different from Zululand, for where kinship and chieftainship are breaking down, an outstanding prophet such as Shembe will acquire a position, aptly described in the laudatory phrase, *"Inkosi yamakosi"*, King of Kings. In Swaziland such a prophet is unthinkable, and therefore does not exist. Shembe's Nazarites have hardly any influence in Swaziland. A Bantu Messiah has no place in a Bantu Kingdom where the King himself is sacral.

Tribal tensions in African Churches

Apartheid—with the Bantu Authorities Act, Group Areas Act, and "ethnic grouping" in the cities—has tended to emphasize the differences between the tribes, their cultures and languages.

The problem of tribal tension is felt in the Reserve. The Paramount Chief of the Swazi was conscious of the weakness represented by the purely tribal Church and was therefore prepared to suggest the substitution of the adjective "African" for "Swazi" in the name of a certain Church. This alteration could be understood by at least some of his people. There are in Swaziland Churches whose leadership is non-Swazi, whose

1. For a list of Swazi chiefs, see Hilda Kuper, *The Swazi*, Ethnographic Survey of Africa (1952), pp. 60–81. Chiefs connected with Zion are in Kuper's book numbered 13, 21, 50, 65–66, 132, 145-46, 165–66. Three princes of the Dlamini royal clan must also be mentioned: Mboko, Zake and Madevu.

2. Cf. Hilda Kuper's admirable chapter, "The Drama of Kingships" in her book, *An African Aristocracy* (1947), pp. 197–225.

headquarters are in Natal or Transvaal, and whose programmes are multi-tribal. Nkonyane's Zion Church is a case in point. From his headquarters and observation post at Charlestown, mid-way between Lobamba, Nongoma, and the Rand, he attempts to balance Swazi and Zulu interests.

With Ma Nku's St. John's Apostolic Church the case is different. Here the leader is a Sotho-speaking Ndebele prophetess from near Johannesburg, who occasionally sends an episcopal representative, Bishop Masango, to Swaziland. Her Church is a recent arrival in Swaziland, where it is led by a young pastor Msibi, who, in the teeth of opposition from Swazi nationalists and intellectuals, has had the temerity to erect his church at a Swazi royal kraal, Kwa Luseni. The church language is, of course, Swazi, but in hymns and testimonies there is surprising scope for the Sotho language.

The use of Sotho in a Swazi ritual has, I think, three functions. By the Sotho phrases the Swazi faithful are reminded of their spiritual relationship to the founding mother of the Church, Prophetess Ma Nku—who has only once—and then briefly—visited Swaziland.[1] (This remarkable woman's position as Church leader, with bishops and presidents and a great number of priests subordinated to her, illustrates the role of women in these movements.) Further, the visitors from the Rand to Swaziland are anxious to demonstrate the super-tribal character of their Church. And, finally, the foreignness of this other Bantu tongue provides a certain mystique, and gives an added quality of holiness to the ordinary home-made Swazi service. Yet, Rev. Msibi, the local preacher, is aware that he is taking a risk, and that pressure from Swazi nationalism may become too strong for these inter-tribal manifestations. In his own mind Msibi seems to be prepared for new departures: Bishop Masango as a Moses has a silver rod, while Msibi, as a local Aaron, has only a black rod. But he has of late had a dream with a revelation of Num. 17. There the rod of Aaron sprouted, put forth buds and produced blossoms. The ecological conditions being what they are, it is probable that these blossoms will in Msibi's case prove to be local and that he may establish his own Swazi church group. Zulu prophets adhering to multi-tribal Churches will be told by prominent Zulus that they are "taking Zulu money out of Zululand to give it to

1. cf. Lekganyane's Church at Morija, Pietersburg, Northern Transvaal. In church services, every preacher, whatever tribe he belongs to, tries to say a few words in Pedi, for the prophet's mother tongue is Pedi.

Sotho or Xhosa", and they try various modern means to meet this criticism.

Personality also plays a part here. One church leader may be able to get away with an approach that others would have to reject as being too daring. President L. M. Makhoba relies on his strong personality and considerable persuasive powers to enlist Christian groups from other tribes into his African Congregational Church, the majority of whose membership is Zulu; "I call the chief and his people and introduce myself, 'I am a Zulu and a son of Zulus. Even if you now speak Xhosa or Sotho, you too are all Zulus, for your forefathers left what was once Zululand. You all come from Zulus.'"

The tribal tension is acutely felt on the Rand, where all tribes meet. It is, of course, experienced not only in the Churches but also on local Advisory Boards—in business, in sport. In the Churches remarkable attempts to overcome these tensions are being made. The way in which the multi-lingual Bantu Church is seeking to overcome its problem of communication in the church services is a striking indication of the inherent vitality of the generous Bantu mind and personality. Translation and interpretation in a European church service is a tedious and sometimes embarrassing business; but in Orlando or Pimville preacher and interpreter manage to create something new. They face one another, the interpreter exactly copying the gestures and tonal inflections of the speaker, from slow deliberate assertions to enthusiastic screams (inspired in both cases by the same Spirit). Soon you are no longer certain who is the speaker and who the interpreter. There is a "give-and-take" between the two, and between them and the responsive audience, which transforms an essentially technical problem into a living act of ritual drama.

With all these attempts by various means to relax the tension between ethnic groups, it must be admitted that the dramatic crises within these Churches in the period under review have occurred precisely over the tribal issue. The Ethiopian Church of South Africa, granted recognition by President Krüger in 1896, and thus the first Church to receive such consideration, was torn by strong tribal interests, for and against something which the Xhosa leaders in the Church termed "Disorder and Zuluism". A tragic outcome of the struggle was the withdrawal in 1953 of the State's recognition of the Church. It did not avail, after the event, that the General Secretary of the Church wrote to the Native Affairs Department: "You Sir, will know just how we feel when this old Church is turned away from Union Buildings."[1] In the same way, in the 'fifties the Independent Methodist Church and with it a great number of other Ethiopian Churches was torn by dissensions between Nguni and Xhosa interests. The struggle between central Sotho leadership and provincial Zulu demands was fought out with great energy also in Mabilitza's Zionist group. Here total rupture was avoided only by making the Zulu leader into an archbishop in 1956 with possibly greater powers than even the constitutional Sotho President.

In its initial conception as "Ethiopian", the Bantu Separatist Church movement looked beyond the horizons of tribe and territory, to all Africa, and even beyond the seas. For the Ethiopian vision included also the Negroes of the New World. The fate of Ethiopia and its noble Emperor before and during the Second World War gave content to this larger vision.

In the 1950's, through the new political pressures in South Africa, the wider interests were lost, and the dominant theme was again nation and tribe. Some Bantu Church leaders still insisted that the horizon should take in the whole of South Africa. In 1958 we heard the Zulu Bishop Masango of Ma Nku's St. John's Apostolic Faith Church from Germiston exclaiming, when opening a new church building at the king's kraal, Kwa Luseni, Swaziland: "This house has no tribal barrier. Here may enter Greeks or Europeans, Swazi or Sotho, for this is the house of the Lord." Similarly, Bishop Jeremiah S. Mncinah, present leader of a Swazi Zion offshoot, informed the Bantu Affairs Department in Pretoria that he had been called to extend his church work on a wider scale, from Swaziland to the Union: "Therefore, as the Lord had said unto Abram on dispensation promise: 'Get thee out of thy country unto a land that I will show thee,' of course, it was thus that Rev. Jeremiah S. Mncinah [was] called out from Swaziland to Johannesburg, Transvaal, and South Africa as the Servant of Jesus Christ's Gospel unto His people in the surrounding Suburbs in Transvaal, South Africa."

But Bishop Mncinah and the others soon found that the wider the horizon of the Church, the more pressing became the problems of unity and of control of the group, and the greater the dangers of break-aways on the periphery of the Church. In that situation the tribal outlook became more reassuring than it had been for a long time. Some of the most realistic of

1. Union Buildings, Pretoria, seat of the National Government.

African leaders decided that the international outlook had become a luxury which they could not afford. In 1958 one of the most gifted African leaders on the Rand, told us: "Internationalism is a weakness in an oppressed people. We express our national aspirations in names such as the Zulu Congregational Church or the Swazi Church of God in Zion." To him, and to many, the African Church had become a symbol of active tribalism.

(3) BANTU MESSIAH

Five Messiahs

The Bantu Messiah groups are strictly limited in number. They form perhaps one per cent of the fifteen hundred Zionist Churches, yet their importance and interest is considerable. They differ fundamentally from the Zionist groups, so that the Zionist leaders are not unnaturally anxious to avoid being identified with the Messiahs. Yet, in current literature one finds two of the Messiahs, Shembe and Lekganyane, brought forward as examples of the Zionist movement. This quite obscures the fact that the Zionists, in their own way, will have Jesus of the Book for their Saviour, while the messianic groups will not. The distinction between the two groups is implied in the question of the utmost theological significance for the faithful in both camps: *"Who stands at the Gate?"* (*esangweni*). Is it this Jesus of the Scriptures, or is it the Bantu Messiah in the person of the Shembe, Khambule, Lekganyane, or John Masowe? (cf. pp. 290-291).

Four Zulu Messiahs are mentioned below (Isaiah Shembe, d. 1935; George Khambule, d. 1950; Timothy Cekwane, d. 1950; and Paulo Nzuza, d. 1959), together with "John Masowe", the Shona prophet.

"John Masowe"—the Secret Messiah—is the foreigner in this exclusive group. Being a Shona, he comes from Southern Rhodesia, whence his "Hosannahs", the Apostolic Sabbath Church of God, followed him via Bechuanaland to Port Elizabeth between 1943 and 1947. Until 1960, when the long arm of the Group Areas Act attempted to send them back, they dwelt as a law-abiding hard-working group of more than a thousand in the Korsten slum, and were known as the Korsten Basket-weavers. Under these bare outlines lies a drama of tremendous strength and suspense. Only an African Selma Lagerlöf, could one be imagined—and why not?—could do justice to the pathos of their great story.

323

To die, in order to rise again from the dead—that is the first necessity for the one who would be recognized as a Messiah. John "died" when he was seventeen, and then rose from the dead. His name was not of course John. While he was a boy in the Rusape district, S. Rhodesia, it had been Shoniwa. Then came the "hunger years" in Rhodesia around 1932. During this time he fell seriously ill and died, and his death is testified to by the neighbours. His grave was being dug when he revived and told the people that he had been before God. Having died, he said, he was now being sent by God into the desert, but would reappear with a message from God to men. He retired to the Marimba mountains for a few days, to return as the Messenger of God, clad in a long white garment and bearing a staff, a Bible, and a new name. He was now "Johannes Masowe", John the Baptist, from the Wilderness, with his message: the Hour of Judgment has come. (Rev. 14: 6–7.)

John was illiterate but not without ideas—though most of them seem to have sprung from the Watch Tower preaching in Rhodesia and Nyasaland of some years earlier.[1] Thus he had an apocalyptic consciousness of the imminence of the Day of Judgment; an assurance that his followers would not die; that government, churches and sacraments are of the Devil; that his followers must not erect church buildings, etc.

John collected a group of fanatic Shona, and through one, Lazarus Chipanga, even succeeded in winning the adherence of some Matabele, no friends to the Shona. This further proof of his powers convinced his followers that he was Messiah, the Messiah of Shona and Matabele. Entering the Union at the head of his faithful in 1943, he lived for a time near Pretoria, and again near Johannesburg in the notorious war-time slum of "Masakeni". Ejected from the Rand, he moved to Bechuanaland where one prominent African generously provided the group with testimonials to show that they were all Bechuana and as such had a right to live and work in the Union. So it came about that they settled in 1947 outside Port Elizabeth.

Here the first crisis arose when the Watch Tower dogma was contradicted by the death of one of the faithful. In the Korsten slum men died irrespective of the Church they belonged to. In consequence, some of the living also left John. But the majority persisted, for John was able to modify his statement: the dead did not actually die—they waited outside the Gate

1. G. Shepperson and T. Price, *Independent African*, Edinburgh, 1958, p. 411.

of Heaven till John Masowe himself should come and bring them into the Kingdom, their Promised Land.

When asked by his people if he was God, John preferred to leave the matter somewhat undecided. He was not, of course, Shoniwa, for Shoniwa *was* dead; but he was John Masowe, the Son of God, sent out by God in order to prepare the judgment. Jesus had come in the person of John Masowe, descendant of the original people of God, speaking the original language of mankind, Shona. Overcoming a certain hesitation on the part of the prophet himself the faithful would sing:

> Mununuri Jesu wauya nasi
> Ugere neso zwino
> Tigere kunewe
>
> (The Saviour Jesus has come to-day
> He is staying with us now
> And we are staying—*with you*)

Yet this Messiah in their midst remains unknown, though the Hosannahs themselves know that Messiah lived there with them in Port Elizabeth. Otherwise, how should they have left their homeland in the Rhodesias? John is the secret Messiah of whom the outside world of Philistines and Midianites (Boers and Britons) remains ignorant. To this Gentile world the Church was known and registered under the South African Companies Act, as Apostolic Sabbath Church Furniture Factory Pty. Ltd., whose head was "Jack Sithole". But Jack Sithole was only another mask facing the wicked world outside. Behind the camouflage, hidden in the white-robed thousands of believers, walked the real Messiah, John of the Wilderness.

Timothy Cekwane, born in 1873, joined Mzimba's Presbyterian Church of Africa, and became a local preacher, an ordinary "Ethiopian" leader. But suddenly one evening in 1909, while Timothy led his customary prayer meeting for the faithful of Heimville in Natal, there appeared in the firmament a miraculous star with a long tail. Moreover it stood still exactly over the place where Timothy prayed upon the mountain. Wild with joy and excitement, the group hailed Timothy as the Elect. The heavens, the stars, Halley's comet itself, yea, the whole cosmos, proclaimed the unique spiritual authority of their leader. Running and dancing over the hills under the stars they sang his praise.

While Timothy prayed for the sick, blood flowed from wounds

325

that opened in his hands to give health to the suffering. Blood
—*there* was the secret! And this Church of the Light became as
if drenched in blood. Dreams, visions, sermons, testimonies—
all is a gushing of blood. Blood on earth and stars above. The
printed constitution of this Ukukhanya Church speaks (p. 5) of
the fact that explains it all—in the year 1873 God made one
drop of his blood descend in the woman Cekwana and she
became pregnant and there was darkness at noon that day.

This is the only Bantu Church which to my knowledge uses
red in its uniform, and it uses nothing else. As a matter of
course, the present local leader in Durban is a butcher. Bible
passages referring to blood were written specifically for this
Church, who, when they hear quoted the words of Revelation
11: 6—of the witnesses who have "power over the waters to turn
them into blood"—are rapt away. To describe the shrieking
hysteria of even a normal service in this Church as "ecstasy"
would be a gross understatement.

There is an apostolic succession of blood in the Church. The
founder claimed to show certain stigmatic phenomena, and the
gift was transmitted in his own lifetime to a woman, his younger
brother's wife. When she died in 1951—only a year after
Cekwane—the Gift of Blood was inherited by Aaron Mjwara,
who when praying can produce blood from his mouth. The
greatest Gift of Blood was withheld from the son of the leader
when he succeeded in 1950, but the Church repeats the dying
founder's final words, pointing to his son: He is my blood—
he is I.

Cekwane is referred to as "the Servant of God", the Man of
Heaven, or Masiliyo, and the constitution draws the parallel
between the Lord of the Book, who preached forty days in
Jerusalem, Judaea, before ascending to heaven, and the Servant
Cekwane, who preached forty years at Heimville, Natal.

George Khambule. One of the amazing documents found
during our research in 1958 into these Churches was Khambule's
diary, which reveals him as the most extravagant of the Zulu
Messiahs. This neatly written notebook holds a record in Zulu
of his visions and revelations, his loves and hatreds between
June 1925 and May 1928, and runs to some 9,100 words. We
made a special study of his Church about 1941, and in 1958
interviewed some of the faithful, notably the pretender to the
vacant episcopal chair, a Zulu policeman in Johannesburg who,
having had similar revelations, helped me in 1958 to under-

stand much that had remained cryptic in the diary. Both Jesus and Khambule visited him in dreams, but the latter was easier to follow, for he spoke Zulu, whereas Jesus spoke English. The diary reveals some hesitation on Khambule's part as to his divinity. Are you king, priest and God? This is the answer, No, says Jehovah Immanuel. A week later he has, however, arrived at a more satisfying solution. "It is wonderful. Who am I? Jehovah—it will be so written that it will be obvious to anybody." The prophet calls himself Nazar—from the Old Testament term Nazirite—or "A and O", or preferably "the Judge".

His fanciful existence included a court of twelve Prophets, twelve Apostles, a General of the Lord, and a General's Clack of the Lord—these last being two young women with whom he had entered into a Heavenly Marriage in addition to his marriage with his first wife. Opposition from European administration and Bantu chiefs forced him to leave Telezini and lead a precarious existence between Natal and the Rand. Since about 1930 his first converts have dwindled to a mere handful but these still believe that the deceased Khambule reveals himself to them in dreams.

Paulo Nzuza resembles Khambule in that he too was a powerful man of the Zulu chief-type who found himself leading the life of a wanderer. At his graveside, June 28, 1958, the obvious parallel was drawn: Moses wandered with his people from Egypt for forty years, but Nzuza wandered for twenty years seeking a place in Natal and Zululand where he could settle with his faithful.

Nzuza's call came when the Holy Ghost was imparted to him at a time and place of great significance. The place was Mbozane, near Stanger, close to the great King Shaka's grave, one of the shrines of Zulu nationalism. The occasion was May 9, 1916—a date which every member of the Church knows by heart, important to us because it lies in those few years after 1913 when it began to dawn on the Bantu that the Natives Land Act of that year had taken away their chance of obtaining land (see below p. 330). As one of several apocalyptic outbursts, there was a corresponding descent of the Spirit upon the whole of Nzuza's Church, thirteen months after his own baptism of the Spirit, on June 17, 1917. This, they insist, was no ordinary visitation but a plenary one, of which there have been no more than two: that to "Saula Paula", or S. Paul, many years ago, and this to Paulo Nzuza and his Church in 1916-17.

327

His people call him merely *Mqhalisi*, the Founder, so that we take a risk in placing him among the Messiahs, especially as we did not study the Church up to the death of the leader, but only up to the date a year prior to this. Nevertheless, though Nzuza had not then gone through the qualifying cycle of death and resurrection, the intensive quality and extensive reach of Nzuza's influence seem to guarantee his rapid acceptance within the Zulu pantheon of Messiahs. At his graveside, young and old prayed: "God of Mfunwa [another name of Nzuza], who revealed thyself at Mbozane, have mercy upon us." Moreover, the spiritual orderliness by which the founder chose to die on the very date—June 17, 1959—on which the Church celebrated the descent of the Spirit upon them and their leader forty-two years before, was taken as an omen.

The powerful posthumous warning, which he delivered through one of the pastors at the graveside, is a further indication of the same tendency: "I shall return in order to kill whoever spoils the affairs of the Church of the Holy Ghost." Messiahship is built into the structure of his theology, and to this we shall return when analysing the Mythical Charter of these groups.

Shembe, father and son. Prophet Isaiah Shembe died in 1935 and then rose again. A few of his hymns in the printed Zulu hymn-book of his Church were written "after his resurrection from the dead". As already pointed out (p. 111) the Church was inherited by one of the sons, Johannes Galilee Shembe, B.A., who has attempted to direct the development of this group over the last twenty-five years: a charming, somewhat disillusioned son of a Messiah, a gifted and interesting personality.

Further to what we have already described in writing of Shembe as Messiah, there have been, in the 1940's and 1950's, two developments: 1. Codification of the dogma. 2. Reflection on, and some scepticism with regard to, the dogma. (1) Recognizing the great volume of testimonies to miracles performed by Isaiah Shembe, Rev. J. G. Shembe decided to collect this material. A special church archivist was appointed whose task it is to collect testimonials, have them typed and filed. Local prophets, chiefs and ordinary Zulu men and women have dictated their experiences of healing and salvation through the "Servant". In an interview which we had with him in 1958 on this subject, J. G. Shembe expressed regret that the Church had nobody who could sort out the mass of material so far collected. "But we want all the personal testimonies just as they were told. Then we shall get real history, you see." The collection is one of the most amazing in the history of African religious movements. It is a record of the effort of the Nazarite faithful to interpret the nature of Isaiah Shembe's personality and to gather his revelations of "God", and it serves the process of the codification of the messianic dogma.

Rev. Simon Mngoma's testimony is representative. He belongs to the leading clergy of the Church. Earlier a member of the African Congregational Church, he decided to turn to Isaiah Shembe in order to find help for a young girl who suffered from hysteria. When face to face with Shembe, he asked himself: "When I looked at him, I was surprised. They had spoken of him being a pastor, yet he is not a pastor, but the Lord." Shembe told him that the girl would recover. "His countenance filled me with awe, he was like Jesus; I have seen Jesus on pictures—here it was only the hair which was not like that of Jesus." Catechist Denis Ngcobo was a boy when he saw Shembe for the first time: "When I saw his face, there came a flash of lightning from his face, and I fell down. And I asked mother, Who is this man? And mother answered me, Jesus. All this makes me say that he is with God (*unoNkulunkulu*)."

Long after his death, and perhaps particularly after his death, the Servant extends his influence. One of Catechist Ngcobo's relatives states that the Father (here the name for Isaiah Shembe) came in a dream to his father, a non-Nazarite. The Servant told the pagan dreamer: "I send you to tell them that they must not say that I am dead. If they say so they are guilty before God. I am not dead. I am still alive. May they not be tired. I shall return. I am still hiding over there, near the mountain". These testimonies as a rule lead to a conclusion, a final oratorical question which gives the clue to the whole problem. Shembe heals and satisfies and overcomes all evil. "Then I asked myself: *Hhawu, kanti si hamba nobani?* Oh, forsooth, with whom are we walking? Could he be any other than God?"

(2) Reflection on the church dogma sets in. The most important is of course the interpretation and teaching given by the son, Rev. J. G. Shembe. In his sermons he invariably returns to the great theme of attempting to determine who Isaiah Shembe was. In personal interviews with him in 1958 we had the privilege of discussing this subject. His one concern is to express his conviction that Shembe makes God real and present to the Zulus. In his Sabbath sermon during the "July" festival of

329

1958, Rev. Shembe put it this way: "Shembe is nothing. He is nothing but dust in the hands of God. Shembe is not God, but the vessel of God. He was just like Moses, but our Moses is among us. Shembe brought him from overseas among us." This re-presentation of God to the Zulus is the theme, now as in 1941, when we first heard him preach on this subject (p. 278). Therefore he can go on to say: "Who Shembe was I do not know. I am his son, but I do not know who he was. Shembe was not born as you and I. He was born of Spirit and was Spirit. He was the Sent (*uThunyiweyo*), sent to the Bantu and to all nations."

Therefore the Nazarites pray in the name of Shembe. Discussing with me in 1958, J. G. Shembe reflected: "There are some Christians who pray in the name of Meshak, and of Shadrach and of Abednego. But my people do not know who these great men were. What is wrong then to pray in the name of Shembe, or in the name of the God of Shembe?" Rev. A. Ngubeni, one of the most trusted of his preachers, develops the theme in a sermon. "Shembe was the name given in heaven. The Jews pray in the name of the God of Abraham and Isaac and Jacob. When they die, they appeal to them. We say, Shembe's God, Shembe who was sent by the God of Senzangakhona and Shaka and Dingaan. You are all Zulus, there is none among you who is white."

Personality and Social Change

The explosive development of Bantu Independent Churches was a reaction to what in African eyes is seen as one of the great crises of this century, the promulgation of the *Natives Land Act* of 1913. From 1913, the burning desire of the African for land and security produced the apocalyptic patterns of the Zionist or Messianic myths, whose warp and woof are provided by native land policy and Christian, or at least Old Testament, material.

It was in 1915 that the springs of Zionism overflowed and, like the Zulus' own beloved Jordan, the Umzinyati river, meandered through Natal and Zululand. Each Church prospered or not according to its success in finding land. Isaiah Shembe and George Khambule found land, though Khambule's first tenure was short-lived. Evicted for disorder, he had to lead his flock from place to place. This was the journey through the Desert towards the Promised Land, which he eventually found in a "Released Area" near Dannhauser and there established his Ekuphakameni, the "Elevated Place".

A subtle consequence of the historical development since 1913 affects the whole ideology of these Churches. Enoch Mgijima called his landless flock the Israelites, for the struggle against the land-possessing Midianites and Philistines had revealed one thing to him: their God Jesus was plainly not the God of the dispossessed; Jehovah was. A. W. G. Champion told me in 1958: "As from 1913 we knew one thing—there is no God with the White man". So Jehovah was chosen, the God of the wandering tribes. The use of Jehovah as the name of God has already had connotations attuned to the racial situation, which were to be powerfully increased in Natal and Zululand about the beginning of the 1920's. At this time Isaiah Shembe set Jesus aside, the White's Sunday-God, and chose the Sabbath-God, Jehovah. Behind the mighty shield of the Name of the Jehovah of the Old Testament, his church sang:

> There is no other name
> By which we can be saved.
> Only the name of Jehovah
> By which we can be saved.
> (Hymn No. 119)

At once a further development took place, behind that shield of the name of Jehovah: the deification of the Bantu Servant himself. One verse in the Old Testament became a cornerstone of the Messianic Churches: The Lord thy God will raise up unto thee *a prophet from the midst of thee, of thy brethren, like unto me;* unto him shall ye hearken. Deut. 18: 15. This was Shembe, or Khambule, or Nzuza. The prophet had one ambition upon earth: to find, like Moses, a land for his people, the Promised Land. In fact, when he died, Shembe left an estate of some thirteen farms.

The changes and upheavals in twentieth-century South African society have thus had a share in producing the Separatist Church movement and, not least, the Messianic groups. Yet our brief sketches of present-day Bantu Messiahs do reveal a further factor. This is the role of the *personality* of the Bantu Messiah himself: his call, his consciousness of being elect and set apart, his experience of "death" and "resurrection". These Separatist Churches are not simply the anonymous effervescence of group forces. Notwithstanding the fact that the subconscious collective mind of the group is a reality and is in close and reciprocal relation with the mind of its Messiah, it is in the deep

331

personal experience of the Messiah himself that the group finds
its origin.

A Mythical Charter

A Mythical Charter of some sort, which is held to legitimate
the Messiah and to authorize his Church, is common to the messianic groups. In the hands of the Messiah himself it becomes the
instrument by which he lifts that burden which, tragically and
paradoxically, oppresses the Bantu in some of these religious
groups: the fateful "curse of Ham". It is a tragic fact that "the
curse of Ham" is here supposed to be a problem particularly
concerned with the African.

Thus John Masowe, for whom Africans are the descendants
of Ham, overcomes the curse by rediscovering that one sacred
language which was spoken before the Tower of Babel. It is
none other than Shona, his mother-tongue. So much was fore-
told by Zephaniah (3: 9–10) and even referred directly to the
fate of Africa: "Yea, at that time I will change the speech of
the peoples to a pure speech, that all of them may call on the
Name of the Lord, and serve him with one accord. *From beyond
the rivers of Ethiopia* my suppliants, the daughters of my
dispersed ones, shall bring my offering." In speaking this
original language, the Hosannahs of John Masowe find themselves back in the *Urzeit*, in the time before the curse and thus
beyond its reach.

Cekwane's Charter was established by the divine drop of
blood by which both the founder and his Church was born.
Here similarly both Church and Messiah are linked with the
First Things.[1] Aaron Mjwara, the present leading charismatic
of the Church, told me at an interview in 1958 that his vision
held two men, Noah and Cekwane, the Man of the Waters and
the Man of the Blood. The first answered prayers for rain (!);
the other could perform the miracle of the angel of the Book of
Revelation (11: 6) and turn water into blood. This visionary
connexion between Noah and the Bantu Messiah was his
Church's Charter, at least to him and his listeners.

No Bantu prophet had devoted so much thought and specu-
lation to the Mythical Charter as Paulo Nzuza. To him and his
flock every personal name in the Old and New Testament is a
golden link, denoting a sacred line through history. For it can
help to solve the basic problem in their minds: Where, in the
History of Salvation, do the Bantu come in?

1. Cf. the author's *The Christian Ministry in Africa* (1960), pp. 282—87.

According to Paulo Nzuza and his docile priests there are three lines that reach back to the Beginnings, and three fore-fathers or archetypes: Jacob, Esau, and Ham or Canaan. And there are three corresponding Churches, and no more.

(1) The Church of the ama-Juda, founded by the Apostle Peter.
(2) The Church of the ama-Gentiles, founded by the Apostle Paul.
(3) The Church of the Canaanites, the Church of the Holy Ghost, founded by Paulo Nzuza in 1916, and centred in the ten-acre colony at Camperdown, near Durban.

Nzuza is anxious to show that the Bantu come of an older generation than do the sons of Isaac the Patriarch, a claim that gives immense satisfaction to the preacher and his congregation. Thus he tackles the problem of Noah's curse upon Ham, for his hearers are sons of Ham and therefore under the curse which turned Canaan into a slave . . . until they discover their salvation in Mqhalisi, in Paulo Nzuza, and his interpretation of the Canaan line.

Officially the Church is called the Church of the Holy Ghost: the name "Canaanites" is kept secret. Additional proof of the genealogical link is found in the colour of the skin, which, coming from one of Noah's sons, gives support to the Church's claim to wield the authority belonging to venerable age. The link between Noah's sons and Paulo Nzuza is supposed to be found in S. Peter's vision (Acts 10: 11–12), where all the nations, "also ours", were included. "This is our chance, our Christmas. We were born then, we who do not follow the Jacob-Moses-John Baptist-Jesus line," Paulo Nzuza's ministers explained to me in Cato Manor, Durban. "We are the Third Church."

The search for a Sacred Genealogy, for a Divine sign, for a primal Tongue—this urge to find for the Bantu Church its own mythical Charter within the earliest chapters of Genesis returns continually as a mighty and weird theme in sermons. In a land of lost unity, it is the Messiah's self-imposed duty to ground his religious group in the Beginning of All Things.

The perspective here is not so much of *Urzeit* and *Endzeit* as of *Urzeit* and *now*; as is dramatically shown by a Nazarite pastor's testimony: A woman complained to Shembe that she was always troubled by a snake that followed her day and night and was driving her to madness. Shembe told her to take a grass rope of the length of the snake and to tie it with a knot

333

at the end as if this were its head. Then she must beat that head and so kill the snake, and afterwards bury it. Thus that snake died. The preacher continued: "Likewise has the knot of Eden been untied by the Lord of Ekuphakameni (Shembe). The God who spoke in Eden is here to-day!"

Moses—Nazir—Messiah

Active Africanization throughout Zionist and Messianic groups shows itself in ritual purification systems, witch-finding and so on, and compels us to recognize the vitality of the Bantu religion. Yet our study shows an equal or greater vitality in the Hebrew myths when transplanted to these new cultures. Biblical personalities become the archetypes of those who fulfil the aspirations of an oppressed people, so that the Bantu prophet becomes a Moses, a Nazir, a Messiah.

Significantly, it is soon after 1913 that some of the great Church leaders, such as Enoch Mgijima, Gardiner Mvuyana, Isaiah Shembe, Paulo Nzuza, and Timothy Cekwane, begin to be regarded as *Moses*. Isaiah Shembe tells his people:

> To-day you are the laughing-stock
> Of all the Nations.
> So wake up Africa
> Seek thy Saviour.
> To-day our men and women
> Are slaves
>   (Hymn No. 46)

Salvation comes, and is specified:

> We ourselves are saved,
> We all Nazaretha
> We shall drink at that rock
> Of Sinai's mountain.
>   (Hymn No. 83)

Sinai's mountain, whither Shembe leads them, is one or other of the two Zulu mountains, Ekuphakameni and Nhlanga-kazi, where twice yearly they stand gathered as a Church under their Moses. J. G. Shembe, in a sermon in 1958, said of his father, "Shembe was just like Moses who was God's great servant." But to his Zulu listeners here was a greater than Moses: "Our Moses brought us God among us Zulus." Similarly, the Shona regard John Masowe as their Moses, who brought his people through to their Canaan, in spite of the surrounding Philistines and Midianites.

Shembe's group call themselves *ma Nazaretha*, the Zulu translation for Nazirite. And Nazar is what George Khambule calls himself in his diary. These names are significant, for it is the Nazir chapter (Num. 6) which provides the blue-print for the constitutions of all the Zionist Churches, and is of particular importance in the Messianic groups. It is as Nazir that the Messiah fulfils his tasks of ritual purification and witch-finding. And as Nazir the most exacting hygienic rules are applied to his person and uniform.

It is as a Nazir purifying his people from sickness and magical dangers that Lekganyane's case is of interest. The spraying of the faithful with water and the burning of paper seem to be commonly understandable symbols of the purifying effects of the two elements, water and fire, and it is in this connexion that the prophet appears as a Nazir.

As Nazir the prophet is supposed to withhold himself from entering into marriage bonds or sexual relationships. John Masowe in the first days of his prophetic enthusiasm told his people that it had been revealed to him that he was not to marry. When in the end he did marry, and on a generous scale, it tended to cause a crisis. G. Khambule's diary is full of his recollections of his Heavenly Marriage, the Wedding of the Lamb, with one Joanah.

The prominent role of John the Baptist in the thought-world of these Churches is due to the fact that he is regarded as the great Nazir. There is achieved a blend of the Hebrew title Nazir and the traditional role of the Zulu witchfinder or *isangoma*. The leading Shembe-ite, Rev. S. Mngoma, testifies that Isaiah Shembe would state when preaching: "To-day the Isangoma of Heaven has come, who knows all the works of men, whatever they do, good or bad." In his diary, George Khambule, too, uses the term "Isangoma of Heaven", in this case referring to his favourite wife.

The Moses-Nazir's identification with the Messiah. When Khambule arrives at the surprising conclusion about himself, "I am Jehovah", or when the Shembes—both father and son —allow themselves to be acclaimed with *"Uyingcwele"*, He is holy, the observer tends to conclude that this is, after all, nothing but a piece of charlatanry. But such an approach does not really meet the problem at the level where these prophets and their groups actually find themselves and their problem can only be understood at *that* level. Development of the prophet into a Messiah seems to follow certain definite steps.

The first is the leader's claim to be a healer, confirmed particularly in his manner of coping with hysteric phenomena. The performance of healing is then dramatized and applied to himself. He "dies" and "rises" again. His acceptance of the role is confirmed by his own prophetic self-consciousness mediated by revelations through dreams. This sequence is at all points met half-way by the expectations and the will to believe of the Church. "Who is this one?" says the healed man. Could he be any other than . . . God? And the believing group in their dream-experience begin to recognize their prophet as the Gate-Keeper of the Gate of Heaven. There is sufficient proof, for the Heavenly Gate-Keeper is the Messiah.

Whether this role is transferable to successors is a problem of some importance in these Churches, where on the one hand the uniqueness of the prophet-Messiah's experience is stressed, and on the other hand the Church should devolve from the leader to his son. In Timothy Cekwane's case (d. 1950) this was solved in a manner which his group of believers found relevant. In his dying moments he pointed to his son and installed him as the new leader, exclaiming, "He is my blood. He is I."

Bantu Messiah and White Christ. "Perhaps we have got the wrong God," an African intellectual confided to me in 1958. "It might have been better if we'd had our own God." This is a burning question discussed both in Mission and Independent Churches. In the Easter Vigil it is always referred to. At Orlando, on that particular night in 1958, I listened in chapel after chapel. Pastor R. of the African Methodist Episcopal Church showed me a cross worked in dark brick upon the white-washed wall of the new-built church. "Has anyone ever seen a cross which was not white?" he asked, and went on: "The white man has corrupted the Cross and made it the sign of the white races—which it is not! With this brick cross we want to show that Jesus Christ is not only the God of Englishmen and Boers, but for all men—for us too." Then on to the great revivalist Nicolas Bhengu. In his sermon he said: "God is a good God. But he is not a European. Anyone who says that is a fool. Jesus has never set foot on the soil of Europe or America or Australia. But—Jesus has been in Africa." One of the prayer-women in the next church, Lutheran, said to me, "I can see Jesus now in Gethsemane, in the garden of sorrows. He looks as though He was white—but no, He is not white! He is the Saviour of the whole world, our Saviour, my Saviour."

Later Pastor Msibi gave his interpretation. He himself is a

specialist in purification rites and preaches an interesting brand of "water-mysticism". Among other things he offers animal sacrifices on an altar outside the church and uses the ashes in his healing rites. Yet he understood well who Jesus was, and expressed his knowledge in a phrase that is unforgettable: *umuntu ungumuntu ngomuntu!* "Man becomes man through Him who became man." We are all no more than potential men; we become men through Him who being found in fashion as a man, humbled Himself—to suffer the death of the Cross.

Yet, this solution is by no means universally acceptable. The intolerable social and economic situation brings up new questions and new answers; an African social worker on the Rand in 1958 summed up his solution: "There is no nation without a God. Each nation maybe has to have its own God. The only one who could bring about a change in our situation would be a great Bantu prophet who would be prepared to suffer like Christ did."

To him, and to many like him, because of the actions of the White caste, the image of the White Christ fades away. The White Christ was, perhaps, only the White's Christ? The longing for a Messiah is at once intensified and baffled. This longing is blood-brother to the yearning in the Negro spiritual:

> Were you there
> When they crucified *my* Lord

Yet the harsh reality of racial conflict made one of the Zulu Messiahs, preaching "on the hills of Ohlange", alter the question in a significant way:

> "Is it that you are Jews?
> Are you not Zulus?
> Were you there when they crucified their Lord?"

In that change of adjective can be read the whole meaning of the Bantu Messiah.

NOTES

Introduction

1. G. Myrdal, *An American Dilemma, The Negro Problem and Modern Democracy*, Vol. II, p. 1064.

Chapter I

1. H. Callaway, *The Religious System of the Amazulu*, 1870, p. 118.

2. E. J. Krige, *The Social System of the Zulus*, 1936, p. 282.

3. Callaway, *ibid.*, p. 375–93.

4. W. M. Eiselen—I. Schapera, "Religious Beliefs and Practices" in Schapera (ed.), *The Bantu-Speaking Tribes of South Africa*, 1934, p. 263 and Krige, *ibid.*, p, 297.

5. M. Gluckman, "Zulu Women in Hoecultural Ritual", *Bantu Studies*, 1935, p. 257, and *passim*, and *idem*, "Some processes of Social Change Illustrated from Zululand", *ibid.*, 1942, p. 254.

6. Krige, *Social System of the Zulus*, p. 283.

7. Eiselen—Schapera, "Religious Beliefs and Practices" in Schapera (ed.), *The Bantu-Speaking Tribes*, p. 251.

8. "The kings said heaven belonged to the royal house." Krige, *Social System*, p. 247. The name for heaven is the same as the royal clan-name, *iZulu*. Cf. Callaway, *Religious System of the Amazulu*, p. 120.

9. The Zulu word for festival is *umkhosi* which first only applied to the First-fruit Ceremonies. Bryant has made it probable that "umkhosi" is connected with *amakhosi*, a reverent word for the ancestral spirits. "The Zulu *Umkhosi* is therefore the great festival of the ancestral spirits of the tribe." Krige, *Social System*, p. 249.

10. Most diviners are women. Bryant put the percentage of women as high as 95 per cent. "The Zulu Cult of the Dead", *Man*, 1917. No. 95.

11. Gluckman, "Zulu Women in Hoecultural Ritual", *Bantu Studies*, 1935, p. 270.

12. H. Ph. Junod, "Les Cas de possession chez les Va Ndau", *Africa*, 1934, pp. 270–98. v. Warmelo, *Contributions Towards Venda History, Religion and Tribal Ritual*, Dept. of Native Affairs, Ethnol. Publications, Vol. III, pp. 141 ff. E. J. and J. D. Krige, *The Realm of a Rain-Queen*, 1943, p. 241–49.

13. Krige, *Social System*, pp. 298 f

14. J. du Plessis, *A History of Christian Missions in South Africa*, 1911, p. 173.

15. *Uplifting the Zulus, Seventy-five Years' Mission Work in Natal and Zululand*, ed. by the Natal Missionary Conference, 1911, p. 8.

16. *Ibid.*, p. 14.

17. du Plessis, *op. cit.*, p. 303, and E. H. Brookes, *A Century of Missions in Natal and Zululand*, 1936, p. 25.

18. du Plessis, *op. cit.*, and Hurcombe, *The Wesleyan Methodist Church of South Africa, Pioneer Missionary Work among the Natives of Zululand and Maputaland* (no year), *passim*.

19. Brookes, *op. cit.*, pp. 23 f.

20. Allison, the pioneer of Wesleyan Methodist mission work in Northern Zululand, severed his connexion with this society and for a while worked independently near Pietermaritzburg. Dr. Alexander Duff, when visiting

South Africa in 1864, had contact with Allison, and the latter was accepted as a missionary by the Free Church of Scotland. *Uplifting the Zulus*, p. 32.

21. Brookes, *op. cit.*, p. 12.

22. *Report, World Missionary Conference, Edinburgh*, Commission I, pp. 228–29.

23. Cf. J. du Plessis, "Missionary Co-operation", in Taylor (ed.), *Christianity and the Natives of South Africa*, 1928, pp. 61 ff. *Uplifting the Zulus*, etc., p. 52.

24. K. G. Grubb (ed.), *The Christian Handbook of South Africa—Die Suid-Afrikaanse Kristen-Handboek*, p. 203.

25. R. H. W. Shepherd, *The Christian Council of South Africa*, Report of Meeting in Johannesburg, January, 1937.

26. G. Warneck, *Outline of a History of Protestant Missions from the Reformation to the Present Time*, 1904, pp. 402 ff.

27. Findlay-Holdsworth, *The Wesleyan Methodist Missionary Society*, IV, p. 322.

28. (Wesleyan) *Missionary Notices*, June–July, 1885, p. 178.

29. J. D. Taylor, *The American Zulu Mission* 1900–01, p. 7 and *idem*, *The American Board Mission in South Africa, A Sketch of Seventy-five Years*, 1911, p. 28.

30. Léenhardt, *Le Mouvement Éthiopien*, 1902, pp. 117 ff.

31. Jacottet, "Native Churches and their Organization", *Report, First General Missionary Conference*, 1904, pp. 108–33, and Lennox, "The Relation of European and Native Churches", *Report, Third General Missionary Conference*, 1909, p. 82–92.

32. C. Lewis and G. E. Edwards, *Historical Records of the Church of the Province of South Africa*, 1934, p. 213.

33. Lennox, in *Report, Third General Missionary Conference*, p. 82 ff.

34. Brookes, *op. cit.*, p. 41, and letter from Rev. Mungo Carrick, Oct., 1946, to the writer.

35. Lord Hailey has shown that the cause of Bantu nationalism in South Africa is to be found in the curtailment of Native lands, through the Land Act of 1913. Hailey, "Nationalism in Africa", *Journal of Royal African Society*, 36 (1937), pp. 134 ff.

36. D. D. T. Jabavu, "Bantu Grievances" in Schapera (ed.), *Western Civilization and the Natives of South Africa*, 1934, p. 287.

37. The figures for Zululand were 400 Europeans and 250,000 Zulus, and the total area of 10,000 square miles, of which the Zulus were restricted to 6,000 square miles. Macmillan, *Complex South Africa*, 1930, pp. 283 f.

37*a*. Cf. J. D. R. Jones, in *Abundant Life in Changing Africa*, Léopoldville—New York, 1946, p. 110.

38. Brookes, *The Colour Problems of South Africa*, 1933, p. 65.

39. The Mines and Works Act, 1911, Amendment Act 1926, ("Colour Bar Act").

40. Brookes, *op. cit.*, p. 10.

41. C. S. Richards, "Economic Revival in South Africa", *The Economic Journal* (London), 1934, p. 624.

42. R. Phillips, *The Bantu in the City*, 1938, p. 66.

43. W. H. Hutt, "The Economic Position of the Bantu in South Africa" in Schapera (ed.), *Western Civilization and the Natives of South Africa*, p. 237.

44. R. Phillips, *op. cit.*, pp. 343–44. Recent developments, after World War II, have shown that the African National Congress under the leadership of Dr. A. B. Xhuma and Professor Z. K. Mathews may attain to new importance.

45. W. E. B. DuBois, *Dusk of Dawn*, 1940, pp. 130–31, quoted after Myrdal, *An American Dilemma*, I, p. 680.

46. W. M. Eiselen, "Christianity and the Religious Life of the Bantu", in Schapera (ed.), *Western Civilization and the Natives of South Africa*, 1934, p. 73.

47. D. G. S. M'Timkulu, "The African", *Race Relations*, 1946, p. 4.

48. Brookes, *A Century of Missions in Natal and Zululand*, 1936, p. 32.

Chapter II

1. C. M. v. Antwerp, *Die Separatistiese Kerklike Beweging onder die Bantu van Suid-Afrika*, 1938, unpublished manuscript, E. Shillito, *Fr. Coillard, A Wayfaring Man*, 1923, p. 107.

2. Findlay-Holdsworth, *Wesleyan Methodist Missionary Society*, IV, p. 322.

3. *Ibid.*, p. 342.

4. R. Allier, *La Psychologie de la Conversion*, II, p. 441.

5. See R. R. Wright, *Information Book for . . . A. M. E. Church*, 1939.

6. General P. J. Joubert signed a statement according to which the "Ethiopian Mission Society"(!) is "a community known to the Honourable Government and is active in the South African Republic". M. Léenhardt, *op. cit.*, pp. 87–88.

7. See Bechler, *Unabhängigkeits-Bewegungen*, pp. 21–24.

8. C. Lewis and G. E. Edwards, *Historical Records of the Church of the Province of South Africa*, 1934, p. 214.

9. Interested Europeans heaved a sigh of relief when seeing Dwane's movement being absorbed by the Church of the Province. D. Kidd (*The Essential Kafir*, 1904, p. 407) writes: "No one who has watched the erratic development of the Ethiopian Church movement could take these people seriously. This strange sect started out with but little in common with the Church of South Africa, and after a short and flickering life has come to rest in the bosom of that Church. A ship will run into any port in a storm, and it is probably a good thing that these unstable people are now under the strong control of rigid ecclesiastical authorities."

10. Lewis and Edwards, *op. cit.*, p. 225. Bechler, *op. cit.*, pp. 30–33. Cf. also F. W. Puller, "The Ethiopian Order", W. M. Cameron, "The Ethiopian Movement and the Order of Ethiopia", *ibid.*, 1904, pp. 375–97, and *The East and the West*, 1903, pp. 75–91. One's judgment on the nature of church secessions is conditioned by one's own position. A. Lea, *op. cit.*, p. 42, believes that "the Order of Ethiopia became but another separatist body", and one A.M.E. historian describes how "Dwane seceded to the Anglican Church (Ethiopian Order)", *Journal of Proceedings*, A.M.E. Annual Conferences, 1939, p. 3.

11. *The Constitutions and Canons of the Ethiopian Catholic Church in Zion*, Bloemfontein, 1918, p. 6.

12. R. H. W. Shepherd, "African Separatist Churches", *International Review of Missions*, 1937, p. 455.

13. Cf. Léenhardt, *Le Mouvement Ethiopien*, pp. 75–76.

14. L. M. Mzimba has developed his ideas on the principles of Bantu Independent Churches in his article, "The 'African Church", in J. D. Taylor (ed.), *Christianity and the Natives of South Africa*, 1928. A characteristic phrase of Mzimba's is this: "The Bantu are determined to have his share not only of the task of living for Christ, but also the blessings and the reward."

340

NOTES

15. *Natal Native Affairs Commission*, 1906–7, Vol. *Evidence*, p. 46. The opposition against allowing Africans going to America became vocal among Europeans at this time. D. Kidd (*Kafir Socialism*, 1908, p. 194) expresses himself in no uncertain terms: "Only the stupid, easy-going, liberty-loving spirit of the Briton would suffer this American peril."

16. Cf. J. Wells, *Stewart of Lovedale*, 1908, pp. 296–97.

17. Lord Acton, *History of Freedom and other Essays*, p. 62.

18. See F. B. Bridgman, in *Report, General Missionary Conference*, 1904, p. 170, and Lea, *op. cit.*, pp. 36–37.

19. Malcolm Spencer, "Social Contribution of Congregational and Kindred Churches", *The Sociological Review*, Vol. XXXV, 1943, pp. 57–59.

20. John Ntekiso first called his offshoot from Goduka's group: The African Caster-oil Dead Church. He explained the name to me: "Dead" stood for the sorrow he felt when the president of his parent church did not follow the "*kongegeshen*" (Constitution). He was killed in body, soul and spirit. "Caster-oil" stood for life and hope. He showed me bottles of the medicine.

21. For the background of the change in financial policy of the mission, linked up with the transfer of the mission work from England to the Methodist Church of South Africa, see *Our Living Message . . . the 117th Report of the Wesleyan Methodist Missionary Society*, 1931, pp. 71–72. The church fee for the Native church members on the Rand was raised from 2s. per quarter to 2s. 6d. Strong opposition occurred and these people went in procession through the streets of Johannesburg. At the head of the procession went a donkey with placards on which was written: "Jesus Christ was sold for thirty pieces of silver. We are sold for thirty pence" (2s. 6d.). The nickname "Donkey Church" has been accepted by the leaders of this section and on some of their churches there has been put, instead of a steeple weather-cock, the picture of a donkey. One of the leaders with a twinkle in his eye, pointed out to me that "the donkey is the most sacred animal in the New Testament. It was used by Jesus. The donkey is slow, but sure, and humble".

22. See E. H. Snelling (publ.), *Statement by the Rev. John Alexander Dowie . . . concerning Conditions in Zion City, Illinois*, 1924.

23. Characteristically on the very same day, May 8, 1904, Dwane's colleague, S. J. Brander, started his Ethiopian Catholic Church in Zion. Brander called himself "Overseer" at that time (he is archbishop now), and both this designation and the qualification "in Zion" were borrowed from Bryant, although Brander's church has since largely developed on Ethiopian lines.

24. Bridgman, in *Report, General Missionary Conference*, 1904, p. 167.

25. A. Lea, *op. cit.*, p. 47, believes that the amaNazaretha or Nazarites are connected with the Church of the Nazarenes, and quotes one authority which speaks of the activities of the Nazarenes in Yugo-Slavia. There is no such connexion. Shembe's church is purely African and purely Zulu.

26. For the discussions in Nat. Repr. Council of this matter, see *Minutes, Native Repr. Council, Pretoria*, 1944, p. 338–49.

27. *Ilanga lase Natal* (Zulu newspaper), June 17, 1939. Lamula's figure about American conditions is derived from the fact that in U.S. "church" is sometimes taken to mean local congregation.

28. Léenhardt, *Le Mouvement Éthiopien*, p. 88.

29. Bridgman, in *Report, First General Missionary Conference*, 1904, pp. 167, 171.

30. Cf. the impression of the Italo-Abyssinian War on the Negroes of U.S.A. See J. Dollard, *Caste and Class in a Southern Town*, 1937, p. 304, and W. L. Sperry, *Religion in America*, 1945, p. 185.

31. The African Orthodox Church claims an apostolic succession back to "St. Peter the Apostle, First Bishop and Patriarch of Antioch". Their Archbishop

Daniel Alexander was consecrated in 1927 (in New York) by an archbishop
of what is described as "American Orthodox Church". Cf. H. R. T.
Brandreth, *Episcopi Vagantes and the Anglican Church*, p. 37 ff.

32. On Garvey, cf. G. Myrdal, *An American Dilemma*, 1944, II, p. 746.

33. Léenhardt, *op. cit.*, p. 110.

34. *Report, General Missionary Conference*, 1904, particularly pp. 171–83.
The decisions of the conference had an interesting sequence in an argument
between representatives of the A.M.E. and M. Jacottet. See Jacottet, *The
Ethiopian Church and the Missionary Conference, An open Letter* . . . (Morija),
1904.

35. See *Notule van die* . . . *Vergaderings van die Sinode van die Neder Duitse
Gereformeerde Sendings-Kerk in die Oranje Vry Stat* 1925, 1928 (where A.M.E.
is referred to as a *"suisterskerk"*), 1931 and 1937.

36. F. Wells, *The Life of James Stewart*, 1908, p. 296.

37. E. Shillito: *Fr. Coillard. A Wayfaring Man*, 1923, p. 228. See also *Report
General Missionary Conference*, 1904, p. 14.

38. *International Review of Missions*, 1937, p. 463.

39. In his *Sketch of Seventy-five years of the American Board of Missions*,
J. D. Taylor has discussed the fact that after the secession of the Zulu Congregational Church from the American Board in 1896, one important section
of the secessionists returned to the mission fold. "It is significant that the
proposal for renewed negotiations with the seceded church came from the
Native Pastorate" (of the mission).

40. Rev. H. Mashite-Maimane, of the Diocese of Pretoria, in an address on
"The African Conception of the Church" at the General Missionary Conference
at Adams, Natal, in 1938, and Rev. M. G. Mpitso, Methodist Church, Pimville,
in an interview which I had in 1940 with the African Ministers' Association,
Johannesburg, of which Rev. Mpitso was then chairman.

Chapter III

1. See W. M. Cameron, "The Ethiopian Movement and the Order of
Ethiopia", *The East and the West*, 1904, p. 378.

2. See Native Affairs Department Memorandum, February, 1913, by R. S.
Merford, "Native Separatist Churches", Native Affairs Department, Pretoria.

3. *Native Affairs Commission*, 1903–5, Vol. II, pp. 215 ff.

4. *Ibid.*, Vol. II., pp. 1061 and 743–44 respectively.

5. *Ibid.*, Vol. II. p. 41.

6. E. A. Walker, *W. P. Schreiner, A South African*, p. 316.

7. Merriman's note on draft letter April 25, 1909, by E. E. Dower, Native
Affairs Department, Pretoria.

8. See *Occupation of Church, School and Mission Sites in Native Areas*,
Pretoria, 1918, p. 9. Goduka's church was a development of Tile's Tembu
Church, founded in 1892.

9. E. H. Brookes, *The History of Native Policy in South Africa*, pp. 74 ff.

10. *Native Affairs Commission* 1903–5, III, p. 165.

11. *Ibid.*, Vol. IV, pp. 960–61.

12. *Ibid.*, Vol. III, p. 530.

13. J. Stuart, *A History of the Zulu Rebellion*, pp. 420–21 *et passim*.

14. *Natal Native Affairs Commissions*, 1906–7, Vol. *Evidence*, p. 243.

15. Secretary for National Affairs, April 29, 1909, to Chief Magistrate of Transkei.

16. See *Occupation of Church, School and Mission Sites in Native Areas*, Pretoria, 1918, p. 9.

17. *Senate Select Committee*, 8/1914, Native Affairs.

18. *Occupation of Church, School*, etc., pp. 9–10.

19. *Senate Select Committee*, 6/1913.

20. *Report of Native Affairs Commission*, 1913–18, p. 7.

21. *Ibid.*

22. *Ibid.*, p. 8.

23. The Native Affairs Commission was formed in 1920 as a result of the Native Affairs Act of that year. Dr. Brookes says in 1933: "The Native Affairs Commission is generally regarded as something of a failure." *The Colour Problems of South Africa*, p. 7. The Commission has briefly expressed its views on the Separatist Churches in its *Report*, 1927–31 (1932), p. 4, and *Report*, 1936 (1937), p. 2.

24. Statement in a letter from Native Affairs Department, to the present writer, October 15, 1941.

25. This should be noted, especially as it has been taken for granted in various statements on Native Separatist Churches in English and other languages that all or most of the applying churches have been "recognized" or are "registered". There exists no machinery for the "registration" of these churches. For names of recognized and applying churches, see Appendix, p. 317.

26. Introduced by Section III of Proclamation No. 234 of 1938, which amended Regulation No. 11 1(c), published under Proclamation No. 123 of 1931, according to which "The right to occupy an allotment shall be liable to be cancelled, if the allotment is used for purposes other than those for which it was granted".

27. The regulation just referred to is now often circumvented in this way: The "church", when not in use for service, is furnished with beds, chairs and tables to show that it is a living-room only. When needed for church services, the furniture is stored elsewhere.

28. According to the latest statistics which have been available to me (1945), the African Methodist Episcopal Church has 113 Marriage Officers, the Ethiopian Church of Africa 34, African Presbyterian Church 9, Lutheran Bapedi Church 5, etc. But certain unrecognized bodies can also count one or two of their ministers as marriage officers.

29. Only recognized churches are given such concessions. The General Manager of the South African Railways and Harbours in a letter of July 21, 1945, informs me that in 1943 the recognized Independent Churches (including the Anglican "Order of Ethiopia") held collectively 453 cards of identification for such concessions.

Chapter IV

1. G. B. A. Gerdener, *Studies in the Evangelisation of South Africa*, 1911, p. 47.

2. J. D. Taylor, "The Rand as a Mission Field", *International Review of Missions*, 1926, and R. Phillips, *The Bantu in the City*, 1938, pp. 248–90.

3. Taylor, *ibid.*, p. 652.

4. Dr. Phillips (in that helpful and well documented book, *The Bantu in the City*, p. 255) refers to a statement by Dr. J. D. Taylor saying that the latter estimates 130 independent churches on the Witwatersrand. Taylor (*International Review of Missions*, 1926, p. 651) gives the figure "about one

hundred and thirty Schismatic Native Churches" *for the whole of the Union,* and arrives at this estimation by a simple medial of a statement in an article by C. T. Loram (*International Review of Missions,* 1926, p. 477): "A conservative estimate puts the number at between 120 and 140".

5. The latest figure available to me, *Journal of Proceedings, A.M.E. Conference,* 1942, p. 52.

6. Minutes of Monthly Meeting of Reef Managers and Superintendents of Urban Native Administration, February 17, 1944.

7. *Libertas Magazine* (Johannesburg), August, 1942.

8. *Libertas, ibid.*

9. Minutes of Monthly Meeting of Reef Managers and Superintendents of Urban Native Administration, February 17, 1944.

10. R. Phillips, *The Bantu in the City,* p. 257.

11. *Report, Fifth General Missionary Conference,* 1921, p. 102.

12. Cf. A. Lea, *The Native Separatist Church Movement in South Africa,* p. 46.

13. Gluckman, "Analysis of a Social Situation in Modern Zululand", *Bantu Studies,* 1940, p. 166.

14. On this term in the first Christian centuries, see A. Harnack, *The Expansion of Christianity,* I, pp. 336–52.

15. See Krige, *Social System,* p. 169.

16. Minutes of Governmental interviews, with Zululand Chiefs, 1944, Chief Native Commissioner, Pietermaritzburg.

Chapter V

1. M. F. Perham, "The System of Native Administration in Tanganyika", *Africa,* 1931, p. 312.

2. On Zulu kingship see Gluckman, "The Kingdom of the Zulu", in Fortes —Evans-Pritchard, *African Political Systems,* 1940, Kuper, *An African Aristocracy,* and Krige, *Social System, passim.*

3. *Ilanga lase Natal* (Zulu newspaper, published in Durban), March 31, 1945.

4. E. B. Gowin's (*The Executive and His Control of Men,* 1915) studies on the size and weight of executives, indicating that the more important executives were heavier and taller than the less important, have been regarded by some as sheer nonsense, by others as true to fact. Cf. W. Albig, *Public Opinion,* 1939, p. 101. But the Bantu, in their social rating, would undoubtedly uphold Gowin's theories! This must however be combined with an important qualification: "A commanding appearance is a high recommendation for a [Bantu] Leader, but it will be of no value, even in a primitive tribe, in the absence of other qualities." Fr. B. Huss, "Native Leadership" (*Southern Cross,* January 21, 1931).

4a. E. L. Roberts, *Shembe—the Man and His Work,* unpublished manuscript, Univ. of Witwatersrand.

5. See B. J. F. Laubscher, *Sex, Custom, and Psychopathology, A Study of S.A. Pagan Natives,* 1937, pp. 32–33. *uMamlambo* is reputed to be a woman of great beauty and sexual attractiveness, and possesses the power to change herself into animals, insects, and medicines. A man who is the partner of a *uMamlambo* rarely cares for women. He is usually known as lucky and wealthy.

NOTES

6. M. Read, "Traditions and Prestige among the Ngoni", *Africa*, 1936, p. 462.

7. A. W. Lee, "The Growth of an African Ministry in the Province of South Africa", *The East and West Review*, 1940, p. 116.

8. *A.M.E. Church, Journal of Proceedings*, 1939, p. 74.

9. *Ilanga lase Natal*, June 9, 1945, art. "*Amabandla azimeleyo*" (Independent Churches).

10. Dube, *uShembe*, p. 34.

11. For comparison with conditions of theological education of the Negroes, see W. A. Daniel, *The Education of Negro Ministers*, 1925, and Mays—Nicholson, *The Negro's Church*, 1933.

12. Alain Locke (ed.), *The New Negro*, 1925, p. 306.

13. G. K. Chesterton, *William Cobbett*, 1926, p. 195.

14. Mays and Nicholson, *The Negro's Church*, 1933, p. 108.

15. This kind of "sheep-stealing" started at the very beginning of the Separatist Church movement. Rev. Chas. S. Morris, of the Negro Baptist Church, who visited Natal in 1899, reported at the Ecumenical Missionary Conference that while in South Africa he received into his church "1200 members, representing seventeen different congregations". Bridgman, who refers to this, says that the "statement carries its own con-condemnation", *Report, General Missionary Conference, Johannesburg*, 1904, pp. 167–68.

16. See *A.M.E. Church, Journal of Proceedings* of Zambesi, Transvaal, etc., Annual Conference, 1942, pp. 4–5.

17. Ch. Cooley, *Social Progress*, 1922, p. 252.

18. M. Edwards, *After Wesley*, 1935, p. 153, and idem, *Methodism and England*, 1943, p. 228.

19. Findlay-Holdsworth, *Wesleyan Methodist Mission Society*, IV, p. 377.

20. According to information supplied by Rev. A. W. Cragg, Secretary of the Mission Society of the Methodist Church of South Africa, in his letter June 5, 1941, to the author.

21. See J. F. Holleman, "Die Twee-eenheidsbeginsel in die sosiale en politieke samelewing van die Zulu", *Bantu Studies*, 1940, p. 35, and E. J. Krige, *Social System of the Zulus*, p. 39.

22. H. Kuper, "Voluntary Associations in an Urban Township", *African Studies*, December, 1944.

23. Some of the aims of the society: promoting the sanctity of married life; "looking after the poor and needy of the church, as well as Dorcas, otherwise known as Tabitha, did (see Acts 9: 36 to the end)". *Constitutions and Canons of the E.C.C. in Zion*, 1918, p. 4.

24. G. M. and P. Wilson. *Analysis of Social Change*, p. 61.

25. E. L. Roberts, *Shembe*, unpublished manuscript.

26. Dube, *uShembe*, p. 100.

27. *The Constitutions and Canons of the Ethiopian Church in Zion*, 1918, Section V.

28. R. M. MacIver, *Society, A Textbook of Sociology*, 1937, p. 250, calls this the "principle of automatic control" by which the large-scale organization is kept flexible.

28. MacIver, *Society*, pp. 347 ff.

29. Krige, *Social System of the Zulus*, p. 264.

30. Sumner, *The Science of Society*, 1927–28, I–IV.

31. J. Dollard and others, *Frustration and Aggression*, 1939, p. 89.

32. J. F. Holleman, "Die Twee-eenheidsbeginsel in die sosiale en politieke samelewing van die Zulu", *Bantu Studies*, 1940.

33. In recent sociological studies of Africa, the concepts of equilibrium—disequilibrium with such corollaries as adjustment and maladjustment, have been used. Cf. Gluckman, "Analysis of a Social Situation in Modern Zululand", *Bantu Studies*, 1940, and G. and M. Wilson, *The Analysis of Social Change*, 1945, pp. 125–57. Originally introduced into modern sociology by Pareto, the equilibrium concept has been valuable for its time. But just as in modern economics this equilibrium concept has become modified and qualified (as "temporary" or "labile" equilibrium; for instance, Hicks, *Value and Capital*, 1945, p. 115) so it has also undergone great changes in the terminology of modern sociology. Myrdal, in his *An American Dilemma*, has freed sociology from the "stable equilibrium" scheme of thinking, and has made a realistic understanding of society possible, through his dynamic interpretation and by introducing more pliant mental tools, such as "the principle of cumulation", *op. cit.*, II, p. 1065. Cf. also Myrdal, *Monetary Equilibrium*.

34. *Report.* . . . Third Gen. Missionary Conference, 1909, p. 91.

35. I borrow this psycho-analytical term from Dollard and others, *Frustration and Aggression*, 1939, p. 50, though conscious of the fact that Dollard uses this term for the aggression release, which, in our case, would refer to the new church of the malcontents, not to the parent church.

36. Dollard, *op. cit.*, p. 89.

Chapter VI

1. *Tambaram Series*, following the Meeting of the International Missionary Council at Tambaram, Madras, 1938, Vol. IV, p. 16.

2. *The Constitutions and Canons of Ethiopian Catholic Church in Zion*, Bloemfontein, p. 4.

3. *Ibid.*, p. 89.

4. *A.M.E. Church, Journal of Proceedings*, 1939, p. 79.

5. B. W. Vilakazi, "The Conceptions and Development of Poetry in Zulu", *Bantu Studies*, 1938, p. 125.

6. M. F. Herskovits, *The Myth of the Negro Past*, 1941, p. 223.

7. Krige, *Social System*, p. 336.

8. Krige, *op. cit.*, p. 341.

9. R. R. Marett, *Threshold of Religion*, London, 1909, p. xxxi.

10. I have not personally been present at any festival on the Nhlangakazi mountain and doubt whether any European has been allowed to attend, other than very casually. Dube, *uShembe*, pp. 62–63, has a few notes on the subject. My material is derived from African observers.

11. W. L. Sperry, *Religion in America*, 1945, p. 190.

12. M. J. Herskovits, *The Myth of the Negro Past*, 1941, p. 208.

13. A. T. Bryant, *Zulu-English Dictionary*, p. 310.

14. Krige, *Social System*, p. 82.

15. Cf. Smith-Dale, *The Ila-Speaking Peoples*. The description of the Mu-ila who "with his fish-spears enters the pool and casts his spears in different directions as if to impale the fish" has a striking similarity with the Zionist prophet entering the pool armed with his Mosaitic *cum* episcopal staff stabbing the snake-like Satan who hides in the water.

16. Krige, *Social System of the Zulus*, pp. 348 ff.

17. Smith-Dale, *The Ila-Speaking Peoples*, I., pp. 388–89.

18. W. C. Willoughby, *Nature-Worship and Taboo*, p. 5.

19. The water-ideology of the Zionists reminds one of G. A. Jung's words (*The Integration of the Personality*, 1940, p. 68): "Psychologically, water means spirit that has become unconscious."

20. Krige, *Social System*, pp. 328–29.

21. Bryant, *Zulu-English Dictionary*, p. 239.

22. H. Webster, *Taboo, a Sociological Study*, 1942, p. 311.

23. Cf. Gluckman, "Zulu Women in Hoecultural Ritual", *Bantu Studies*, 1935, p. 263.

24. Krige, *Social System*, p. 167.

25. *Ibid.*, p. 388.

26. J. Stuart, *A History of the Zulu Rebellion*, 1906, pp. 103, 108.

27. Cf. for instance, Dube, *uShembe*, p. 75.

28. Dube, *ibid.*, p. 113.

Chapter VII

1. Dube, *uShembe*, 1936, p. 23.

2. E. L. Roberts, *Shembe*, unpublished manuscript.

3. F. Melland—C. Young, *An African Dilemma*, London, 1937, p. 127.

4. A. I. Richards, "A Modern Movement of Witch-finders", *Africa*, 1935, pp. 448–61.

5. E. J. and J. D. Krige, *The Realm of a Rain-Queen*, p. 212.

6. Dube, *uShembe*, p. 67.

7. See Callaway, *Religious System of the Amazulu*, pp. 284 ff.

8. Cf. E. L. Roberts, *Shembe*, unpublished manuscript.

9. Cf. p. 24, and Krige, *Social System*, p. 315.

10. For the concept of *scale*, see G. and M. Wilson, *The Analysis of Social Change*, 1945, p. 24 ff.

11. Audrey Richards says of the *Bamucapi* of N. Rhodesia that "the success of their charlatans was due to their clever blend of the old and the new", and she speaks of "the cleverness of a technique" used by these men. *Africa*, 1935, p. 460.

12. *The Dynamics of Culture Change*, p. 36 and pp. 94–99.

13. Evans-Pritchard, "The Morphology and Function of Magic", *American Anthropologist*, October, 1929.

14. Krige, *Social System of the Zulus*, p. 286.

15. Callaway, *Religious System of the Amazulu*, pp. 228–46.

16. Malinowski, *The Sex-Life of Savages in Northern Melanesia*, 1929, p. 387.

17. Callaway, *Religious System of the Amazulu*, p. 259.

18. Allier, *La Psychologie de la Conversion*, I, p. 373.

19. Allier, *op. cit.*, I., p. 371, 379, 381, 396.

20. Smith-Dale, *The Ila-Speaking Peoples of N. Rhodesia*, II, p. 134.

21. Geza Roheim has very carefully worked out the dreams in a primitive tribe, also the connotations of the red colour. *The Eternal Ones of the Dream: A Psychoanalytic Interpretation*, 1945, pp. 220–1.

22. Dube, *uShembe*, pp. 8–10.

23. R. Allier, *op. cit.* I, p. 373.

24. R. Firth, "The Meaning of Dreams in Tikopia", *Essays Presented to C. G. Seligman*, 1934, p. 74. Tikopia belongs to the British Solomon Islands Protectorate.

25. Brookes, *The History of Native Policy in South Africa*, 1924, p. 437.

26. A.M.E. Church, *Journal of Proceedings*, 1939, pp. 67–68.

27. G. E. Phillips, *The Old Testament in the World Church*, 1942, pp. 6 ff.

28. Dube, *op. cit.*, p. 90.

29. Williams—May, *I Am Black*, p. 205.

30. W. Sachs, *Black Hamlet*, 1937, p. 116.

31. Dube, *uShembe*, pp. 34–35.

32. Dube, *ibid.*, p. 35.

33. G. Asmus, *Die Zulu, Welt und Weltbild eines bäuerlichen Negerstammes*, Essener Verlagsanstalt, Essen, 1939, pp. 17–18. Almost the entire edition of Asmus's book was destroyed during the war. Only a few copies still exist. It would be valuable to have the book published anew, in English or Afrikaans.

34. L. Mqotsi and N. Mkele, "A Separatist Church, *I6andla lika Krestu*", *African Studies*, 1946, pp. 124–25.

35. For similar reactions among U.S. Negroes, see H. Powdermaker, "Negro Aggression and the Cultural Process", *The American Journal of Sociology*, 1943, p. 755.

36. G. K. Meek has found that the Gobir of Northern Nigeria compare their good spirit Ndseandsu to "the Mother Hen that gathers its chickens underneath its wings". He thinks that this may be New Testament influence, via the Copts. Meek, *The Northern Tribes of Nigeria*, 1925, Vol. I, p. 73. The role of the heaven-bird in Zulu religion and of lightning in Shembe's thinking seems, however, to make Shembe's hymn nativistic. One Zuionist dream stereotype is God on His Throne with a large bird at his side. This bird catches the evil-doers and throws them into a deep pool of water in which they drown.

Conclusions

1. K. S. Latourette, "The Church in the Anglo-American World, The Post-War Situation", *International Review of Missions*, 1947, p. 236.

2. "That the Congo Protestant Council set up a permanent commission to study profoundly the separatist movements that exist and to discover, if possible in time, tendencies that may indicate the formation of other such movements". *Abundant Life in Changing Africa, Report of the West Central Africa Regional Conference* (of Protestant Missions), Léopoldville, 1946, p. 181.

MESSIANIC AND ZIONIST CENTRES IN NATAL AND SWAZILAND.

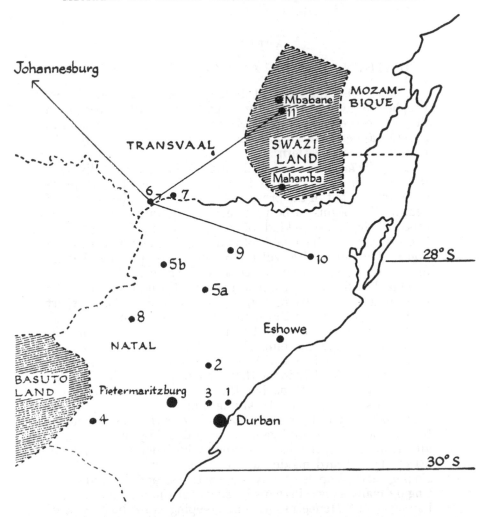

1. Ekuphakameni } Shembe's holy
2. Nhlangakazi } places
3. Camperdown: Nzuza headquarters
4. Himeville: Cekwane headquarters
5a. Telezini: Khambule's first headquarters
5b. Spookmill: Khambule's final headquarters
6. Charlestown: Nkonyane Zionist headquarters

7. Groenvlei, near Wakkerstrom: the Jordan of Nguni Zionism with strategic position related to 10 and 11 and the Rand
8. Besters: Msibi Zionist headquarters
9. Vryheid: Mdlalose Zionist headquarters
10. *Nongoma:* Zulu Paramount Chief's headquarters
11. *Lozitahlezi-Lobamba:* Swazi royal capital

349

HEATHEN DIVINER AND CHRISTIAN PROPHET

I work out the parallel between *isangoma* and Zionist prophet, following it step by step: (1) the call to become a diviner, respectively to join a Zionist church; (2) similarities in general appearance, behaviour and activities; and (3) the parallel in group pattern.

1. (*a*) *Callaway's* classical description of the Zulu diviner's (*isangoma*) initiation relates that the person is at first apparently robust, but in the process of time begins to be delicate of health.[a] He begins to be particular about food, and abstains especially from certain kinds of meat, for instance mutton. "His body is muddled, he dreams of many things, and he becomes a house of dreams." He will often tell his people that he has dreamt that he has been carried away by a river.

(*b*) At last the man (or woman) is very ill, and his people take him to a diviner (*isangoma*) to be examined. This expert probably says: "As for this man, I see nothing else but that he is possessed by an ancestral spirit." Your people (= the ancestral spirits) move in him. They are divided into two parties; some say, No, we do not wish that our child should be injured. We do not wish it! It is for that reason and no other that he does not get well. If you bar the way against the *idlozi* (= ancestral spirit), you will be killing him.

(*c*) "His body is dry and scurfy. He shows that he is about to be a diviner by yawning again and again, and by sneezing again and again. . . . In the middle of the night, when the people are asleep, he is heard making a noise, and wakes the people by singing. His sleep is merely by snatches, and he wakes up singing many songs. Perhaps he sings till the morning, no one having slept." He feels something creeping in his body. One of my informants likened this feeling to the sensation of being troubled by fowl-lice (*okuhambisa okwoбukhuphe*). He now realizes that he has been entered by an ancestral spirit and eventually this spirit is located in the shoulders.

(*d*) He goes to an old diviner and is instructed in the method of divining: He stays with a "Father" for a considerable period,

[a] Callaway, *Religious System of the Amazulu*, pp. 259 ff., and M. Kohler, *The Izangoma Diviners*, Dept. Nat. Affairs, Ethnological Publications, Vol. IX, Pretoria, 1941.

perhaps up to two years. Every morning they go together to the river to undergo purification by vomiting.

(*e*) They have also to enter the river and find the place where a snake (called *inhlwathi*) is supposed to be. If and when the "snake" is found, the diviner moves him aside and takes home some of the white earth found under the snake. He smears his face with the clay.

(*aa*) "I was ill',—that is the starting point of all Zionists when they wish to explain why they joined their new church: "I was ill—I was prayed for—and now I am well." It is characteristic that Zionists as a rule, at least when they first join a church, belong to the same somatic type as the diviner, thin, nervous, highly strung. In this state of hysteria, the person concerned is constantly dreaming night after night, and becoming just as much a "house of dreams" as any diviner. As to food he will especially avoid pork, and reason given is that it is forbidden in the Old Testament.

(*bb*) In a series of dreams he is now shown that he ought to go to certain people dressed in white robes who are accustomed to assemble near a river. During the contact with other Zionists he eventually becomes possessed by the "Holy Spirit", which is shown by the fact that an angel appears to him in his dreams, dictating his future activities.

(*cc*) Instead of sleeping during the night, he lies awake yawning or singing. He becomes more and more filled by the Spirit, a state which can especially be felt in the shoulders.

(*dd*) At dawn the novice goes with the teacher to the river. To the Zionist novice the pool in the river (*amanzi amaningi*) becomes the most common symbol in his dreams, and when staying at the prophet's kraal he has to go to the river as a rule every morning for purification rites.

(*ee*) But whereas the diviner goes to the place where the *inhlwathi*-snake hides, the Zionist knows that his "Bethesda"—pool is full of dangerous snakes and terrifying creatures, whom only the Lord of the Water can calm and bind. The white earth taken from under the *inhlwathi*-snake will make the diviner fit to have clear distinct dreams. White ashes mixed with water fulfil the same function for the Zionist.

2. A heathen diviner has to wear long hair (*umyeko*). Most of the Zionists forbid their people to cut their hair, but of course, in their case the authority is the commandment in Judges 13: 5, or 1 Sam. 1: 11. Whereas the diviner is clad in her white goat-skin strips, the Zionist is particular about

his white uniform with green or sacking sashes which he has to wear.

3. As to behaviour and activities after initiation, some general characteristics will be mentioned here. (*a*) Not only throughout the initiation period (*ukwethwasa*), but continually, as long as he or she is a diviner, the person concerned will dream during the night about water, rivers, the ancestral spirit (in the form of a snake). This is, of course, characteristic also of the Zionist, except that instead of an ancestral spirit, an angel appears. (*b*) When awakening before dawn the diviner yawns and cries and makes a variety of noises. Anyone who has lived for some time at a Zionist prophet's kraal will hear him yawn and snort very loudly at dawn, noises which are supposed to be the sign of inspiration by the Holy Spirit. Persons living in the neighbourhood of a diviner or a prophet will be made aware of his awakening by these evidences. (*c*) Visiting a stream in the morning and undergoing early vomiting ceremonies have already been mentioned as typical of the initiation period for both groups; as a matter of fact such ceremonies will continue for as long as diviner and prophet are active as such. (*d*) The chief activity of the *isangoma* is divining (*ukubula*). A special study has been made here of the parallelism between *isangoma*-divining and Zionist prophesying, p. 256. (*e*) As to food taboos, the *isangoma* must not eat mutton (which would make the spirit dumb).

The Zionist on the other hand, may eat mutton, but not pork. As the reason for this taboo one is referred to Lev. 11: 7 and Mark 5.

4. As far as is known to me the *group organization* of the diviners has not yet been studied in detail. On the basis of some observations I made in Zululand I might, however, venture to point out some of its typical features.[a]

(*a*) The diviners band together in fairly distinct groups. The younger diviners and the novices owe allegiance to the one who has initiated them, called "the Father" (*uBaba*), whether man or woman.[b]

(*b*) Not only do the novices stay with the "father" for a

[a] See Junod's remarks on "the society of the exorcized" among the Thonga (*A South African Tribe*, II, pp. 500–03).

[b] A psycho-analytical study of Zionist group life—which has not been attempted here but which would be valuable and revealing—would benefit very much from Jung's distinction between *anima* (the woman in a man) and *animus* (the man in a woman). Cf. his *The Integration of Personality*, 1940, p. 19.

considerable time during the initiation period, but also on other occasions, times of crisis, do heathen diviners meet together as a group.

(c) When a diviner marries, the "Father", together with all those who have been initiated, will attend. On one occasion at Ceza, sixteen diviners, being spiritual sons and daughters of the same "Father", came together to a wedding of a colleague, and they performed special dances after the general wedding dances.

(d) Likewise, at the burial of a diviner, her (or his) colleagues will congregate and perform special rites and dances.

(e) Each diviner group has its particular songs, especially in honour of the spirit of the "father"-*isangoma*, and such songs differentiate this group from the others.

(f) Most of the heathen diviners are women.

(g) Driven by the *idlozi* (ancestral spirit), these people will wander about, one day here, another day there, in constant vagrancy.

(a) To me it has become evident that the congregations of Zionist type are moulded on this *isangoma* group pattern rather than on the congregational pattern of the historical Christian churches. The bond between leader and followers does indeed point in this direction.

(b) The "Bethesda" type of congregation, where the faithful live for months and years at the prophet's place, being prayed for, going through purification rites and in all sorts of ways being in intimate contact with the Leader, is developed on the *isangoma-amathwasa* pattern.

(c-e) The coming together of the faithful for weddings and funerals, is, of course, characteristic not only of the Zionists, but of all Christian churches among the Zulus. The Zionists, however, congregate on a group pattern, which is distinct from that of the other churches.

(f) As pointed out in Chapter V, some 80 per cent. of the members in churches of Zionist type are women. In many cases these women have earlier been diviners or have had some other hysteric disorder (such as *amandawe*-possession). v. Warmelo relates that in a group of 400 *malcpc*-possessed, only four were men, the rest women.

(g) The nervous hysterical people to be found among the Zionists, as among the diviners, are vagrants. They claim that the Holy Spirit always is moving them to change abode. The prophet and his female attendants rove about from Zululand to Johannesburg.

LIST OF NATIVE SEPARATIST CHURCHES AS ON AUGUST 1, 1945[a]

The A1 Zion Elected Church.

Abantu Independent Methodist Christian Church of South Africa.

Abyssinian Baptist Church.

Abyssinian Methodist Holy Church of Christ.

The Acts of Apostolic in Jerusalem Church.

Afrikaanse Matieve Evangelic Kerk.

African Apostolic Catholic Church in Zion.

African Apostle Church.

The African Apostolic Church.

African Apostolic Church in Sabbath.

African Apostolic Church of Christ in Zion.

African Apostolic Church in Sabbath South Africa.

African Apostolic Church in Zion.

African Apostolic Church of South Africa.

African Apostolic Church Union of South Africa.

African Bakgatla National Church.

African Baptized Apostle Church.

African Baptist Church.

African Baptist Church of Christ.

African Baptist Mission Church.

African Baptist Church in Zion.

African Baptist Sinoia Church.

African Baptist Sinoai Apostolic Church Beira.

The African Baptist Zion Church.

African Bavenda Church.

African Bechuana Church.

African Bethal Mission.

African Board Apostolic Church in South Africa.

African Brethren Apostolic Bantu Church.

African Casteroil Dead Church.

African Cathedral Episcopal Church.

African Catholic Apostolic Church in Zion.

African Catholic Bantu Church.

African Catholic Episcopal Church.

[a] In certain cases, the same name—for instance, "Holy African Apostolic Church in Zion"—is used by two or more organizations. I have, however, not reiterated these names. On May 30, 1947, a list with 123 new names of churches was sent to me by the Secretary for Native Affairs. These churches are *not* included in the list published here.

African Catholik Church of Gaza.
African Catholic Church of Christ.
African Catholic Church of God.
African Catholic Church of South Africa.
African Catholic Mission.
The African Christ Holy Apostolic Prophets Church of God.
African Christian Apostolic Church (two churches).
African Christian Apostolic Church in Zion.
African Christian Baptist Church of South Africa.
African Christian Catholic Baptist.
African Christian Christ Church.
African Christian Church.
African Christian Missionary Church.
African Christian Union Church of South Africa.
African Church.
African Congregational Ethiopian Church.
African Congregational Church.
African Congregational Church of the Colony of Mocambique.
African Congregational Church (Gardiner Mvuyana).
African Congregational Methodist Church.
African Congress Catholic Church.
African Convent Catholic Church of Christ.
African Correctly Apostolic Jerusalem Church in Zion.
African Emmanuel Church.
African Empumulanga Mission.
African Ethiopian Apostolic Church of South Africa.
African Ethiopian Apostolic Kamazi Church of South Africa.
The African Ethiopian Bantu Church of South Africa.
African Ethiopian Church.
African Ethiopian National Church.
African Evangelistic Band.
African Faith Mission.
African Free Bapedi Church.
African Free Catholic Church.
African Free Congregation Church.
African Free Ethiopian Church.
African Free Presbyterian Church of South Africa.
African Heaven Baptist Church of South Africa.
African Holy Apostle Church in Zion.
African Holy Baptist Church of South Africa.
African Holy Baptist Church in the Zion of South Africa.
African Holy Catholic Church.
African Holy Independent Church.

355

African Holy Messenger Church in Zion.
African Independent Apostle Church.
African Independent Baptist Church.
African Independent Ethiopian Church.
African Independent Mission Church.
African Lutheran Church.
African Methodist Church of South Africa.
African Methodist Episcopal Church.
African Mission Catholic Church.
African Mission Church.
African Mission Home Church.
African Mission Society.
The African Mission Zion Apostolic Christian Church.
African National Baptist Church Association.
African National Church (Bethal Baptist).
African National Church.
African National Ebenezer Church.
The African National Tembu Church.
African Native Apostolic Church.
African Native Catholic Church.
African Native Church.
African Native Free Church.
African Native Methodist Church.
African Native Mission Church.
African Native Ndebele Church No. 1.
African Natural Presbyterian Church.
African Orthodox Apostolic Church.
African Orthodox Church.
African Pentecostal Baptist Church.
African Pentecost Church of Christ in Zion.
African Pentecostal Church of Christ in Zion.
African Pentecostal Church.
African Pentecostal Faith Mission.
African Pentecostal Mission.
African Presbyterian Bafolisi Church.
African Presbyterian Natural Church.
African Province Ethiopian Catholic Church.
African Province Church.
African Reform Church.
African Sabbath Mission Church.
African Seventh Church of God.
African Seventh Church of God Laodicean Mission.
African Seventh-Day Adventists.

African Seventh Day Zulu Shaka Church of Christ.
The African Sixth Church of God Philadelphia.
African Two Church of Christ in Smirna.
African Zulu Congregational Church.
African United Brethren Church of St. Moravian.
African United Church.
The African United Church of Christ.
African United Church of Christ in Zion South Africa.
African United Ethiopian Church.
African United Gaza Church.
African United Evangelists Church.
African United Zulu Congregational Church.
African Zion Baptist Jerusalem Apostolic Church.
African Zion Baptist Church.
The African Zion Native Ministers Association.
African Zulu Methodist Church.
African Zulu St. John Baptising Church.
Afro-Athlican Constructive Gaathly.
Algemene Volks Kerk.
Alliance Nazareth Baptist Church of Christ.
Allmount Mount of Olives Baptist Church.
Almighty God Church.
Ama-Kushe.
Ama Yoyopiya.
Ama-Ziyone.
American Ethiopian Church.
Anglo-African Church.
Apostles Brethren Church.
Apostles and Christian Brethren Church.
Apostles Church of the Full Bible of South Africa.
Apostles Church.
Apostle Church in Zion.
Apostle Mission Church.
Apostles and Symbol Brethren Church of South Africa.
Apostle Zion City in Jerusalem.
Apostle Zion Church.
Apostolic Acts Church of Africa.
Apostolic Assembly Faith Church of South Africa.
Apostolic Association of South Africa.
Apostolic Baptist Church in Zion.
Apostolic Belliel Ugarete Church in Zion.
Apostolic Bethal Ndebele United Church of South Africa.
Apostolic Beth Peori Church in Zion of South Africa.

Apostolic Bethlehem Church in Zion, Krugersdorp.
Apostolic Brethren Church in Zion.
Apostolic Christian Church in Zion of South Africa.
Apostolic Christian National Zion Church of South Africa.
St. Apostolic Church of Christ in Zion.
Apostolic Church City in Zion.
Apostolic Church of Christ in Zion.
Apostolic Church of Great Britain & Northern Ireland.
Apostolic Church of Jesus Christ.
Apostolic Church Messenger in Zion.
Apostolic Churches Ministers Association in Africa.
Apostolic Church of South Africa.
Apostolic Church in Zion of the New Jerusalem Mission in
    Basutoland.
Apostolic Church in Zion.
Apostolic Church in Zion Amen.
Apostolic Church of Zion in South Africa.
Apostolic Church in Zion in South Africa.
Apostolic Church of Witness in Jerusalem.
Apostolic City in Zion Church of South Africa.
Apostolic Congregational Jerusalem Church of South Africa.
Apostolic Ephesian Foundation Church.
Apostolic Faith Assembly.
Apostolic Faith Church Association in Zion of South Africa.
Apostolic Faith Nazareth of South Africa.
Apostolic Faith Church.
Apostolic First Assembly of Holy Spirit Catholic Church in
    Zion.
Apostolic First Assembly of South Africa.
Apostolic First Christian Church of South Africa.
Apostolic Fountain Catholic Church.
Apostolic Full Gospel Mission of South Africa.
Apostolic Galelea Church of Christ in Zion, South Africa.
Apostle Gaunar Church Zion.
Apostolic Great African Church.
Apostolic Heaven Church in Zion.
Apostolic Holy Church in Zion.
Apostolic Holy Messenger Church in Zion.
Apostolic Holy Spirit Church in Zion of South Africa.
Apostolic Holy Zion Mission in South Africa.
Apostolic Jerusalem Christ Church of South Africa.
Apostolic Jerusalem Church in Sabbath.
Apostolic Jerusalem Church in Zion.

Apostolic in Jerusalem Church in Zion of South Africa.
Apostolic Jerusalem United Christ Church in Zion of South
    Africa.
Apostolic Messenger Light World Church in Zion.
Apostolic Mission Church.
Apostoliç Native Baptist Church.
Apostolic Prophetic Church of South Africa.
Apostolic Society New Jerusalem Church.
Apostolic Temba Church.
Apostolic Tzaneen Church in Zion.
Apostolic South African Zulu Church.
Apostolic United African Church of South Africa.
Apostolic United Faith Coloured Church.
Apostolic United Faith Native Church of South Africa.
Apostolic Zion Church.
Apostolic Zion New Jerusalem Church.
Assemblies of God Church.
Assembly of God in Mozambique and South Africa.
Bakwena Lutheran Church.
Banner of Faith Mission.
Bantu African Church.
Bantu Apostolic Church of Africa.
Bantu Baptist Church.
The Bantu Baptist Nazareth Church of Christ.
Bantu Bible Holy Cross Church of South Africa.
Bantu Cathedral Episcopal Church of Kushe.
Bantu Christian Catholic Church.
Bantu Christian Church.
Bantu Church Apostolic Church of South Africa.
Bantu Church of Christ.
The Bantu Church of South Africa.
The Bantu Congregational Church of South Africa.
Bantu Constitutional Luther Church of Africa.
Bantu Customers Church to Almighty God.
Bantu Dependent Church.
Bantu Dutch Reformed Church.
Bantu Free Methodist Church.
Bantu Holy Cross Church of South Africa.
Bantu Methodist Episcopal Church of South Africa.
Bantu Methodist Church.
Bantu National Church of Christ (Lamula's).
Bantu Ngqika-Ntsikana Church.

Bantu Reform Church.
Bantu Reformed Apostolic Church.
Bantu Reformed Methodist Church under the Bantu Nation, South Africa.
Baptist Apostolic Church of South Africa.
Baptist Church of Christ.
Baptist Church of the Seventh-Day Adventists of Africa.
Baptist Gospel Apostolic Church of South Africa.
Baptist of the Seventh-Day Adventists.
Basuto Native Baptize Church of Christ.
Basuto Redemption Episcopal.
Batho Reformed Church of South Africa.
Bauenda in Zion Apostolic Church.
Bechuana Methodist Church.
Bechuana Methodist Church in Zion.
Berean Bible Readers Society.
Bethal Apostolic Baptist Church.
Bethal Church.
Bethal Methodist Ethiopian Church.
Bethel Native Church.
The Bethlehemo Apostles in Zion of South Africa Church.
Bethlehem Christian Church of Central Africa.
Bethlehem Church of God in Zion.
Bethlehem Damascus Apostolic Church in South Africa.
Bethlehem Holy Apostolic Church in Zion.
The Bethlehem Holy Spirit Apostolic Church in Zion of South Africa.
Bethlehem of Judia Church in South Africa.
The Bethlehem of Judea Church Apostolic Church in Zion, South Africa.
Bethesda Zion Apostolic Church of Africa.
Bible Standard Church of America.
Brethren Holy Apostolic Prophet Christ Church of God of South Africa.
Brethren Mission Church.
Catholic African Union.
Catholic Apostolic Church of Zion.
Catholic Apostolic Church of Witness in Zion of South Africa.
The Catholic Church of South Africa King George Win the War.
Catholic Evangelist Kingdom of God Apostolic Church in Zion.
C.C.A. St. Sugustibe Church of South Africa.
Central African Church.
Christ Apostolic Holy Spout Church in Zion of South Africa.

Christ Apostolic Zion Church of South Africa.
Christ Assemblies of South Africa.
Christ Baptist Church of Africa.
Christ Divine Mission.
Christian African Catholic Church.
Christian African Catholic Church in Zion.
Christian Apostolic Faith Assembly Church in Zion of South
    Africa.
Christian Apostolic Faith Church in Zion.
Christian Apostolic Church.
Christian Apostolic Church of South Africa.
Christian Apostolic Church in Zion.
Christian Apostolic Church in Zion, America.
Christian Apostolic Heaven Church in Zion.
The Christian Apostolic Holy Spirit Church in Zion of South
    Africa.
Christian Apostolic Indhlu ka Jacob Church in Zion South
    Africa.
Christian Apostolic Jerusalem Church in Zion.
Christian Apostolic Nationality Church in Zion.
The Christian Apostolic Stone Church in Zion of South Africa.
The Christian Apostolic Topian Church.
Christian Apostolic Zulu Church of Zion.
Christian Bavenda Church of South Africa.
Christian Bethlehem Church.
Christian Brethren.
Christian Brethren Baptism Church of South Africa.
The Christian Catholic Apostolic African Church in Zion of
    South Africa.
Christian Catholic Apostolic of God Church in Zion of South
    Africa.
Christian Catholic Apostolic in Zion.
Christian Catholic Apostolic Church in Zion.
Christian Catholic Apostolic Church in Zion of South Africa.
Christian Catholic Apostolic Holy Spirit Church in Zion.
Christian Catholic Apostolic Nazareth Church in Zion of South
    Africa.
Christian Catholic Church in Zion.
Christian Catholic Church in Zion of South Africa.
Christian Catholic National Church in Zion.
Christian Church.
Christian Church Mission of South Africa.
Christian Church Saturday.

Christian Church of South Africa.
Christian Congregational Baptist Mission.
Christian Evangelical Mission Church.
Christian Galilee Apostolic Church in Zion.
Christian Holiness Church.
Christian Holy Apostles Catholic Antioch Church in Zion of
    South Africa.
The Christian National Apostolic Church in Zion of South
    Africa.
Christian Native Church of South Africa.
Christian Native Union Church of South Africa.
Christian Nissi Native African Church.
The Christian Pentecostal Church of Christ.
Christian Zion Apostolic Church.
Christian United Church.
Church of African Mission Homes.
Church of the Apostolic Jerusalem Christ Church of South
    Africa.
Church of Christ.
Church of Christ, South Africa.
Church of Christ for the Union of the Bantu.
Church of Christian Catholic Apostolic.
Church of the Christian Evangelist.
The Church Council of the Peace on Earth Mission of South
    Africa.
Church of Cush.
Church Emmanuel Full Gospel of Zion.
Church Ethiopian of Africa.
Church of God.
Church of God Apostolic Jerusalem in Zion.
Church of God Apostolic Zion in Jerusalem.
Church of God in Christ.
Church of God and Saints of Christ.
Church of God in South Africa.
Church of the Holy Ghost.
Church of the Holy Kingdom of Christ the Saviour.
Church of Israel.
Church of Jehova under the Apostle Law.
Church of Native Independent Gatcon Congregationalists.
Church of the Nazarenes.
The Church of Pleasant Living Congregation in Zion South
    Africa.
Church of the Prophets.

Church of Zion Mission.
The City of Jerusalem Zion Church.
Congregation Evangelist Apostolic Church of South Africa.
Congregational Apostolic Evangelica Church.
Congregational Catholic Apostolic Church in Zion of South Africa.
Congregational Church of Christ.
Congregational Church in Zion.
Congregational Gaza Church.
Congregational Union African Church.
The Corner Stone of the Apostle Church in Zion.
Corner Stone of Apostolic Bethlehem in Zion.
Corner Stone of Zion.
The Chronicles Church.
Cross of Jesus Church.
Demasek Apostolic Church in South Africa.
East African Church of Nyasaland in the Union.
East African Gaza Church.
East Heathlon Church.
East Pentecostal Mission Church.
East Star Baptist Church of Portuguese East Africa.
Eastern Star Nazareth Baptist Church of God.
Eden Lamb Mission of South Africa.
Emmanual Mission.
Empumalanga Gospel Church.
Ephesian's Mission Church.
Epifania African Church.
Epifania Star Mission.
Episcopal Egraja Auzo Africana Church.
Estas Catholic Apostolic Church in Zion.
Ethiopian African Church of Zion in South Africa.
Ethiopian Apostolic Church of South Africa.
Ethiopian Apostolic Orthodox Church in Christ.
Ethiopian Baptist Church of South Africa.
Ethiopian Catholic Church.
Ethiopian Catholic Church in Christ.
Ethiopian Catholic Mathew's Church.
Ethiopian Catholic Church in Africa.
Ethiopian Catholic Church of South Africa.
Ethiopian Catholic Church in Zion.
Ethiopian Catholic United Taperonakeel Church.
Ethiopian Christ Church of South Africa.
Ethiopian Church.

Ethiopian Church of Abbyssinia.
Ethiopian Church of Africa (Ethiopian Church African).
Ethiopian Church of Basutoland.
Ethiopian Church of Christ in Africa.
Ethiopian Church of Christ by Religion.
Ethiopian Church of Christ in South Africa.
Ethiopian Church of God the Society of Paradise.
Ethiopia Church Lamentation of South Africa.
Ethiopian Church of St. James.
Ethiopian Church in Zion.
The Ethiopian Congregation Apostolic Church in Zion.
Ethiopian Holy Baptist Church in Zion.
Ethiopian Holy Orthodox Church of South Africa.
Ethiopian Independent Church of Africa.
Ethiopian Messanger Catholic Church in South Africa.
Ethiopian Methodist Church of Africa.
Ethiopian Methodist Christian Church of South Africa.
Ethiopian Methodist United Church.
Ethiopian Mission of South Africa.
Ethiopian National Church.
Ethiopian National Theocrasy Restitution of South Africa.
Ethiopian Ngcayupa Memoria Church.
Ethiopian Orthodox Catholic Church.
Ethiopian Reformed Salatuel Church in Zion.
Ethiopian Springfield Catholic Church.
The Ethiopian Star Church of God.
Evangelic Apostolic Church in Christ.
Evangelic Apostolic Church in Zion.
Evangelic Mission Church of South Africa.
Evangelist Catholic Church.
Ezekiel Apostoli Church in Zion.
Filadelfia Church of Africa.
The Fire Baptized Holiness Church of God.
First African Church of Christ.
First Apostolic Church of God.
The First Apostolic Church of Christ in Zion of South Africa.
First Apostolic Jerusalem Church in Zion of South Africa.
First Apostolic Zion Gaza Church of South Africa.
First Catholic Apostolic Church Jerusalem in Zion of South
    Africa.
The First Century Gospel Church.
First Church of God, Asia in Efese Church in South Africa.
First Jerusalem Holy Apostolic of Bethlehem Church in Zion.

First Kappadocian Apostles of Jerusalem in Zion.
The First Mission Apostolic Baptist Church.
First Native Church of Christ.
First New Church of Christ.
First Public Apostolic Church in Zion.
Followers of Christ.
The Foundation Apostolic Church of South Africa.
The Free Congregational Church of South Africa.
Free Independent Bechuana Church of South Africa.
Free Methodist Episcopal Church.
Free Sabbatarian Mission of the Seventh-Day Observers Church
    of United States of America in Southern Africa.
The Free United Church of Christ in South Africa.
Full Branch of Ethiopian Church Basutoland.
Full Branch of Union Brethren Mission Church.
Full Gospel Christian Mission.
Full Gospel Church.
Full Witness of Jehova Bible Students Apostolic Society
    Church of Africa.
Gaza Church.
Gaza Mission Church.
Gaza Zimbabque Ethiopian Church.
The General Apostolic Church in Zion.
The General Church of New Jerusalem Apostolic.
General Church of the New Jerusalem Mission of South Africa.
General Convention Church of New Jerusalem.
General Faith Assembly Church in Zion.
General Faith Assembly Zion Church of the Innumerable
Company.
Genesis Apostolic Church in Zion.
Glory Bantu Church.
Gospel Catholic Church of South Africa.
Gospel Messenger Church.
Great George 5 National Church.
Griqua Independent Church.
Head Church of Gods Students Bible in Christ of Natives.
Head Mountain of God Apostolic Church in Zion.
Heaven Apostolic Jerusalem Church in Zion.
Heaven Twelfth Apostle Church in Zion.
Hephzibah Faith Mission Association.
Hill of Zion Apostolic Church.
His Zion City Apostolic Church of South Africa.
Holy African Apostolic Church in Zion.

Holy Apostolic Church.
Holy Apostolic Church of South Africa.
Holy Apostolic Church in Zion.
Holy Apostolic Bethlehem Church in Zion.
Holy Apostolic Jerusalem Church in Zion.
Holy Apostolic Mission Church in Zion of South Africa.
Holy Baptist Church of Africa.
Holy Baptist Church in Zion.
Holy Catholic Apostolic Church in Zion.
The Holy Catholic Apostolic Church in Zion of South Africa.
Holy Catholic Church in Zion.
Holy Catholic Episcopal Church.
The Holy Christ Church of Witness.
Holy Christian Apostolic Church in Zion.
Holy Christian Church of God in Sabbath South Africa.
Holy Christian Church in Zion.
Holy Church of Christ of South Africa.
Holy Communion Jerusalem Church of South Africa.
Holy Cross Apostolic Church Zion of South Africa.
Holy Cross Catholic Apostolic Church in Zion.
Holy Independent Batua National Church of South Africa.
Holy Independent Catholic Church of South Africa.
Holy Independent Church of South Africa.
The Holy Jerusalem Christ Twelfth Apostolic Church in Zion
    of South Africa.
The Holy Lamb Mission Church.
Holy Messenger Apostolic Church of God.
Holy Mission and Kingdom of Christ Evangelist Church.
Holy Missionary Bethesda Church.
Holy Missionary Evangelist Church.
Holy National Church of South Africa.
Holy National Church of Ethopia in South Africa.
Holy Native Apostolic Church of Africa.
Holy Sabbath Church.
Holy Sabbath of God's Church.
Holy Spirit Jerusalem Church in Zion.
Holy Trinity Church of God.
The Holy Union Apostolic Church in Zion of South Africa.
Holy Zion Apostolic Zululand Church in South Africa.
Home Natives Co-operative Society.
Immanuel Missionary Church of United States America.
Independent African Church.
Independent Bantu Methodist Church.

Independent Church of South Africa.
Independent Church of Zion.
Independent Congregational Church (Coloured).
Independent or Congregational Church.
Independent Ethiopian Congress Mission.
Independent Methodist Church of South Africa.
Independent Native Presbyterian Church.
Independent Presbyterian Church.
Independent Presbyterian Church of South Africa.
Independent and United National Church.
Inter-Communion Church of South Africa.
International Baptist Church of God.
International Foursquare Gospel.
International Holiness Church.
International Missionary Alliance.
International Missionary Society of Seventh-Day Adventist
  Reform Movement.
Jacob Mission Church (Apostolic) of South Africa.
St. James Church of Ethiopia.
Jerusalem Apostolic Kuphiliswa Church in Zion.
Jerusalem Apostolic Church in Africa.
Jerusalem Apostolic of the Lamb Church.
Jerusalem Christ West Zulu Church Holy South African
  Apostolic.
Jerusalem Christian Church in Zion of South Africa.
The Jerusalem Christian Twelve Apostolic Church in Zion
  South Africa.
Jerusalem Meeting Apostolic of Jesus Christ Son of God.
Jesus Christ Church in Zion.
St. John's Faith Mission.
St. John's Fifth Mission.
King of Salom Melchezedeck Church.
Klopiso Apostolic Faith Church.
Kopano Thatano Native Church.
Kush Apostolic Church.
Kushe Lamentation Church in Apostles.
Kush Nineveh Church.
Kushe Zulu Church.
Kereke ea Kopano ea Africa Church.
The Later Light Church in Zion.
League of African Bantu Churches of South Africa.
League of African Bantu Churches of South Africa.
Lott Carey Baptist Mission of South Africa.

Luso African Congregational Church.
Lutheran African Mission Church.
Lutheran Bapedi Church.
Lutheran Bapedi Church of South Africa.
Luz Episcopal Church (of Mozambique Colony).
Mabboko Jerusalem Christ Church in Zion.
Magana National Church Association.
Matthews Apostolic Church in Zion in South Africa.
Mayen Church.
Medium Catholic Apostolic Church in Zion of Africa.
Melchizedek Ethiopian Catholic Church.
Messenger Apostolic Church in Zion.
Messenger Apostolic New Jerusalem in Zion.
The Messenger of the Covenant Church of Jerusalem.
Messenger Holy Apostolic Church in Zion.
Methodist African Church.
Methodist Church African Mission.
Methodist Episcopal Church.
Metropolitan Church Association.
Mission Church of Israel.
The Mission of Jehovah's Last Message to All Nations.
Modern Mission.
Moriana Episcola Apostolic Church in Zion.
The Moriana Church of Homeland in Zion.
Moshesh Bereau Bible Readers Church.
Mount Zion A.M.E. Church.
Namagna Methodist Church of South Africa.
Die Namakwa Independente Kerk van Zuid-Afrika.
National African Church of Salom.
National Baptist Church of South Africa.
The National Church.
National Church of Africa.
National Church of Africa's Union.
National Church of God of South Africa.
National Church of God Apostolic in Jerusalem Church.
National Church of Ethiopia in South Africa.
National Convention Church of the New Jerusalem.
National Coptic Church of Africa.
National Native Apostolic Church.
National Protestant Church in Zion.
National Swazi Native Apostolic Church of Africa.
The Nations Apostolic Nazareth Church in Zion.
The Nations Church of Christ in Africa.

Native African Christian Church.
Native Apostolic Nazareth Church.
The Native Branch Apostolic Church Zion of South Africa.
Native Catholic Episcopalian Church.
Native Christian Baptist Church of South Africa.
The Native Church of Christ.
Native Congregational Church.
Native Congregational Church of South Africa.
Native Congress Catholic Church.
Native Denomination Church of South Africa.
Native Methodist Church of South Africa.
Native Mission Church.
Native Modern Religious Society of East Africa.
Native Nation Independent Congregation.
Native Nation Union Church.
Native Nineveh Church.
Native United Ethiopian Church.
The Native Zulu Apostolic Church.
Nazaretha (or Shembeites).
Nazareth Apostolic Church in Zion.
Nazareth Baptist Church of South Africa in Sabbath.
Nazareth Church.
Nazareth Ekukanyane Bantu Church of South Africa.
Nazareth Mission Apostolic Church of South Africa.
The New African Native Presbyterian Church.
New African Christian Apostolic Church in Zion.
New African Ethiopian Church.
New African Independent Ethiopian Church.
New African Jerusalem Church in Zion.
New African Pentecostal Baptist Church of South Africa.
New African Zion Apostolic Church.
New Apostolic African Church.
New Apostolic Church.
New Apostolic Christian Mission Church in Zion.
New Bantu Apostolic Church of Africa.
New Bantu Methodist Christian Church.
New Baptist Church in Christ.
New Baptist Mission Church.
New Bethlehem Church in Zion of Apostolic Faith in South
    Africa.
New Catholic Church.
The New-Christian Apostolic Church Heaven in Zion Home.
The New Christian Catholic Apostolic Church in Zion.

The New Christian Dependent Apostolic Church in Zion.
New Church.
New Church Baptist Mission.
New Church of Christ.
New Congregational Church of Christians of Africa.
New Creation Baptist Church Star of South Africa.
New Ethiopian Catholic Church of Africa.
The New Faith Gospel Apostolic Church of Jesus Christ.
New Full Gospel Apostolic Church.
The New Full Gospel Apostle Church of Christ.
New Galelic Holy Apostolic Church in Zion.
New Holy Gospel Christian Church of Africa.
New Independent Ethiopian Church.
New Jerusalem Apostolic Church in Zion.
New Jerusalem Church (or New Church of Christ).
The New Jerusalem Church in Christ.
The New Jerusalem Eleventh Apostolic Church in Zion of
    South Africa.
New Jerusalem Holy Trinity Church.
The New Jerusalem Sabbath Apostolic Church in Zion South
    Africa.
New Jerusalem Zion.
New National Church of Ethiopia.
New Native Church of Christ South Africa.
New Pentecost Church in Zion of South Africa.
New Progressive Baptist Church.
New Progressive Christian Church.
New Zion Temple Church.
Nomination Congregation Church of South Africa.
Nova Hierosolyma.
Ntsikena Memorial Church.
Nyassaland Church of South Africa.
The Old Apostolic Church of Africa.
Old Emmanuel Apostolic Church of God in Zion.
Only Church of Christ.
Order of Ethiopia.
The Pamphilia Tabernacle.
St. Paul's Apostolic Faith Mission.
Pentecost Christ Church.
Pentecost Christian Church of Zion of South Africa.
Pentecost East Star Jerusalem Church in Sabbath.
Pentecost Holiness Bafolisi Church.
The Pentecostal Baptist Apostolic Church of South Africa.

Pentecostal Baptist Church.
Pentecostal Christian Church.
Pentecostal Christian Fellowship.
Pentecostal Church of Christ of South Africa.
Pentecostal Holiness Church.
Pentecostal Sabbath Mission.
St. Peter's Apostolic Church.
St. Peter's Covenant Church of Christ.
St. Phillip's Ethiopian Church of South Africa.
Pilgrim Holiness Church.
The Poor Christ Church.
Presbyterian Apostolic Church of South Africa.
Presbyterian Christian Apostolic Church of Christ in Zion.
Presbyterian Church of Africa.
Presbyterian National Church of South Africa.
Priest African Ethiopian Church.
Protestant Episcopal Church.
Refartion (Reformation) Mission Baptist Church.
Regular Baptist Christian Church of South Africa.
Regular Church of Christ of South Africa.
Remnant Church of God.
Return Church of Africa.
Revelation Baptist Mission Church.
The Rhodesia Mission.
Sabbath Church Zion Message of God to African and to Zulu
    Man.
The Sabbath Church in Zion of South Africa.
The Sabbath Christian Apostolic Church in Zion.
Saratile Church of South Africa (Mission of God).
Sardis Five Church of God in South Africa.
Seventh Church of God.
Seventh Church Sabbath.
Seventh-Day Baptist Church.
Seventh-Day Baptist Church of Christ.
Seventh-Day Baptist Church of London.
Shaka Zulu Church.
Shebanbiah Church.
South African Apostolic Native Church in Zion.
South African Baptist Church Mission.
South African Baptist Missionary Society.
South African Barolong Church.
South African Baroling Methodist Church.
South African Ethiopian Catholic Church.

South African Evangelical Mission Church.
South African Gaza Mission.
South African Native Baptist Association.
South African Native Faith Healing Church.
South African Native Mission.
South African National Apostolic Church.
South African National Ethiopian Church.
South Africa National Ethiopian Church of Africa.
South African Seventh Church of God.
South Africa Zulu Church.
South African Zulu Native Baptist Church.
Star Baptist Church.
The Star Nazareta Church in Zion of Sabbath.
Sun Light Four Corners Apostolic for Witness of God Church.
Sun Light Four Corners Apostolic for Witnesses of God Jehova.
The Supreme Apostolic Church of South Africa.
Tembu Catholic Church of South Africa.
The Temple of God in Africa.
Temple of God of Africa.
The True (Truth) Zion Church of God.
Twelve Apostolic the New Jerusalem Zion Church of God.
Twelfth Apostolic Church in Zion.
Uhlanga or Church of the Race.
Ukuhlupeka Kuka Krestu Zinyana Apostol Zion.
Ukukanye Mission.
Union Apostolic Church of South Africa.
Union Brethren Mission Church.
United African Apostolic Church.
United African Missionary Society.
United Apostolic Church.
United Apostolic Church of South Africa.
United Apostolic Faith Church.
United Bantu Lutheran Church.
The United Bantu Presbyterian Church of South Africa.
United Catholic Church of Christ.
United Church of the Brethren in Zion.
United Church of Ethiopian in South Africa.
United Ethiopian Catholic Church of Africa.
United Ethiopian Church.
United Free Independent Church.
United Central African Church.
United Christian of Abyssinia of South Africa Church.
United Christian Church.

United Churches of Christ.
The United Church in Ethiopia in Zion.
United Independent National Church of God.
United National Catholic Church in Zion.
United National Church (Lutheran).
United National Church in Africa.
United National Congress Church.
United Native Baptist Church.
United Sabbath Christian Apostolic Church in Zion.
Universal African Church.
Universal Church of Christ.
Universal Mission Church.
Universal National Christian Union.
Unto The Church of God Apostolic Jerusalem in Zion
Volks Kerk van Zuid-Afrika.
Vula Singene Yehova e-Zion.
Watch Tower Movement.
The Witness of Apostolic Church in Christ.
Zinyana Apostolic Zion.
Zion Apostle Jerusalem of God in South Africa.
Zion Apostolic Assembly Church.
Zion Apostolic Baena Church.
Zion Apostolic Brethren Church of South Africa.
Zion Apostolic Christ Church.
Zion Apostolic Church of Christ.
Zion Apostolic Church in Galali.
Zion Apostolic Church of God of South Africa.
Zion Apostolic Church in Jerusalem.
Zion Apostolic Church of South Africa.
Zion Apostolic City Church.
Zion Apostolic City of South Africa.
Zion Apostolic Faith Mission.
Zion Apostolic Gaza Church of South Africa.
Zion Apostolic Jerusalem Church.
Zion Apostolic Jerusalem Church of God in South Africa.
Zion Apostolic New Jerusalem Government Church.
Zion Apostolic New Jerusalem in South Africa Church.
Zion Apostolic Old Mission Church of South Africa.
Zion Apostolic South African Church.
Zion Apostolic Swaziland Church of South Africa.
Zion Apostolic Union Church.
Zion Apostolic Weseyterian Catholic Church of South Africa.
Zion Baptist Zinai Church in South Africa.

Zion Bethal Apostolic Church.
Zion Brethren Mission Apostolic Church in South Africa.
Zion of Christ Africa Apostolic Church.
Zion Christian Church.
Zion Church of Christ Apostle of South Africa.
The Zion Church of Christ in South Africa.
Zion Church of South Africa.
The Zion City Apostolic Church of South Africa.
Zion City Apostolic Paulus Church in South Africa.
Zion City Christian Church.
Zion Congregational Church of South Africa.
Zion Elected Church of South Africa.
Zion Free Church Impumalanga Gospel of South Africa.
Zion Gospel African Church.
Zion Holy Church of South Africa.
Zion Holy Church Nation of South Africa.
Zion Jerusalem Apostolic Church in South Africa in Transvaal.
Zion Kingdom of God.
Zion Kingdom of God Salvation in South Africa.
Zion Maboko Church of South Africa.
Zion Mission African Apostolic Church.
Zion Revelation Apostolic Church of South Africa.
Zi zi Apostolic Church in South Africa.
Zulu or African Ethiopian Church.
Zulu Congregational Church.
Zulu Ethiopian Church.

LIST OF RECOGNIZED BANTU CHURCHES IN 1960

African Catholic Church
African Church
African Congregational Church
African Gospel Church
African Methodist Episcopal Church
African Orthodox Church
Bantu Methodist Church of South Africa
Lutheran Bapedi Church
Lutheran Bapedi Church of South Africa
Native Independent Congregational Church

The official list of Churches in South Africa, *May*, 1960, has more than 2030 *Bantu Separatist Churches*—the full list also including Mission Churches. The string of names is just the same as in 1949, "only more so". There does not seem to be much point in adding here another 20 pages of names to the list already published.

374

SPECIAL BIBLIOGRAPHY

Aldén, K., "The Prophet Movement in Congo", *International Review of Missions*, 1936.

van Antwerp, C. M., *Die Separatistiese Kerklike Beweging onder die Bantu van Suid-Ajrika*, University of Cape Town, 1938, unpublished MS.

Axenfeld, K., *Aetiopianismus*, Koloniale Abhandlungen 6, Berlin, 1906.

Cameron, W. M., "The Ethiopian Movement and the Order of Ethiopia", *The East and West*, 1904.

Dlepu, B. S., "The Native Separatist Church Movement", *Report, General Missionary Conference*, 1925.

Dube, J., *uShembe*, Pietermaritzburg, 1936.

Eberhardt, Jacqueline, "Messianisme en Afrique du Sud", *Archives de Sociologie des Religions*, 1957.

Emmet, Dorothy, "Prophets and Their Societies", *Journal of the Royal Anthropological Institute*, Vol. 86, 1956.

Gollock, G. A., *Sons of Africa*, 1928.

Gutmann, B., "Sektenbildung und Rasseerlebnis in Ostafrika", *Evang. Missionsmagazin* (Basel), 1934.

Hill, F., "The Native Separatist Church Movement", *Report-General Missionary Conference*, 1935.

Jabavu. D. D. T., *An African Independent Church*, Lovedale, 1942.

Jacottet, E., "Native Churches and Their Organization", *Report, First General Missionary Conference*, 1904.

Knoob, Willi J., *Die Rolle des Propheten in den Afrikanisch-Christlichen Sekten*, manuscript, 1959.

Lea, A., "Native Separatist Churches", in J. D. Taylor (ed.), *Christianity and the Natives of South Africa, A Year-Book of South African Missions*, Lovedale, 1928.

—— *The Native Separatist Church Movement in South Africa*, Cape Town- Johannesburg, 1926.

Léenhardt, Maurice, *Le Mouvement Éthiopien au Süd de l'Afrique de 1896 à 1899*, Cahors, 1902.

Lerrigo, P. H. J., "The Prophet Movement in Congo", *International Review of Missions*, 1922.

Linington, P. A., *A Summary of the Reports of Certain Pre-Union Commissions on Native Affairs: Church Separatist Movement*, Pretoria, 1924.

Loram, C., "The Separatist Church Movement", *International Review of Missions*, 1926.

Mqotsi, L., and Mkele, N., "A Separatist Church, *16andla lika Krestu*", *African Studies*, 1946.
Mzimba, L., "The African Church" in J. D. Taylor (ed.), *Christianity and the Natives of South Africa, A Year-book of South African Missions*.
Neame, L. E., "Ethiopianism: The Danger of a Black Church", *Empire Review*, 1905.
Norton, G. R., "The Emergence of New Religious Organizations in South Africa", *Journal of the Royal African Society*, 1940.
Omoyi, B., *A Defence of the Ethiopian Movement*, Edinburgh, 1905.
Peleman, Dom M., O.S.B., *De Ethiopische Beweging in Zuid-Afrika.—Bijdrage tot de Studie van het Zuid-Afrikaansch Protestantisme*, no year.
Platt, W. J., *From Fetish to Faith*, London, 1935
du Plessis, J. C., *Ethiopianisme en die Naturelle Problem*, 1936.
—— *"Hoe die Ethiopische Beweging in Suid-Afrika begin het"*, *Sending Instituut Jaarblad*, 1937.
du Plessis, J. S., "Die oorsake van Separatisme in die Sending-velde van Suid-Afrika", *Op die Horison*, 1939.
Roberts, Ester Lindsay, *Shembe, the Man and His Work*, unpublished MS., Witwatersrand University.
Roux, Edw., "The Ethiopian Movement", *Trek*, Johannesburg, July 27, 1945.
Roux, H. A., *De Ethiopische Kerk*, 1905.
Shepherd, R. H. W., "The Separatist Churches of South Africa", *International Review of Missions*, 1937.
Schlosser, Katesa, *Propheten in Afrika*, Braunschweig, 1949.
—— *Eingeborenenkirchen in Süd- und Südwestafrika*. Ihre Geschichte und Sozialstruktur, Kiel, 1958.
Schneider, Théo, *Les Eglises indépendantes africaines en Afrique du Sud*. Verbum Caro, Bâle, Vol. (Nos. 21–24), 1952.
Smith, C. S., *A History of the African Methodist Episcopal Church*, 1922.
Stead, W. F., "Order of Ethiopia in its Relation to the Church", *African Monthly*, Vol. III, 1907–8.
Sundkler, B. G. M., "Black Man's Church", *Libertas Magazine*, Johannesburg, 1945.
—— "Separatisme en die Sending", *Op die Horison*, Stellenbosch, 1940.
Welbourn, F. B. *East African Rebels: A Study of Some Independent Churches*, London, S.C.M. Press, 1961.

INDEX OF NAMES

INDEX OF SUBJECTS